THE WORLD
OF ROME

**PHOENIX
PRESS**

HISTORY OF CIVILIZATION

For more than thirty years this distinguished series has provided the general reader with a comprehensive picture of the world's greatest civilizations. The series is free from commitment to any single interpretation of history, and seeks to go beyond the standard works of reference. It presents individual and original evocations, by leading scholars in many countries, of the culture and development of a nation, groups of nations or period of history.

Michael Grant is a highly successful and renowned historian of the ancient world. He has held many academic posts including those of Fellow of Trinity College, Cambridge; Professor of Humanity at Edinburgh University; Vice Chancellor of The Queen's University, Belfast and Vice Chancellor of the University of Khartoum. He is a Doctor of Letters at Dublin and a Doctor of Laws at Belfast. He has also been President of the Classical Association of England, the Virgil Society and the Royal Numismatic Society, and is a Medallist of the American Numismatic Society. He lives and writes in Italy.

A SELECTION OF WORKS BY MICHAEL GRANT

The Twelve Caesars
The Classical Greeks
The Climax of Rome
The Fall of the Roman Empire
The Roman Emperors
The Rise of the Greeks
The Myths of the Greeks and Romans
The History of Ancient Israel
The Jews in the Roman World
The Roman World
Cleopatra
Cities of Vesuvius

THE WORLD OF
ROME

Michael Grant

PHOENIX
PRESS

5 UPPER SAINT MARTIN'S LANE
LONDON
WC2H 9EA

A PHOENIX PRESS PAPERBACK

First published in Great Britain
by Weidenfeld & Nicolson in 1960
This paperback edition published in 2000
by Phoenix Press,
a division of The Orion Publishing Group Ltd,
Orion House, 5 Upper St Martin's Lane,
London WC2H 9EA

Second impression 2000

A CIP catalogue record for this book
is available from the British Library.

Printed and bound in Great Britain by
Clays Ltd, St Ives plc

ISBN 1 84212 037 9

To ANNE-SOPHIE

CONTENTS

LIST OF PLATES

ix

LIST OF ILLUSTRATIONS IN TEXT

LIST OF MAPS

FOREWORD

THIS book is intended to give a picture of the world of the Romans during the three hundred and fifty years when, at the height of their unparalleled power, they made their greatest impact on the world, and received most from it in exchange. After a sketch of the historical background I shall try to single out the achievements and activities in the Roman empire which look to me, for good or ill, most fundamental to our understanding of its place in history.

Imperial Rome has seemed, to the people of many later centuries, a peculiarly enthralling and moving theme, and that is what it remains—unique, terrible, and rich in allurements and astonishments. I shall be happy if in this book I can transmit even a small charge of its versatile, potent magnetism. The material that has come down to us, though in many respects fragmentary, is nevertheless massive; and, from the sometimes bewilderingly contradictory variety that it offers, no two writers will ever make the same personal selection. My own account of this Roman Experience, perhaps because I have spent seven years in near and middle eastern countries, dwells more than most upon its inextricable, creative fusion of elements originating not only from Italy and the mainland of Greece but from farther Mediterranean coasts as well.

Political, social and economic conditions will first be briefly surveyed, and then something will be said of the more intimate thoughts, feelings and achievements both of the majority among the great populations of the empire and of their minority: that is to say, attention will first be directed to the religious hopes and beliefs w ich preoccupied millions, and then to the intellectual and artistic creations of a few small, talented groups and individuals.

The story runs from 133 BC to AD 217. The selection of any starting-date cannot help being somewhat artificial; but the year chosen here witnessed the first notable protests by Romans against parochial narrowness, and strainings after a new sort of state capable of ruling the empire that they had now won. Moreover, within the same few months, the rapid process of imperial expansion reached its climax with Rome's annexation of a region which was to exert great influence upon its affairs, the province of Asia in western Asia Minor (Anatolia). The book ends with the decline of the Roman Peace and of its characteristic institutions. As a terminal date I have chosen, among several possible dates during this process, the year which brought an end to the last stable imperial dynasty before the troubles preceding the transference of the world-centre from Rome to Constantinople. However, in order to present as self-contained an account as possible, I have on occasion strayed rather beyond these inevitably arbitrary limits, and indeed text and illustrations alike include comparative material drawn not only from the immediate aftermath of the period under discussion, but from various other epochs up to the seventeenth and eighteenth centuries.

The illustrations include sixty-four pages of photographic plates; they will be found between pages 234 and 235. These plates are supplemented by forty-five line drawings at appropriate points in the text—all drawn by Mr Dick Hart except numbers ix, xi and xiv, drawn by Mrs Campbell, and numbers xxii, xxiii, xxv, xxvii, xxxvii and xlii to xliv which are included by kind permission of Messrs Longmans Green & Co Ltd—and by five maps and a town-plan executed by Mr F. V. Botley. Since there seems no point in keeping secrets from those readers who do not know Latin or Greek, quotations from all ancient authors are given in English; but for those who wish to look at the original writings, references to quoted passages are added in the Notes which follow the Epilogue. I am grateful to the following for permission to quote from copyright works:

Penguin Books for *Tacitus: Annals of Imperial Rome* and *Cicero: Selected Works*, Robert Graves and Penguin Books for *Suetonius: The Twelve Caesars* and *Apuleius: The Golden Ass*, Ronald Latham and Penguin Books for *Lucretius: The Nature of the Universe*, E. V. Rieu and Penguin Books for *The Four Gospels*, Messrs William Heinemann for various translations from the *Loeb Classical Library*, Lady Dunsany for *The Odes of Horace* by Lord Dunsany, The Executor of R. C. Trevelyan and the Cambridge University Press for *Translations from Horace Juvenal and Montaigne* and *Translations from Latin Poetry*, C. Day Lewis and The Hogarth Press for *Virgil: The Aeneid*, C. Day Lewis and Messrs Jonathan Cape for *The Georgics of Virgil*, J. H. Oliver and

The American Philosophical Society for *The Ruling Power*, T. R. S. Broughton and The Johns Hopkins Press for *Economic Survey of Ancient Rome*, Paul MacKendrick and Messrs D. Van Nostrand, Princeton, for *The Roman Mind at Work*, N. Lewis and M. Reinhold and the Columbia University Press for *Roman Civilisation*, E. P. Barker and the Oxford University Press for *The Letters of Seneca*, F. H. Cramer and The American Philosophical Society for *Astrology in Roman Law and Politics*, A. S. L. Farquharson and The Clarendon Press for *The Meditations of the Emperor Marcus Aurelius*, Gilbert Highet and Messrs Hamish Hamilton for *Poets in a Landscape*, Messrs Macmillan & Co for *The Odes of Horace*, translated by Sir Edward Marsh, W. H. Auden and Messrs Faber & Faber for *Collected Poems*, F. O. Copley and the University of Michigan Press for *Complete Poems of Catullus*, Rolfe Humphries and Messrs Charles Scribners' Sons for *The Aeneid, A Verse Translation*, M. L. Clarke and Messrs Cohen and West Ltd for *The Roman Mind*.

My very many debts to other modern writers, inevitable for anyone who tackles however inadequately this many-sided theme, I cannot set down here. But I want to express my gratitude to Professor Sir Ronald Syme, editor of this series, for his advice, and to those who helped in the search for photographs; among them, not only the representatives of museums and galleries from which the objects illustrated have come, but also the following: Professor Giovanni Becatti, Professor Carl Bluemel, Professor Laura Breglia, M. Jean Charbonneaux, Father J.-A. Festugière, Mr J. P. Gillam, Herr Ludwig Goldscheider, Mr M. R. E. Gough, Mr D. E. L. Haynes, Professor Gilbert Highet, Dr Seton Lloyd, Dr René Naccache, Mr G. H. Robertson, Mr Graeme Shankland, Messrs Thames and Hudson Ltd, Professor J. M. C. Toynbee, Mr John Ward-Perkins and Mr W. H. N. Wilkinson. I want also to express my thanks to Miss Vanessa Jebb and Miss Sarah Marris for their work in collecting these illustrations. Finally, I have to record acknowledgements to my fellow-author of *Romans*, Mr Don Pottinger, and to its publisher Messrs Thomas Nelson and Sons Ltd, for the adaptation of certain material in the historical sketch which comprises the first chapter of the present book.

For certain of the amendments incorporated in this revised edition I am grateful to Mr. P. A. Brunt and Professor Sir Mortimer Wheeler.

MICHAEL GRANT

Part I
THE ROMAN EMPIRE

CHAPTER 1

HISTORICAL SKETCH

For their first four centuries the energies of the Romans were absorbed in asserting control over Italy south of the river Po. Within this area they established a complex network of unequal alliances which increasingly developed, not into the genuine confederacy that had once seemed possible, but into an empire controlled by themselves.

Then, within little more than a hundred years (241–133 BC), the power of Rome was rapidly extended over an enormous variety of peoples outside Italy. Writing of Roman rule during the central part of this period, a contemporary Greek statesman and historian, Polybius, ascribed his choice of subject to the belief that everyone must be curious to learn how the Romans, 'in less than fifty-three years, succeeded in subjugating to their sole rule nearly the whole inhabited world—an achievement unprecedented in history'.[1] Alexander the Great, dreaming of world unity, had almost for a brief moment brought it within reach; his diffusion of Greek as second language over huge areas of the middle east was lasting. And now for a second time something not far from world unity was being attained, by force once again, yet on a much more durable basis.

The only other potential world power was China, but China's world and Rome's were beyond each other's reach. Carthage had controlled the western Mediterranean, but Carthage had been defeated by Rome in three Punic Wars (264–41, 218–201, 149–46 BC) and was no more. Of the three eastern states which, in the Hellenistic epoch following the classical age of Greece, had divided most of Alexander's inheritance, the Macedonian kingdom had fallen to Rome; the centralized realm of the Ptolemies had been restricted to little more than Egypt; and the great State of the Seleucids, though still ruling from Syrian Antioch vast areas of south-west Asia, had been eliminated from the crowded and varied peninsula of Asia

Minor—meeting-place of Europe and Asia, and during ancient times almost a continent in itself.

These victories brought the Romans a long series of annexations. The First Punic War had extended their dominion beyond the Italian peninsula, giving them the important granaries of Sicily (241 BC) and Sardinia (231 BC). Large areas of Spain, though its annexation remained incomplete for two centuries to come, fell into Roman hands during and after the Second Punic War; within only nine years Rome derived 130,000 pounds of silver and 4,000 pounds of gold from Spanish mines. Then, after repeated wars with the successor states of Alexander, increasing Roman impatience with Greek disputes and methods led to further annexations: Macedonia became Roman in 148 BC, and Achaia (Greece) in 146 BC. This last step, with its ominous indication that romantic Roman Hellenism, exemplified at the beginning of the century by Flamininus 'liberator of Greece' (Plate 10a), had now worn thin, was heralded by the sack of the leading commercial city of Corinth. The same violently decisive year witnessed the final destruction of Carthage, undertaken by Scipio Aemilianus of the long pre-eminent family of the Cornelii. This act of annihilation gave Rome its province of Africa, initially an area of about 5,000 square miles—roughly corresponding to the modern Tunisia—which included three large districts contributing to its new rulers vitally important quantities of corn.

Africa was Rome's fifth province; but the climax of this series of annexations was reached when it gained its even richer sixth possession, on the farther coast of the Aegean where the Attalid dynasty of Pergamum had broken away from the Seleucids. In 133 BC the last monarch of Pergam um, insuring against social upheaval, had bequeathed his kingdom to the Romans. This comprised the heavily populated western part of Asia Minor (Map 4), full of famed and still-growing cities and agricultural resources, and noted for its textile and other industries. Stamping out a revolution in which slaves and nationalists united, Rome took over its heritage—a source of fabulous profit for its officials and financiers, and of potent influences upon its culture, religion and racial composition. The former royal capital Pergamum and other Greek cities officially remained 'free', but— like the 'free' cities in other Hellenized parts of the empire—came under Roman control, though in such cases this was generally exercised with a respect for appearances.

During this period of annexations the effective ruler of Rome was the Senate, the dominant partner in the 'Senate and People'. Its three hundred members, jealously restricted, with very few exceptions, to a small number of families within the landed aristocracy, remained senators for life and held the two annually elected consulships and other leading official posts. Among the arrogant, aggressive individualists who comprised the Senate there were no political parties in the modern sense; amid interminable quarrels men gathered to their support whatever social and economic groups they could. Nevertheless, the Senate maintained a sufficiently united front to eliminate any rival aspirations to the control it monopolized. The Second Punic War, won by senatorial management, had delayed for a whole century incipient moves towards a more democratic régime, and although not the Senate—which was theoretically an advisory body—but the People's Assembly was 'sovereign', the growing complexities of foreign affairs had made the Assembly willing to give the Senate its head in foreign and financial policy.

However, the control exercised by the Senate was limited by the rise, resulting from the wars, of another important class, occupied mainly in business. This class comprised the 'knights'. Remaining outside the offices of state reserved for senators, but often not far behind them in wealth, the knights sought power and profit rather than official grandeur. They controlled numbers of financial agents known as *publicani*, entrusted by the government with contracts for construction, army supply, mining operations, and above all the collection of taxes.

After the wars of the third and second centuries BC, Italian smallholdings on the old subsistence basis had gradually diminished in favour of huge cash-crop ranches and mixed farms. The absentee capitalist landlords of these plantations found that land was the safest investment and that grazing paid better than growing corn. Such estates, increasingly staffed by numerous slaves provided by the wars, dispossessed the free poor, who drifted to the cities, unemployed, starving and violent. To help them, and to renew the prosperity of Italy, the high-minded young nobleman Tiberius Sempronius Gracchus revived the ancient revolutionary potentialities of his office of Tribune of the People. This office, though designed centuries earlier to protect the lower classes, had long since succumbed obediently to the senatorial machine. But Tiberius

Gracchus, familiar with Greek ideas of popular sovereignty, ignored the Senate, instead proposing to the Assembly, first, that land occupied—at present precariously—by the state's tenants should be confirmed in some cases but limited in others; and secondly that the surplus thus created should be rented to the landless poor. He took the alarming step of securing the deposition of a conservative fellow-tribune, but when in defiance of custom Tiberius stood for immediate re-election he and three hundred supporters were killed. This, the first bloodshed in Roman civil strife for nearly four hundred years, inaugurated a century of political violence.

Tiberius's more forcible and influential though not much more worldly-wise brother Gaius, tribune in 123 BC and again in 122 BC, proposed novel trading colonies not only in south Italy, but also on the north African coast, near the site of Carthage—an idea distasteful to traditionalists—and tried to limit the rocketing prices of corn. He also resuscitated his brother's land-laws; but this disturbed Rome's so-called confederates or 'allies'—virtually its subjects—in Italy, who, increasingly ill-treated by the Roman authorities, feared for the loss of their lands. So Gaius offered full Roman citizenship to all Latins (the central, nuclear group in the 'confederacy') and half-citizenship to other Italians. He also sowed future dissensions between Senate and knights by proposing that the latter should be given the lucrative tax-farming of recently acquired Asia (p. 4)—and that these knights, instead of senators as hitherto, should be judges in the Court which had, a quarter of a century earlier, been set up to protect the provincials from misgovernment by examining charges of extortion brought against Roman governors. Yet no class liked the favours to the others; so in 121 BC Gaius found himself a private citizen. A brawl led to the first emergency decree that the Senate ever passed. Then, amid heavy fighting, and the repression that followed, Gaius and three thousand others lost their lives.

Soon afterwards, in order to safeguard their communications with Spain and protect their long-established ally Massilia (Marseille) against the Gallic tribes in its hinterland, the Romans annexed the southern regions of Gaul (121 BC). The new province, named after Narbo (Narbonne) where a colony of Roman citizens was settled (118 BC), became second only to Italy in Roman culture and urbanization. But trouble now came from beyond the southern frontier of the empire. By allowing Italian traders to be killed (112 BC), Jugurtha, king of semi-dependent Numidia in north

Africa, offended the Roman knights. Reluctantly declaring war, the Senate entrusted the command to Quintus Metellus of the now dominant clan of the Caecillii. Metellus fought two promising campaigns, but his tough, sly subordinate and protégé Marius—from a farming family of Arpinum—intrigued against Metellus with trading and popular interests so that the Assembly made him consul (ignoring the Senate, and thus foreshadowing party struggles), and appointed him to supersede Metellus. Raising a part-volunteer army, Marius wore down Jugurtha, who was captured (105 BC) and put to death. But Italy was now threatened, not only by a slave war in Sicily, but by two huge German tribes on the trek, the Cimbri and Teutones, who humiliated several quarrelling amateur Roman generals and at Arausio (Orange) in 105 BC destroyed 80,000 legionaries. However Marius, four times successively elected consul though he was a 'new man' (member of a family that had never held a consulship), annihilated the tribes in turn at Aquae Sextiae (Aix-en-Provence) (102 BC) and Vercellae in north Italy (101 BC). A notable military innovator, he developed earlier experiments in the use of the cohort (600 men) as chief tactical unit. The now largely professional ten-cohort legions developed a formidable *esprit de corps*, and became more dependent on their generals than on the state.

In riots during Marius's sixth consulship (100 BC), a tribune, Saturninus, seeking to distribute state lands, was stoned to death. Disappointed beneficiaries from among the Italian 'confederate' subjects of Rome flocked to the capital, but the government unwisely rebuffed them and expelled all non-Roman Italians from the city (95 BC). When the Confederates' spokesman Drusus was obstructed and then murdered, they openly revolted, and the desperately fought Marsian War followed. This was also called the 'Social' War, from *socius* the Latin for ally; but nearly all Rome's oldest Latin confederates or allies remained loyal, the rebels being the warlike highlanders of central Italy, among whom were the Marsians in a northern and the Samnites in a southern group. These rebels called their movement *Italia*; some among them were fighting to win Roman citizenship for themselves, but others—notably the Samnites whose rivalry had been crushed in the fourth century BC—sought to break Roman power. Rome won, by resisting tenaciously—and by conceding the main issue at stake: all men south of the river Po became citizens, and the many inhabitants of fertile Transpadane

7

Gaul, between the Po and the Alps, acquired 'Latin status' through which, as an intermediary stage towards citizenship for their whole community, the officials of each self-governing town obtained the franchise.

Marius wanted the command against the king of Pontus, a large area of northern Asia Minor rich in timber and pasturage, capable of threatening Roman communications with the east. This monarch, the charming, murderous, imperialistic half-Hellenized Iranian Mithradates VI (Plate 10*b*) had overrun the greater part of the peninsula and instigated the murder of its Italian residents. However, the Roman command against Mithradates went not to Marius but to the impoverished patrician Sulla, who after a sharp struggle in the streets of Rome asserted his claim by placing himself at the head of his army outside the capital and then (ominous precedent) marching on the city. Marius armed slaves to support his cause but was outlawed and fled to north Africa. Perhaps the best Roman general since the elder Scipio who had won the Second Punic War, Sulla left for the east and took back Greece from Mithradates. Meanwhile Marius, mentally unhinged, returned to the capital. After organizing unprecedented massacres he died early in his seventh consulship (86 BC), and his supporter Cinna (consul 87–84 BC) was murdered. Their successors, backed by many Etruscans, Samnites and Roman knights, failed to prevent Sulla's return.

After three years of civil war, and a blood-bath of thousands of opponents which provided land for his 120,000 demobilized soldiers, Sulla had himself appointed to the ancient emergency office of dictator (81 BC), waiving the original six-month time-limit of this office pending the completion of national recovery. Nevertheless, this brilliant, cruel, mystic and dissolute man, far from intending to overthrow the traditional machinery of senatorial control, meant to enlist the support of the aristocracy so that the system should work. Liberally replenishing the decimated Senate from his supporters, he arranged that office, in the official career—the tenure of the quaestorship, a post held by twenty young men each year—should be the sole qualification for future admission to its ranks; and the criminal procedure, expanded and improved, was placed under the Senate's sole control.

Sulla also tried to guard the Senate against future autocrats and subverters (such as himself) by limiting the duration of overseas commands, preventing recurrent consulships, tightening treason laws and discouraging tribunes—whose office he made a disqualification from all other posts. Sulla was also the first Roman to systematize the architecture of a large area of the city. At the age of fifty-nine, weary of war, power and Rome, and without aspiring to the final solution of life-long rule, he announced an un-Roman abdication into private life. In retirement, he hunted, wrote, drank with theatrical friends, and soon died. He was given a splendid funeral.

The next years witnessed the rise of the affable, ambitious millionaire Crassus—patron of senators and knights—and the arrogant, shifty young Pompey. Both had won reputations fighting for Sulla, and Pompey had eliminated in Spain Marius's gallant supporter Sertorius, an unequalled leader of guerillas (76–72 BC). Subsequently Crassus had broken 90,000 rebellious, dangerously menacing slaves under the Thracian gladiator Spartacus; and Pompey had finished them off.

As consuls, each with an army behind him, Crassus and Pompey undermined Sulla's work by showing that the Senate could not control them. Then, against the Senate's wishes, the Assembly gave Pompey wide, un-Republican powers to deal with the pirates who had for long dislocated all communications in the eastern Mediterranean (67 BC), and with the still unsuppressed Mithradates of Pontus. Pompey's appointment was supported by an unprecedentedly eloquent 'new man', Cicero from Arpinum (Plate 20a), friend of the knights, and by the penurious aristocrat Caesar (Plate 1). But in Pompey's absence Catiline, another blue-blooded pauper and an ex-tough of Sulla's, having been disappointed for the consulship mobilized the support of displaced persons and debt-ridden land-owners in favour of a programme of debt cancellations and then of armed revolution. Cicero, consul in 63 BC, arrested six of Catiline's fellow-conspirators and had them executed. First, however, he received the backing of the Senate, led by the crafty, austerely principled Cato the Younger; Caesar, in diplomatic opposition, advocated more moderate penalties. Early in the next year Catiline fell fighting against an army of the Republic near Pistoria (Pistoia).

Pompey was an outstanding commander with an instinct for amphibious warfare. In the east he achieved unprecedented successes, finally putting an end to Mithradates, settling Judaea, and abolishing the once great Seleucid monarchy. This involved the annexation of its nucleus, heavily populated Syria. The Syrian city-states, whose autonomy Pompey confirmed, continued their traditional carrying-trade astride the caravan routes, and controlled prosperous wool and linen-weaving, purple-dyeing and glass-blowing industries; and Syria possessed great military significance as bastion against the power which was becoming Rome's arch-enemy, the semi-feudal Iranian monarchy of the Parthians across the Euphrates. Pompey had ensured that all the lands of hither Asia should look westwards to Rome rather than eastwards to Parthia; and his settlement was the basis of subsequent Roman rule throughout the area.

He returned to Rome without dictatorial intentions. Yet, although his successes had brought into the Treasury a sum perhaps roughly the equivalent of twelve million pounds, and had raised the annual national income by seventy per cent to an equivalent of some eight and a half million pounds, the ratification of his arrangements was blocked by the Senate—while Cicero talked only of his own successes. Thereupon Pompey, Caesar and Crassus united in the unofficial but irresistible First Triumvirate, cemented by Pompey's marriage to Caesar's daughter Julia. Cicero's ideal 'Harmony of the Orders', which depended on the free working of the Republican institutions, was frustrated, and the death-throes of the Republic had begun.

The division of spoils by the First Triumvirate gave Caesar the consulship (59 BC), followed by a military command for five (later increased to ten) years in Illyricum (Yugoslavia) and Gaul on both sides of the Alps (France and north Italy). Appeals from Gaulish chieftains against their fellow-Celts the Helvetii took him to the Rhine. Then, often by brutal methods, he reduced the disunited tribes of northern France and Belgium (58–57 BC), and conducted success-ful amphibious operations on the Atlantic seaboard (56 BC). With the central tribes thus encircled, Caesar twice invaded Britain (55–54 BC). He landed five legions (28 warships, 540 transports) and took Wheathampstead, capital of the temporary British generalissimo Cassivellaunus, but effected no conquests. He was then confronted by a formidable coalition of central Gallic tribes. Beating off a large relieving army, he finally captured their leader Vercingetorix in 52 BC at Alesia (Alise-Sainte-Reine). The newly-conquered territories of northern and central France, and the borderland up to the Rhine, were made into the new province of Gallia Comata ('long-haired' Gaul). This, with its population of perhaps five millions, did not take long to form a vigorous provincial culture, to develop the great potential resources of its agriculture, stock-breeding, mining and metallurgy, and to create important industries for the production of pottery and glass.

Meanwhile Cicero had been exiled to Epirus (58–57 BC) for his execution of the Catilinarians; when allowed to return he was powerless. Although subjected to many strains the Triumvirate was reaffirmed at Luca (Lucca) in 56 BC. Pompey received the governorship of Spain for five years, but exercised it by proxy from Rome, surrounded by unprecedented grandeur and hordes of dependants ('clients'). In 53 BC Crassus was killed at Carrhae (Haran) across the Euphrates fighting against the Parthians, and the Triumvirate was at an end. Next year, amid increasing gang warfare, Pompey became sole consul—a precedent for emperors. His wife, Caesar's daughter, had died (54 BC), and Pompey was pressed by a conservative clique of senators into a breach with Caesar in order to limit the latter's tenure of his Gallic governorship and prevent him from becoming consul again. Whatever the constitutional rights and wrongs—and they are still disputed—the Republic crashed. A government designed for a modest city-state had failed to prevent violence and corruption, or to control the commanders who could not be dispensed with in so enormous an empire.

Caesar crossed the Rubicon (49 BC) and occupied Italy, from which Pompey withdrew to the Balkans. Pursuing him there after a rapid expedition to Spain, Caesar was victorious at Pharsalus in Thessaly (48 BC), owing to the courage of his veterans in withstanding cavalry. On landing in Egypt—long since semi-dependent on Rome—Pompey was murdered. After a winter campaign there, alleviated by the company of the twenty-two-year-old Cleopatra whom he confirmed as Queen, Caesar overwhelmed Mithradates's son Pharnaces at Zela in Asia Minor (47 BC). Then he returned to Rome, and in further lightning wars crushed Pompey's sons in north Africa in 46 BC (Thapsus—his strategic masterpiece) and in Spain in 45 BC (Munda —a grim soldiers' battle). Although no military innovator, Caesar possessed a startling sense of the moment to strike, a perfect comprehension of supply problems, and the supreme power of utilizing and inspiring his unequalled legionaries.

Ruler of the whole Roman world, he caused his dictatorship, which he had held at intervals since 49 BC, to be extended for life. A month later, amid grandiose building schemes, plans to resettle his ex-soldiers in commercial colonies, and preparations for an eastern expedition emulating Alexander, he was struck down by Brutus, Cassius, and others who had enjoyed his favour or his pardon but could not endure autocracy. In spite of his clear, swift vision, intense intellect and will of steel, the programme of reforms launched by his initiative had included no far-reaching reconstructions of the machinery of the state, which after his death reverted to anarchy.

Encouraged by Cicero's courageously vituperative *Philippics*, the Senate rallied against Antony's attempt to succeed to Caesar's power and defeated him in 43 BC at Mutina (Modena). But Antony then allied himself with the cold-bloodedly ambitious twenty-year-old Octavian (the later Augustus; Plate 2a)—adopted in his great-uncle Caesar's will as his principal heir, and probably also, as Octavian claimed, as his son. Together with the unimpressive Lepidus, who had succeeded Caesar as chief priest, Antony and Octavian formed the Second Triumvirate, a dictatorial committee appointed by due processes of law to 'reform the state' and avenge Caesar's murder. Among the 2,000 executed (including 300 senators) was Cicero. The triumvirs—principally Antony—crushed the Republican cause at Philippi in Macedonia (42 BC), and Brutus and Cassius committed suicide.

After the Treaty of Brundisium (Brindisi) in 40 BC between Antony and Octavian, the latter strengthened his hold on Italy and the western provinces. The surviving son of Pompey, Sextus, who had blockaded the peninsula, was eliminated in a naval battle off Naulochus in Sicily (36 BC). Octavian then doubled his army by taking over the twenty-two legions of Lepidus, who was forced into seclusion. Meanwhile Antony had consolidated his control of the eastern provinces. Ignoring his wife Octavia (Octavian's sister) he bestowed the headship of an oriental hierarchy of princes upon the ambitious, intellectual Cleopatra—to whom, in his infatuation, he was suspected of sacrificing Roman interests.

Antony lost many Roman soldiers in a disastrous large-scale invasion of Parthian-controlled Armenia (36 BC), whereas Octavian crossed the Adriatic to fight more successful campaigns in Illyricum and Dalmatia (35–34 BC). Octavian then induced the Senate to deprive Antony of his triumviral powers and to declare war on Cleopatra. She and Antony were decisively defeated in a naval battle off Actium in Epirus (31 BC); each side shipped nearly 40,000 legionaries, but Antony's crews, sapped by propaganda attacking his sybaritic oriental siren, failed to fight. He and Cleopatra withdrew to Egypt where, as Octavian prepared the *coup de grâce*, both committed suicide (30 BC). Egypt, with its enormous, bureaucratically exploited wealth—the country could send Italy enough corn to satisfy Rome's needs for four months of every year—was in Octavian's possession; and so was the entire Roman world.

Augustus, for it was by this name with antique religious associations that the new autocrat chose to be called (27 BC), maintained unchallengeable authority because, in spite of careful lip-service to Republican institutions, he controlled the army and the empire's financial resources. Chief among the friends whom he needed to help him in his vast task were the unfailingly competent Agrippa (d. 12 BC), almost co-regent, and the debauched but watchful Maecenas (d. 8 BC). Although no emperor or ruling house officially existed, Augustus aroused speculation about the succession by marrying his amusing, immoral daughter Julia first to a nephew Marcellus (d. 23 BC), then to Agrippa, and finally to his own stepson Tiberius. Augustus worked Tiberius even harder than his other helpers, but only reluctantly envisaged him as his successor (AD 4), after the premature deaths of the two sons of Agrippa and Julia. Augustus was a simple-living small-townsman of literary tastes who combined a romantic admiration for Greek culture with an intense feeling for Rome and Italian tradition. But efficiency was what concerned him most, and for this he had a remarkable talent. During his long reign he took in hand all branches of the Roman administration and transformed them into an organism capable of bearing its imperial responsibilities; the ingenious self-praise of his Acts survives on an Ankara temple.

Provided that his own glory was not forgotten, Augustus preferred peaceful to warlike methods. Yet the reign saw much fighting—largely conducted by Agrippa and the brothers Tiberius and Drusus (the elder)—and consequent imperial expansion. The eastern frontier was pushed forward to include not only Egypt but a huge strategic tract of central Asia Minor, inhabited by the descendants of Celtic immigrants. This was formed into the province of Galatia (25 BC) (Maps 4, 5). Also annexed were Numidia in north Africa, the territories bordering on the Danube from Switzerland to the Black Sea, and western and central Germany where Roman troops reached the river Elbe (9 BC). The Elbe-Danube frontier thus achieved was shorter than the previous Rhine-Danube line. But for the sake of economy the army was maintained at too small a strength, and the instability of territorial gains when no central reserve existed was shown by serious rebellions first in Pannonia-Illyricum between the Danube and the Adriatic (AD 6), and then in Germany (AD 9). The first of these rebellions frustrated a Roman plan to conquer Bohemia, and the second threw back the borders to the Rhine. A notorious bone of contention was still the mountainous land of Armenia, which changed hands rapidly between puppets placed there by Rome and Parthia in turn. After a show of force by Tiberius, Augustus attempted a diplomatic settlement with the Parthians (20 BC) and claimed that Armenia was now his, but the country did not remain under his control.

The next four reigns provide the long series of harrowing court melodramas described by Tacitus's *Annals* and Suetonius's *Lives*. Each emperor began with protestations of Republican and Augustan correctness, and then, under the pressure of his enormous power, degenerated to massive murders among the ruling class. Tiberius (AD 14–37; Plate 11a) was an efficient provider of order, justice and economy, but was glum, misanthropic and intolerant of public relations and hypocrisy. Irritated by his imperious mother Livia and by hostility within his own family, he retired to Capreae (Capri) in AD 26 and ruled the empire through the Praetorian Prefect— commander of the imperial bodyguard—Sejanus. But Sejanus, having removed Tiberius's heirs, was himself struck down, as prelude to a final holocaust of spyings, persecutions, vengeance and suicides.

Tiberius's grand-nephew Gaius ('Caligula', AD 37–41) emerged from an unhealthy upbringing and a disturbing illness as a fidgety, neurotic sadist. After his murder, the Guard secured the succession for his uncle Claudius (AD 41–54), a man of learning and shrewdness, concealed by a ridiculous appearance and behaviour. The reign of Claudius was noteworthy for the extension of Roman citizenship in the provinces—in which the emperor, born at Lugdunum (Lyon), was especially interested—and for the creation of an inner imperial cabinet of ex-slaves. These men from Asia Minor and the Levant, enjoying unprecedented power and wealth, competed or co-operated with the emperor's third and fourth wives, Messalina, who was without sexual restraint, and the ruthlessly ambitious Agrippina the younger. Agrippina poisoned Claudius and secured the succession for her own son by a former marriage, Nero (Plate 11*b*).

Nero drew, painted, modelled and wrote poetry. His eager participation in musical and theatrical contests scandalized the Senate. But his policy of free food and entertainments and his personal appearances as a charioteer delighted the populace, who did not find his self-indulgence and cruelty offensive. Begun under the good, if ineffective, influence of the philosopher Seneca and the Prefect of the Guard Burrus, his reign deteriorated when the horse-breeder Tigellinus succeeded as Prefect and chief adviser. To facilitate marriage to the dazzling Poppaea, Nero caused the murders of his mother Agrippina and his high-minded wife Octavia. The Great Fire of Rome in AD 64 (probably accidental) was officially attributed to the Jewish sect of the Christians, whose first persecution now occurred. But then, after the discovery of a conspiracy led by the aristocratic Piso, many of the ruling class were struck down. The emperor went to display his dramatic talents in Greece, but revolts broke out in Gaul and Spain, and Nero, deserted after his return by army and Senate, fled from Rome and took his own life (AD 68).

During these four reigns of members of Augustus's family, imperial scandals made little impact on the provinces, which amid improving material conditions and commercial development continued to be well governed. Warfare during this half-century was mainly defensive. Though a great commander, Tiberius did not venture, after his accession, to leave Italy. His reign opened with three years' expensive amphibious campaigning in northern Germany under his popular nephew Germanicus; but the emperor recalled him before any annexations could be made. In the Danube lands Tiberius created a system of highways, and Claudius opened up the Brenner and Great St Bernard routes across the Alps. In Africa prolonged fighting on the Sahara border under the generals of Tiberius was followed by the annexation of Mauretania by Claudius, who also suppressed the 'client' kingdoms of Thrace. But Augustus had bequeathed advice not to extend the frontiers any farther, and usually this advice was respected. The main exception was Britain—already trading extensively with the empire—which the generals of Claudius annexed as far as the Severn and the Trent (AD 43–52). Being himself, like Caligula and Nero, unfit to take the field, Claudius did not like entrusting commands to others; so, in order to acquire a military reputation, he took part briefly in the conquest of Britain. In Nero's reign a revolt under Queen Boudicca (Boadicea) of the Iceni caused heavy losses before it was suppressed.

As regards the Armenian throne, Augustus's successors at first—in face of a strong Parthian monarch, Artabanus—continued his policy of using the minimum military effort to maintain Roman authority. Then Nero, nervous of campaigns by his publicity-minded general Corbulo, successfully arranged a long-lasting diplomatic solution by staging, at Rome, a magnificent coronation of Parthia's nominee Tiridates as king of Armenia (AD 66). But an even more serious area of disturbance was among the restless Jewish population of Palestine, where Jesus taught and was crucified under Tiberius and, some thirty-five years later, moderate and extremist Jews joined in a national uprising (Plate 11c) which Vespasian had begun to put down at the time of Nero's death.

The Year of the Four Emperors, theme of Tacitus's *Histories*, showed that emperors need not have Julian or Claudian blood, and that they could be appointed away from Rome—by the legions. The elderly aristocrat Galb a (Plate 12a, b) led the Spanish army to Rome. But he seemed miserly to the jealous Praetorian Guard, who lynched him and proclaimed Otho, a man of fashion (January AD 59). Meanwhile, however, the army on the German frontier had declared for one of its commanders, Vitellius, whose generals successfully launched a two-pronged invasion of Italy. Otho committed suicide. Yet before the year was over the gluttonous Vitellius had also met his death, after defeat by the forces of the governor of Judaea, Vespasian (Plates 2b, 3).

This sensibly frugal, bourgeois, facetious Italian (AD 69–79) founded a new (Flavian) dynasty. After suppressing a national Germano-Gallic revolt, he restored the ruined imperial finances, reorganized the army, and created a new aristocracy of provincial origin. Following the brief reign of his popular but prodigal son Titus —noteworthy for a catastrophic eruption of Vesuvius (AD 79)—the latter's able, priggish, cruel brother Domitian gave the principate a more frankly monarchical character. His high-handed measures incurred the hatred of the Senate, in whose ranks developed an opposition party. The repressive measures directed against them turned into a reign of terror during the last years of Domitian, who was then himself assassinated (AD 96). The Flavian dynasty had advanced and fought on several of the borders of the empire. In Asia Minor, Vespasian united the central and eastern areas and created a road system covering the frontier. The English lowlands were safeguarded by the Scottish campaigns of Agricola, who defeated the momentarily combined Highland chiefs in AD 83 or 84. Similar protective advances carried the German frontier to the Neckar. Beyond the lower Danube, Domitian began to iace a new danger from Decebalus, wealthy king of the Dacians (AD 86–9).

After Domitian's murder, his well-meaning elderly successor Nerva (AD 96–8) encountered trouble from the Praetorian Guard, which had not been in the plot. So Nerva adopted, and thus secured as his successor, the most competent man available—the great soldier Trajan (AD 98–117), descendant of Roman settlers in Spain and the first emperor to have come from outside Italy (Plate 4a, b). In a series of major campaigns Trajan reduced and annexed Dacia, seizing important treasures and mines which, for once, more than paid for the wars. He also overran a large part of the Parthian empire, capturing its capital Ctesiphon (Kut) and sailing down the Tigris to the Persian Gulf. Not only a conqueror, Trajan, acclaimed 'best of rulers', was kind and unassuming, devoting great care to the welfare of Italy and the provinces.

When Trajan died in Asia Minor, another Spaniard, Hadrian (Plate 5) succeeded him. This able, restless, extraordinarily versatile administrator, soldier, sightseer, and patron and practitioner of the arts completed a reorganization of the public service, separating the civilian from the military career. However, he spent more than half his reign traversing and benefiting the empire, throughout which he put into effect a provincial's new conception of partnership between Rome and the provinces. His visit to Britain led to the construction of a fortified wall from the Solway to the Tyne (c. AD 122–9). On his accession Hadrian had evacuated the Mesopotamian and Armenian conquests of Trajan, whose communications had been threatened by widespread Jewish revolts; these savagely recurred in Hadrian's last years. Antoninus Pius (AD 138–61; Plate 12d), member of a family which in the previous century had migrated from Nemausus (Nîmes) to Italy, had been adopted by Hadrian shortly before the latter's death. During his peaceful reign this unbrilliant but devoted, tolerant and economical ruler retreated from the cosmopolitanism of Hadrian and spent nearly all his time in Italy, where his centralized government was human and painstaking. A minor expansion was attempted only in Britain, where revolts caused a new fortified line to be established between the Forth and the Clyde (*c.* AD 142–3).

At Hadrian's wish, Antoninus had adopted his nephew and son-in-law, the young Marcus Aurelius (AD 161–80; Plates 6*b*, 7*a*) and the insignificant Lucius Verus, and they reigned jointly until Verus's death in AD 169. Though providing the noble spectacle of a Stoic philosopher ruling in accordance with his principles, Aurelius had to spend nearly all his reign fighting. When Parthia forcibly reopened the Armenian question, Roman commanders destroyed its two principal cities, Ctesiphon and Seleucia-on-the-Tigris, and a vassal state in north-western Mesopotamia changed hands. A more novel and ominous threat was provided by mass movements among the south German peoples; at a time when the Roman empire was devastated by plague the Marcomanni and the Quadi swept through the provinces into northern Italy (AD 167). Raising funds by desperate means, Aurelius, though deficient in military reserves, gradually drove the invaders back and was intending to advance the frontier to a straighter line along the Carpathian and Bohemian mountains when he died. His son and successor the savage, unstable Commodus (AD 180–92; Plate 8*a*), although he raised the soldiers' pay, was unwise in his rapidly changing choices of advisers. The last of these, with the help of the emperor's ex-mistress, arranged for his assassination.

Within a few months after the murder of Commodus, two more emperors, Pertinax and Didius Julianus, had been acclaimed and murdered. Didius Julianus had set a sinister precedent when he bought the throne by auction from the Praetorian Guard. The fierce, extremely capable north African Septimius Severus (AD 193–211; Plate 13*b*), governor of Upper Pannonia on the Danube, only asserted his claim against the nominees of rival armies after four years of civil war which were as ruinous as the wars after Nero's death. Building roads, repairing frontier defences, and mobilizing three new legions, Severus aggressively reoccupied large areas of Mesopotamia, and invaded the north of Scotland (AD 209). To achieve these ends and lavish privileged treatment upon the army, taxation was doubled. True to his own provincial origins and those of his wife Julia Domna (Plate 13*c*), who was a Syrian patroness of letters, Severus taxed Italians as heavily as provincials, and the Praetorian Guardsmen, previously drawn in large part from the home country, were now recruited from the provinces. His son Caracalla (AD 211–17; Plate 9), though abandoning his father's plans in Britain, intensified Severus's other policy, raising army pay by one half as much again; but the attempt of this restless tyrant to win eastern laurels ended in assassination.

Throughout an empire as large as it had ever been except for a very brief period under Trajan, stability of a sort had returned under the Severi. Yet their régime, supported as it was by the constantly worsening methods of a police state, soon became far more grim and careworn than the Antonine Age which they claimed to revive. Moreover, the lull was shortlived. After a brief period of orgiastic eastern despotism under Elagabalus (AD 218–22), and a respite under his correct cousin Severus Alexander—ominously broken in the east by the rise of a new Sassanian monarchy, more formidable than its Parthian predecessor—the empire foundered into anarchy. Yet it miraculously survived Sassanian and German onslaughts and internal disintegration through the efforts of military geniuses such as Claudius Gothicus (AD 268–70) and Aurelian (AD 270–5), only to become the totalitarian monarchy of their fellow-Illyrians Diocletian (AD 284–305) and Constantine (AD 306–37). But the west never recovered from third-century invasions and civil wars, and Constantine, the first emperor to embrace Christianity as his State religion, moved the capital from Rome to Byzantium. Renamed Constantinople, this city stood at the focal point where Europe is closest to the lands of Asia Minor, which continued, almost undamaged, to be a reservoir of men and riches for the Byzantine empire which now began—and lasted for over a thousand years.

Part II

STATE AND SOCIETY

CHAPTER 2

THE RULERS AND THE EMPIRE

BEFORE the democratic movement of the Gracchi (pp. 5 f.), and again for thirty years after them, the essential feature of the political history of Rome was the monopoly of power by the Senate. Although this body was too narrow in its interests, too selfish, and too persistently riven by faction to be well-suited for governing an empire, its predominance continued, not so much (as Polybius claimed) because the constitution possessed effective balances,[1] as because an ancient tradition of service was still sometimes apparent among Roman senators, and the members of their inner circle continued to display a flair for politics. By prestige, bribery, the purveyance of food and entertainments, and the satisfaction of great armies of 'clients'—who depended upon them for subsistence and gave political support in return—the nobles had long been accustomed to induce the Assembly of the Roman People to elect them to the consulships which were the principal offices of the state. In the century before the Gracchi, 159 out of 200 consuls were provided by 25 families, and 99 by only 10 families. Twenty-three of these consulships were held by Cornelii, the house of the Scipios, who were, at this period, the most successful and influential of the great clans.

However, the reforms of the Gracchi gave much greater coherence and self-consciousness to the 'knights', those of the gentry who were not senators and who since earlier in the second century had been gaining ever more influence through their financial operations (p. 5). These measures foreshadowed a major rift in the governing class. There was not usually, it is true, a simple line-up between the Senate on the one hand and the whole order of knights on the other, but the possibilities of paralysing dissensions were greatly increased; and the new breach of upper-class unity—on a larger scale than the inter-clique breaches of the previous centuries—contributed to the violence that followed. The whole incident of the Gracchi rocked Roman society, politics and economics to their foundations. In particular, Rome began to breed a new type of party man, the *popularis*, who ostensibly admired the Gracchi but, lacking their ideals, cynically claimed an interest in the rustic or urban poor in order to supplant the dominant oligarchy by his own kind of oligarchic clique.

Yet for a time the Senate remained the arbiter of events, though not, perhaps, with quite the same easy assurance. The dominant house was no longer the Cornelii but the Caecilii Metelli. This family, often more sympathetic to knights than to ultra-conservative senators, were elected by the Assembly to six consulships within fifteen years (123–109 BC). But then, in defiance of the traditional ruling groups, the middle-class Marius and the poverty-stricken aristocrat Sulla used their new-style, semi-professional armies to give themselves a power that no Roman had possessed before. Sulla, indeed, used his power to shore up the senatorial oligarchy for the future. But he failed and, in the forty years that followed his abdication, politics were corrupt, chaotic and violent; a characteristic feature was the mobilisation of trade-guilds or clubs (collegia) as political pressure groups. A surviving document purporting to be advice to the 'new man' Cicero, standing for office, from his brother, Quintus, may be fictitious, but its summing-up of late Republican politics is accurate: 'The city is Rome, a state formed of an assemblage of all nations, a state in which many intrigues, much deceit, many vices of every kind abound, in which the arrogance of many, the perverseness of many, the malevolence of many, the pride of many, the hatred and vexation of many must be endured.'[2] Yet the 'many', if we limit the term to those of political importance, were still relatively few—the small nexus of oligarchic groups who were now attempting, by all means at their disposal, a final desperate reassertion of their traditional control.

Their failure was symbolized by the dictatorial alliance of the First Triumvirate between Pompey, Crassus and Caesar (60–59 BC). The next generation believed that this was the moment, and this was the deed, that set events moving inexorably towards the Civil Wars which finally destroyed the traditional system.[3] After the death of Crassus, vainly seeking military glory (53 BC), it only remained for the two survivors to fall out, as they did, to give the winner, Caesar, sole control of the government. Then at last the protracted death-throes of the Republic were at an end. For Caesar brushed aside the pretensions of the previously ruling groups. Contemptuous of this time-wasting Republicanism, he replaced it by open autocracy:

'Titus Ampius has recorded some of Caesar's public statements which reveal a similar presumption: that the Republic was nothing—a mere name without form or substance; that Sulla had proved himself a dunce by resigning his dictatorship; and that, now his own word was law, people ought to be more careful how they approached him. Once, when a soothsayer reported that a sacrificial beast had been found to have no heart—an unlucky omen indeed—Caesar told him arrogantly: "The omens will be as favourable as I wish them to be; meanwhile I am not at all surprised that a beast should lack the organ which inspired our finer feelings." . . . During one of his Triumphs, he had ridden past the benches reserved for the tribunes of the people, and shouted in fury at a certain Pontius Aquila, who had kept his seat: "Hey there, Aquila the tribune. Do you want me to restore the Republic?" For several days after this incident he added to every undertaking he gave: "With the kind consent of Pontius Aquila".[4]

Caesar had stopped short of accepting the title of King, with its unwelcome tyrannical associations dating from the semi-legendary Tarquin. Yet, in the last months of his life, he accepted the title 'dictator for perpetuity',[5] which deprived leading Romans indefinitely of their traditional access to the highest honours and pickings. Aristocratic Romans, and bourgeois Italians, were more vigilant than the other peoples of the empire about infringements of what they regarded as their 'freedom'—their right to be governed not autocratically but in accordance with the laws of the Republic; for many of them Caesar had gone too far, and so he died. Nevertheless there had existed, and continued to exist, a widespread feeling that a 'saviour' was needed to rescue Rome and its homeland from the protracted chaos which the Republican government had been powerless to avert.

Both of these apparently contradictory requirements were satisfied by Augustus. On the one hand, he supplied the autocratic firmness and control necessary for natural recovery. But at the same time he dressed his constitutional settlement in the most elaborate Republican forms; it was called the 'Restoration of the Republic'[6] (*respublica* signifying constitutional government), and he described his own position by the term *princeps* which lacked dictatorial trappings; his specific powers were ostensibly renewable. In his *Acts* and on his coins he stressed that he was the Liberator who had saved the lives of citizens, that he held no post 'contrary to ancestral tradition', that he had 'transferred the state from his own control to the free will of the Senate and Romanle' Peop'[7]—and to those traditional components of the Roman state, the S.P.Q.R., there are many honorific

25

references on his coins.[8] It may seem surprising that in spite of their vigilant Republicanism many members of the Italian governing class were satisfied by what seems to us a fiction. Yet the Romans, although their intense anxiety to preserve everything good in the past made them instinctively averse to open changes, had a fairly impressive record for modifying their institutions when this was necessary. Clear-cut breaches of past custom could scarcely be admitted, owing to the widespread belief that any departures from tradition must necessarily be for the worse, and this feeling was never more apparent than under Augustus himself.

> Injurious Time, what age escapes thy curse?
> Evil our grandsires were, our fathers worse:
> And we, till now unmatched in ill,
> Must leave successors more corrupted still.[9]

And yet, even Cicero—no constitutional innovator himself—had recognized, when it suited him, that institutions needed to be accommodated to new demands.[10] Caesar, too, was well aware that the Romans had always borrowed serviceable ideas and had never shrunk from adopting novel expedients to meet new facts and needs. This was the middle course between conservatism and revolution which Augustus shrewdly steered, well aware that if he gave the Roman people peace they were prepared, after a generation of civil war, to regard his careful, archaic application of Republican forms as salvation. The Roman world was going through one of those phases in which order seemed more important than freedom—though, seeing that Roman *Libertas* never meant complete political self-expression, Augustus was able to claim that he had restored the latter too.[11] Not everyone agreed; there was a series of conspiracies, real or alleged. But on the whole, during his long reign, critical comments were silenced, or at least muffled so that few of them have reached posterity. From Tacitus, however, writing a century after his death, we have an acute, disillusioned summing-up of the causes of Augustus's success:

'He seduced the army with bonuses, and his cheap food policy was successful bait for civilians. Indeed, he attracted everybody's goodwill by the enjoyable gift of peace. Then he gradually pushed ahead and absorbed the functions of the Senate, the officials, and even the law. Opposition did not exist. War or judicial murder had disposed of all men of spirit. Upper-class survivors found that slavish obedience was the way to succeed, both politically and financially. They had profited from the revolution, and so now they liked the security of the existing arrangement better than the dangerous uncertainties of the old régime.'[12]

At the same time, it was an essential feature of Augustus's 'restored Republic' that the Senate should be cherished and encouraged to play a central part in the system, in collaboration with himself; that is to say, under his direction. A very large proportion of influential Romans were among the 600 active senators—of whom 500 were in Rome at any given time, while the rest were engaged in provincial duties. The senators stood for vested interests, since there was a property qualification for their appointment; and their ranks were increased each year by the enrolment of some twenty sons of senators, men of about twenty-five years of age approved by Augustus for future responsibilities. Yet there was room for 'new men', too, and even, as time went on, for foreigners (p. 37), and if they were capable they advanced: promotion was open to merit, and able 'new men' were judiciously blended with the sons of the traditional ruling families.

This Senate of the emperors undertook a good deal of business, but its role in important matters was not glorious. The reason is made painfully clear in a long series of scenes presented by Tacitus and Suetonius. The senators might be urged to debate more freely, but little encouragement to do so was provided by the sudden transformations, from time to time, of great generals or administrators from the emperor's closest friends into imprisoned, executed and unmentionable traitors. It was on account of such disasters, as well as because of the opening of the career to merit, that very few of the leading Romans of AD 100 could trace their descent from the Republican aristocracy.

Nevertheless, an emperor wanted his doings to appear to the Senate in as favourable a light as possible, since its members included so many of the men whom he needed to help him. The result was that most rulers of the first and second centuries AD took immense pains to maintain the Republican façade and present themselves as moderate, constitutional rulers. Tiberius tried particularly hard. Such was his hatred of flatterers that he refused to let senators approach his litter, whether in greeting or on business. Indeed one day, when an ex-consul seeking to apologize for tactlessness tried to embrace his knees in suppliant fashion, the emperor retreated so hurriedly that he fell over backwards. And if anyone, either in conversation or a speech, spoke of him in too fulsome terms, Tiberius would interrupt and sternly correct the phrase.[13] Once, when addressed as 'My Lord and Master', he gave warning that no such insult must ever again be thrown at him. Another man referred to 'your sacred occupations', and a third said that he had 'approached the Senate by the emperor's authority'; Tiberius made them change these words to 'your laborious occupations' and 'at the emperor's instance'. He was, moreover, quite unperturbed by abuse, slander, or lampoons on himself and his family, and would often describe liberty to speak and think as one pleases as the test of a free country.

These efforts by Tiberius to seem un-autocratic failed to impress leading Romans. According to Tacitus this was because his words only concealed, in hypocritical fashion, a savagely evil personality and policy. More probably the failure was due to his glum grimness of manner, and—at the back of all this modest behaviour—to an honest impatience with eyewash, which caused him to fail in public and private relations where the more genial Augustus, better at saying the right thing, had succeeded.

Under Tiberius, therefore, we find fresh stirrings of opposition among leading Romans. As time went on, this opposition, based originally on rancorous resentment, was stiffened and dignified by doses of Greek philosophy. The Cynic school had always been opposed to monarchy, and the Stoics to bad monarchy. But during the first century AD these two doctrines tended to become indistinguishable from one another and to form a general décor for the upper-class Romans who opposed good and bad imperial governments alike. Indeed a philosophically-minded group caused particular irritation to one of the best and most considerate emperors, Vespasian, who felt obliged to take punitive action. The movement reached its height under his son Domitian. But in the enlightened atmosphere of the second century AD systematic opposition, resulting in the loss of aristocratic lives, ceased to occur.

The Roman principate had been born convulsively among blood-lettings, of which the young Augustus did his share and more. These circumstances, increasing the necessity for rulers to display a Republican face, prevented the establishment of any firm rules or overt understandings about the imperial succession. However glaring the limelight in which the younger relatives of Augustus might find themselves, there could be no open admission that he was founding a dynasty or that the succession would pass automatically from one ruler to another. So although he pointed the way by ultimately adopting his stepson and long-standing collaborator Tiberius as his son and conferring upon him a share of his own powers, the deterioration of Augustus's health towards the end of his life created a tense situation.

'In the capital the situation was calm. The titles of officials remained the same. Actium had been won before the younger men were born. Even most of the older generation had come into a world of civil wars. Practically no one had ever seen truly Republican government. The country had been transformed, and there was nothing left of the fine old Roman character. Political equality was a thing of the past: all eyes watched for imperial commands. Nobody had any immediate worries as long as Augustus retained his physical powers, and kept himself going, and his House, and the peace of the empire. But when old age incapacitated him, his approaching end brought hopes of change. A few people started idly talking of the blessings of freedom. Some, more numerous, feared civil war; others wanted it. The great majority, however, exchanged critical gossip about candidates for the succession.'[14]

Tiberius duly succeeded to the principate, but only after a series of painful embarrassments. And the problem of the succession remained, throughout the first century AD, acutely difficult. In AD 68–70, after Nero, the last ruler of Augustus's house, had perished, the absence of a recognized or obvious successor created the ruinous chaos of the Year of the Four Emperors. But when the next dynasty, that of the Flavians, had gone down in violence, the elderly Nerva (AD 96–8) anticipated trouble by adopting as his son and, by unmistakable implication, as his successor, the senator who seemed best suited for the post—Trajan. The principle of adoption, fortified by blood relationships and marriage ties, held good and proved highly successful until Marcus Aurelius, for all his philosophy, lapsed from it, designating as his successor his worthless son Commodus. This disastrous decision contributed substantially to the collapse of the western provinces during the century that followed. For, although the accession of Commodus was not contested, his irresponsible rule and consequent murder (AD 192) set a precedent for the future by precipitating a catastrophic series of civil wars. When these had continued for nearly four years, and Septimius Severus, though dominant in Rome, had not yet overcome his rivals in Gaul and the East, there occurred one of those occasions on which the ordinary people of Rome made their feelings heard. They had, it is true, heckled emperors before in the Circus or Amphitheatre, notably Tiberius when he did not show enough interest in the proceedings. But now they shouted for peace (AD 196); and the senator and historian Dio Cassius of Nicea heard and recorded the demonstration as 'something that increased our apprehensions still more'.[15]

Yet popular alarm or pacifism was wholly ineffective, and during the third century AD unending succession struggles (almost always deliberately provoked by revolts) continued to drain and devastate Italy and the empire. At the same time formidable external threats menaced the German and eastern frontiers. To deal with these dangers, very large amounts of money were needed. They could have been raised without all this misery—and the emperors could even have afforded a few glory-bringing aggressive foreign campaigns as well—if only gigantic sums had not been drained away on civil wars. These civil wars were caused by the failure of the imperial system to regulate the succession to the throne; and it was largely due to this failure that, during the terrible decades of the 'military anarchy' (AD 235–84), the relatively prosperous conditions which had hitherto favoured the Roman principate ceased to exist.

The failure to achieve a stable imperial succession impinged violently on the provinces during the third century AD, but until then, except for periods of civil strife after the murders of Nero and Commodus, the results of this constitutional problem had not greatly affected their peace and prosperity. In these vast and varied territories beyond the borders of Italy the Roman government, until the chaos of the third century, maintained the even tenor of its unprecedentedly efficient, if not remarkably imaginative, rule.

The whole population of the empire in the time of Augustus may have been between seventy and ninety millions, of whom from thirty to fifty millions were in Europe, perhaps the same number or rather fewer in Asia, and something short of twenty millions in Africa (Maps 1–5). Most of the provinces of the empire had been acquired as a direct or indirect result of the powers of conquest and unilateral decision which were so highly developed in the Romans. That was how they had won Sicily, Sardinia and Corsica, Spain, Macedonia, Africa, Pontus (northern Asia Minor), Crete, Cyprus, Illyricum, Cilicia (south-eastern Asia Minor), Syria, Gaul, Egypt and most of the Danubian and German territories—with Britain and Dacia (Roumania) to come. Other lands, however, had been left as bequests to Rome by their former monarchs, who hoped in this way to win peace in their time and a safe passage, after their deaths, for their supporters. Asia, the greatest of all the provinces, and later Bithynia (north-western Asia Minor) and Cyrene, came into Roman hands in this way. But other important provinces became possessions of Rome by a less decisive transition, seeing that even before annexation their Greek or native monarchs had already been 'client-kings' dependent on Rome. The corn-producing Bosphorus (Crimea) was almost unique in retaining client, as opposed to subject, status throughout the principate; whereas the client-kingdoms of Galatia, Noricum (in central Europe), Mauretania, Judaea, and the Nabataean Arabs (north-western Arabia) were in due course absorbed into the empire. In Britain, even before its partial annexation by Claudius, certain of the princelings had already been semi-dependent upon the emperors. For there were client states of many nuances of autonomy; beyond the truly client kings there was sometimes, in west and east alike, a penumbra of semi-clients, less dependent on Rome and tied to its rulers by economic rather than political bonds, comparable to the 'banana imperialism' of today. Such, in the time of Augustus, was king Tincommius in Sussex, Hampshire and Berkshire, who, however, was apparently regarded as a traitor by his compatriots, since he fled to Rome.

Communications with such a distant chieftain might sometimes be erratic, but within the empire they were admirable. From the time of Augustus onwards maritime links were enormously improved in speed and security alike (p. 63). But the most important means of communication and organization was provided by the amazingly comprehensive network of excellently constructed roads extending throughout Italy and over all the provinces of the empire. Already in the Republic the Via Egnatia had been constructed from Dyrrhachium (Durazzo) to Thessalonica (Salonica) and the Via Domitia from the Rhône to the Pyrenees. Thereafter road-building by the emperors was on an immense scale. In the single province of Britain alone, 6,500 miles of roads were constructed within one hundred years after the initial conquests of AD 43, and of those perhaps no less than 6,000 miles were completed during the first four decades of that period (Plate 46a). Such roads display a magisterial control of nature. For example, the Via Domitiana, a branch of the Via Appia passing through Cumae to Puteoli (Pozzuoli) and Naples, over-coming the difficulties of marshes, a sandy shore, a river of fluc-tuating course, and thick woods, cut straight through a mountain; its severed heights were linked by a great viaduct (Plate 46*b*).

On solidly and powerfully constructed roads such as these, built primarily for troop movements, Caesar travelled 800 miles in 8 days; Galba, in Spain 332 miles from Rome, received the news of Nero's death in 7 days. Moreover, this mighty network of road-communications also did a great deal to foster trade (p. 63). No less impressive were the bridges which carried the roads over rivers (Plate 48*a*; p. 271) and the aqueducts which conveyed water over land and river alike (Plate 49*a,b*; p. 272).

The governors sent to rule the most important of these provinces were Roman senators, men who had done their term of metropolitan service as consul or praetor. They therefore belonged to the inner circle of people and families who shared, at first absolutely and then under imperial supervision, the control of Rome's destinies.

When the east had received its first Roman governors in the second century BC, their ability to keep their hands off public funds was noted to exceed that of the Greeks—and our informant, Polybius, is a Greek himself, from Megalopolis in Arcadia:

'Among the Greeks, members of their governments, if they are entrusted with no more than a talent, though they have ten copyists and as many seals and twice as many witnesses, cannot keep their faith; whereas among the Romans those who as officials and legates are dealing with large sums of money maintain correct conduct just because they have pledged their faith by oath. Whereas elsewhere it is a rare thing to find a man who keeps his hands off public money, and whose record is clean in this respect, among the Romans one rarely comes across a man who has been detected in misconduct of this kind . . .'[16]

A famous example and model of such integrity was Cato the elder, skinflint though he was. As Cicero said:

'The most eminent men in the country, during the best period of our history, counted it among their most honourable and splendid achieve-ments to protect from injury and to maintain in prosperity those guests and retainers of theirs—the foreign nations who had been received as friends into the Roman Empire. That wise and distinguished man Marcus

Cato Sapiens, history tells us, made many and lasting enemies by standing up for the unfortunate Spaniards, among whom he had served as consul [195 BC].'[17]

In the last century BC, on the other hand, when Rome and Romans had become more cynical and predatory, the standard of honesty and responsibility among governors was very low; they were mostly corrupt and rapacious, regarding their year of office as a period for making large illegitimate profits. The Greeks or others, who, subject to these proconsuls, controlled the provincial communities, usually endured the burden more or less willingly since they owed their positions to Rome and could pass on much of the cost to the lower levels of the population (p. 103). They were also consoled by the amateurishness of the governors, none of whom stayed long enough for his depredations to go really deep. Still, the general practice of the Republic, that Italy should provide the men and the provinces the money, was generally interpreted as meaning that, over and above the tribute (land-tax) paid by provincials, a large proportion of these funds should find its way into the pockets of provincial governors and, to a lesser extent, of their subordinates.

During the second and first centuries BC the Roman government initiated and elaborated laws aimed at limiting and controlling the improprieties of its representatives in the provinces. But the Extortion Court thus established was all too often totally incapacitated by bribery, and Cicero, in his courageous attack upon one of the most unscrupulous—and best protected—governors, Verres in Sicily (70 BC), deplores the discredit which had fallen upon the institution in the eyes of provincials:

'I asserted my belief that, one of these days, communities from the provinces would send deputations to the people of Rome requesting that the extortion law and its court should be abolished. For if no such court existed, they suppose that each governor would only take away with him enough for himself and his children. At present, on the other hand, with the courts as they are, a governor takes enough for himself, and his protectors, and his counsel, and the president of the court, and the judges! In other words, there is no end to it. A greedy man's lust for gain they could satisfy, but they cannot afford a guilty man's acquittal. How peculiarly glorious our courts have become, how scintillating is the prestige of our Senatorial Order, when Rome's allies pray that the courts which our ancestors created for their benefit should be struck out of existence!'[18]

Probably Cicero, in this eloquent speech which so greatly increased his reputation (and served as a model for Burke's prosecution of Warren Hastings) somewhat exaggerates the startling list of crimes attributed to Verres. But when allowance is made for that, it is still clear that many governors behaved deplorably—with the active or passive connivance of powerful leaders of Republican Rome, who sometimes arranged, as in the case of Verres, that the normal tenure of one year should be extended.

The provincials suffered also from the onslaughts of Roman financiers belonging to, or depending on, the important Order of Knights (p. 5). In the immensely wealthy province of Asia, corporations directed by knights, with their own couriers, banks and probably shareholders, were authorized by the Roman authorities to farm the taxation. As under the previous régime of the kings of Pergamum, the main tax was fixed at ten per cent on all agricultural produce. The corporations of tax-collectors made bids to the Roman government for five years' income, and the successful bidders guaranteed an agreed sum to the treasury: what more they collected was their margin of profit. The state could, itself, not have collected this money since it did not yet possess a civil service capable of doing so; but the delegation of the process to tax-farmers inevitably led to arbitrary exactions. Members of the Senate were officially not allowed to take an active part in such financial transactions. Yet when Cicero was governor of Cilicia he found that the high-minded Stoic senator Brutus, the man who, according to Shakespeare, was above wringing 'from the hard hands of peasants their vile trash', had charged Cypriots forty-eight per cent interest and wanted this sum collected by force and bloodshed. Cicero wrote to his friend Atticus, a great financier himself (who was always urging Cicero to help Brutus), expressing his shock and embarrassment.[19]

Cicero was a hesitant, timid man, but occasionally he was so moved by a cause that he showed determination; and he showed it here. This was in keeping with his own conduct as governor of Cilicia, which at that time extended far into the interior of Asia Minor. He worked strenuously, fought to maintain public security— seeking a somewhat tenuous military glory against some tribesmen— and, unlike so many others, was in a position to claim that he had extracted no improper gains from his province. His only profit, one regarded as legitimate, comprised the proceeds (at famine prices) from the large amount of corn which governors were allowed to requisition, ostensibly for their own table; and even these perhaps not wholly creditable, but legally defensible, savings were lost to Cicero once the Civil War started, since Pompey laid hands on them. Cicero also proved unwilling to help Caelius Rufus, the fashionable young man who was his political informant at Rome, either with a free gift of panthers for his electioneering show, or with a financial contribution from the provincials. Cicero describes the situation in his Cilician province to Atticus, with a typical mixture of vanity, the human desire to criticize one's predecessor, and real humanity:

'So I sit down on the high road to scribble you a summary of what really calls for a long epistle. You must know that my arrival in this province, which is in a state of lasting ruin and desolation, was expected eagerly. I got here on 31st July. I stayed three days at Laodicea, three at Apamea, and as many at Synnada. Everywhere I heard the same tale. People could not pay their taxes: they were forced to sell out their investments; groans and lamentations in the towns, and awful conduct of one who is some kind of savage beast rather than a man. All the people are, as you may suppose, tired of life. However, the poor towns are relieved that they have had to spend nothing on me, my legates, or a quaestor, or anyone. For you must know that I not only refused to accept pay, or what is a proper perquisite under the Julian law, but that none of us will take firewood or anything beyond four beds and a roof; and in many places we do not accept even a roof, but remain mostly under canvas. So extraordinary throngs of people have come to meet me from farms and villages and every homestead. Upon my word my very coming seems to revive them. Your friend Cicero has won all hearts by his justice and self-restraint and kind bearing.'[20]

Even with Cicero, however, the overriding consideration was, too often, the effect of his actions on his Roman career, of which he regarded this governorship as an irritating and painful interruption. Yet the desire of a few men like him to rule decently pointed the way to a better future.

During the later Republic, governors were generally bad; from the time of Augustus onwards they varied from bad to conscientious. When Tiberius told them that 'a good shepherd shears his flock but does not flay them',[21] he was instructing them to maintain what had already, since the beginning of the principate, become required practice. Under the system established by Augustus, senior senators who had served as consuls or praetors were carefully groomed and chosen for provincial governorships, of which the old rascalities diminished. Africa and Asia came at the head of the 'senatorial provinces'—still governed by 'proconsuls', usually for only one year at a time. But Augustus himself, 'at the request of the Senate' (probably confirmed by a Law of the Assembly), and on a basis which was at first temporary but in fact became permanent, took over, as supreme governor, the principal military provinces. These included Spain and the regions bordering on the Rhine, Danube and Euphrates. Following and expanding certain late Republican precedents for governorships *in absentia*—Pompey had governed Spain in this way—Augustus controlled his provinces through 'legates' who like the proconsuls were of high senatorial rank, but unlike them often retained their posts for several years at a time.

Augustus also strengthened the provincial administration by his reorganization of the Order of Knights. This was still limited, like the Senate, to the well-to-do, though its property qualification was less than theirs. Augustus used the knights to provide the nucleus of a new Imperial Civil Service existing alongside, and supplementing, the traditional official career of the senators. He posted knights in the provinces as his personal representatives (procurators), with tax-collecting and other financial duties under his close supervision. They were also allowed certain 'plums', such as the governorships of small provinces—notably Judaea, when it passed into Roman hands (p. 46)—and one large one: the rich territory of Egypt which, after its conquest from Cleopatra, remained under the emperor's personal control, and was entrusted by him to a prefect chosen from among the knights.

What did the Romans feel about the peoples whom they ruled?

In one sense, xenophobia was not very strong in the Roman empire. That is to say, anyone who had learnt the Greek or Latin language and absorbed enough of the prevalent culture to participate in current activities was able to make good. The proof is provided at the very top of the pyramid, by a long list of non-Italian emperors. The first of them was Trajan, whose Roman ancestors had settled in Spain and had no doubt intermarried with Spaniards. The list of foreign rulers continues with his compatriot Hadrian, with Antoninus Pius whose ancestors had come from Gaul, with Septimius Severus who was a north African married to a Syrian, and with Elagabalus who was himself a Syrian; followed by emperors who themselves came from Thrace, from Arabia, and from the Illyrian provinces bordering on the Danube and on the Dalmatian coast. But even before emperors came from the provinces, many other political and military figures had been of provincial origin. Thus the home of Caesar's chief adviser Balbus was the partially Semitic Gades (Cadiz) in Spain, described as containing more capitalists than any city of the empire except Patavium (Padua); a Roman knight, Theophanes, Pompey's historian, came from Mitylene, and his grandson Q. Pompeius Macer became a senator under Tiberius (p. 101); the principal secretaries of Claudius and Nero were orientals (pp. 98 f.); Tiberius Julius Alexander, Prefect of Egypt from Nero to Vespasian, was a renegade Jew; Domitian's Commander of the Guard, Crispinus, was an Egyptian; legionary commanders came from Gaul and other provinces (p. 51); and one of Trajan's principal generals, Lusius Quietus, was a Berber (p. 43).

In AD 48 Claudius addressed the Senate in favour of admitting Gaulish chiefs to their membership. The speech, in addition to an imperfect account by Tacitus (p. 101), has survived in a verbatim reproduction at Lyon.[22] With a characteristic blend of liberal practicality and antiquarian learning he points out that this sort of receptiveness had been typical of Roman history from the very beginning. In support of this thesis, he is able to cite not only Julius Caesar, who had himself admitted to the Senate a few Gallic notables—perhaps of Roman origin—but also the legendary or semi-legendary kings of Rome, of whom Numa Pompilius was reputed to be not a Roman but a Sabine, Tarquinius Priscus the son of a Corinthian immigrant to Etruria, and Servius Tullius the son of a slavewoman or refugee in the same country. Many of the greatest masters of the Latin language also came from outside Italy (pp. 213 ff.), and the best of 'Roman' sculpture, architecture and painting was almost all the work of non-Roman hands (pp. 237 ff.): the most noteworthy school of imperial sculpture was at Aphrodisias in south-western Asia Minor, and the most famous architect of metropolitan buildings, Apollodorus, was a Greek or more probably a Hellenized Syrian from Damascus.

Yet behind this impressive picture of internationalism there were serious racial tensions. The most significant of these, because it concerned the two chief peoples of the empire on whose collaboration the whole structure depended, was the tension between Romans and Greeks. Psychologists might describe the attitude of the Romans towards their Greek neighbours and subjects as the manifestation of a love-hate relationship. On the one hand educated Romans felt a passionate admiration for Greek culture, and a consciousness of inferiority to its possessors. On the other hand they retained a widespread suspicion of its unmanly cleverness, and a strong distaste for contemporary Greeks, who seemed light-weight, unsound and unprincipled. Already in the second century BC Rome had rung all the changes on these attitudes—and had moved all the way from the sentimental 'liberation' of Greece in 194 BC by the philhellene Flamininus (Plate 10*a*) to the increasing loss of patience manifested in their dissolution of the Achaean League and sack of Corinth (146 BC). During the latter part of this period Rome had witnessed a deep cultural fissure between the supporters of Cato the elder, who despite his own debts to Greek literature stood for the retention of the 'pure' Italian, crude, western tradition, and Scipio Aemilianus who gathered round himself the leading Greek thinkers of the day such as the historian Polybius and the Stoic philosopher Panaetius.

These conflicting tendencies could even be detected existing together within the breast of a single Roman. Indeed, they are found together in Cicero, where they correspond with his two great talents —for studious popularization of Greek philosophy, and for public Roman oratory. Yet it would be an over-simplification to say that when Cicero is philosophizing he is pro-Greek and when he is delivering an oration he is anti-Greek. The truth rather is that he is the one or the other as befits the actual case, in either genre, which he is arguing at the time. When he is attacking Verres, for example (p. 33), he is afraid that his support of the oppressed Sicilian Greeks may make him seem too philhellene to his Roman audience. So he affects an elaborate ignorance about the works of art which he claims that Verres has stolen:

'One was a marble Cupid by Praxiteles—I learnt the artist's name, you will understand, in the course of my investigations as prosecutor. . . . Other statues were called the Basket-Bearers; but the sculptor—who was he? now who did they say he was? Oh yes, thank you—Polyclitus. . . . It is indeed astonishing what delight a Greek will take in these things of which a Roman thinks so little.'[23]

This from a man who was an enthusiastic collector of Greek sculpture! Elsewhere in these speeches, it is true, Cicero must instil in his hearers sympathy for his Greek clients, the Sicilians who were oppressed by their Roman governor Verres. But his tribute to them is somewhat backhanded, for he says that they are good, industrious people—unlike other Greeks.[24]

But Cicero appeared in a far more pro-Greek light eight years later, when it was his task to assert the disputed claims to Roman citizenship of Archias, a Greek or Greco-Syrian poet of Antioch. The written oration as it has come down to us—no doubt, like the Verrines, in a form more elaborate than the speech that he actually delivered—contains a brilliant eulogy of the profession of the liberal arts: a profession understood by his audience as Greek, and exemplified by Cicero's Greek client:

'If anyone thinks that the glory won by the writing of Greek verse is naturally less than that accorded to the poet who writes in Latin, he is entirely in the wrong. Greek literature is read in nearly every nation under heaven, while the vogue of Latin is confined to its own boundaries, and they are, we must grant, narrow.'[25]

However, the trouble usually was that the Greeks whom Cicero encountered, apart from a sprinkling of learned men or devoted secretaries, failed lamentably to square up to the picture of the ideal Hellas which he so passionately cherished. This became apparent when, in 59 BC, he spoke in defence of Lucius Valerius Flaccus, a governor of Asia who was accused of robbing provincials—that is to say, leading citizens of the Greek cities. Allowing for an element of exaggeration since it was Cicero's professional duty to discredit their evidence, we cannot fail to detect a sincere gusto in the slashing attack which, although himself an abstainer from similar plunderings (p. 34), he directs against the Greek character:

'This I can say of the whole race of Greeks. I grant them literature, I grant them a knowledge of many arts, I do not deny the charm of their speech, the keenness of their intellects, the richness of their diction; finally, if they make other claims I do not deny them. But truth and honour in giving testimony that nation has never cherished: the meaning, the importance, the value of this whole matter they know not. Whence comes that saying, "Testify for me and I'll testify for you"? It isn't thought to be Gallic, is it? or Spanish? It is so entirely Greek that even those who do not understand Greek know the Greek words for this expression. . . . And Greeks never trouble to prove what they say but only to make a display of themselves by talking. A Greek witness takes the stand with the intention of doing harm, he does not think of the worth of his oath but of words that may injure; to be beaten, to be refuted, to be worsted in an argument, he regards as a disgrace; he protects himself against this and cares for nothing else. So the witnesses selected are in each case not the best and most influential men but the most pert and most talkative.'²⁶

This contempt and distrust of the Greeks was scarcely mitigated by Cicero's occasional assurance that it was only the Greeks of Asia Minor (or Asians of Hellenic culture and some Greek blood) to whom he was referring, and that the Greeks of the homeland were better. This distinction, and indeed the general rise of anti-Greek feeling at Rome, had been encouraged by an event which shocked Rome profoundly—the massacre of Italians, at the orders of the Hellenized Iranian Mithradates VI of Pontus (Plate 10b), by the Greek city-governments of Asia (88 BC). The Greeks may, looking to the future, have been unwilling to comply—Tralles hired a native Asian to do the job for them—yet at many cities, including Ephesus and Pergamum, Italian refugees were torn from the sanctuaries and butchered, according to the lowest contemporary estimate, to the number of 80,000. Another reason why the more law-abiding sections of the Roman population felt disgusted with the Greeks and Hellenized Asians was because they collaborated in various ways with the pirates who, until Pompey and then Augustus put them down, infested the Mediterranean. For example, Attaleia and Side on the south coast of Asia Minor were openly in league with the pirates, for whose prisoners Side, like the island of Delos, provided a vast slave-market.

Thus Cicero's voluminous works contain a great many derogatory remarks about the Greeks whose culture he so greatly admired. Something of the same duality is apparent in the policies of Augustus, who deliberately exalted Italy at the expense of the provinces, and yet built for the god Apollo, borrowed from Greece, a resplendent shrine on the Palatine which symbolized the emperor's desire to recreate in Roman guise the classical Hellenic culture. Lucretius and Cicero had regarded it as their patriotic mission to make the best of Greek philosophy available for the Romans—and so to 'free' Rome from Greece—and in the same way, Horace, following the Augustan trend, declares it his task and privilege to recreate in himself, in Roman guise, the Greek poet Alcaeus.²⁷ The emperors Nero and Hadrian were openly philhellene: Nero repeated Flamininus's gesture of 'liberating' Greece (p. 38), and Hadrian showered favours on the Greeks and their cultural institutions. Yet only a few years before Hadrian's reign, under the uncompromisingly pro-Roman Trajan, the satirist Juvenal went right back to the anti-Hellenic tradition, which had existed continuously at Rome ever since contact between the two races had begun. Juvenal venomously attacks the Greeks who were to be seen in the capital:

> . . . eager to worm their way
> Into great houses and become their masters.
> A quick intelligence, a shameless boldness,
> Ready speech more torrential than Isaeus—
> Say now, what do you think that man to be?
> He brings with him any character you please: . . .
> All sciences the famished Greekling knows:
> Bid him ascend to heaven, to heaven he mounts . . .
> Should you laugh,
> Your Greek will be convulsed with a loud guffaw,
> He weeps, if he sees tears in a friend's eye,
> Yet feels no grief . . .
> Night or day he is able to compose
> His looks after the face of another man;
> Is ready to fling his hands up and applaud
> If his friend has belched finely, if he has jetted
> A good straight stream, or if his golden cup,
> Turned upside down, is drained with a loud smack.
> Moreover there is nothing sacred to him,
> Nothing from his lasciviousness secure,
> Neither the matron of the family,
> Nor yet the virgin daughter, no nor even
> The still unbearded son-in-law, nor the son,
> Chaste hitherto. Or in default of these,
> He will debauch the grandmother of his friend.[28]

And even the Italian rustic, says Juvenal, now imitates the Greeks: 'puts on foppish Greek slippers, and adorns his wax-anointed neck with prize-medallions.'[29] Leading Greeks were uncomfortably aware of what Romans thought of them (p. 57).

Yet neither Rome nor Greece finally conquered the other. The division between the main western and eastern cultures of the Mediterranean region remained fundamental, and the disunity which this division engendered was one reason for the empire's eventual failure to weather its storms. The same division initiated, along its frontiers, age-long tensions between Croats and Serbs, Poles and Russians, producing among these people the basic, permanent fission between

the Roman Catholic Church—Christianity in the Latin form which
gave it power—and Greek Orthodoxy.

If the appreciation of the Greeks by the Romans left a good deal to
be desired, relations between Rome and the native, 'barbarian'
populations of Asia Minor, Syria and Egypt were rudimentary. The
Romans only learnt of these populations through the medium of the
Greeks who controlled the cities and led the civilizations of those
countries. The Augustan geographer Strabo of Amaseia in Pontus
suggests that ethnic divisions between the native peoples of Asia
Minor tended to become blurred,[30] and there can be equally little
doubt that the Greek communities of the peninsula had intermarried
with these peoples. Some Greeks, notably Dio Chrysostom of Prusa,
regarded this as a racial danger to Hellenism. Cicero records the
derogatory sayings that he had heard concerning the peoples in the
hinterland of the Asian province.[31] 'He's the lowest of the Mysians'—
that is to say, of the low. 'If you want to risk a life in any experiment,
use a Carian' (this was as old as Plato).[32] 'A Phrygian is usually
improved by whipping.'

Moreover, the slave parts in Greek comedies were taken by
Lydians. This became increasingly apposite, in the time of the
Roman empire, since a very large proportion of the slave population
of Rome came from Asia Minor. So, therefore, did many of the
freedmen, the great new middle-class of Rome (p. 96). This is
symbolized by the Asian origin of Trimalchio and his friends in the
Satyricon of Petronius (p. 64). Naturally, therefore, this great influx,
which meant in the end that a large proportion of the Roman people
were of Anatolian origin, aroused echoes of Cicero's charges of
frivolity, acquisitiveness and untrustworthiness.

A great many also of Rome's slaves were Syrians, and these too
were clever and versatile enough to figure largely among the number
of freedmen and freedwomen. The Syrian population of the capital
was singled out for attack by that hater of foreigners Juvenal:

> Long since into Tiber
> Syrian Orontes has come flooding in,
> Carrying language and manners on its flood,
> The flutist, and the harp with slanting strings,
> Outlandish drums too, and the girls whose trade
> Is to accost one at the Circus doors.[33]

But it was the Egyptians that Juvenal detested most, and his hatred was evidently based on a period of unhappy residence in that country. His fifteenth satire describes an allegedly recent incident of lynching and cannibalism caused by the fanatical religious feelings which were particularly associated with Egypt (p. 161). What Juvenal means to say is that from among such people barbarism is always pressing in upon civilization; he hated the Egyptians for what he regarded as their paradoxical mixture of feebleness and violence, leading, as he saw it, to the worship of animals and killing of men, to abstention from vegetables and the eating of human flesh. The remarkable school of portrait-painters of Egypt has left us with some vivid presentations of the facial types of this period (Plates 17, 18a, 19a). We cannot generally tell if the people thus depicted on their mummy-cases are Greeks or Egyptians; they are mostly upper-class, and Hellenized—they wear Greek and not Egyptian jewellery—but racial mixtures were both ancient and continuous.

Certain of these mummy-portraits are dark and negroid, and Alexandrian sculptors had during the last centuries BC developed a special penchant for the rather sentimental and mannered, not unsympathetic representation of negroes (Plate 19b). They were popular among artists because of the opportunities that they provided for psychological virtuosity and extreme, sometimes grotesque, naturalism. Graceful boys are particularly often represented— melancholy slave-singers for example—but Hadrianic art also includes portraits not only of slaves but of more distinguished figures, perhaps visiting chiefs. In literature, however, except for two Carthaginian poems praising a black hunter Olympius,[34] they usually receive a mildly contemptuous treatment. (The terms 'Moor' and 'Ethiopian' were loosely used. But the true 'Moor' was a Berber with little or no negro blood such as Trajan's Libyan consul and cavalry leader Lusius Quietus, employed to stamp out Jewish revolts (AD 116–17) but executed under Hadrian in AD 118.)

A contemptuous attitude towards coloured people is particularly to be expected from satirists such as Martial and Juvenal, who imply their utilization at Rome for immoral purposes. The latter says it was bad luck to meet a negro at night; he also writes of a dinner-party at which the host and leading guests were waited on by a choice slave from Asia, but the poor guests by a black slave. Earlier, in a gastronomic poem *The Salad* (*Moretum*), of which we do not know the author, there is a description of just such a girl:

> At times he shouts for Scybale.
> She was his only servant; African
> By race; all things about her bearing witness
> Where she was born: hair curly; her lips thick;
> Her colour dusky; with broad chest and breasts
> Low-hanging, and with belly somewhat pinched;
> Thin legs, feet large and broad. Her tough-skinned heels
> were seamed with many a crack. . . .[35]

It was from Alexandrian writers and artists that Rome adopted the methods and tones of describing such negroes in words and sculpture. But if there must, then as now, have been a considerable negroid population of Egypt, no less than one-seventh of the total population of that country in Roman times was Jewish. The extreme hostility between these Jews and the Egyptian Greeks (as well as the native Egyptians) brought the Jews ultimately into grave racial disputes with the Romans too. When Pompey conquered Jerusalem in 63 BC his entrance into the Holy of Holies—an outrage to Jewish feelings— was a significant omen of the disastrous relations between the two races which were to develop during the two centuries that followed. The Romans felt repelled by the 'otherness' of the Jews, who, in Palestine and throughout the near east, alone refused to enter into the new, international cosmopolitanism of the Roman empire—in contrast with the situation of their similar settlements today, which form international groups in national states. In 139 BC they were expelled from Rome, probably for proselytizing. In 59 BC Cicero explains the reasons why Roman patience might, and would, break down:

'Even while Jerusalem was standing and the Jews were at peace with us, the practice of their sacred rites was at variance with the glory of our empire, the dignity of our name, the customs of our ancestors. But now it is even more so, when that nation by its armed resistance has shown what it thinks of our rule. How dear it was to the immortal gods is shown by the fact that it has been conquered, let out for taxes, made a slave.'[36]

Yet Pompey and Augustus, even if they did not handle Jewish politics with their usual care or skill, were tolerant of the Jewish religion. A harsh penal action by Tiberius, who expelled the Jews from Italy and sent four thousand to serve as military police in fever-ridden Sardinia, was due to an alleged attempt by some of them to obtain money under false pretences from a Roman lady. But the storm-centre of the Mediterranean was Alexandria, where a very large Jewish quarter adjoined the palace quarter. Perhaps, out of the seven or eight million Jews in all countries outside Palestine, no less than a million lived in Egypt, many of them descended from settlers of the time of Alexander and the first Ptolemy—from ex-soldiers with no special reputation, at first, as financiers and traders. The hostility between Jews and Greeks in Egypt was intense—far the most serious inter-racial tension of the empire. Arising at least as early as the opening years of the third century BC, pagan anti-Semitism sprang from Jewish exclusiveness, and from the consequent resentment of the city Greeks against people refusing to share in their social interests and amusements. The Jewish case on the other hand is put for us, in Greek, by Philo of Alexandria and the pro-Roman Pharisee Josephus.

For a time the Jews had their own client-state in Palestine—under Herod the Great (43–4 BC), at the end of whose reign Jesus was born (not in AD 1 as medieval theologians computed), and then again under Archelaus (4 BC–AD 6). While the Jews thus enjoyed self-government, it seemed to Rome that, cherishing this position, they would be less tiresome than the Greeks, and more likely to support the ruling power. So Augustus, while curbing the Alexandrian Greeks, confirmed Jewish privileges. But blunders under Tiberius's governor Pontius Pilatus led to a massacre of Samaritans on Mount Gerizim, and when, during an active phase of rioting in Alexandria under Caligula (AD 38), a disastrous visit by the popular, ambitious, extravagant Jewish prince Agrippa I had resulted in a pogrom, Rome's prefect of Egypt, Aulus Avillius Flaccus, decided to blame the Jews and support the Greeks against them. In Antioch, too, there was, at the same time, something like a Greco-Jewish war. However, Caligula's decision to erect his own statue in the Temple at Jerusalem was, fortunately for peace, averted by his death. Claudius's reversal of his anti-Jewish policy is shown by edicts (recorded by Josephus) in which the emperor raps the Alexandrian Greeks severely over the knuckles for their persistent anti-Semitism. Here, too, is his warning after a riot which shortly followed his accession:

'As for your quarrel or breach of the peace, or, if I must be blunt, war, with the Jews, while reluctant to look into the responsibility for it too deeply, I have stored up within me an implacable anger against any who start further trouble. I tell you frankly that if you do not stop this suicidal and bigoted squabbling with each other, I shall be forced to demonstrate what a humane prince can be like when he turns to righteous indignation.'[37]

And in AD 53 two anti-Jewish leaders, whose case Claudius had heard, were put to death—and canonized as anti-Semitic nationalist martyrs.[38] Yet it was the same emperor who had precipitated the future breach in relations between Jews and Romans by annexing Judaea, on the death in AD 44 of its ruler Agrippa I whom he himself had wisely installed three years earlier.

The Roman governors who followed (in this province knights, not senators, in rank) were often unable to conceal their antipathy for their subjects; they showed Roman rule at its most tactless. The Jews felt infuriated at the obligation to pay tribute. They also detested the sight of a Roman garrison in the Tower of Antonia commanding the Temple, and the insulting facts that the vestments of the High Priest were in Roman hands and that Roman governors could intervene in Jewish courts. There followed three prolonged revolts of appalling carnage and savagery—in AD 66–70, in 115–16 and in 132–5. In the first of these revolts, of which (as in the second) the leaders issued their own coinage (Plate 11c), a million Jews were said to have perished after Titus's siege and destruction of Jerusalem (AD 70; Plate 37a)—described by Josephus, who sided with the Romans against the fanatical Zealot leaders of his compatriots. In the two later revolts, sparked off respectively by Greco-Jewish disputes and by Hadrian's foundation of a Roman colony on the site of Jerusalem, the Jews of Cyrene, Egypt and Cyprus joined those of the homeland.

The complete failure of understanding on both sides is echoed, early in the second century AD, by Tacitus. Although he knew more about the Jews than any other Roman writer with the possible exception of Juvenal, his account of their history and institutions is strangely perverse. He describes most of their customs as 'base and abominable, owing their persistence to the depravity of the Jews . . . the ways of the Jews are preposterous and mean'.[39] Soon afterwards, following the third revolt and virtual extirpation of the Jewish national home, Hadrian imposed severe penal laws prohibiting circumcision, but these were allowed to lapse by Antoninus Pius. Henceforward the Jews enjoyed toleration. But the Greeks never loved them, and against the torrent of Jewish apocalyptic literature, much of it directed against the Greeks (pp. 60 f.), stand papyri inscribed with the 'Pagan Acts of the Martyrs'. In the surviving fragments of these Acts, dating from a number of reigns, the Alexandrian Greeks season their attacks on Rome with savage vituperations against the Jews for their alleged predominance in the emperor's counsels. Many of the pagan sects of this period, too, were violently anti-Jewish, those of dualistic tendencies identifying the 'accursed god of the Jews' with the evil power Saturn and with the Devil.

As regards the less civilized native populations of Europe, the Roman record, apart from savagery during warfare, is better. The peoples of the western provinces gradually became Romanized, and an occasional sneering reference to Gaulish trousers seen in the capital and the Senate is immaterial in contrast to Rome's general, if cautious, receptiveness towards the more advanced elements of these peoples. True, those of the natives who rejected such opportunities found the Romans and their supporters unaccommodating. The Augustan geographer Strabo, himself a Greco-Asiatic, has little sympathy for defeated and enslaved rebels from Corsica, finding them astonishingly brutish. Either, he complains, they are as savage as wild animals or as tame as sheep. Some of them die in captivity. 'The rest are so apathetic and slow-witted that their angry purchasers, though they have bought them for a song, repent of their bargain.'[40] Strabo is also shocked, but not impressed, by the Cantabrian rebels from northern Spain who 'on being crucified after capture still kept on shouting their victory slogans from the cross'.[41] Julius Caesar, although deliberately clement to Roman citizens, was second to none in brutality towards his Gallic enemies, though he took trouble—as a successful general must—to see their points of view.

But it was towards the end of the first century AD that Roman interest in the innumerable, mysterious peoples beyond the western frontiers became intense. On the Columns of Trajan (Plate 38) and Marcus Aurelius (Plate 39a, b) we see vigorous, dramatic, clearly differentiated types of barbarians, just as in the third century BC sculptors at Pergamum had excelled in depicting the Gaulish invaders of Asia Minor. By Trajan's time the nations beyond the Rhine and the Danube had already been the subjects of an eloquent ethnological study by Tacitus, the *Germania* (c. AD 98). There was an established tradition of ethnographic writing, in which the Ionian Greeks, such as Hecataeus of Miletus (c. 500 BC), had been pioneers.

Posidonius (p. 137) in the first century BC had written informatively about Spain, and his data had been used by Strabo—who remarked that the Romans, regarding geography as difficult and abstruse, did little to add to such Greek sources. Tacitus for his part depended on the polymath Pliny the elder (d. AD 79), but while he does not add much up-to-date information his attitude to the Germans is individual and noteworthy. Up to a point, he dramatizes them as 'noble savages', selecting for description those of their qualities which resembled the simple, tough habits of the early Romans. For, writing at a time when Trajan commanded on the Rhine and was soon going to fight beyond the Danube, Tacitus saw the Germans, whom the passage of over two centuries since the victories of Marius (p. 7) had not enabled Rome to conquer, as the deadliest of national enemies—far more dangerous than the oriental Parthians, whom Augustan poets had denounced as the most formidable and treacherous of foes. After another three-quarters of a century the German invasions of the empire under Marcus Aurelius and his successors were to prove the forecast of Tacitus correct. But Tacitus does not merely idealize the capabilities of the Germans; he also dwells on their vices—fecklessness of many kinds and chronic disunion—which he sees as Rome's great hope. 'Long may it last, I pray, and persist among the nations, this, if not love for us, at least hatred of each other: since now that the destinies of the Empire have passed their zenith, Fortune can guarantee us nothing better than discord among our foes.'[42]

Such being the attitude of Romans to other peoples, it was not always easy for their government to make the provincial see that Roman rule was beneficial to them. No conscious attempt was made to Romanize the cultures of the Greek and other non-Roman populations of the empire; and in the east Romanization made hardly any progress. It progressed greatly in the west, but this happened by the indirect means of the Latin-speaking traders, soldiers, and settlers who penetrated far and wide. Moreover, all alike could see the impressiveness of the Roman idea manifested in the power, law and peace of imperial rule. And in case the advantages of these manifestations should not be sufficiently apparent, the Roman government was at great pains to explain to the subject populations of the empire, from Portugal to the Euphrates and from Britain to the Sahara, how well they were being governed.

In this process the imperial currency played an important part.

For, in the absence of modern media of communication, the only official announcements which the central government could be sure that very many people would see were those on the enormous network of official coinages that circulated throughout the empire (p. 65). If people could read, they could read the inscriptions on an imperial coin, and whether they could read or not they could see its design. Particular attention was lavished on the coin-portraits of the emperor (p. 240): these are startlingly well done at almost every successive epoch (Plates 11*b*; 12*a*, *b*, *d*; 13*b*). It was of primary importance to bring the features and personality of the Father of the Country himself to every home and shop in the empire. The subjects of Rome, unlike many Greeks of earlier centuries, were not generally fastidious enough to look for great artistry in the reverse designs of their coinage. But this deficiency was counterbalanced by their susceptibility to *news*—and there was no better medium for the diffusion of news than the coinage. So with news its reverse is crammed. In contrast to our modern currency, a single denomination of the Roman coinage, within a single year of an uneventful reign (that of Antoninus Pius), was issued with no less than one hundred and fifty different reverse 'types'.

For example, what should make Roman rule tolerable to the provincials was the gift of the Roman Peace itself; this was demonstrated to the world by the designs on innumerable coins. Another popular theme was timely imperial benefaction. Thus Tiberius refers to 'the Restoration of the Communities of Asia' (CIVITA-TIBVS ASIAE RESTITVTIS, Plate 11*a*). Under Tiberius this province experienced severe earthquakes, the worst damage occurring at Croesus's ancient capital of Sardes (AD 17). The emperor remitted taxes and provided huge sums for reconstruction. Sometimes, too, such messages to the general public were presented in the form of Personifications, often referring to qualities claimed by the imperial government. Thus Galba's design LIBERTAS PVBLICA not only points a contrast between the reigning emperor and his tyrannical predecessor Nero but also stresses that all citizens of Rome, and in a wider sense all the populations of the empire, enjoy their full rights under the law (Plate 12*a*). Another personification with a wide appeal was Fairness, *Aequitas*—more frequently found on the coinage than the colder conception of Justice. First appearing under Galba,[43] the name of *Aequitas* is often accompanied, from the beginning of the third century onwards, by three figures (Plate 13*c*).

These represent the gold, silver and bronze coinages themselves, and stress the honesty of the government in maintaining their weight and purity—at a time when, in fact, these were not being maintained, and when the psychologically unwise debasement of the gold and silver was shortly going to precipitate a grave economic crisis (p. 67).

Hadrian personifies, on a great series of coins, not only imperial qualities but geographical entities—the whole world and each individual province under Roman rule.[44] This is to remind the Romans and their subject peoples that he, a provincial by origin, regarded the empire not as an Italian possession but as a living organism of which every part existed in its own right and enjoyed imperial attention. One group of issues commemorates the visits of this greatest of imperial travellers to no less than eighteen territories, which are personified in the full dignity of their national costume. Antoninus Pius promptly retreated from this cosmopolitan attitude, but when Septimius Severus shows AFRICA on his coins, again in national dress (Plate 13b), this means no conquered province, not just another benefited territory, but tells the world that this is the country of the emperor's origin and special favour—and that the provinces may now expect the same treatment as Italy (p. 19).

Those are a few instances of the massive, long-lasting, loud and varied numismatic self-praise by the Roman government. Naturally enough the same theme predominates in literature, since the authors were for the most part members or dependants of the Roman governing class. Differ though they might, and did openly, regarding the merits of individual emperors (especially dead ones), writers of the imperial age are almost unanimous in their expression of the benefits of Roman rule to the provincials. Characteristic is a paean of the Pax Augusta by Velleius Paterculus, no great writer but a loyal senior officer of Tiberius.[45] In the hands of a genius, this somewhat threadbare genre could be transformed out of all recognition. One of the most significant successes of the imperial régime lay in the profound admiration for Roman rule overtly expressed by Virgil:

> Others, no doubt, will better mould the bronze
> To the semblance of soft breathing, draw from marble
> The living countenance; and others plead
> With greater eloquence, or learn to measure,
> Better than we, the pathways of the heaven,
> The risings of the stars; remember, Roman,

To rule the people under law, to establish
The way of peace, to battle down the haughty,
To spare the meek. Our fine arts, these, forever.[46]

Yet this, from the complex, humane mind and heart of Virgil, is not a straightforward panegyric. He warns Romans to make sure they govern well; Kipling's *Lest We Forget* recaptured something of the spirit.

Nearly a century and a half after Virgil, one of the many doubts which tormented the historian Tacitus concerned this point; were the grievances which provincials undoubtedly felt (pp. 59 ff.) justi-fied? There is therefore special interest in the reasoned defence of Roman imperialism which, in the Year of the Four Emperors (AD 68–70), he attributes to Cerialis, commander in Gaul and the Rhineland, addressing the defeated rebel tribe of the Treveri (Trier):

'There were always kings and wars throughout Gaul until you sub-mitted to our laws. Although often provoked by you, the only use we have made of our rights as victors has been to impose on you the necessary costs of maintaining peace. For you cannot secure tranquillity among nations without armies, nor maintain armies without pay, nor provide pay without taxes. Everything else we have in common. You often command our legions; you rule these and other provinces; we claim no privileges, you suffer no exclusion. You enjoy the advantage of the good emperors equally with us, although you dwell far from the capital: the cruel emperors assail those nearest them. You endure barren years, excessive rains, and all other natural evils; in like manner endure the extravagance or greed of your rulers. There will be vices so long as there are men, but these vices are not perpetual and they are compensated for by the coming of better times: unless, maybe, you hope that you will enjoy a milder rule if Tutor and Classicus the rebel leaders reign over you, or that the taxes required to provide armies to keep out the Germans and Britons will then be less than now! For, if the Romans are driven out—which Heaven forbid—what will follow except universal war among all peoples? The good fortune and order of eight hundred years have built up this mighty fabric which cannot be destroyed without overwhelming its destroyers.'[47]

With such words, continues the historian, Cerialis calmed and encouraged his hearers—who were fearful of sterner measures. Instead of acting harshly, he had soberly explained to them why the only alternative to Roman rule was anarchy. Tacitus himself, though a great admirer of military glory, was feeling towards the ideas of provincial partnership which Hadrian was about to put into effect. But Rome did not only have Romans to speak on its behalf. In the east, where the Greek governing classes owed their position to Roman rule (p. 101), there was no lack of propagandists for the régime, including some of the greatest orators, writers and philosophers of the day. In harmony with the Hellenic tradition, their exposition and arguments are more high-flown and learned than those of Cerialis, though their theme is the same. In this spirit, like Epictetus before him (p. 200), the popular philosopher Aelius Aristides of Hadriani in north-western Asia Minor offers praises to Rome under Antoninus Pius (AD 156):

'Now all the Greek cities rise up under your leadership, and the monuments which are dedicated in them and all their embellishments and comforts are beautiful suburbs which redound to your honour. The coasts and interiors have been filled with cities, some newly founded, others increased under and by you. . . . Taking good care of the Hellenes as of your foster-parents, you constantly hold your hand over them, and when they are prostrate, you raise them up. You release, free and autonomous, those of them who were the noblest and the leaders of bygone days, and you guide the others moderately with much consideration and forethought. As on holiday the whole civilized world lays down the arms which were its ancient burden, and has turned to adornment and all glad thoughts—with power to realize them. All the other rivalries have left the cities, and this one contention holds them all, how each city may appear most beautiful and attractive. . . . Gifts never cease from you to the cities, and it is not possible to determine who the major beneficiaries have been, because your kindness is the same to all. Cities gleam with radiance and charm, and the whole earth has been beautified like a garden. . . . Thus it is right to pity only those outside your hegemony —if indeed there are any—because they lose such blessings.

'It is you again who have best proved the general assertion that Earth is mother of all and common fatherland. Now indeed it is possible for Hellene or non-Hellene, with or without his property, to travel wherever he will, easily, just as if passing from fatherland to fatherland. Neither Cilician Gates nor narrow sandy approaches to Egypt through Arab country, nor inaccessible mountains, nor immense stretches of river, nor inhospitable tribes of barbarians cause terror, but for security it suffices to be a Roman citizen, or rather to be one of those united under your hegemony. Homer said, "Earth common to all", and you have made it come true. You have measured and recorded the land of the entire civilized world; you have spanned the rivers with all kinds of bridges and hewn highways through the mountains and filled the barren stretches with posting stations; you have accustomed all areas to a settled and orderly way of life.'[48]

The provinces, like Italy, had suffered terribly during the civil wars, and were so impressed by the Roman Peace brought by Augustus that the majority of the population were prepared to welcome the imperial system without dwelling too much upon its less attractive features. Tacitus remarks of the closing years of the Republic:

'In the provinces government by Senate and People was looked upon sceptically as a matter of sparring dignitaries and extortionate officials. The legal system had provided no remedy against these, since it was wholly incapacitated by violence, favouritism, and—most of all— bribery.'

So the new order 'was popular in the empire'.[49] Moreover, provincials were now in a better position to ensure that their complaints against Roman governors were heard at the capital. This could best be done by inducing a well-placed Roman to take the matter up at the highest level. It had long been customary for whole communities, in the fashion of private individuals, to make themselves the 'clients' of eminent Roman patrons who looked after their interests; and now this custom became more effective. Of the resultant appeals by provincials we hear a good deal from Tacitus. Indeed, a complaint from the province of Africa was taken up in the Senate—under the presidency of the emperor and in co-operation with Pliny the younger—by the historian himself.

This kind of collective action by whole provinces was facilitated by the establishment of provincial Councils consisting of local notables. These Councils, it is true, were set up by Augustus and his successors to act as focuses of pro-Roman feeling; one of their principal tasks was to organize the official worship of Rome and the emperor. But they served also to canalize the pride taken by provincials, whether Greeks or westerners, in their own culture and nationality. One of these provincial organizations was the Council of the Three Gauls at Lugdunum, of which the Altar of Rome and Augustus appears on the latter's coins.[50] This was a bold imperial experiment and gesture of confidence, since the Gallic aristocracy who monopolized this Council's membership held longest to anti-Roman feelings and led the revolts of the first century AD (pp. 51, 59). Tacitus and Pliny the younger stress the part that these Councils played in organizing the prosecution of bad proconsuls and legates, and although this was entirely subordinate to the main functions of these bodies, their existence proved a check upon the relatively few officials who defied imperial vigilance against oppressive government. The sanctions established against such misuse of powers were gradually incorporated into laws and decrees which protected not only Romans from office-bearers in the capital[51] but also provincials from bad governors and imperial agents. Under Commodus, for instance, the tenants of an olive-producing imperial estate, the Saltus Burunitanus in Africa (north-western Tunisia), complained vigorously against the local agent of the emperor, who was accused of collusion with the lessor of the estate in compelling the tenants to undertake unjustified work.[52] Commodus sent a soothing answer, in which he ruled that the agent might not demand more than thrice two days' work in each year.

But more important than the attitude to Rome of the provinces as such, or of individuals or groups of provincials with grievances, was the relation between the central power and the self-governing cities throughout the Greco-Roman world: the heirs to the classical Greek city-states and, before them, to the Sumerian city-states of the third millennium BC. The empire had to be subdivided into manageable parts, and into smaller, more self-sufficient organisms than a provincial government, and the long-established Greek institution of the city-state fulfilled the need. For these cities were the units in which a man lived and died; to them he devoted his keenest interest and foremost patriotic feelings. In the third century BC city-states, differing greatly from one another in importance, had become more numerous than ever—largely owing to a new proliferation of them in western Asia Minor. There and elsewhere, the Romans found this city-structure so convenient that they even extended it to the mountainous central parts of the same peninsula, and to Gaul—both regions in which, hitherto, the tribe rather than the town had been the normal unit. The whole history of Roman rule, no less than of the earlier Greek ascendancy, can be described with some justice as a history of cities.

Among them the Romans deliberately encouraged, within the loose framework of the province, a very wide variety of local privileges and gradations of autonomy. The monarchs of the successor-states of Alexander had done the same, but not so skilfully as Rome, which systematically interpreted the autonomy of its subjects as meaning, not necessarily freedom in international relations or in defence or from imperial taxation, but as nevertheless quite a substantial amount of self-government within the larger whole. It seemed to the Jewish historian Josephus that Cerialis (p. 51) was right, and that the Romans were ready to concede anything provided only the tribute was paid. Exceptional was the status of certain favoured cities, particularly in Greece and Asia Minor, which were nominally 'free', and sometimes also 'bound by treaty' to Rome. Athens, Rhodes, Antioch and Nicopolis—founded by Augustus beside the site of his victory at Actium—were conspicuous among them, but there were a good many more.

Yet the amount of self-government allowed even to cities that were not 'free' was very considerable. Many of them possessed considerable strips of hinterland, and treaties and charters negotiated with Rome regulated their local rights, including a limited jurisdiction. In the last resort, it is true, the government could always interfere, for example in the overriding emergencies of the Civil Wars at the end of the Republic, or later in the name of imperial security. But generally, in the prosperous years of the early emperors, their central government was at pains not to appear too heavy-handed; its relations with the cities elaborately exemplified the doctrine 'Divide and Rule', and this was put into effect in a sensibly empirical fashion.

So under Rome the city-state knew a second flowering; prosperous local bourgeoisies clung passionately to the city ideal on which their position depended (p. 101), and anonymous Jewish oracles classed Greeks with Romans as the hated partners in authority (pp. 60 f.). In the second century AD, however, the relationship of the cities with Rome, based as this was upon a reasonable degree of non-interference by the ruling power, began to break down. This was partly because the city governments were sometimes reckless and irresponsible in public finance. Trajan and his successors at Rome had learnt by experience the difference between the expert and the amateur in government, and they now intruded agents into the affairs of cities and showed an increasing tendency to expand their civil service into a bureaucracy which could handle many matters hitherto left to the less efficient attention of the local authorities. Trajan was alarmed by financial irregularities in the communities of Bithynia and Pontus, territories of northern Asia Minor which were on the lines of communication towards his projected eastern campaigns. He therefore initiated the practice—or possibly developed a practice introduced by Domitian—of sending out into the provinces high Roman officials with special powers of intervention. One of these was Pliny the younger, from whom we have a collection of letters to the emperor requesting his guidance, sometimes a little fussily; and Trajan's replies have also survived.

PLINY TO TRAJAN

'The citizens of Nicomedia, Sir, have expended three million three hundred and twenty-nine thousand sesterces on an aqueduct; but they abandoned it unfinished, and it has actually been pulled down. They made a grant of two hundred thousand sesterces for another aqueduct, but this likewise is discontinued; so that after having thrown away an immense sum they must incur fresh expense in order to be accommodated with water. I have personally visited a most limpid spring from which the water may be conveyed over arches (as was done in their first design), so that its supply need not be limited to the level and low parts of the city. There are but very few arches remaining; others can be erected with the square blocks of stone which have been pulled down from the former work; some part, I think, may be built of brick, as that will be the easier and cheaper method. But, first, to prevent another failure, it will be necessary for you to send here an inspector of aqueducts or an engineer. I will venture to affirm one thing—the beauty and usefulness of the work will be entirely worthy of your reign.'

TRAJAN TO PLINY

'Care must be taken to supply the city of Nicomedia with water—you will, I am convinced, set about the work with all due diligence. But it is most certainly no less incumbent upon you to ascertain whose fault it is that the Nicomedians have up to the present squandered such large sums. They must not be suffered to commence and then abandon aqueducts by a system of collusion. You will let me know the result of your enquiry.'[53]

The phrases of Pliny and Trajan display a fluctuation between the traditional Roman reluctance to interfere in detailed matters and a paternalistic desire for efficiency, characteristic of the times.

But the letters exchanged between Trajan and his governor also hint at a continual undercurrent of suspicion, at Rome, about possible breaches of the peace (cf. pp. 106–108). And at about the same time Juvenal writes a terrifying account, with evident truth underlying the satire, of a fight for religious reasons between two

56

neighbouring Egyptian villages, Ombi and Tentyra.[54] Units of this small size were non-Greek, but the Greek or Hellenized controllers of the larger eastern communities, the cities, were as aware as the Roman government itself that local breaches of the peace might have disastrous effects on their relations with Rome. Sometimes, therefore, they felt obliged to remind their compatriots of the brutal facts concerning Rome's power over them all. In this vein the biographer Plutarch of Chaeronea in Greece (c. AD 40–112) warns against the Roman boot on the neck, the dread chastiser, the axe that cleaves the neck.[55]

His contemporary Dio Chrysostom ('Golden Mouthed'), the romantic, serious, slightly priggish preacher-philosopher of Prusa near the Sea of Marmora, urges the peoples of Nicaea and Nicomedia, and those of Ephesus and Smyrna, to stop bickering with one another. The disturbances which caused the Romans so much displeasure could readily come from inter-city quarrelling—which in any case, as Dio points out, could only be for an 'ass's shadow'. Dio, who depended on Rome when the Prusans demonstrated against him (p. 106), emphasized to the cities how ridiculous and humiliating such quarrels were, and how they unnecessarily increased the extent to which the Greeks were at Rome's mercy. 'Is it possible that you are not aware of the tyrannical power which your own strife offers those who govern you?'—and the rivalries, he says, for honorific titles, between one Greek city and another 'excite laughter, especially at Rome—and what is still more humiliating, are called "Greek failings".'[56] In another speech, addressed to the Rhodians, Dio castigates his audience for giving new names to old statues so as to honour their contemporaries with a minimum of expenditure. This custom he describes as a combination of meanness and adulation. That is not the way, he says, in which the people of Rhodes ought to preserve and justify their status of a 'free' city bound by treaty to Rome. What they ought to do instead was to safeguard their dignity and, with their dignity, the honour of Hellas.[57]

Such words may sound a little too much like a lecture. Yet a sad day had come for the Greek cities when, in the course of the second and third centuries AD, their governing classes gradually lost interest in local political life. Petty duties proved too irritating and unrewarding, the tenure of official posts—which they were now strenuously urged by Rome to accept—far too expensive; and Roman interference, even if necessary to check local inefficiency

(p. 55), had taken the point and the fun out of Greek city-life. This withdrawal of the Greek bourgeoisie meant the end of Rome's Hellenic Renaissance, of the 'fair appearance of a union of self-governing cities' under Roman rule. The city-structure, which had for so long been the basis of Mediterranean civilization, had received a mortal blow. Marcus Aurelius remarked, 'What does not benefit the hive is no benefit to the bee';[58] and no confidence was now felt at Rome that these provincial bees could be relied upon to work for the hive's interests. So in the third century AD Rome's inter-ference in the affairs of the Greek cities became all-embracing and continuous. For this reason, and because of successive military crises, oppression increased. This heavier hand was noticeable in day-to-day procedures. For instance, the requisitioning of animals for state-transport (*angareia*), a legacy from the Persian and Greek monarchs of the middle east which Claudius and other emperors tried to alleviate, gradually became increasingly burdensome, and, before AD 250, intolerable.

The monarchs of client-kingdoms dependent on Rome spoke to their subjects in the same terms as Dio used to the Asian provincials. Herod the Great of Judaea (d. 4 BC), for example, regarded it as his mission, in spite of contrary advice from the more nationalistic priesthood, to educate his subjects into accepting a compromise with Roman power. Herod sought to do this through the adoption of Greek culture, an easier medium for an understanding with Rome than the more alien Jewish civilization could provide. Some such prudent accommodation to imperious historical facts was inevitable —whatever the inmost thoughts of men like Herod and Dio, and whether or not they shared the hatred and profound contempt which many of their compatriots undoubtedly felt for their Roman rulers.

The more thoughtful Greek and Latin writers sometimes take the trouble to record such anti-Roman sentiments. Already in the last years of the Republic attention had been called to the hostile feelings that might be expected from Rome's subjects. Cicero feels that the entire empire is detested everywhere, and he can understand why;[59] he puts much of the blame on Sulla (p. 8).[60] But according to the historian Sallust, who gives a vivid and sometimes sympathetic portrayal of the enemies of Rome, the trouble had started much earlier.[61] Cato the elder observed that the Rhodians had every right to want freedom and therefore to pray for Roman defeat;[62] and it had long been said that Roman justice was only the right of the stronger. We learn of Greek propagandists for Parthia, and of bitter anti-Roman pamphleteers such as Metrodorus of Scepsis in north-western Asia Minor.[63] The Augustan historian and rhetorician Dionysius, who came from Halicarnassus in the south-west of the same peninsula, protests against a tendency to call the Romans barbarians—saying that this could not be so, since they were an offshoot of the Greeks![64] A second-century writer from the same peninsula, Aelius Aristides, preferred to call the Greeks their 'foster-parents' (p. 52).

Tacitus repeatedly notes discontent against Rome in the western provinces. Although he observed that it was cheap, easy and conventional to accuse great empires, no other writer produced more telling accounts of provincial grievances—as well as showing how they could be refuted (p. 51). Tacitus was quite aware that the ultimate sanction was force, and that its abuses were not always concealed. A revolt in Gaul under Tiberius could be caused by excessive taxation; the weak have no rights; appallingly heavy-handed behaviour sometimes came to light or was alleged, for instance in the treatment of the British queen Boudicca (Boadicea)—treatment which helped to make her rebel;[65] and in the *Agricola* Tacitus tells further stories of oppression and exploitation in the same province of Britain.[66]

Such evidence from the western provinces is particularly valuable since their natives, other than the highly Romanized who tended also to be the most pro-Roman, were too inarticulate to leave us much evidence for themselves. The Greek or Graecized easterners were both far more articulate and felt the ideological conflict more intensely. Yet even among them the extent of anti-Roman feeling is by no means easy to assess, since the vast majority of Greek writers—like the vast majority of Latin writers—belong to the educated, prosperous and loyal classes, and therefore do not usually (even by the indirect methods of Dio Chrysostom) reflect whatever virulently anti-Roman sentiments existed. In general, therefore, we have to rely for this very important topic on 'the low murmur of inscriptions', on accidental discoveries of private documents—especially papyri preserved by the Egyptian soil—and on subversive compositions of more or less proletarian origin and circulation that were passed from hand to hand. These often took the form of religious tracts, oracles and prophecies. Such were the Acts of the Pagan Martyrs (pp. 46 f.) and innumerable 'Sibylline' Oracles in Greek verse.

It is not surprising that these anti-Roman Oracles often have a Jewish tinge, since Judaea was so unsatisfactory a feature of the Roman imperial record (p. 46). The three Jewish revolts formed a terrible background for many of the apocalyptic, ecstatic Oracles. Redolent of hatred for Roman ways, the fourteen miscellaneous books which survive predict bloodthirstily the downfall of Rome and of its insufferable arrogance.

> God's revelation of great wrath to come
> In the last time upon a faithless world,
> I make known, prophesying to all men. . . .
> On thee some day shall come, O haughty Rome,
> A fitting stroke from heaven, and thou the first
> Shalt bend the neck, be levelled to the earth,
> And fire shall utterly consume thee, bent
> Upon thy pavements. Thy wealth shall perish,
> And on thy site shall wolves and foxes dwell,
> And then shalt thou become all desolate
> As though thou hadst not been. . . .
>   Near at hand
> Is the end of the world, and the last day
> And judgment of immortal God for such
> As are both called and chosen. First of all
> Inexorable wrath shall fall on Rome:
> A time of blood and wretched life shall come.
> Woe, woe to thee, O land of Italy,
> Great, barbarous nation. . . .
> And no more under slavish yoke to thee
> Will either Greek or Syrian put his neck,
> Barbarian or any other nation,
> Thou shalt be plundered and shalt be destroyed
> For what thou didst, and wailing aloud in fear
> Thou shalt give until thou shalt all repay.[67]

And this fate, claims another Oracle, will be brought upon Rome by a king from the Rising Sun, by whom the west will be enslaved

'For all the wealth that Rome took from tributary Asia, three times as much shall Asia take from Rome, in requital for her accursed arrogance: and for all the men from Asia made household slaves in Italy, twenty times so many men of Italy shall serve in Asia as penniless slaves, and a thousandfold shall be the requital. . . .'[68]

The same oriental or Hebrew background is detectable in further promises that the Greek world, a partner in the iniquities of the ruling race, will share Rome's utter downfall and destruction.

When millions were under the rule of a foreign race, it was perhaps inevitable that many people should be discontented. The effectiveness of Roman administration and publicity could not always conceal a widespread feeling that

> Earth is sick
> And Heaven is weary of the hollow words
> Which States and Kingdoms utter when they talk
> Of Truth and Justice.

Yet how widespread or acute such discontent was, our evidence is too fragmentary to tell us. Probably there was a great deal of grumbling. But it rarely became desperate or united enough to lead to the joint action which the emperors were at such pains to avoid.

Throughout the Roman epoch agriculture remained the basis of Italian and imperial economics. But Gaius Gracchus (123–2 BC), seeking to remedy unemployment due to dispossessions and flights from the land, pointed the view to the future by attempting a commercial solution. For he planned to settle many of the urban unemployed, together with some wealthier people, in colonies upon trade-routes—not only in Italy itself, but also a new foundation (to be called 'Junonia') in north Africa near Carthage. Owing to opposition at Rome his attempt failed. Yet within a very few years, the first of many such overseas colonies had been founded, at Narbo (Narbonne; pp. 6, 78). For trade was now taking its place alongside agriculture as an important economic factor; and in spite of widespread piracy and repeated civil wars, the last period of the Republic witnessed continuous developments in inter-regional commerce. For these developments, Rome's annexation of wealthy countries such as Asia, Gaul and Egypt was largely responsible. From tribute, extortion, plunder and banking profits, great stocks of capital had accumulated. In spite of the hazards attending sea communications (Fig. i; cf. Plate 64b), luxury rapidly increased from the second century BC onwards, and more and more money was made by the great financiers of the late Republic such as Crassus and Atticus. Admittedly the former of these, and many other men with great business interests, were senators, belonging to an Order whose members were not supposed to engage directly in coarse pursuits such as trade (p. 75). But that was easily overcome by transparent fictions. Cicero remarked:

'Trade, if it is on a small scale, is to be considered vulgar; but if wholesale and on a large scale, importing large quantities from all parts of the world and distributing to many without misrepresentation, it is not to be greatly disparaged. On the contrary, it even seems to deserve high respect if those who are engaged in its pursuit, satiated or rather I should say satisfied with the fortunes they have won, make their way from the port to a country estate, as they have often made it from the sea into port . . .'[69]

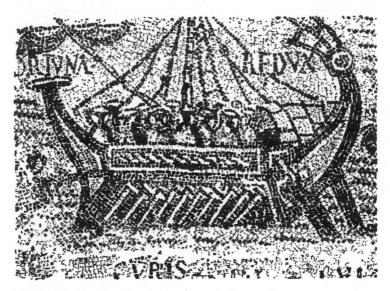

Fig. i. Mosaic of ship with cargo of wine, 2nd century AD. From Theveste (Tebessa in Tunisia)

During the last two centuries BC, the exports of Italy, especially pottery, wine and oil, and iron goods manufactured at Puteoli and Capua, were distributed over the whole Mediterranean area. This extension was aided not merely by the normal processes of trade but by influential backing within the Roman government; late in the second century BC, for example, the authorities forbade the potentially competitive production of wine and oil in Gaul. Rome, economic as well as political centre of the empire, had its principal harbour first at Puteoli—by 125 BC inferior only to Delos (successor to Rhodes) as a commercial entrepôt—and then, under the principate, at Ostia (Plate 11*b*). Served by a net-work of lighthouses (Fig. ii), the main provincial harbours receiving Roman exports, as well as conducting their own regional trade, were Narbo (Narbonne) and Arelate (Arles) in Gaul; Utica (replaced by Carthage), Cyrene and Cirta (Constantine) in north Africa; Athens, Delos and Ephesus (soon superseded by Smyrna) on the Aegean; Antioch and Apamea on the Syrian coast; and in Egypt Alexandria, three weeks away from Ostai by sea. To these and many other cities flocked the Italian businessmen—merchants, bankers and owners of workshops and large estates—of whom, with their families, king Mithradates VI of Pontus was said to have massacred 80,000 in Asia Minor alone (p. 8).

Fig. ii. Reconstruction of late Roman lighthouse. Dubrae (Dover)

Throughout the Mediterranean area the Augustan Peace brought a new security and freedom of intercourse, encouraged by widespread road construction (p. 32) and the removal of pirates from the seas. The most comprehensive compliment that Augustus ever received was paid him during the last days of his life, off the Campanian coast. When the ship on which he was making for Capreae sailed by Puteoli, it passed a merchantman that had just arrived from Alexandria. Dressed in white, decked with garlands, and burning incense, the crew and passengers of the Alexandrian ship saluted Augustus, calling out that it was to him that they owed their lives, their liberty and their prosperity.[70] These favourable circumstances created by the efforts of Augustus gave an immense impetus to commerce and manufacturing. Italy still took the lead, for example, with new industries for woollen goods at Pompeii and in the north, glass-blowing—recently invented at Phoenician Sidon—in Campania, and metal-working at Rome. The pottery of Arretium (Arezzo), its red glazing a trade secret, was widely exported; a single mixing bowl had a capacity of 10,000 gallons, and a single workshop employed fifty-eight slaves. Increasing its export-trade throughout the west and extending it in the east (in spite of Nero's failure to complete a Corinth canal), Italy also bought goods on a large scale from the provinces, importing slaves, grain, metals, marble, linen, papyrus, furs and ivory.

The internal commerce of the empire was more important than foreign trade, but a large quantity of luxury articles were fetched from abroad: frankincense from Somaliland, amber from the Baltic via Carnuntum (Petronell) and the north Italian entrepôt Aquileia, pepper and jewels via Aden from India, relations with which were facilitated by the discovery of the monsoon; and silk from China for weaving and dyeing in Syria (and incorporation at Cos into half-silk goods with a linen warp). Along the route from China, middlemen soon handled a flourishing trade in silk, for which a route avoiding Parthian intervention was kept open. Early in the second century AD —or perhaps already under Augustus—a certain 'Maes called Titianus', probably a Syrian, led an expedition which penetrated as far as Tashkurghan in Chinese Turkestan.[71]

Amid all this activity there were exciting, if still hazardous, opportunities to make money. Petronius has commemorated the financial vicissitudes and triumphs, in the early principate, of his Asian freedman Trimalchio, settled in Campania:

'I conceived a passion for business. I will not keep you a moment—I built five ships, got a cargo of wine—which was worth its weight in gold at the time—and sent them to Rome. You may think it was a put-up job; every one was wrecked, truth and no fairy-tales. Neptune gulped down thirty million in one day. Do you think I lost heart? Lord, no, I no more tasted my loss than if nothing had happened. I built some more, bigger, better and more expensive, so that no one could say I was not a brave man. You know, a huge ship has a certain security about her. I got another cargo of wine, bacon, beans, perfumes, and slaves. Fortunata did a noble thing at that time; she sold all her jewellery and all her clothes, and put a hundred gold pieces into my hand. They were the leaven of my fortune. What God wishes soon happens. I made a clear ten million on the voyage. I at once bought up all the estates which had belonged to my patron. I built a house, and bought slaves and cattle: whatever I touched grew like a honey-comb. When I came to have more than the whole revenues of my own country, I threw up the game: I retired from active work and began to finance freedmen.'[72]

Although active state intervention was at this time still limited, trade figured in the calculations of emperors. For political reasons they held it their most essential duty to provide the people of Rome with cheap corn—imported from the great granary countries such as Africa (Tunisia) and Egypt. Moreover, the mines of Spain, which were the most important source of metals, came under imperial influence, which Tiberius converted into imperial control. These and other mines provided the metals for the new coinage which Augustus had established. This was based on standard, interrelated gold and silver denominations, upon which depended novel token currencies composed of bright yellow brass and red copper (Plates 11*a*, *b*; 12*a*, *b*, *d*; 13*b*, *c*); sometimes the three main metals, gold, silver and *aes* (brass and copper) are personified as a trio on the coinage itself (Plate 13*c*; cf. p. 49). These major components in the monetary system were supplemented by bronze issues of provincial governments in addition to local currencies produced by scores of cities in the east and west alike; though in the western provinces the local issues gave way to imperial under Claudius. This empire-wide system of currency, in addition to conveying political propaganda far and wide (p. 49), bore the brunt of the vast new expansion of trade.

Although during the first and second centuries AD the ownership of land came to be concentrated in ever fewer hands, the imperial economy continued to develop, as the peaceful conditions and new roads encouraged the larger-scale organization of industry. Aelius Aristides, in his speech of AD 156 in praise of Rome, was justified in declaring that every Greek and barbarian could easily travel to whatever destination he chose, and that neither the Cilician Gates nor the tracks of the desert need make him afraid (p. 52). Fresh sources of raw materials were tapped: Trajan's conquests in Dacia opened new goldfields; iron and lead came from Britain. Gaul developed glass and bronze factories, and above all important potteries, successively at La Graufesenque in the south and Lezoux in the Auvergne; in the second century AD the main output was from Rheinzabern and Trier in the Rhineland which, with Colonia Agrippina (Cologne) as a glass-blowing centre, became the principal industrial region of Europe. Many military camps on the Rhine and Danube and in Africa were transformed into cities. Meanwhile, the export trades of Asia and Syria—notably in textiles—continued to flourish and expand, and there too urbanization progressed, until the towns in some parts of Syria, where people had a genius for trade, stretched almost uninterruptedly as one great urbanized area.

Amid such developments, although Rome with its great markets

(p. 268) and its port of Ostia now safe for large ships (Plate 11*b*) retained its preponderance in the Mediterranean world, the increasing tendency to decentralization had begun to deprive Italy of its economic supremacy. This decentralization was also one of the factors which kept economic development, vigorous though it was, from expanding unrestrictedly. Other limiting ιactors were the essentially agrarian basis of the empire, the high costs of land-transport, and the relative immaturity of banking, which although moneylending was extensive never achieved large-scale credit organizations or syndicates (possibly because the state was jealous). Other restrictive factors included the stagnation of techniques—partly owing to the employment of slave-labour (p. 118)—and, during the first century of the principate, the outflow into foreign countries, notably India (p. 64), of large quantities of precious metal currency. 'So much,' says Pliny the elder, 'do our luxuries and our womenfolk cost us.'[73]

The extent of these luxury purchases from abroad was due to the fantastic extravagance of major sections of the upper class. Developing during the first century BC, and then deplored (without effect) by Augustus and Tiberius, this unrestrained taste for luxury reached its climax under Caligula, Claudius and Nero, who gave an imperial lead in the matter, as countless stories by Suetonius, Tacitus and the elder Pliny indicate. In the less extravagant atmosphere encouraged by such emperors as Vespasian and Trajan, the Treasury evidently imposed restrictions on this export of the national currency. Henceforward, for example, Roman coins are no longer found in huge quantities in southern India as hitherto. The restrictions are of importance because—like earlier interventions by Tiberius to set money in circulation during a financial crisis (AD 33)—they foreshadowed a general decline of *laisser aller* economics in favour of government intervention and control. For one thing, this tendency expressed itself in increased public works and in other measures of improvement and relief. For example, Nerva introduced, and Trajan developed, a scheme for maintaining (and possibly educating) poor Italian boys, from the proceeds of land mortgages, for which the state advanced money at low rates of interest—thus helping farmers as well as the recipients of the charity (Plate 12*c*). Then, to keep alive the memory of Antoninus's wife, Faustina the elder, the scheme was extended to girls (Plate 13*a*). But state action of a more fundamental kind developed during the same period, when it became clear that the national finances were inadequate, if left to themselves, to maintain increased expenditure on the military activities held to be necessary (pp. 17 f.). In such circumstances, the lack of central financial reserves meant a hand-to-mouth existence for the state, which gradually and surreptitiously debased the gold and silver currencies without admitting that they had begun to possess a token character. The danger of national bankruptcy was ever present in the minds of Trajan, who fought huge wars, Hadrian who sought maximum efficiency, and Aurelius who had to surmount a perilous threat from the north (p. 18). So Trajan's interventions in the affairs of Greek cities (p. 55) were part of a wider pattern. He and his successors were moving step by step towards completer control of the national economy and revenue through more stringent assessment and enforcement of taxation, increased direction or compulsion of labour, compulsory state leases, and armies of officials to enforce these requirements.

Under Septimius Severus and his successors such measures were greatly intensified. As the grim third century wore on, and taxation was shortsightedly raised to ruinous levels, the economy of the west fell headlong. This was an epoch of ceaseless insecurity and disturbance, with consequent shrinkage of industries and of urban and cultivable areas, amid widespread failure of confidence caused by the progressive deterioration of the currency (p. 50). The policy of debasement had, indeed, been a psychological error. In other respects, however, it would not be just to blame intensified state-control for the general recession of the imperial economy in the third century AD. Rather was this due to the inability of Rome to maintain the peace in its provinces, particularly in the west, because the exchequer could not afford the double burden of the civil wars continually produced by the lack of a succession system and the aggressive wars which many emperors still pursued from a desire to be thought glorious (pp. 18, 30). With these factors present, the Roman government calculated that it could not make both ends meet without the rigorous, dictatorial regimentation which was foreshadowed by the paternalist second-century emperors, developed by Severus, and savagely intensified thereafter. This decision enabled the empire to survive, but the trading prosperity of the second century AD was never quite recaptured in the east, and in most of the west never at all. The only exceptions might be found in outlying territories such as Britain, which reached the peak of its development in the third and fourth centuries AD.

CHAPTER 3

CITIZENS OF ROME

THE social pyramid of ancient Rome was a great deal higher and steeper than those of the most highly developed European countries today—perhaps about as steep as the British pyramid in the eighteenth century. Something has been said already of the ruling class: of its small, warring, shifting groups which dominated the Republic, and were then utilized by Augustus to help govern the empire under his direction (pp. 5, 27). We have seen that many of these senators and knights attained unprecedented degrees of luxury and extravagance (p. 66). Others, of course, led more sober lives. How, in general terms, were such men trained for their responsibilities?

In the earlier years of the Republic, the education of upper-class children had been conducted by their fathers and mothers, who inculcated in them the traditional Roman virtues. Emphasis was laid on the examples set by the great national heroes of the past, and children were required to memorize the Twelve Tables, which were the source of all subsequent Roman Law. Boys accompanied their fathers to the Forum and elsewhere, and were placed in informal apprenticeships to leading men, so as to learn and imitate their ways. In the third and second centuries BC, however, although the old family traditions remained a haunting, frequently evoked memory, education was gradually institutionalized under the influence of Greece, and Greek slaves and freedmen became school teachers at Rome. A freedman named Spurius Carvilius opened a fee-paying school in *c.* 250 BC, becoming the first *litterator*, or primary-school teacher; and the writers Livius Andronicus and Ennius gave literary instruction in Roman private houses as forerunners of a new type of school master, the *grammaticus*, or secondary-school master. These *grammatici* taught 'the knowledge of right speaking' and also, as the second part of their task, the interpretation of Greek, and eventually Latin, poetry—since it was held that only through poetry were the higher levels both of public speaking and of intellectual life as a whole attainable (p. 215). Cato the elder firmly though vainly resisted this trend, advocating a more specifically Italian curriculum of oratory, agriculture, law, medicine and military studies. The Greek system prevailed, and at least the most famous *grammatici* attracted good pay, although school-mastering as a whole remained arduous, inglorious and ill-paid, and, in its primary branch at least, far from well conducted.

But what particularly disturbed Cato and those who thought like him was the threat that the more advanced forms, too, of Greek education would become established in Rome—as was already happening in his day. The foundations of the European university system had been laid at Athens in the fourth century BC by the Academy of Plato, the Lyceum of Aristotle, and the rhetorical school of Isocrates. Isocrates, who favoured the regular lecture as opposed to the dialogue or seminar group of Plato, had sought to find a general education suitable as a background for his principal subject, which was rhetoric. This, the teaching of oratory—the art of persuasion—was placed at the centre of the curriculum because it was held to be the key to practical public life. The Romans, too, accorded rhetoric this same pre-eminent position in their own educational system; and in the second century BC the *rhetor*, or teacher at university level, came to Rome. The enthusiasm with which young Romans flocked in 168 BC to hear Crates of Mallus, librarian at Pergamum—who had to stay in Rome because he had slipped in the opening of a Palatine sewer—caused conservative elements to impose a ban on rhetoricians, and those who sought to adapt this Greek technique to Latin encountered similar difficulties in 92 BC. But during the years that followed, this type of higher education, in both languages, became established in the capital. Imposing a classical framework of fixed forms for all categories of literary production—within which frame, but not outside it, variation might and should take place (p. 211)—the system aimed at the formal education of the mind by inculcating clarity and sharpness of oratory as a reflection of clarity and sharpness of thought.

Cicero was insistent that the Isocratean breadth of studies should not be lost. In his highly polished works on educational subjects (the *De Oratore, Orator*, and *Brutus*) he often stressed that no man can be that paragon of public life, the good orator, without being the possessor of a wide and liberal culture; moreover, he must be a good man also (p. 194). These were the twin bases of the *humanitas* which was his great contribution to education. His contemporary Varro advocates a teaching programme including grammar, dialectic, rhetoric, geometry, arithmetic, astronomy, music, medicine, architecture.[1] Philosophy does not appear in this list; to study that subject, as well as rhetoric in its more advanced forms, young Romans went on to the supreme university town of Athens, or to one of the other Greek centres of higher education such as Rhodes, Mitylene, Ephesus, Pergamum, Tarsus, Smyrna, Alexandria, Apollonia (in Illyricum) or Massilia (Marseille). But Varro's broad curriculum never came into effect on any appreciable scale, and at the beginning of our era the *rhetors* had begun to concentrate almost exclusively on instruction in rhetoric, which was conducted by teaching declamation. Soon after Augustus, fashionable literary criticism turned from poetry (p. 222) and concentrated on these rhetorical arts, and late in the first century AD Rome's greatest educationalist, Quintilian, though objecting to the ridiculously specialized and unreal factors in these declamation courses,[2] accepted without question the supremacy of rhetoric as a subject of higher education.[3] The philosophers had for centuries been of a different mind, and Quintilian was reacting against a recent expression of their view by Seneca—who had criticized rhetoric because it was taught 'not for life but for the school'.[4] But the real reason why rhetoric had assumed elements of unreality and fantasy is pointed out by Tacitus. In the *Dialogue on Orators*, which is usually believed to be an early work of his, one of the speakers recalls that rhetoric had originally been chosen as the chief educational subject because it was, in those days, a necessary training for Greek and also Roman public life. Now, however, that the vigorous, excitable deliberations of the governing class had been replaced by the calm process of imperial government, the speaker points out that rhetoric no longer performed the same central function:

'Rhetoric is not a quiet and peaceable art, or one that finds satisfaction in moral worth and good behaviour; no, really great and famous oratory is a foster-child of licence, which foolish men called liberty, an associate of sedition, a goad for the unbridled populace. . . . It is a plant that does not grow under a well-regulated constitution.'[5]

And yet, although its chief *raison d'être* had vanished with the establishment of the principate, rhetoric remained the basis of Roman education throughout the whole of antiquity. Even in the fourth century AD the rhetorician Libanius voices the belief that this study alone, in the last resort, distinguishes civilized men from barbarians, and the recipient of his letters, Basil the Cappadocian, despite contrary influences among fellow-Christians (p. 188), is its equally ardent supporter.[6] Rhetoric had been maintained in this position by the active support of the emperors. Long ago, Polybius had expressed surprise at what he regarded as the chief flaw in an otherwise effective Roman educational system, namely that the authorities did not intervene in its conduct[7]—in extreme contrast, for example, with the practice of the Jews.[8] But in the first century AD this was changed at Rome, the pioneer in such intervention being Vespasian who established Quintilian himself as the first state-salaried professor of rhetoric and literature. Hadrian endowed Rome with an Athenaeum—on the Athenian model but with the addition of law to its curriculum—and in his reign it was already exceptional for the Greek directors of the great Athenian philosophical schools not to be Roman citizens. Antoninus Pius and Marcus Aurelius established imperial Chairs at Athens; and professors, although still classed by Juvenal with the attendants at public baths, received notable tax-immunities. Indeed, during the second and third centuries AD, the state control of important educational institutions was ever on the increase, until it became complete and universal. School-teaching at primary and secondary levels had previously been left to local initiative; at Comum, for example, a scheme was sponsored by Pliny the younger.[9] But now these levels of education, too, increasingly occupied the attention of conscientious emperors. For example, Nerva and Trajan arranged for the education of orphans to be defrayed from the proceeds of land mortgages (Plate 12c; p. 66). Trajan is praised by Pliny for his generosity in this field,[10] and under Hadrian there was schooling for the children of miners at Vipasca in southern Portugal.

Yet such extensions of the benefits of education below the higher social classes remained ineffective, patchy and rare. In the fourth century AD, Vegetius could not assume that new recruits for the army would be literate enough to keep their unit's books.[11] In spite of the protests of Epicurus and his disciple Lucretius (p. 156), the belief of Plato and Aristotle that truth was the preserve of the élite continued to prevail in ancient times; there was no free public education. A considerable number of Greek cities, it is true, had extended

schooling to the children of all free-born citizens. But even there it
became increasingly difficult for the lower classes to participate and
achieve reasonable standards; and the custom did not extend at all
widely to Rome, Italy and other Latin-speaking areas. It is also true
that wealthy homes provided vocational training for slaves; we have
evidence for this in the imperial household, as well as from Egypt,
and from Dorylaeum in the hinterland of the Asian province.[12] But
here again only the few and unusually privileged were normally
included, for the practice was felt by emperors to be in need of
rigorous restriction. Domitian, for example, ruled as follows (AD
93–4):

I have decided that the greed of physicians and teachers—who, not for
the sake of culture but for the sake of increasing their gain, are most
outrageously selling instruction in their art (which ought to be transmitted
only to certain freeborn youths) to many domestic (?) slaves sent to them
for training—must be rigorously curbed. Therefore, whosoever of them
takes a fee for teaching slaves is to be deprived of the privileges granted
by my deified father Vespasian. . . .'[13]

The exclusion from formal education of all but a minute proportion of those who were not well-off must be accounted one of the
principal failures of the Roman régime. Nor was education systematically extended to women. In Greek cities, schooling for girls, even at
secondary level, had long been fairly widespread, notably at Teos
(on Asia Minor's Aegean coast) in the third century BC.[14] There were
even women professors at the Athenian Academy (the last of them,
Hypatia of Alexandria, was lynched by a Christian crowd in AD 415).
At Rome, by a paradox, although upper-class women figured more
prominently in public life—we have an extraordinary letter from
Cicero about female influence in Brutus's family council,[15] and the
power of empresses was notorious—yet their formal education had
generally been small. There were certainly learned women, for
example Cicero's literary friend Caerellia, and imperial patronesses
of writers, such as Sabina and Julia Domna, wives of Hadrian and
Severus respectively. Girls of good family might, and sometimes did,
study with boys, and Antoninus Pius even developed a scheme for
female orphans (Plate 13a; p. 66). Yet women's education never
became usual—as Seneca confirms when he tells us how his
mother acquired a liberal education in spite of obstruction by her
husband.[16]

The full benefits of education were reserved for men—and indeed for men who were destined to govern the empire. These young Romans went at the age of seven to their primary schools, and at twelve to secondary schools, where they remained until they formally assumed adult status (*toga virilis*). Then came their higher, rhetorical training, followed perhaps by a year or two at Athens, Rhodes or elsewhere. By this time they had acquired an education in Greek and Roman literature, Greek philosophy, Roman law, public speaking and some rather superficial military and political history. They were accustomed to riding, pig-sticking and other hunting, and to the use of arms; and they had probably heard a good deal from their fathers, and the friends of their fathers, about public and private business and military affairs.

But this educational system concentrated in a remarkably one-sided fashion upon the purely verbal discipline of rhetoric, and tended in consequence to become a purely literary education, with facility in speaking or rhetorical writing as the ideal accomplishment. One of the most noteworthy psychological phenomena of history is the strange, continued passion of the practical and shrewd Romans for the fascination of rhetorical effect. This passion inevitably led to the decline or exclusion of other studies. In general, the ready-made sets of arguments and modes of treatment employed in the rhetorical courses excluded observation and experience, destroyed curiosity, and blunted distinctions between true and false.

Particularly disastrous was the exclusion of science from the curriculum. The syllabus had no room or time for it; Varro's suggestion that geometry and astronomy should be included (p. 70) was an unrealized ideal. Rome hardly produced any original scientific thinkers of her own, as Pliny the elder was painfully aware:

'More than twenty Greek authors of the past have published observations about these subjects. This makes me all the more surprised that, although when the world was at variance and split up into kingdoms sundered limb from limb, so many people devoted themselves to these abstruse researches, especially when wars surrounded them and . . . pirates, the foes of all mankind, were holding up the transmission of information—so that nowadays a person may learn some facts about his own region from the notebooks of people who have never been there more truly than from the knowledge of the natives—yet now in these glad times of peace, under an emperor who so delights in the advancement of letters and science, no addition whatever is being made to knowledge by means of original research, and in fact even the discoveries of our predecessors are not being thoroughly studied.'[17]

Yet distinguished Greek and oriental scientists still existed, though they were far fewer than in the third century BC when the scholarship of Alexandria was at its height. There was Dioscurides of Anazarbus in south-eastern Asia Minor, a botanist of the early principate whose treatise on medicinal plants remained a standard work until the sixteenth century. There was the even more influential Galen of Pergamum, whose medical writings were translated by the physician of Henry VIII, Thomas Linacre; and Galen's contemporary, Ptolemy of Alexandria, the mathematician and astronomer whose theory of the movements of the heavenly bodies was in large part accepted until Copernicus and Kepler. Hero, of the same city, described the use of the piston in a fire-engine which incorporated a boiler generating steam pressure. There were also other Greeks and easterners. But their aims were generally completion and improved arrangement rather than originality. Sometimes, too, they were affected by forgetfulness of Aristotle's general principles, or by current reactions against abstract science and mathematical formulae —too rational for the age—or by the unscientific influences of religion, against which the Epicureans protested: influences such as had earlier caused the rejection of the heliocentric theory of Aristarchus of Samos (c. 310–230 BC) in favour of the traditional geocentric hypothesis, which continued to hold the field until Copernicus. In due course Origen of Alexandria (c. AD 185–254), although the first great scholar among the Greek Christians, was even to reimpose the belief that epilepsy and sleep-walking were of demoniac origin, so that epileptics must be excluded from the Eucharist.[18]

And meanwhile it was 'at Rome above all', as Constant Martha pointed out, that 'every man who ventured on a scientific explanation of a natural phenomenon seemed to be encroaching on the limitless power of the gods. In order to engage in science a man had to have the courage to declare his impiety. That is why the Romans remained so long in ignorance.' The separation of science from religion, which had been the great achievement of the Greeks, was at an end; and the Roman government, which sponsored the national religion and had leanings towards Stoic determinism, showed only a very limited interest in science. It was interested in building, and produced magnificent builders and civil engineers who executed the plans of Greek and oriental architects (pp. 32, 271); it studied the art of war, and produced great military engineers. Yet if the whole field of science is considered, the number of inventions during the Roman period remains very small indeed. It is true that the Greek scientific achievement had been dauntingly large. The Greeks had discovered the essential notion of a scientific theory and a mathematical proof, and had shown how to turn pregnant speculations into useful and empirically tested scientific ideas. Now the time had come to convert many of these ideas to practical use. But this was not done: the ancients never entered the industrial age. Yet they had reached its threshold. For instance, it was only a very short step from Hero's researches to the construction and employment of a steam engine. But this step was never taken in Roman times, and was left for James Watt 1,700 years later.

Somehow or other the necessary drive and incentive were lacking; and one important reason for this was the exclusion of science from respectable education. 'The meaner sort of mechanic,' Aristotle had observed, 'has a special and separate slavery',[19] and Cicero concludes that 'all mechanics are engaged in vulgar trades; for no workshop can have anything liberal about it'.[20] The laboratory was not a place, in fact, for leading Romans; and any tendencies towards abstract science that they might have possessed would have found equally little appreciation. Roman reliance on slave labour was another discouragement to inventiveness, since it both allowed techniques to stagnate and caused social prejudice against the manual efforts which might have improved them (p. 118). There are also stories about the fears of emperors regarding the economic dislocations likely to be caused by inventors. Tiberius was alleged to have killed a man who invented an unbreakable sort of glass, because his discovery would have cheapened the value of the imperially owned metals;[21] and when Vespasian was offered a labour-saving machine for transporting heavy columns, he was said to have declined it with the words: 'I must always ensure that the working classes earn enough money to buy themselves food.'[22] Such stories have a large enough grain of truth in them to suggest that conditions were unfavourable to scientific discovery.

The Roman educational programme also differed from the Greek in its exclusion of physical training, and its rejection of music and dancing. Or rather, the last two subjects could be learnt at Rome, but not as part of the regular curriculum. Quintilian approved of the teaching of music—as an aid to oratory—provided it was old-fashioned and martial.[23] When Nero introduced a new five-yearly stage-competition at Rome, it was objected that: 'emperor and Senate . . . have given immorality a free hand. They are compelling the Roman upper-class to degrade themselves as actors or singers on the stage. It only remains for them to strip and fight in boxing-gloves instead of joining the army.'[24] For the gymnasium, too, though fashionable in more advanced circles, never achieved public recognition as part of a liberal education. Nor is it hard to see why the painting, sculpture and architecture of the imperial age were achievements in which leading Romans had no part, except as users and patrons (p. 235), since these arts, also, formed no part of their training. Cicero, in the passage quoted above, includes architecture —with medicine and teaching—among socially undistinguished professions. Pliny the elder observes that, although painting was permissible as a preliminary step in a liberal education, no wellborn Roman had been a painter for centuries.[25] And if you are a sculptor, adds Lucian: 'You will be just a worker, one of the masses, cowering before the distinguished, truckling to the eloquent. . . . Even though your art will be generally commended, no sensible observer will be found to wish himself like you.'[26]

Those whose education has just been discussed were the apex of the social pyramid. They formed part, however, of a larger privileged class, those who enjoyed the advantages of Roman citizenship.

When the emperor Claudius had held a census in AD 47, the population-figure which his officials recorded was 5,984,000.[27] This may represent the grand total of Roman citizens at the time, including wives and at least older children. If we accept the rough estimate of 70–90 millions for all the inhabitants of the empire (p. 30), it is clear how small a proportion were citizens. On the other hand, the number of citizens and their relatives had risen by nearly a million during the three-quarters of a century since the census of Augustus in 28 BC.[28] Earlier statistics, hard to interpret though they are, suggest that the citizen body, after rallying from its numerical decline during the second century BC, had not greatly increased during the forty years before Augustus. This is perhaps not surprising in view of the civil wars that raged throughout most of the period. It is true that during our own recent World War the birth-rate, in

Britain at least, rose rapidly; whether the Romans likewise augmented their birth-rate in time of crisis cannot be determined, but if so any such rise during the first century BC was more than offset by the greatly increased incidence of sudden death.

In origin, Roman citizenship had been a privilege for the free inhabitants of Rome, and long after the establishment of the Roman confederation in Italy large areas of the peninsula had still been excluded from its benefits. In order to break the great revolt (90–88 BC; pp. 7 f.), Rome had been obliged to concede citizenship to all Italians south of the river Po (89 BC), together with a half-way step towards the franchise for Transpadane Gaul (Italy north of the Po) which reached full Roman citizenship in 49 BC. So what was, in origin, a municipal Roman franchise had now developed into a quasi-national citizenship of Italy. In the later Republic, and still in the early years of the principate, Italy was raised by this privilege above the rest of the empire. The glorious homeland remained the centre of the empire and the mainstay of its political, military, agricultural and economic strength.

> Hail, great mother of harvests! O land of Saturn, hail!
> Mother of men! For you I take my stand on our ancient
> Glories and arts, I dare to unseal the hallowed sources,
> And sing a rural theme throughout the cities of Rome.[29]

Romans, no doubt, looked down even upon Italians; but less than Italians looked down upon provincials. The benefits conferred by the franchise will be described shortly (p. 79), and Italy possessed other solid advantages too. No legionaries were stationed on its soil; membership of the military *corps d'élite*, the Praetorian Guard, was long reserved for its sons; and—most important of all—it was exempted from the direct tribute or land-tax which was levied on all provincial communities except a few sharing this cherished 'Italian right' of exemption.

The expansion of the citizen body between the beginning of Augustus's sole rule and the census of Claudius can partly be accounted for by the return of peace and prosperity to Italy. But the increase is also due, in part, to the steady though cautious extension of the franchise to selected communities and individuals in the provinces. When in 118 BC, despite senatorial objections to overseas colonies, a citizen-colony was founded at Narbo Martius (Narbonne) in the south of France (p. 6), this, like the numerous similar foundations that were to follow in many provinces, was granted a fully-fledged self-governing administration—modelled on such Italian towns as already had full Roman citizenship, and equivalent to them in the rights of its citizens. Then Marius, who like other war-lords of the late Republic had to find land to preserve his ex-soldiers' loyalty to himself, created a further precedent by settling many of them abroad—in North Africa and Corsica. He did not, however, make these settlements into fully-fledged, self-governing colonies; and it remained for Caesar, Antony and Augustus to establish citizen-colonies in the provinces on a considerable scale. Caesar, in thus 'refounding' Carthage and Corinth, drew to some extent upon civilians in order to strengthen the commercial element, but this proved exceptional. The great bulk of the settlers were ex-soldiers. Very many of them were settled in the provinces of western Europe, as well as in Italy. Other colonies were founded in north Africa, the Balkans, Syria and northern Asia Minor; and in the mountainous central areas of that peninsula (Pisidia) a further group of citizen communities were established by Augustus.

In hill-stations such as those the settlers were expected to perform military service, when necessary, against rebellious local tribes. Elsewhere, too, not all settlers were free from cares. 'Even after your official discharge and further service as a reserve', complained a spokesman to his fellow-mutineers on the Danube (AD 14), 'you are dragged off to a remote country and "settled" in some water-logged swamp or untilled mountainside.'[30] Not every retired soldier would make a competent or willing civilian settler—that had already been learnt in Italy during the last years of the Republic (pp. 8 ff.). Yet on the whole this massive settlement was a potent factor in cementing loyalty to the emperor. Just as the ex-soldiers of Marius, Sulla, and Caesar, after their settlement on the land, had remained loyal to the generals who had settled them, so too most of the veterans of imperial armies, established in citizen-colonies, felt a positive loyalty to their emperor and described him as their benefactor and patron.

Although the establishment of a pension scheme for soldiers reduced large-scale settlement, veteran colonies continued to be established until the time of Hadrian, when the tendency to recruit legionaries locally made such settlements unnecessary. Although some colonies failed and came to an end, most of them survived and, as one generation succeeded to another, increased in size. Moreover, many of the original settlers had already played their part, in their own persons, in increasing the citizen-body before they arrived, for if they were not born citizens they had obtained the citizenship on joining the legions. Morcover, the inhabitants already living on the sites chosen for colonies were often promoted to the same citizen status as the new settlers; and the Romanization developed by such settlements led, indirectly, to further enfranchisements, for which Romaita was one of the criteria. Members of auxiliary units, too—the successors of the old allied contingents, as numerous under the principate as the legionaries themselves (p. 91)—gained the franchise after serving their full term with the colours. In these ways many provincials became citizens. In the eastern provinces Roman citizens still only comprised a minute proportion of the population—although important individual Greeks and orientals were granted the franchise—but the west became increasingly Roman in civil rights as in civilization. This process, referred to approvingly in a speech made by Claudius before the Senate (p. 101), was assisted by the conferment *en bloc* of citizen rights upon chosen native communities, sometimes after the intermediate stage of 'Latin rights' (p. 8).

Until the second century AD, Roman citizens continued to enjoy prestige and privilege far exceeding those of the other populations of the empire. Pride in this status was of great antiquity and supported by every racial, patriotic, religious and legal sanction. Historians associated this feeling particularly with the satisfaction which Romans had felt in achieving their liberation from the autocratic rule of the kings (50 BC): 'the Roman people were not living under a monarchy but were free. They had resolved to throw their gates open to enemies sooner than kings.'[31] Thereafter, a jealous solicitude for certain rights due to the average citizen was a marked trait of the Roman character, and is one of our most valuable heritages from Rome. During the Republic the basic rights of a citizen were two: the right of appeal (*provocatio*) to the Assembly of the Roman People, and the vote (*suffragium*) in that Assembly. Both rights were ascribed to a very early date; both were regarded as mainstays of freedom, and illustrated as such on the Republican coinage (Plate 10c, d). The right of appeal remained the basic privilege of a citizen. This right was believed to have been allowed, in remotely ancient times, to all Romans condemned, for whatever reason, to the capital penalty; in due course the same right was extended to those condemned to other sentences too. A magistrate who disregarded the appeal and carried out a capital sentence was guilty of murder, unless the right had been suspended by the proclamation of a state of siege or super-seded by the emergency appointment of a dictator. Under the emperors, if not earlier, the principle was extended to civil appeal (*appellatio*), by which controversies were referred from a lower to a higher magistrate. But, likewise in the imperial epoch, the old right of *provocatio* to the Assembly was replaced by the vesting of appellate jurisdiction in two new High Courts of Justice under the chairman-ship in the one case of the consuls, presiding over the Senate, and in the other of the emperor himself. These new courts eclipsed in importance the old public law courts and the special permanent criminal courts that had been established from time to time since 149 BC to deal with specific offences—principally those affecting the state—such as extortion.

The right of appeal to the emperor was particularly cherished. An extension of this right seems to have been claimed by the Roman citizen St Paul when he was brought before Porcius Festus, governor of Judaea, to answer complaints from the Jewish community:

'Festus, willing to do the Jews a pleasure, answered Paul, and said, Wilt thou go up to Jerusalem, and there be judged of these things before me? Then said Paul, I stand at Caesar's judgment seat, where I ought to be judged. . . . I appeal unto Caesar. Then Festus, when he had conferred with the council, answered, Hast thou appealed unto Caesar? unto Caesar shalt thou go.'[32]

As no decision had been given, there could be no appeal, properly speaking, in Paul's case; yet even so a citizen could insist on being heard by the emperor, and Paul successfully asserted his right to be tried by Roman law under imperial direction. He was also appar-ently protected against arbitrary flogging without trial. And even emperors, whatever influence they exerted upon the workings of the law, for a long time remained subject to it in theory, and sometimes in practice. Pliny the younger praises Trajan for not being above the law,[33] and until the end of the second century AD or later, it was only when suspicions of treason were uppermost in an emperor's mind that this concept faded from view.

Well might Cicero, greatest of advocates in the law courts, point out that the rights and privileges of the citizen, upon whom the whole Roman system was based, depended ultimately upon the incom-parable majesty of the Roman law as their ultimate safeguard and supreme sanction:

'Law is the bond which secures these our privileges in the commonwealth, the foundation of our new liberty, the fountainhead of justice. Within the law are reposed the mind and heart, the judgment and the conviction of the state. The state without law would be like the human body without mind—unable to employ the parts which are to it as sinews, blood and limbs. The magistrates who administer the law, the jurors who interpret it—all of us in short—obey the law to the end that we may be free.'[34]

And subject to the (at first) relatively rare autocratic incursions of the emperors into his daily life, the law remained the protector of each citizen.

Roman law displays practical common sense at its highest and best, embodied in thought and language of extreme clarity and sharpness. Its exponents were reluctant (like the English) to specify the principles on which they proceeded. They were interested in generalizations not for their own sake, but in order to solve each new set of problems that arose. And few of the generalizations which, as they grappled with successive situations, they offered, have since been discarded. Of all sets of laws ever compiled theirs comes nearest to universal acceptability. The Romans were themselves aware that this was what made them unique among peoples. They were the first nation to treat law in a scientific way; and to nothing like the same extent did the legal frameworks of other countries—including the numerous codes still operating among those of their subjects who were not Roman citizens—exemplify the systematic, practical reasoning of which their own law was the embodiment. What later jurists found especially valuable was their idea of law as *written reason*, embodying the principles of natural justice and keeping free from considerations of theology.

Their greatest success was in the treatment of law affecting the relationship of one man with another. From very early times they devoted most attention to the law regulating these relations, deriving from it many of their ideas of citizenship upon which our own ideas about how members of a community should live with one another are based. For this emphasis there was a historical cause, relating to a fundamental feature of Roman society. In law as in education (p. 68), the Roman family, under the exceptionally autocratic powers of its head, had from the first been a very powerful entity. The relations between one family and another had been almost like the relations between one independent state and another; and the law which regulated them was not regarded as subject to governmental or other vagaries. This body of legislation was rarely altered to any great extent; for depending as it did upon careful analyses of day-to-day life, and upon the principles underlying the activities which this contained, the occasions for amendment were relatively few.

So this greatest of Roman achievements, one of the outstanding creations of the human mind, has had a continuous history of over two millennia; during long periods the survival of civilization has seemed to depend upon its maintenance. Yet, in spite of the stability of its fundamental framework, there was slow, careful development over the centuries. The drafters of the Twelve Tables, who in the fifth(?) century BC blended ancient, oracular custom with progressive professional thought, were already no novices. During the last centuries before our era, however—about which we begin to be better informed—although a father's control over the property of his descendants always remained great, his power over their persons was gradually limited. Meanwhile, too, the natural acuteness and precision of the Romans in matters of law was being enriched and fertilized by the impact of Greek philosophical ideas, including that of the 'natural', universal law (p. 193) which played its part in formulating the dominant Roman principle of fairness (*aequitas*). The Civil Law was a national, Roman creation, but Hellenism was a great factor in universalizing its provisions and facilitating the acceptance of its main principles, alongside less adequate local codes, throughout the empire. The first systematic treatise was that of Quintus Mucius Scaevola (consul 95 BC)—who had read the Greeks—and the middle years of the same century witnessed the elaboration of the full juristic method.

But the classical period of Roman law came later than the classical period of Latin literature. Roman law is like Roman architecture in that the second century AD witnessed the zenith of its creative evolution. As jurists began to eclipse the declining profession of advocate, there came into being the codifications for which—preferring to work from practical matters and single decisions—the Romans had hitherto been disinclined. The earliest of the great names of this epoch was that of the north African Salvius Julianus (*c.* AD 100–169), who worked for Hadrian—one of the greatest instigators of humanitarian legislation (p. 117)—and was famous for his concise, lapidary formulations. Salvius's younger contemporary, Gaius, gained fame, among later generations, for his elementary textbook the 'Institutes' (*Institutions*). But this climactic period of legal process continued during the subsequent years which saw the waning of Antonine peace and stability. For further striking advances took place, and existing principles were worked out over the whole field of the law, during the last years of the second century AD and the first years of the third—under Septimius Severus and Caracalla. This was the age of the brilliantly logical, profoundly fair Papinian (d. AD 212), and of his Syrian junior contemporary Ulpian (d. AD 228) who was famous for the sheer clarity of his legal exposition. Such were the men who developed, ensured and safeguarded the legal conditions in which Roman citizens could enjoy their rights and privileges; and it was not their fault that despite their efforts the empire, a prey to dissensions and invasions, was already heading towards tyranny. But in the Middle Ages, again, it was the Roman jurist who led movements to liberate the individual from feudalism and from ritualistic irrationalities such as trial by ordeal.

Though the Roman citizens retained their right of appeal, the later Republic and principate witnessed a gradual whittling away of the privileges which had raised them, corporately, above the subject peoples of the empire.

There were many stories about their successful assertions of rights in earlier days. In the distant past, the lives and properties of plebeians had been protected by the inviolable Tribunes of the People, whose establishment—traditionally ascribed to the fifth century BC—was the result of revolts by the people against oligarchic control. The tribunes were able to exercise a veto (*intercessio*) against actions by officials, elections, laws and senatorial decrees, and they could enforce their own rights and the decrees which their electors, the plebeians, passed at meetings (*concilium plebis*). During the fourth and third centuries BC, by a gradual process of compromise, the tribunes had been brought into co-operation with the Senate. From that time onwards, although the people through the Assembly had been theoretically sovereign, its sovereign decisions had in fact almost always been guided by the wealthy and aristocratic classes. The Assembly had voted only on business presented to it by officials, and had usually acted in accordance with the advice of the Senate. Furthermore, the extension of Roman territory during the past two centuries BC, which made full-scale attendance impracticable, had contributed to the Assembly's decay; and so had the unwillingness of the governing class to consider reforms. Those who attended still voted, indeed, concerning many important matters—including the election of the consuls and other senior officials—but the votes were 'organized' by every sort of corruption and pressure from leading politicians and noblemen. Indeed, the 'freedom' of the people was not interpreted as it is in western democracies today. 'It is danger-ous,' remarked Ennius, the father of Roman poetry, 'for a plebeian to mutter aloud'[35]—unimportant citizens even found it difficult to speak in the Assembly. Their 'freedom' as citizens meant equality of personal rights before the law rather than freedom to govern. Ancient man could not claim the individuality of his modern counterpart; civilization was too precarious and hard-won to be imperilled by individuals.

There had, it is true, been two moments when a sort of democracy seemed to be emerging—in the third century BC between the First and Second Punic Wars, and a hundred years later during the activities of the Gracchi. But both developments were blighted: on the earlier occasion by the crisis of the Second Punic War and its victorious conduct by the Senate, and in the time of the Gracchi by their failure to revive tribunician authority in the interests of democratic reform (p. 6). Their not very judicious methods rallied sufficient support round the conservative leaders to defeat the attempt, and led to the official curtailment of the power of the tribunes, which reached its nadir under Sulla. Only occasionally, both before and after Sulla, the Assembly reasserted itself, for instance in the conferment of special military powers upon Marius and then Pompey (pp. 7, 9). Yet even these revolts were instigated from above, and not truly popular. At most times the lower classes more or less voluntarily fell in with the manipulations of those more powerful than themselves.

But in the last years of the Republic these manipulations included a vigorous deployment of the nuisance-value of the tribunes—who thus enjoyed a sort of Indian summer—and also a thorough exploita-tion of the capacity of the proletariat for violence. The Republican government had, on earlier occasions (186, 64 BC), suppressed the clubs (*collegia*) which helped to instigate such violent movements, but at the end of the Republic anarchy was almost complete. In these circumstances Cicero, in his recipe for the ideal state, reacted strongly against democracy:

'My granting the people the freedom to vote is so managed that the possession and use of political power shall be in the hands of men of goodwill [*boni*; i.e., the upper class] . . . so that liberty may consist in the very fact that the people are given an opportunity of honourably gaining the favour of those men.'[36]

In more philosophical terms, he argues that any more literally interpreted kind of 'equality' is undesirable and dangerous:

'For that equality of legal rights of which free peoples are so fond cannot be maintained: since the people themselves, though free and unrestrained, give very many special powers to many individuals, and create great distinctions among men and the honours granted to them. Besides, what is called equality is really most inequitable. For when equal honour is given to the highest and the lowest—for men of both types must exist in every nation—then this very "fairness" is most unfair; but this cannot happen in states ruled by their best citizens.'[37]

As he expresses such sentiments during the crises and riots of the late fifties BC, Cicero is thinking of the Sovereign People in terms of the gangs of destitute thugs, the 'dregs of Romulus', who were mobilized at frequent intervals to intervene forcibly in metropolitan politics. The Law of Nature which made all men Brothers (p. 193) was, at such times, almost as far from his thoughts as it was from theirs.

When Augustus controlled the empire, it became clear that he agreed with Cicero's view that democracy was out of the question. Remembering the anarchic use that many a war-lord had made of the tribunes in his political sparrings, Augustus deprived their office of all its significance, instead incorporating 'tribunician power' without office among his own titles, where it appears continually on his coinage; and subsequent emperors followed the same practice (Plates 11*a*; 12*a*, *b*, *d*). The purpose of the Roman rulers in claiming this power was to emphasize that they themselves were the people's best protectors. Indeed, whereas the citizenry's right of appeal was scrupulously maintained, it was now to the emperor and not the Assembly that they appealed (p. 80). At the same time their second basic right of Republican times, the right to vote, rapidly vanished. At the outset the Assembly and its powers and elections were ostensibly maintained—Augustus even announced an abortive desire to permit votes *in absentia*—but there was never much opportunity to register any vote or appoint any candidate contrary to the emperor's wishes. Under Tiberius, elections were transferred from the Assembly to the Senate, and although the Assembly retained a nominal existence until the third century AD we do not hear of its exercise of judicial or legislative functions after the end of the first century. In other citizen communities of Italy active elections for the annual appointment of the chief municipal officials continued for a time. For example, the seven thousand scrawls that have been preserved on the walls of Pompeii include a large number of electioneering notices and appeals—'Primus the fuller asks for support for Lucius Ceius Secundus as *duumvir* [chief official]' and so on; and the novelist Petronius tells how rival candidates at another town, perhaps Puteoli, tried to ingratiate themselves with the voters (p. 121). But at Rome an election had graver implications for public security and imperial prestige, and a few early experiments with uncontrolled elections, resulting in riots, convinced Augustus and his successors that—even if not crudely 'fixed'—the choice of officials should not be left too much to chance.

However, imperial policy regarding the Roman lower classes did not limit itself to a mere negative deprival of political power. The policy had a more positive aspect also—namely the provision, to make them happy, of cheap food and spectacular shows. Already in the later Republic high-minded statesmen such as Cato the younger, as well as more opportunistic politicians, had felt that the only sound and safe policy was to keep the populace quiet by entertaining them and subsidizing their food supply. Public shows became ever more spectacular, and from 62 BC a monthly ration of corn (five pecks) was delivered to some 320,000 applicants at less than half the normal market price. In 58 BC Cicero's enemy Publius Clodius over-trumped Cato by giving this corn away free of charge, diverting for this purpose more than one-half of the revenues from Pompey's recent conquests in the east (p. 10). This was like the economic, as opposed to the political, solution envisaged in our own century by certain colonial powers for their African territories. The feeling was that the rank and file, indeed that the bulk of the Roman citizenry, must be kept out of politics—for which, except in its lowest forms, they were not regarded as suitable—and that this could be ensured if their standard of living was raised (by subsidization) and if they were kept amused.

That is the background against which the imperial policy of emasculating the Assembly and tribunate must be seen. Augustus brought out the point quite explicitly in his *Acts* which we can see today affixed to the walls of his temple at Ancyra (Ankara). True, he makes play with the imposing formula 'The Senate and Roman People', but he goes into careful details about the character of the favours which he showered on the latter:

'To the Roman populace I paid out three hundred sesterces per man in accordance with the will of my father [sc. adoptive father, Caesar], and in my own name in my fifth consulship I gave four hundred sesterces apiece from the spoils of war; a second time, moreover, in my tenth consulship I paid out of my own patrimony four hundred sesterces per man by way of bounty, and in my eleventh consulship I made twelve distributions of food from grain bought at my own expense, and in the twelfth year of my tribunician power I gave for the third time four hundred sesterces to each man. These largesses of mine reached a number of persons never less than two hundred and fifty thousand. In the eighteenth year of my tribunician power, as consul for the twelfth time, I gave to three hundred and twenty thousand of the city populace sixty *denarii* apiece. . . .'[38]

—and the list goes on.

Caesar had set new standards of expense for public displays, and there again Augustus, economical though he was by nature, considers that no outlay is too high to be devoted to such a purpose. This is part of the expenditure which he proudly records:

'Three times in my own name I gave a show of gladiators, and five times in the name of my sons or grandsons; in these shows there fought about ten thousand men. Twice in my own name I furnished for the people an exhibition of athletes gathered from all parts of the world, and a third time in the name of my grandson. Four times I gave Games in my own name; as representing other magistrates twenty-three times. . . . On twenty-six occasions I gave to the people, in the circus, in the Forum, or in the amphitheatre, hunts of African wild beasts, in which about three thousand five hundred beasts were slain. I also gave the people the spectacle of a naval battle beyond the Tiber.'[39]

These were the bloodthirsty means (p. 123) reckoned by Augustus, according to his own account, to be necessary for the conciliation of the Roman people to his régime.

All subsequent emperors agreed that this dual formula of 'bread and entertainments' was the right one, and participation in politics the wrong one, for the Roman proletariat. The popularity of a ruler in the capital very largely depended on the efficiency and lavishness with which he put the formula into practice. Nero, in particular, was so generous in these respects, and was therefore regarded as so indispensable, that the metropolitan crowds persuaded him to postpone his plans for a foreign tour. Not only did he arrange expensive shows for them, but he loved riding and driving chariots so much that he keenly participated in the races himself. He also wore his front hair set and crimped in steps, like a charioteer's, and that is how it appears on coins (Plate 11b). The reverse of the coin illustrated here reminded those who saw it that their food-supply had been much improved by the great new harbour (constructed by Claudius) which Nero had opened at Ostia. In the same spirit other coins, depicting buildings reconstructed after the Great Fire, show not only antique shrines but the splendid Provision-Market (Macellum) which Nero himself had completed five years earlier and now presumably hastened to rebuild.

The same two themes, of subsidized food and amusements, recur very often on the imperial coinage, as ever larger sums were spent on these items. Titus depicts the Colosseum itself.[40] Trajan remained famous for centuries because of his patronage of the Games, still commemorated by tokens issued nearly three hundred years after his reign.[41] Later in the second century AD, not long before the number of national festival-days in the year had risen to 130 (an increase of 37 from the time of Claudius, and twice the Republican total), even the enlightened Antoninus Pius creates a precedent by depicting, with the inscription 'The Generosity of the Emperor', one of the elephants which he had procured for slaughtering in the arena (Plate 12d)—perhaps to celebrate the ninth centenary of Rome (AD 148). On the millenary of the city, Philip the Arabian enlarged on this theme by displaying on his coinage a great variety of animals. Coins also frequently show scenes of imperial largesses: the distributions to the civilian populations of Rome. Since however pieces with this design, though often repeated, usually survive today in much smaller numbers than many other coinages, the original issues are likely to have been of limited size and not intended for circulation much beyond the capital. For it was the Roman proletariat who benefited from this policy, as they benefited, also, from the ever-increasing material comforts of Rome, notably the great Baths of Titus, Trajan and Caracalla (Plate 64a; pp. 279 ff.).

Though the Baths were no doubt good for the bodies of the 'free' Roman people, their exclusion from government and their dependence on largesses and on often horrible amusements degraded their minds; and the rich and clever despised them more and more. When a Circus audience cheered a team which he did not support, the emperor Caligula was quoted as expressing regret that the population did not possess but a single neck, so that he could sever it.[42] In literary circles there was often a markedly anti-democratic trend. When Horace writes 'I hate the profane crowd, and I keep it away',[43] he is using the imagery of the hierophant of poetry whose holy rites must not be desecrated; but he is also echoing Cicero's disgust with the dregs of Romulus. Petronius shows a certain genial, if contemptuous, sympathy with the Italian community which he depicts; unlike almost any other writer, he even takes the trouble to reproduce their uneducated speech. Tacitus loathes all mobs, civil or military alike, and especially the population of the capital—where 'all degraded and shameful practices collect and flourish'.[44] Though he notes that even humble clients (or slaves) are capable of courage, he sees the metropolitan crowds in general as corrupt, hysterical, superstitious and servile. So does his even more embittered contemporary, Juvenal. Juvenal also passionately dislikes the rich and aristocratic, whom he blamed for the discomforts of his earlier life; but in one Satire after another he ruthlessly analyses the humiliations —inflicted by others but also self-inflicted—of the poor, or more particularly of the lower middle-class like himself, whose parasitic dependence has made themselves responsible for their own unhappiness. To Trebius, hanger-on of Virro, he writes:

> If you're not yet ashamed of following this career
> And think the height of bliss is eating another man's bread
> I'd be afraid to trust your honour even on oath. . . .
> He shows good sense to treat you so. If you can endure
> The worst, then you deserve it. Later you'll shave your head
> And offer it to be slapped, you won't shrink from the cruel
> Lash of the whip, to earn such a dinner and such a friend.[45]

What was said of Heine is true of Juvenal: 'much as he hated an arbitrary absolutism, he hated equally the pettiness of mind which it bred among the people.' Nor do the philosophers of the principate mostly rise above this emphasis on degradation. Seneca, like Cicero, loves humanity (p. 196), yet is not fond of the malodorous crowd. Epictetus (p. 199), who had started life as a slave, strikes a more sympathetic and unfamiliar note: 'If you fall in with a crowd, call it

Games, a festival, a holiday, try to keep holiday with the people. For what is pleasanter to a man who loves his fellow-men than the sight of large numbers of them?'[46] Yet he, too, has something of the spirit of Horace, for he also feels that the philosopher would be well advised to shun ordinary people until he himself has his own elevated principles firmly fixed within him: 'remember that the man who brushes up against someone covered with soot cannot help getting some soot on himself.' When we read this, from one of the most enlightened of pagan thinkers, it is possible to grasp the excitement with which, at the same epoch, increasing numbers were beginning to read what Matthew had said about Jesus, who 'when he saw the multitudes, *was moved with compassion on them*, because they fainted, and were scattered abroad, as sheep having no shepherd'[47] (p. 185).

The powerless, exploited, often destitute proletariat of the empire included a large number of Roman citizens. It was inevitable in these circumstances that the citizenship should gradually lose its character of a privileged caste. Aelius Aristides flatteringly grouped citizens and all other subjects together as beneficiaries of the imperial favour (p. 52). But in reality there was already beginning, in his day, to be a new privileged class—namely the imperial bureaucracy which grew out of Augustus's civil service and, during the second century AD, tended both to expand and to raise itself more and more above the other citizens.

However, the bureaucracy did not for long reign unchallenged, for another inner circle of the citizen body which gained ever-increasing power from the last years of the second century AD was the army. This had begun to exchange amateur for professional status nearly three hundred years earlier, under the direction of Gaius Marius (p. 7). That notable military innovator, as well as endowing the legions with an increasingly vigorous *esprit de corps*, had paved the way for their professional character by abandoning earlier property qualifications—which had restricted soldiering to men of some substance—so as to include in their ranks, with no distinction of equipment, those who had no possessions at all. Since these looked to their generals, not to the government, for reward and plunder, the Republic split apart amid the conflicting ambitions of military men each followed loyally by his own legions. Caesar, in particular, wrought his legionaries—many of them from Cisalpine

Gaul, now in Italy (49 BC)—to an unprecedented pitch of efficiency, and so bequeathed to his imperial successors the human weapon through which, behind their civilian Republican façade, they autocratically controlled the empire.

Augustus came into possession of something like sixty legions, but at the end of his reign there were only twenty-five. Each legion, at full strength, consisted of about 5,000 men, with a small bodyguard of 120 cavalry. On this reckoning the legionaries under Augustus totalled about 128,000. But he also developed the Republican custom of employing contingents of non-citizen allies, and created

Fig. iii. Part of frieze showing light warship (*liburnica*), later 1st century BC. Vatican Museum, Rome

from these a second branch of the army—cavalry as well as infantry—nearly equal to the legionaries in number and not far behind in efficiency (Plate 38a). These auxiliary units were at first stationed near their own homes, but later this practice was abandoned. The military organization was completed by the creation of the first regular fleet (Fig. iii), of three 1,000-man units (*cohortes urbanae*) under a City Prefect to keep order in Rome, and of nine Praetorian cohorts —each between 500 and 1,000 men strong—which did duty as the emperor's guards, orderlies and *aides-de-camp*. The Praetorians, under their powerful Prefect, were Italians (from the most urbanized regions) until the second century AD, when elements from the Romanized areas of Spain, Noricum and Macedonia began to be added. In the early principate the legionaries were still mainly recruited in Italy, but with increasing admixture from the more advanced regions of Spain and particularly Gaul, so that the Italian element slowly diminished until, at the end of the first century AD, it vanished altogether. The less Romanized regions of the same countries provided large quotas to the auxiliaries.

In keeping with Augustus's foreign policy, most of the legions were concentrated near the frontiers, in the neighbourhood of the Rhine, the Danube and the Euphrates; the only other districts which possessed large garrisons were north-western Spain and Egypt. There

Fig. iv. Reconstruction of frontier fort, early 4th century AD. Deutz (bridgehead opposite Colonia Agrippina)

was no central reserve; and the army as a whole, which now enjoyed regular terms of service and a pension scheme, tended, for reasons of economy, to be too small to deal with any serious threat from outside. Under Augustus's successors army service increasingly took the form of frontier patrol-work—which emphasized still further the absence of a central reserve—and the field-forces in the border areas gradually assumed the more static appearance of garrisons enclosed in fortresses (Fig. iv). Soon these great concentrations in the frontier areas began to tempt their commanders to seek imperial power. The first tragic results were seen in the Year of the Four Emperors, when Galba, Vitellius and Vespasian were brought to the throne by the legionaries in Spain, Germany and Judaea respectively. Tacitus sees to the full the grave implications of these events for the future, and in a series of dramatic scenes depicts the collapse of the traditional rule of law at the hands of these rebellious armies.[48]

The Praetorian cohorts, for their part, had murdered Galba, and even earlier, under Prefects who were second in power only to the emperor, they had shown how dangerous they could be to the throne. In due course it was they who became the most powerful, cynical and capricious emperor-makers. The climax of this ruinous development occurred in AD 193, when the Praetorian Prefect Laetus, only three months after arranging the murder of Commodus in favour of Pertinax, had Pertinax assassinated. Thereupon the Praetorians put the empire up to auction between Sulpicianus, Prefect of the City, and an even wealthier elderly Senator Didius Julianus—'a most disgraceful business and one unworthy of Rome'.[49] This dangerous custom of supplementing the pay of the army by special gifts (*donativa*) had been gradually growing ever since the beginning of the principate. Money-presents were distributed on imperial accessions, adoptions and other joyful occasions. Most of the money went to the Praetorians, whose salaries were already thrice those of the legionaries and whose *donativa* obeyed the same proportion. In AD 136, when Hadrian adopted Aelius Caesar (who died before him), the sums distributed to the soldiery had reached the astronomical proportions of 300,000 *sestertii*[50] (a *sestertius* being worth perhaps sixpence or rather more), with the Praetorians as principal beneficiaries. Now the empire itself was auctioned to Didius Julianus and each guardsman was reported to have received 25,000 for himself.

But Didius only remained emperor and alive for two months. His successor, Septimius Severus, controller of the twelve legions on the Danube, before entering the city summoned the Praetorians to meet him unarmed, surrounded them with his legionaries, and dismissed them with ignominy. This decisive step was followed by the reconstruction of the Guard at an increased strength of 15,000 men. But, whereas hitherto it had largely consisted of Italians, this formation was henceforward to be recruited from the frontier legionaries, and Severus, treating it as a training-school for officers, drafted into its ranks the pick of his men from the Danube garrisons. This served notice that the primacy of Italy was at an end; and a legion was stationed at Albanum (Albano) near Rome.

The steps taken by Severus to satisfy his troops amounted to a militarization of the whole Roman imperial structure. Not only did he increase the size of the army, but he made various new concessions to the soldiers, who were allowed to marry during their service and on their discharge enjoyed special benefits. Commodus had raised their pay by twenty-five per cent; Severus raised it by thirty per cent again; his son Caracalla instituted yet another increase of fifty per cent. The first and last acts of Severus's reign symbolized the new power and spirit of his government. In AD 193 he entered Rome in full armour accompanied by his entire force, and on his deathbed in 211 he was quoted as advising his sons to heap riches on the soldiers and not to trouble about the rest of the population. This was the policy which he, with his outstanding ability and ruthless clarity of purpose, deemed necessary to maintain his own power against

Fig. v. Bronze statuette of Roman soldier, 2nd century AD.
From Velia (Castellammare di Veglia)

external threats. It marked the beginning of a new era; from now on the privileged class was no longer the Senate, no longer the citizen-body—whose rights, *de facto* obsolete, Caracalla extended *de jure* to the whole empire (AD 212)—no longer even the elevated bureaucracy but a democratized, non-Italian cadre of officers, and the troops whom they commanded. Gifts increased, but under Severus's successors the formula, far from assuring loyalty, proved useless and lethal; the increased power of the soldiers made them all the more willing to make and unmake emperors.

In this, as in earlier periods, the role of the army is duly recorded, in propagandist form, not only on sculptural reliefs and in many other media (Plates 37a; 38a, b; 39a; Fig. v), but in great numbers of different coin designs. Some themes, certainly, are omitted. Thus, although there are frequent celebrations of imperial largesses to the civilian populations of Rome, there is dead silence about the catastrophically large *donativa* to the troops. And only Claudius, on a single coinage, is maladroit enough to commemorate openly the understanding with the Praetorian Guard which enabled him to succeed to the throne.[51] In their titles, too, which appear upon the coins, emperors lay greater stress on their civilian powers than on their commandership of the army. Military matters are often mentioned, but they are mentioned in such a way as to stress, not the autocratic supreme command, but Victory: she is never long absent, recurring in countless different guises, all clearly understandable even by the most unlettered of Rome's subjects (Plate 12b). Sometimes the victories thus recorded had not yet occurred, but were hoped for in the future; and, in the same spirit of wishful thinking, coins of the Civil Wars of AD 68–70 celebrate the often non-existent 'Concord of the Praetorians', 'Loyalty of the Praetorians', 'Loyalty of the Army'—a theme which returns with especial urgency at the worst period of chaos, disloyalty and unrest in the third century, for instance under Gallienus (253–68) and Quintillus (270). Nerva (AD 96–8), though harassed by the Praetorians who were not consulted about the murder of his predecessor Domitian, had paid tribute to a more theoretical pattern of society by balancing *The Concord of the Armies* with *The Forethought of the Senate*—which had long since become the dutiful servant of the emperors, just as the citizen-body as a whole was before long to lose its privileged position, first to the emperor-controlled bureaucracy, and then to the army.

But who, now, were the Roman citizens, thus in process of losing the privileged position which they had once possessed? A long time ago the solid, conservative Italian small farmer, backbone of the Republic during its earlier, formative periods, had been badly hit by the economic troubles of the second century BC—a time of great estates run by slave labour (pp. 5 f.)—and was shattered by the holocausts of bloodshed, the financial upheavals and the political chaos of the century that followed. Many families had died out; of the rest, a very few moved upwards and became prosperous, or even extremely rich; many moved downwards, and gravitated to the cities and the starving, turbulent crowds that filled them. The Roman social pyramid had become steeper still. There were very rich and very poor, and the middle class between them had lost much of its substantiality.

Yet already a new middle-class was arising, largely composed of freed slaves and their descendants. Of the slave system something will be said later (p. 109); here it must be noted that a conspicuous feature of the system, from very early times, was the frequency with which slaves were freed. This could happen for many reasons, but especially because of the custom that slaves could themselves purchase their freedom from their savings (*peculium*)—as the lawyers recorded, this was their chief incentive to hard work. As early as 357 BC a government tax of five per cent was levied on each act of liberation, and the income from this tax was placed in a special treasury reserved for national emergencies. By 209 BC 4,000 lbs. of gold had accumulated in this fund, a figure from which it has been deduced that every year must have witnessed the emancipation of about 1,350 slaves.

A freedman could not officially be enfranchised, and in other respects, too, his freedom was not complete. He owed deference and service to his former master, to whom he stood in the relationship of client to patron. He could not bring a legal action without a senior official's leave; if he died intestate or without heir, his property reverted to his former master. Though a freedman could serve as an assistant to a senior functionary or priest, he himself was not eligible for the higher ranks of the army or of an official career in Rome or other citizen communities. Nevertheless, every son born to the freedman after his liberation was a free man exempt from all such restrictions, and a full citizen. This feature of Roman history marked a significant deviation from the maxim attributed by Plato to one of his speakers that: 'any meddlesome interchange between the social classes would be most mischievous to the state and could properly be described as the height of villainy'.[52]

During the middle years of the Roman Republic, slaves were usually prisoners of war, coming from many lands, often with as good an education as their masters. So the Roman citizen population was steadily augmented and altered by the admixture first of Italian, and then of Greek and Semitic and Asian blood. Evidence of some official apprehension about these new elements is apparent in a decision to restrict all freedmen to four of the thirty-five Roman tribes, that is to say, to the four Urban Tribes (? *c.* 220 BC). Since voting in the Assembly was often by tribes, the effect was to restrict the freedman to a limited number of 'constituencies' and thus to limit his voting influence and that of his children. Similarly, in 169 BC, it was arranged that all the more impoverished freedmen should be confined to a single tribe.

Nevertheless, the Roman readiness to liberate slaves and to extend citizen rights to their children is very liberal in comparison with the practice of other ancient states. As time went on, the great number of freedmen produced by this policy began to transform Roman society —and, in particular, to make it more oriental in character. Juvenal, like most Romans who belonged or aspired to the higher ranks of society, deplored the situation. His famous complaint about Orontes flowing into Tiber (p. 42) correctly noted that the more advanced type of slave, who found it easiest to earn liberation, was usually from the eastern provinces—Syria or Asia Minor—urban, sharp and prolific, but lacking the more solid, Nordic-type virtues of the western barbarians, who became rustic slaves and were never freed. Juvenal was writing after AD 100, but the process was already well under way during the Republic. According to one calculation nearly half a million slaves were freed during the years 80–50 BC alone. And this figure refers to formal procedures only; a good many additional emancipations were undertaken by more informal methods, and before the end of the Republic the praetors had extended a measure of protection to the ex-slaves who were in this somewhat precarious situation.

Augustus tackled the whole complex sociological problem. According to his custom he both tightened procedures—limiting liberations both by will and in the testator's lifetime—and at the same time offered concrete, stable advantage to those who, according to proper legal processes, became its beneficiaries. Augustus may have felt some desire for racial 'purification'; but in all probability his motive was not so specifically racial as has been believed. His intention was primarily to restrict the numbers of new citizens at least to the extent that their cultural absorption should be possible, and that their minds should be capable of appropriate attunement to the political requirements of the régime. Thus he restricted the social aspirations of freedmen by refusing to allow their intermarriage with the families of senators; and limitations on succession and litigation were further defined. Similarly, he conferred statutory freedom upon informally liberated slaves, but he did not permit them to receive legacies or make wills, though their children were treated as 'Latins' who could become full Roman citizens.

His general object was to have enfranchisement regarded as a reward for merit; and alongside these restrictions he offered marked incentives to such freedmen as were prepared to collaborate with him. The effect of his recognition of their status was to encourage them to have more children, and they grew into a powerful middle-class, the cosmopolitan successor of the Italian middle-class of the Republic. They were, it is true, still excluded from the higher levels of office (the employment of one of them, Licinus, as an imperial agent in Gaul proved a failure). But Augustus added more important posts to the junior positions in which they had served during the Republic. They were now given responsible jobs in the Roman navy, and in the *vigiles* who acted as fire-brigade and police. They were also allowed to be in charge of city-wards, as officials whose duties seem to have been less concerned with the general regimentation of the populace than with the maintenance of the Roman holy places— and these holy places included shrines where a cult and statue of the emperor's genius served as reminders that the presiding freedman had his place in the imperial régime. In other parts of Italy, Rome, too, the various offices concerned with the worship of the emperor now became open to freedmen, who, in these capacities, were entitled to call themselves *Augustales*. Former slaves also became doctors, jurists, school teachers, artisans, shopkeepers, bailiffs, jockeys, auctioneers, copyists, dancers and pimps.

Many of these freedmen benefited greatly from the wave of commercial prosperity brought by the Augustan Peace. Of this type of New Rich, usually from the east, Petronius's *Banquet of Trimalchio* provides a famous burlesque, and there are caustic comments on the same topic in Juvenal. But between the lifetimes of the two authors, one writing under Nero and the other under Trajan and Hadrian, the freedmen, though they still could be very rich and powerful, had reached and passed their apogee as a political force. For Claudius had introduced the custom of employing freedmen as his principal ministers and political advisers—talented easterners of gigantic wealth, and of power unequalled by any senator, such as Claudius's three State Secretaries: Pallas (finance), Narcissus (secretary of state) and Callistus (petitions). Their foibles and vicissitudes are given the fullest dramatic attention by Tacitus, who regarded their rise as a horrible portent. From him, too, we hear of Nero's powerful and intimate freedmen such as the dancer Paris, and Helius who begged him to return from his Greek tour. Another of them was Epaphroditus, who acted as inquisitor upon conspiring senators, owned and freed the philosopher Epictetus (p. 199), and returned to his post of financial secretary under Domitian—who killed him, apparently because Epaphroditus had helped his former imperial master, Nero, to commit suicide. But emperors such as Vespasian, Trajan and his successors thought it unwise to rely so much upon ex-slaves; and the State-Secretaryships were henceforward filled from the higher social class of the knights.

However, in view of Rome's traditional policy of freeing many slaves, the knights, too, were very often descended from freedmen. So were numerous members of the Senate. When that body discussed possible restrictions on the arrogance of freedmen, it was pointed out that 'most knights, many senators are descended from former slaves. Segregate the freed—and you will only show how few free-born there are'[53] (AD 56). Possibly—though this can only be a guess—ninety per cent of the population of Rome in AD 100 were non-Italians of slave origin. The Romans of the principate were a new, cosmopolitan race, different in ethnic composition from the Italians who had fought for the empire in the earlier centuries of the Republic. Whether this must be thought a change for the better or worse depends upon the point of view (or race) of the historian who is considering the matter. If any generalization about so many millions of people may be possible, the new, oriental, darker Romans were more excitable, less industrious, less grimly pertinacious, and with less team spirit than their forerunners, but also quicker-witted, more spiritual, and more humane.

CHAPTER 4

SUBJECTS AND SLAVES

THE city-states of the eastern Mediterranean, in the time of the great kingdoms of Alexander's successors which were in due course obliterated by Rome (pp. 3 f.), differed little in outward structure but a great deal in substance from the city-states of classical Greece such as fifth-century Athens. Each of these communities still had its own Assembly, town council, presiding officials, powers of jurisdiction, and internal and external quarrels. But the Assemblies were losing ground; and whatever manifestations of life they might still display, each city was governed, in effect, by an upper-class, prosperous clique in sympathy with whichever of the Greek monarchies was the city's suzerain. These huge continental empires, in which communications were necessarily slow, would not tolerate the variations of policy which they felt that a democratic system might well introduce in the cities under their control.

Besides, the governing classes of the cities were themselves very fearful of revolution. During the third century BC, as the gap between rich and poor widened, such fears became increasingly acute. What the richer people were afraid of was a movement for the redistribution of land or for abolition of debts. Visions of egalitarian Utopian societies which inspired the first Stoics and Euhemerus of Messene (*c.* 300 BC), and the picture of a Communistic Sun-State described a generation or two later by Iambulus, seemed to bring the danger nearer. And it was a very real danger, for in the period that followed there were many proletarian outbreaks. These outbreaks included two *coups d'état* at Sparta which, although slaves had no part in them (they had their own rebellions, p. 113), bore all the other signs of class revolution. At this epoch the whole aristocratic structure of ancient society seemed to be cracking and perhaps on the verge of disintegration, and it was to avert proletarian revolution that in 133 BC king Attalus III bequeathed his immensely prosperous bureaucratic kingdom of Pergamum to Rome (p. 4). The immediate aftermath was just such a revolt as he had feared—part nationalist, part socialist—under Aristonicus.

Rome suppressed the rising, but felt as little inclined as the monarchs before them to allow democracy its head in the eastern cities. Thus Cicero blames the downfall of the classical Greek city-states upon their democratic Assemblies; and he comments on the hatred and vindictiveness which, in his own day, the populations of the cities felt against the symbols of power—the name, the land-tax, the tithe and the port-dues of Rome.[1] The emperors agreed with Cicero's diagnosis. Accordingly, throughout the period of Roman rule, power in the eastern cities was left in the hands of narrow, mainly hereditary, cliques of property-owners. 'The greatest and most powerful men in each city,' said one of their number Aelius Aristides in his Address to Rome in AD 156, 'guard it for you.'[2] Life and property were far more uncertain than they are in most parts of the civilized world today, and these local oligarchies and Rome's governors, as was noted by the tenants of the Saltus Burunitanus (p. 54), collaborated to keep the lower classes in order. In AD 62 there were adverse comments in the Senate about a rich Cretan, Claudius Timarchus, who had boasted that he could make or break a Roman governor.[3] But usually the governor dominated his local collaborators.

The emperors did their best to bolster up their supporters in the cities by admitting a good many of them to Roman citizenship (p. 79)—and even a few to membership of the Senate. The first of these, under Tiberius (AD 15), was Quintus Pompeius Macer, grandson of Pompey's friend Theophanes of Mytilene. The experiment was unsuccessful, since Macer was involved in a conspiracy in AD 33. But Claudius repeated and continued the process—and extended this liberal policy to the less developed communities of the west. For in his speech of AD 48 (p. 37), recorded without great accuracy by Tacitus,[4] he recommends the Senate to admit to its number certain Gallic chieftains, putting forward the arguments for a generous policy of admitting to the Senate (as a reward for their services) the non-Roman governing classes who maintained pro-Roman régimes in the provinces against the pressures from below. He is speaking of Gaul, but oriental senators also soon began to be found in greater quantity, increasing during the Antonine period. This was the greatest reward that the pro-Roman aristocracies of the Greek cities could receive—though the prize became somewhat tarnished when the Syrian Elagabalus (AD 218–22) threw down all racial barriers to senatorial admission, describing the members as slaves.[5]

This pro-Roman ruling class in the cities comprised members of the local Councils, which ceased to be mere committees of the popular Assemblies and became permanent and irresponsible governing bodies eclipsing their Assembly in power. It is true that for propaganda reasons the cities had to call themselves 'democracies' since this term still retained glamour as a popular ideal. But the Assemblies were only retained to 'elect' to office, by acclamation, the lists of candidates proposed by the Council, and to pass decrees ratifying what the Council had resolved. The pro-Roman Plutarch of Chaeronea saw that appearances must be properly maintained and that a little trouble should be taken to make it seem that all Assembly business was not decided beforehand—even to the extent of preparing, in advance, fictitious disputes for the rulers to have with one another in public.

'When the populace are suspicious about some important and salutary measure, the statesmen when they come to the Assembly ought not all to express the same opinion, as if by previous agreement, but two or three of the friends should dissent and quietly speak on the other side, then change their position as if they had been convinced; for in this way, since they appear to be influenced only by the public advantage, they draw the people along with them.'[6]

While they were in office the members of these Greek or Hellenized local ruling classes had to spend a good deal of money upon cheap food and amusements for the urban proletariat as well as upon other public services. As at Rome (p. 87), this was a form of social insurance, aimed at conciliating the populace that was thwarted in so many other ways. But the expense proved so burdensome that during the second century AD the Roman government started bringing pressure on provincial notables to prevent them from evading their responsibilities (p. 57). During the preceding centuries, however, these oligarchies had been able to make their monopoly of local power worthwhile by introducing legislation to concentrate the ownership of land among ever fewer owners, and to support their own class interests in other ways as well. For example, local codes of law favoured land-owners and creditors, and flat rates of taxation (resembling the flat rate of the imperial tribute and customs duties) meant that the poor man paid the same arithmetical proportion of taxes as the rich man—who, moreover, by his control of the administrative system, was able to command many resources of graft and legal privilege.

For example the city administrations, that is to say the magnates, were entrusted with the collections of the Roman tribute itself. Yet in the eyes' of their increasingly humanitarian and bureau-cratically efficient patron and partner the imperial government, the local governing groups sometimes treated their dependent populations with an embarrassing excess of heavy-handedness. This appears clearly from the description of Rome by Aelius Aristides as 'a secure refuge against the power of the local rulers'.[7] The fact was that, in the second century AD, the emperors often had to intervene to protect the underprivileged. It is true that at the same time, by increased grants of imperial favours, they shored up their alliances with the local oligarchies, on whose collaboration, after all, the whole structure depended. Yet the Roman authorities were obliged to set some limit upon the privileges of these oligarchies in order to protect the small man whom, in the interests of stability and humanity alike, they could not just turn over to the local rich; and their interventions to this end were among the encroachments which accelerated the breakdown of local self-government (p. 58).

The ever-increasing gap between rich and poor tended to take the form of a sharp contrast between town and country. As in classical Greek times, the self-governing city-states of the Roman empire mostly controlled strips, varying greatly in size, of rural land. The cities were economically parasitic on the country. Land was always the best investment, and a community's trade and industry largely depended on the incomes which the urban aristocracies, as absentee landlords, drew from the peasantry. Thus the population of the rustic areas and villages round a town was in most cases reduced to an even lower standard of living than the proletariat within its walls. For the peasantry, who could rarely attend meetings in town, had no say in civic affairs, and so amounted to little more than a large dis-franchised class. Thus at Smyrna we read of the 'upper city' as opposed to the underprivileged 'men of the seashore', while at Prusias ad Hypium (Cierus) in Bithynia inscriptions record a distinction between 'those on the register' and 'those who inhabit the rural district'.[8] These impoverished or destitute countrymen were often reduced to the age-old custom of selling themselves or their children as slaves—a custom which Rome probably did not suppress, although classical Roman law, while permitting the prevalent custom of exposing infants (especially girls),[9] frowned on the sale of 'free' children into slavery.

There in Asia Minor, as in many other parts of the east, these rustic, native populations (p. 42) differed in race and culture from the city people, who, unlike them, were Greek or at least Hellenized. None of the indigenous languages of Asia Minor have survived at the literary level, but inscriptions in the Phrygian tongue, for example, are found until the end of the first century BC, and throughout the principate the survival of the native races in the countryside is demonstrated by the continuing and sometimes increasing strength of the local native religions (p. 168). The villages lived a curiously separate life from the Hellenized towns to which they belonged. The cities very rarely intervened in their affairs, in which members of the civic aristocracy took little interest. So, below the surface of the city organization, the villages possessed a local, largely non-Greek political life of their own.

There was a tendency, on the part of the Romans, towards urbanization. In the east as in the west the imperial government liked to promote tribal units, when they were sufficiently advanced and 'safe', to the status of a city with its much greater political, economic and cultural possibilities. But this movement, although deliberate, did not go very deep, and in the third century AD, as the authority of the Hellenized ruling class waned (pp. 57 f.), the Greek façade crumbled and the countryside began to assert itself. The process is apparent on the coinages which the Romans permitted many of the eastern cities to issue until c. 268–275 AD. Apart from a few veteran colonies clinging more or less feebly to Roman models, the inscriptions of these issues are normally in Greek, and their designs, though artistically poor, are Greek-inspired. But the third century AD brings a gradual de-Hellenization of style which reminds us how the traditions of the long-neglected and oppressed rural areas were at last coming into their own at the expense of the urban organism, the city-state, that had long been so characteristic of the Greco-Roman civilization.

Evidence about relations between the social classes throughout the empire is difficult to obtain, because most of our literary sources reflect the views of those in power. At most, an occasional grumble is reported. For the rest it is possible by a laborious study of casual literary, and accidental documentary, material to build up some sort of a picture. This material suggests that, at any rate in the east and probably in the west also, the administrative achievement and propaganda of the Romans did not succeed in making the masses content with the men of property who governed them.

Even in Italy, the great harbour town of Puteoli in AD 58

'sent two opposing delegations to the Roman Senate, one from the town Council and one from the other citizens. The Council complained of public disorderliness, and the populace of embezzlement by officials and leading men. There had been riots, with stone-throwing and threatened arson.'[10]

And the novelist Petronius makes one of his characters, Ganymedes, who speaks uneducated Latin, illustrate economic class-feeling at the same or a neighbouring town:

'None of you care all the time how the price of food pinches. I swear I can't get hold of a mouthful of bread today. And how the drought goes on. There has been a famine for a whole year now. Damn the authorities, who play "Scratch my back, and I'll scratch yours", in league with the bakers. So the little people come off badly. . . . Lord, things are worse every day. This town goes downhill like the calf's tail. But why do we put up with a chief official not worth three peppercorns, who cares more about putting twopence in his purse than keeping us alive? He sits grinning at home, and pockets more money a day than other people have for a fortune. . . .'[11]

Even more discontented were the labourers on an estate of Commodus in Africa (p. 54). But on the whole there is far less articulateness about class-feeling in the west than among the eastern populations, to whom words—in Greek—came more readily and have, in some cases, survived the pressures which made it harder for the case of the poor man to be presented and preserved. In the east, dissatisfaction was acute, and became more acute: under the Flavians, and then under Trajan and Hadrian, the tempers of the eastern crowds grew worse rather than better. As Greek writers such as Lucian and Plutarch[12] understood, there was continuous tension between rich and poor. Towards the end of the second century the oppressed peasantry became even more surly and unreliable. In Asia Minor, and no doubt elsewhere, there were special corps of rural police which, acting on the basis of secret lists of potential criminals in governors' offices, struck down or arrested malcontents, robbers and Christians.

In the towns discontent took various different shapes. One of them was traditional: although the Assemblies of the cities had lost their sovereign power, they still provided occasion for inflammatory speeches proposing the old radical panaceas such as cancellation of debts and redistribution of lands. The emperors took this sort of disturbance seriously enough to suspend certain local Assemblies and deport their left-wing politicians to the islands.[13] Rome was very sensitive about potential class disturbances in the cities. In a curious exchange of letters with Pliny the younger, governor with special powers in Bithynia and Pontus (p. 56), Trajan even invokes security hazards in order to veto his representative's useful plan for a local fire-brigade at Nicomedia:

'You are of the opinion it would be proper to constitute a guild of firemen in Nicomedia, as has been done in several other places. But it is to be remembered that societies of this sort have greatly disturbed the peace of your province in general, and of those cities in particular. Whatever title we give them, and whatever our object in giving it, men who are banded together for a common end will all the same become a political association before long. It will therefore be better to provide suitable means for extinguishing fires, and enjoin owners of house-property to employ these themselves, calling in the help of the populace when necessary.'[14]

Mob action by the guilds and clubs which now proliferated, or by claques at theatres and circuses, seemed an ever-present danger: the flash-point of class-hatred was low. Prosperous collaborators with Rome such as Dio Chrysostom of Prusa would find their houses attacked,[15] while Antoninus Pius sharply rebuked the people of Ephesus for 'not properly appreciating' the splendid building activity of their local millionaire Vedius Antoninus—whose money they would have preferred to earmark for free distributions and amusements.[16] There were also demonstrations by groups of commercial and industrial workers against authorities and employers. Although slave-workers were not in a position to strike, countries such as Asia Minor, with industries not greatly relying on slave-personnel, produced labour disputes which provide something of an analogy to the modern strike. Again Ephesus is to the fore with a bakers' protest, reproved by an imperial edict:

'Thus it comes about at times that the people are plunged into disorder and tumults by the unrestrained evil speaking of the seditious groups of bakers in the market-place, for which they ought already to have been arrested and put on trial. Since, however, it is necessary to consider the city's welfare much more than the punishment of these men, I have resolved to bring them to their senses by an edict. I therefore order the Bakers' Union not to hold meetings as a faction nor to be leaders in recklessness, but strictly to obey the regulations made for the general welfare and to supply the city unfailingly with the labour essential for bread-making. When from this time forward any one of them shall be caught in the act of attending a meeting contrary to orders, or of starting any tumult or riot, he shall be arrested and shall undergo the fitting penalty.'[17]

These bakers were concessionaires of the city, or working under a special authorization of their civic authorities. They seem to have gone on strike with the assent of their union; and apparently striking was not punishable unless accompanied by sedition. Similarly, in a building dispute at Miletus, a group of workmen under a certain leader were tempted to abandon their contract through discontent.[18] Ordinary workers were involved in such manifestations, but the protests are non-proletarian in the sense that they were organized by, and needed organization by, leaders of higher social grade; the bakers responsible for the trouble at the bakeries of Ephesus were owners of bakeries, and indeed similar protests came from a group of builders at nearby Pergamum, and from shipowners at Arelate (Arles) in Gaul.

Our evidence is insufficient to tell us if such strikes were frequent in Asia—they were certainly infrequent elsewhere—and to what extent they involved or aroused strong class-feelings. But the basic economic reasons for discontent in the first century AD are clearly indicated by a story of the wonder-working sage Apollonius of Tyana and his intervention at Aspendus on the south coast of Asia Minor:

'When Apollonius got to Aspendus . . . there was nothing for sale but cattle fodder and starvation rations, for the rich had cornered the grain for export. Old and young, furious with the governor, had lit a fire to burn him alive, though he had fallen at the feet of the emperor's statue. . . . Apollonius turned to the crowd and signalled that they should listen. They fell silent in wonder . . . and even shifted their fire to the nearby altars. The governor, encouraged, said X and Y (naming names) "are responsible for this famine, for they have locked up the grain in their warehouses all over the province". The men of Aspendus wanted to track these plantation-owners down, but Apollonius shook his head and signed to them to get those responsible to give up the grain voluntarily. When the guilty ones arrived, he almost burst into speech against them, in his sympathy with the tears of the crowd of women and children, and with the moaning of the old men half-dead with hunger. But he kept his vow of silence and wrote his accusation on a slate which he gave to the governor to read, as follows: "Apollonius to the grain merchants of Aspendus: the earth is the mother of us all, for she is just, but you in your injustice have acted as though she were your mother exclusively. If you do not stop, I will not let you exist upon her." In terror they filled the market-place with grain, and the city came back to life.'[19]

Feeling between the social classes was particularly strong in Judaea. At the higher levels, it assumed a religious form: those who monopolized the important offices, and especially that of High Priest, were more or less resolutely Sadducee, whereas the lesser priests and Levites were mostly Pharisees (the Essenes, the third sect described by Josephus as important—but ignored by the New Testament—were monastic in character, p.184). But far below all, whipped up by the radical, puritanical, anarchistic Zealots who saw all priests and other Jewish and Roman notables alike as poisonously corrupt, were hosts of penniless, downtrodden outcasts, such as the 'destitute sailors of Tiberias' who clashed with the aristocracy under Nero. Jewish literature has much to say concerning the gulf between the rich and the desperately poor; and it is a theme often dwelt on by Jesus, who told the parable of Lazarus, and, for all his message *Render unto Caesar* as regards this world, assured the crowds: 'Again I say unto you, It is easier for a camel to go through the eye of a needle, than for a rich man to enter into the kingdom of God'[20] (p. 185).

But class-contrasts and oppression were perhaps to be seen at their worst in Egypt, where the city-system scarcely existed and the country was maintained, without the customary provincial organization, as a source of imperial revenue. Evidence here is plentiful owing to the properties of the Egyptian soil, which has preserved many papyri. These contain a host of complaints against the avoidance of state burdens by the rich and their robbery of the peasant, in spite of attempts by Roman governors to check both these abuses. In Egypt there was ruthless exploitation, exacerbated by the exemption of the privileged from poll-tax, by an elaborate system of compulsions and collective responsibilities, and by lapses on the part of Roman officials from the relatively high standards of honesty generally prevalent under the principate. In AD 55–60, Egyptian villages were depopulated by the flights or deaths of their taxpayers, and when agriculture had a bad year increasing numbers of peasants went underground. Revolts occurred in AD 152–4 and 172, and in the third century AD the treatment of the poor went from bad to worse. A surviving papyrus shows a personal expense account jotted down at this time, in which there are indications of disbursements to police, military police, informers, and soldiers, as well as the payment of another unspecified bribe.[21] Whether the 'free' *fellahin* and small native traders of Roman Egypt were better off than they had been under the Ptolemies who had ruled them before is very doubtful; at all events their lives were far from pleasant, and their resentment was great.

In general the ancient world assumed the existence of slavery, and the Roman world was no exception. But Rome was exceptional both in utilizing slaves more extensively than any previous empire, and in introducing many modifications into their employment, which was for a long time extraordinarily brutal but subsequently became a great deal more humane.

There had been slaves at Rome from a very early date. Enslavement for debt, for example, which had supplied a high proportion of the slaves of pre-classical near-eastern civilizations, is provided for in the Roman Twelve Tables attributed to the fifth century BC, and was therefore probably of more antique origin still. Some centuries before the Twelve Tables, the custom of employing slaves on a really substantial scale had come west with the Greek colonists of South Italy and Sicily, and with the Phoenicians who settled at Carthage. Then, from the third century BC onwards, slaves flooded into Rome from all quarters as a result of victorious wars. For example, there were 75,000 enslaved prisoners from the First Punic War, 30,000 from a single city—Tarentum—in the second of those wars, many Asiatics after Rome's successes against the Seleucid king Antiochus III (189–8 BC), 150,000 slaves from Epirus in 167 BC, a similar number after Marius's victory over the Germans (102–1 BC), perhaps nearly half a million in Caesar's Gallic Wars. They were

sold in the great slave-markets such as Capua (Fig. vi) and Delos.
The markets were also kept well-provided by the pirate kidnappers
who, with the collaboration of eminent Romans, infested the Mediterranean; as well as by the exposure and sale of children by the
destitute rural populations (pp. 103 f.).

The best qualified of the enslaved, and their children, were allotted
civic or domestic duties (Plate 18*b*), or even became professional men
such as philosophers, teachers, artists and architects; while those

Fig. vi. Part of funeral stele showing sale of slave, later 1st century BC.
Museo Campano, Capua

who were unlucky, barbarous or criminal, experienced the rigours
of gladiatorial schools and the horrors of mines and quarries. Moreover, after the Punic Wars, the free tenant farmer in Italy was
gradually eliminated by great cattle-ranches run for absentee
landlords by gangs of slaves (pp. 5 f., 95 f.). During the last two
centuries BC Sicily, north Africa and above all Italy possessed
economies which were more firmly grounded on slave-labour than
ever, in any country, before or since. Italy remained the chief slave
centre until the second century AD. By then the supply of slaves
from prisoners-of-war was drying up (the last big haul was after
Trajan's Dacian wars), and the tenant-farmer, so characteristic of
later European society, was beginning to come into his own again.

It is not possible to estimate with accuracy the number of slaves in Italy or Rome at any one time. In Augustus's time they may in Italy have numbered two million or more, and formed from one-quarter to one-third of the total population; these conjectural figures may be compared with the former slave-holding states of the USA where in 1850 there were 51 slaves to every 100 free men. At Rome, out of about one million inhabitants, perhaps a quarter were slaves. Many of them came from Europe, many more from Asia Minor and Syria, and perhaps one-eighth from outside the empire. Important Romans may have averaged four or five hundred slaves apiece. In even greater contrast to the ancient tradition exemplified by Regulus, who in the third century BC had owned one slave and one hired hand, Pliny the elder quotes the case of Gaius Caecilius Claudius Isidorus who claimed in his will to own slaves to the number of 4,116.[22] But by far the largest slave-owners were the emperors, whose households and bureaucracies continually increased. In the provinces, the degree of reliance on slaves varied from region to region. Spain was well-known for its hordes of slaves, and there were large slave-holdings in the province of Africa; but Egypt had many more free poor than slaves, and though the prosperous Hellenized cities of Asia Minor had their quota there were not many in their industries or agricultural areas (p. 106).

The ancient attitude to slavery, as reflected in the practice of the Greco-Roman world, had been adequately defined, less than a century before Rome gained her first great windfall of overseas prisoners, by Aristotle: 'from the hour of their birth some are marked out for subjection, others for rule'.[23] Yet the problem was increasingly discussed, and within a few years the founders of the Stoic philosophy expressed their conviction that slavery was a conventional, artificial, unnatural state of affairs; in other words that slaves, being human beings, were equal to free men (p. 196). But when, soon afterwards, Rome became a large-scale employer of slaves and afraid of social disorders, its influential Stoic friends such as Panaetius in the second century BC went half-way back to the point of view of Aristotle. Like other philosophers of the time these new Stoics, though they might make no theoretical difference in their own minds between the essential human condition of slave and free, were content to regard slavery as a misfortune like any other, and to leave it at that. In the early years of the Roman principate the Hellenized Jewish philosopher Philo of Alexandria still regarded it as axiomatic that civilization could not exist without slaves, and accordingly drew the conclusion that their acquisition was permissible according to the moral law.

The treatment of their slaves by numerous Romans, especially in Republican times, was, according to modern ideas, frightful and unspeakable—one of the worst blots on the history of the human race. Although slavery was endemic in the ancient world, it is difficult to think of any ancient people, except possibly the Assyrians, who can have exceeded many slave-owning Romans in the scale of their callous brutality, although this has perhaps been outdone in the twentieth century. Since the expectation of life even among free Roman citizens was probably no higher than that of Liverpool and Glasgow in the mid-nineteenth, or India in the early twentieth century, slaves clearly survived for a very much shorter time; at a rough guess their average age of death was twenty-one. The worst atrocities of ill-treatment occurred among the slaves who, under the Republic, were herded in great barracks and concentration camps on the large ranches and plantations, and who worked in the agonizing squalor of the mines, from which pathetic epitaphs have come down to us.[24] 'What malignant breath,' writes Lucretius, 'is exhaled by gold mines! How it acts upon men's features and complexions! Have you not seen or heard how speedily men die and how their vital forces fail when they are driven by dire necessity to endure such work?'[25]

An example of the viewpoint of Republican days in one of its more thoughtful forms is provided by Cato the elder's work *On Farming*. Writing in the second century BC, Cato's sole motive is profit. Slaves, of whom he bought a great number from among prisoners of war, are to be treated like animals, though more anxiety is felt concerning the welfare of the ox, which was not so good at looking after itself. Some of the slaves were evidently kept in chains,[26] and when they were too old to work, and therefore to be fed, Cato got rid of them with complete callousness. Yet he goes on to say that the best principle of management is to treat both slaves and animals well enough to give them the strength to work hard. The foreman, therefore, should not be vindictive when he punishes the slaves:

'When at home, a slave had to be either at work or asleep. Indeed Cato greatly favoured the sleepy ones, accounting them more docile than those who were wakeful, and more fit for anything when refreshed with slumber than those who lacked it. Being also of the opinion that the greater cause of misbehaviour in slaves was their sexual passions, he arranged for the males to consort with the females at a fixed price and permitted none to approach a woman outside the household. . . . He also lent money to those of his slaves who wished it; they would buy boys and, after training and teaching them at Cato's expense, would sell them again after a year. Many of these Cato would keep for himself, crediting the trainer-slave with the price offered by the highest bidder. . . .'[27]

There is no trace of humanity in Cato, but his common-sense efficiency meant that the worst ill-treatment was avoided. However, there was nothing to stop other masters, if they wished, from working their slaves to death, and that is what often happened. The cumulative result of an appalling amount of ill-treatment was that a great many desperate slaves deserted and went underground. This was one of the principal reasons why, at certain moments during the second century BC, it seemed that classical society would founder completely and be engulfed (p. 100). Terrified of the huge numbers of slaves whom they had come to possess, and often lacking Cato's powers of management, the Roman slave-masters oscillated between violence and weakness. *Every slave we own*, went the saying, *is an enemy we harbour*; and indeed the deserters were forming openly rebellious bands which sometimes reached the size of armies. In the massive revolts that followed, the Romans had to exert several full-scale military efforts, and it was recorded, perhaps without exaggeration, that more than a million slaves met their deaths.[28] Rebellions had occurred at intervals since 198 BC, but the first large-scale rising broke out on Sicilian plantations in 135. It was sparked off by an unusual degree of ill-treatment, including the withdrawal of food and clothing allowances—cynical owners said that if their slaves wanted new clothes they must rob passers-by. The story of this slave-war is told by a Sicilian historian of the first century BC, Diodorus.

'Never had there been such an uprising of slaves as now occurred in Sicily. In it many cities experienced terrible misfortunes, and untold numbers of men, women and children suffered most grievous calamities; and the whole island was on the point of falling into the power of the runaways who set the complete destruction of their masters as the goal of their power. To most people these events came to pass unlooked for, and unexpectedly; but to men of competent political judgment their occurrence did not seem unreasonable. For on account of the immense wealth of those exploiting this rich island, practically all the very wealthy revelled in luxury, arrogance and insolence. Consequently, as the slaves' hatred of their masters increased *pari passu* with the masters' cruelty towards their slaves, the hatred burst forth one day at an opportune moment. Then, without pre-arrangement, many thousands of slaves quickly gathered together to destroy their masters. . . .

'The Slave War broke out from the following cause. The Sicilians, being grown very rich and elegant in their manner of living, bought up large numbers of slaves. They brought them in droves from the places where they were reared, and immediately branded them with marks on their bodies. Those that were young they used as shepherds, and the others as need required. . . .

'Oppressed by the grinding toil and beatings, maltreated for the most part beyond all reason, the slaves could endure it no longer. Therefore, meeting together at suitable opportunities they discussed revolt, until at last they put their plan into effect. There was a Syrian from Apamea named Eunus, a slave of Antigenes of Enna. A kind of magician and conjurer, he claimed to foretell future events from divine revelations in his dreams, and he imposed upon many by his cleverness in this. . . . Before the revolt he used to boast that the Syrian goddess had appeared to him and told him that he would be king; and he repeated this not only to others but even to his own master. . . .'[29]

The devices which Eunus employed to assert his leadership included a spectacular fire-breathing act, performed by the secretion in his mouth of a nut filled with sulphur.[30] His governmental machinery included the issue of coins, on which he called himself king Antiochus in memory of his Syrian homeland.[31] These talented slave-leaders seasoned their religious appeals with calls to eastern national sentiment, and created organizations determined by the social patterns that they had known at home. Before the rebellion was suppressed—after immense loss of life—in 131 BC, the slave army had swollen to 70,000 and its victories had stimulated outbreaks in other parts of the empire. Curiously enough Eunus was allowed by the Romans to die a natural death in captivity; they also refrained from a general massacre of their prisoners, preferring to restore them to their owners. But at the time of the German invasions of Gaul the Sicilian slaves rose again (104–100 BC), and 17,000 Roman soldiers were needed to put them down. The last great outbreak was led by the courageous, humane Thracian gladiator Spartacus, whose slave army 90,000 strong—he rejected many additional volunteers— terrorized the entire Italian peninsula (73–71 BC). The war ended with the execution, by Crassus, of the 6,000 slaves whom he captured.

With their crucifixion along the Appian Way, from Capua to Rome, the age of the great revolts was at an end. They had provided the most serious threat to Rome since Hannibal.

But new and less ruthless ideas were in the air, though at first they were cautiously expressed. The Stoic Posidonius, contemporary of Spartacus, saw that the ill-usage of slaves by individual masters was a danger to the whole community.[32] In the same period it came to be realized that, since the slave had a soul, he might be allowed to take part in religious activities; at the Temple of Hope at Minturnae the active helpers include as many slaves as free and freed together.[33] Except during short periods (in 64–58 BC and under Caesar), they were also allowed to belong to clubs (*collegia*), organizations for mutual help which had sprung up everywhere. Moreover, in the writings of the encyclopaedic scholar and farmer Varro (116–27 BC) the naked profit motive of Cato has given place to more sophisticated welfare economics. Varro looked upon slaves as articulate implements—differing from their voiceless counterparts, such as a pitchfork, in that they need psychological study and sensible, unbrutal handling.[34] Cicero knew that his Brotherhood of Man could not, in practice, make slaves the same as free men, yet his genuine humanity impelled him to be kind, considerate, and even affectionate to them. When a slave who served as his reader, Sositheus, died, Cicero wrote: 'I am more upset about it than anyone would suppose I should be about a slave's death.'[35] He also corresponded affectionately with his devoted secretary and slave, later freedman, Tiro; and his disgust with the appalling Sassia, who tortured her slaves to excess,[36] is genuine as well as forensic. Although slaves had to be regularly tortured before they were allowed to give evidence—otherwise it was thought they would be incapable of telling the truth—nevertheless, in this age of dawning humanity, there were lines short of the worst brutalities that had to be drawn.

But the lines became arrestingly clearer a century later, in the works of the other great Roman popular moralist, Seneca of Corduba (Cordova). This extraordinary man combined concessions to human weakness, in his capacity as Nero's millionaire minister, with a warmth of human feelings which is none the less authentic for being the product of the study. His *Moral Letters* to his friend Lucilius— letters intended, unlike most of Cicero's, for publication—contain an epoch-making statement of his attitude to slavery, in which the Human Brotherhood is brought into relation with the daily life of a Roman gentleman. He does not, it is true, propose that all slaves should be freed, but he insists on their treatment as human beings:

'I'm glad to learn, from visitors of yours who come here, that you live on friendly terms with your slaves. That squares with your sensible outlook no less than with your philosophy. "They're slaves." Perhaps, but still fellow-men. "They're slaves." But they share your roof. "They're slaves." Friends, rather—humble friends. "They're slaves." Well, fellow-slaves, if you reflect that fortune had an equal power over them and you. . . . Please reflect that the man you call your slave was born of the same seed, has the same good sky above him, breathes as you do, lives as you do, dies as you do! . . . Treat your slave with kindness, with courtesy too; let him share your conversations, your deliberations, and your company.'[37]

Such sentiments were now gaining currency among cultured Romans, and Pliny the younger translated them into the more personal language appropriate to the manner of his correspondence—reflecting, for example, in more elaborate and sensitive terms than Cicero, upon the unhappiness which he has felt when slaves dear to him have died.[38] From this century onwards we find epitaphs to the souls of dead slaves; the branch of the emperor's slave household at Carthage owned its own cemetery, and slaves belonged to associations defraying the funerals of members of their community.

The spread of more humane ideas among the upper classes resulted in enactments by Augustus and his successors affording increased protection against the maltreatment of slaves. For example, Claudius deprived masters of the power to kill or discard sick slaves arbitrarily. But inevitably there came clashes between, on the one hand, this increasing sensitiveness and benevolence, and at the other extreme the strict letter of the law, and the severe customs and policies which went with it. For the law set a gulf between slave and free: 'the main distinction in the law of persons is that all men are either free or slaves'.[39] The slave was, in principle, a human chattel which could be owned and dealt with like any other piece of property. He was at the mercy of his owner, without rights. But if he was a thing in law, he was a man in fact—and a man whose contribution to economic and social life enforced recognition of his personality. That is where the dilemma arose.

It is brought out with keen dramatic force by Tacitus. The occasion is the murder, in AD 61, of the City Prefect Lucius Pedanius Secundus by a male slave whom he had either broken a promise to liberate or disappointed in a love affair. According to tradition, reaffirmed by a senatorial decree of Augustan date, such a happening meant the torture and execution of every slave in the dead man's household—including, by a decree of Nero, those who were due for liberation in his will. The decision to inflict this penalty in AD 61 caused great public outcry, but the Senate was not to be moved.

'There were protesting cries of pity for the numbers affected, and the women, and the young, and the undoubted innocence of the majority. Yet those favouring execution prevailed. However, great crowds ready with stones and torches prevented the order from being carried out. Nero rebuked the population by edict, and lined with troops the whole route along which those condemned were taken for execution. Then it was proposed that the ex-slaves, too, who had been under the same roof should be deported from Italy. But the emperor vetoed this—the ancient custom had not been tempered by mercy, but should not be aggravated by brutality.'[40]

Tacitus does not state his own verdict; he has given the arguments for severity, and none for mercy, yet he records that the crime had been committed under provocation.

After this critical case under Nero, legislative reforms against the abuse of slaves continued. Vespasian protected female prostitutes from victimization. Domitian, though much of his other legislation was reactionary, proceeded against the castration of slaves for commercial purposes. Hadrian forbade masters to kill their slaves and ordained that:

'recourse should be had to torturing only when there is a suspect under indictment, and when other evidence brings the proof so close that only the confession of slaves appears necessary (to complete it); and then the inquiry must be limited to those slaves who could have been near enough to see anything material.'

This and other significant legislation by Hadrian—as well as administrative action, such as the banishment of Umbricia for five years for cruelty to slaves—reflects the constant readiness of that emperor to support the under-privileged, and also his clear understanding of the humane basis that, in his age, a slave society and economy needed. His successor Antoninus Pius continued the same process by further enactments punishing those who killed or maltreated slaves. He ordered that if the cruelty of masters was found to be unendurable they must sell their slaves, seeing that: 'it is to the masters' interest that relief against cruelty, hunger or intolerable wrong should not be denied those who seek it with just cause.'[41] And Septimius Severus and his sons, despite the autocratic tendencies of their régime, produced further legislation of the same humanitarian character, in keeping with their egalitarian views (p. 19).[42]

For although, under such a social system, severe sanctions—for instance in regard to the household of a murdered master—were still felt to be necessary, the jurists of the later second and early third century AD echoed the Stoic view that slavery was a convention contrary to natural law (p. 196): 'Slavery is an institution of law common to all peoples [*ius gentium*], by which, in violation of the law of nature, a person is subjected to the mastery of another.'[43] 'As far as Roman law [*ius civile*] is concerned, slaves are regarded as nothing, but not so in natural law as well; because as far as the law of nature is concerned, all men are equal.'[44]

A Greek in Rome in the middle of the second century AD was struck by the lack of outward distinction between slaves and free men. For instance, their clothes were the same; a proposal in the Senate to differentiate them had been defeated for the significant reason of public security—'then they would see how few we are' (p. 99). But Juvenal was obviously right to remark that a rich man's slave was better off than a destitute citizen. Marcus Aurelius, though he recognized only free men as his equals, could even ask: 'In what other universal constitution beside ours can the whole race of men have a share?'[45]

One of the most disputed problems of antiquity concerns the changing role of the Roman slave in the national economy. It has rightly been pointed out that cheap slave labour ruined Italian agriculture, exhausted the soil, and stagnated techniques; that many slaves could not handle complicated processes; and that the consequent degradation of manual skill discouraged interest in technology (p. 75). Yet the versatility of some slaves must not be underestimated—nor must the likelihood that, in the conditions prevailing in antiquity, slavery increased the available surplus in the hands of the propertied classes more than could have been done by other accessible means. Even during the later Republic, when the use of slaves in agriculture and industry had enormously increased, it is probable that they numerically exceeded free labour only on the cattle-ranches. The subsequent replacement of slave gangs by free tenants (p. 110) suggests that under the principate, when the influx of war-prisoners first diminished and then ceased, slaves were neither abundant nor cheap.

So the slave society was gradually running its course. But in the harsh political conditions of the third and fourth centuries AD there were regressions from the improving standard of treatment. Even the Christian Fathers, with both the New Testament and the humane provisions of imperial paganism behind them, did not unequivocally denounce the slave-structure of society, and did not, indeed, advance beyond the dilemma between traditional practice and moral rejection which has been noted in the pagan jurists. It was not until the nineteenth century that the anti-slavery movement—stimulated by Christian ethics —achieved notable successes; though slavery still exists in the world today.

The visible and practical sign of the Roman will to power was Roman cruelty. This found expression in savage, primitive floggings (Fig. vii) often resulting in death; crucifixions, tortures, burnings and buryings alive, hurlings from the Tarpeian rock, revengeful massacres of prisoners, drowning in sacks, brutal punishments by heads of families and school-masters. It was not for nothing that the axe and rods (*fasces*) were the emblems of Roman authority. And although certain Romans, rising above the bloodstained world in which they lived,

Fig. vii. Figurine (originally suspended from string) of slave being flogged. From Priene (S.W. Asia Minor)

protested against this cruelty and legal improvements followed (p. 117), the slaves were always the worst sufferers. The most hideous feature of this subject remains to be considered. This was the Roman entertainment with which the Circus alone could compete in its immense popularity—the massacre of slaves in gladiatorial combat (Fig. viii). These bloodthirsty contests were not of Greek origin but came to the Romans from Etruria, where they may originally have

Fig. viii. Mosaic of fighting gladiators. Galleria Borghese, Rome

formed part of the ceremonies at a chief's funeral. The first recorded instance of their appearance in Rome was at the funeral games of a nobleman in 264 BC, when only three pairs of gladiators fought. In 160 BC we hear of a gladiatorial bout competing successfully for public attention with a play by Terence. A century later, at the games given by Julius Caesar as aedile, the number of gladiators had risen to 320 pairs; and the construction of permanent amphitheatres soon followed (p. 274). Cicero discussed gladiatorial combats with feeble excuses, suggesting that they promoted courage and endurance, yet criticizing them as inadequate entertainment.[46]

Contests between gladiators formed an integral part of the programme of food and amusements which emperors felt obliged to offer the people of Rome. Augustus's own enumeration of his efforts in this direction quotes a total of 10,000 combatants (p. 87), some of whom fought in the first permanent amphitheatre, made partly of stone. The private reactions of imperial personages towards such combats varied from boredom (Marcus Aurelius found them 'wearisome') to keen appreciation—although, whatever their thoughts, they did not usually dare to suppress or diminish the bloodshed. Tiberius alone felt such distaste that he not only cut down expenditure on Games, but often stayed away. To his son Drusus the younger, however, fell the extraordinary distinction of shocking even the Roman public by the extravagance of his fondness for this slaughter.

The critical public who watched such performances in the Italian towns—their advertisements are still to be seen on the walls of Pompeii—are exemplified in Petronius's novel by one of Trimalchio's dinner-guests, Echion:

'Our good Titus has a big imagination and is hot-blooded . . . he is all against half-measures. He will give you the finest blades, no running away, butchery done in the middle, where the whole audience can see it. . . . After all, what has Norbanus ever done for us? He produced some decayed twopenny-halfpenny gladiators, who would have fallen flat if you breathed on them; I have seen better ruffians turned in to fight the wild beasts. He shed the blood of some mounted infantry that might have come off a lamp; dunghill cocks you would have called them; one a spavined mule, the other bandy-legged, and the holder of the bye just one corpse instead of another, and hamstrung. One man, a Thracian, had some stuffing, but he too fought according to the rule of the schools. In short, they were all flogged afterwards. How the great crowd roared at them, "Lay it on!" '[47]

In thousands, gladiators fared worse than that and lost their lives. At Rome the decision whether a defeated gladiator should survive was referred to the emperor. The winner was richly rewarded, and lived to fight again. Although straightforward gladiatorial combats never palled, the emperors tried to think of novel forms of massacre for the amusement of their people. For example, large-scale naval fights were arranged by Julius Caesar and Augustus. The most lavish of such spectacles was organized by Claudius in AD 52, when, although the nineteen thousand combatants 'were criminals, they fought like brave men. After much blood-letting, they were spared extermination'.[48] Nero was more interested in Greek entertainments of a less bloody character; nevertheless he hit on the idea, to tickle jaded senses, of arranging for fashionable women to fight against each other in the arena. Domitian later set women to grapple with dwarfs.

It was Domitian's father Vespasian and brother Titus who gave the city its monumental Colosseum (Plates 50a and 51a, p. 275; cf. Plate 51b, Pula in Yugoslavia), with room for 45,000 seated and 5,000 standing. Titus inaugurated the building with exhibitions lasting for over 100 days. Then, during four months of AD 107 alone, Trajan, to celebrate his Dacian victories, sent 10,000 gladiators into the arena—a number equal to the figure for Augustus's whole reign. A recently discovered inscription gives a few figures relating to his entertainments in AD 108–113. Mentioned there are two minor shows, one with 350 pairs of gladiators and the other of 202, and a major event which lasted 117 days and brought into action 4,941 pairs of gladiators. Altogether, between AD 106 and 114, over 23,000 performers seem to have fought.[49] The Dacian prisoners were available for this purpose, and Trajan was notoriously fond of the Games; his panegyrist the younger Pliny echoes the lame explanations of Cicero.[50] But imperial affection for this sort of entertainment was carried a good stage further by Commodus, who as well as organizing contests between cripples—whom he finished off himself—was a keen performer in more orthodox gladiatorial contests. He boasted of having fought personally in no less than 1,000 combats, 365 of these in the reign of his saintly father Marcus Aurelius. Not long afterwards the future emperor Gordian I gave gladiatorial Games every month of his year of office as aedile, employing a total of from 4,000 to 5,000 combatants.

And yet already a century and a half before these displays Seneca, in pursuance of his enlightened views about slaves in general (p. 196), had expressed unequivocal disgust about the horrors of the arena.

'I've happened to drop in upon the midday entertainment of the arena in hope of some milder diversions, a spice of comedy, a touch of the relief in which men's eyes may find rest after a glut of human blood. No, no: far from it. All the previous fighting was mere softness of heart. Away with such bagatelles: now for butchery pure and simple! The combatants have nothing to protect them: their bodies are utterly open to every blow: never a thrust but finds its mark. Most people prefer this kind of thing to all other matches, whether part of the programme or by special request. Naturally so. The sword is not checked by helmet or shield. What good is armour? What good is swordsmanship? All these things only put off death a little. In the morning men are matched with lions and bears, at noon with their spectators. These pit butcher actual against butcher prospectively and reserve the winner for another bloody bout: death is the fighters' only exit. "But this, that, or the other fellow has committed highway robbery!" Well? "And murder!" As a murderer, then he deserved what he's getting: what's your crime, unlucky creature, that you should watch it? "Kill! Flog! Burn! Why does he jib at cold steel? Why boggle at killing? Why die so squeamishly?" The lash forces them on to the sword. "Let them have at each other in the nude—get in at the bare chest!" There's an interval in the display. "Cut a few throats meanwhile to keep things going!" Come now, can't you people see even this much—that bad examples recoil on those who set them?'[51]

In the same spirit, the more enlightened of the Greeks rejected gladiators with horror. Nevertheless, the taste for such amusements gradually spread even in the Greek lands of the Roman empire and one by one the cities constructed their own amphitheatres. It is true that in the second century AD a Cynic philosopher, Demonax from Cyprus, successfully vetoed a proposal to have gladiatorial games at Athens. Yet it was not until the early years of the fifth century, nearly a hundred years after the empire had become officially Christian, that gladiatorial games ceased in the western provinces; in the east they had ended a generation earlier. This was during the lifetime of St Augustine, who describes better than anyone else the irresistible excitement and fascination that these sanguinary performances exerted on one of his friends.[52]

Contests between wild animals were also very popular: in a single day of Titus's reign 5,000 were massacred. Seneca disliked this sort of amusement scarcely less than gladiatorial combat, and wrote with equal hatred of that other horrifying Roman custom—introduced

Fig. ix. Relief showing fight with wild beasts. Sofia Museum

in the second century BC and only terminated by Constantine in AD 326—of arranging for human beings to be slaughtered in the amphitheatre, not only as hitherto by armed gladiators, but by wild beasts[53] (Fig. ix)—a practice from which the modern bullfight is descended. Augustus made this sort of penalty and entertainment more spectacular by erecting in the Forum a pillory which collapsed and dropped its victim, the bandit Selurus, into a cage of wild beasts. But Seneca himself lived, as an adult, through the reign of the emperor Caligula, in whom—if only a little of the gossip retailed by Suetonius is true—the native Roman streak of sadism expressed itself by acts of appalling cruelty; the sight of people torn to pieces by animals seems to have given him the keenest pleasure.[54] Some of those condemned to this fate were unarmed, condemned criminals (Fig. x); for example, the Christians whom Nero butchered as scapegoats for his suspected incendiarism (p. 186) and whom other

Fig. x. Relief of condemned men in amphitheatre. From Miletus (Balat, S.W.
Asia Minor); Istanbul Museum

rulers martyred at Lyon, Carthage and many other places. But some
of those set to encounter the wild beasts were skilled and armed
huntsmen, that is to say, members of the gladiatorial profession.

Gladiators were slaves. On the one hand, they enjoyed a passionately
personal admiration such as the public now reserve for film-stars and
popular singers; girls at Pompeii scrawled lovesick tributes on its
walls. On the other hand, these men lived lives of almost inconceiv-
able harshness and continuous mortal danger, only mitigated,
perhaps, by the hope that they had the organizers of shows on their
side, since these received a discount on gladiators returned to the
schools unhurt. In the second century AD, the doctor Galen of
Pergamum described a member of one of the great elaborately
organized imperial schools of gladiators, with his short expectation of
life, his overfed, battered and disfigured body and his dreadful
wounds.[55] In temperament, they varied, as our records show, between
suicidal despair and *prima donna* tantrums if they were not allowed to
fight. Emperors and Senate busied themselves with their terms of
service.[56]

Human immolation also assumed *recherché*, dramatic forms. The
Colosseum was the scene of theatrical performances in which the
murders were not fictitious but real. Under Domitian the public was
able to see plays in which one criminal plunged his right hand into a
fire, and another prisoner was crucified. Such spectacles in the

amphitheatre outbid the Circus Games and in the end cleared the theatres, which fell into disuse during the half-century after Commodus. In this period, too, Tertullian saw a performance of the *Death of Hercules*, in which the actor representing Hercules was actually burnt to death as part of the show. With sombre, eloquent gusto Tertullian writes of the greatest of all spectacles that was to come, the Last Judgment in which all Roman monarchs, officials, professors and performers—even those in the less lethal branches of their profession—will be enveloped in a far greater holocaust than any which they themselves had perpetrated. 'How vast the spectacle that day, and how wide. What sight shall wake my wonder, what my laughter, my joy and exultation, as I see . . . the magistrates who persecuted the name of Jesus liquefying in fiercer flames than they kindled in their rage against the Christians!'[57]

Part III

BELIEFS

CHAPTER 5

FATE AND THE STARS

THE ever-recurrent horrors and brutalities described in the last Chapter were ultimately of Etruscan origin, and could not have happened in classical Greece where—for all its faults—there had always been a certain number of people, including men in high places, who tried to think and live on more reasonable, rational lines. This tendency had gone along with progress in exact science, which reached its highest point in the Hellenistic Alexandria of the third century BC. From then onwards, throughout the Roman period, the rationalistic approach was in increasing disfavour. The scientifically minded were a tiny, almost swamped minority (p. 75) in a world in which, on the one hand, the sports of the amphitheatre came to be almost universally enjoyed, and, on the other, ordinary human knowledge had ceased to be regarded as important; faith in human effort and inquiry had been lost.

The Roman age was a time not only of uncontrolled bloodlust but of pessimism and nerve-failure regarding the powers of man to work out his own future. The existence and propaganda of the imperial government claiming the support of the old gods (p. 154) did not remove the deep-seated feeling that every man was adrift, and everything hazardous. So the presiding deity of nerve-failure was Fortune. 'Throughout the whole world,' says Pliny the elder, 'at every place and hour, by every voice, Fortune alone is invoked and her name spoken: she is the one defendant, the one culprit, the one thought in men's minds, the one object of praise, the one cause. She is worshipped with insults, counted as fickle and often as blind, wandering, inconsistent, elusive, changeful and friend of the unworthy. . . . We are so much at the mercy of chance that Chance is our god.'[1] Pliny wrote in the first century AD, but he is probably drawing on Greek sources of a good many years earlier; for Fortune's cult, as Polybius shows, had swept conqueringly over the Mediterranean

129

world as early as the third and second centuries BC.[2] To millions it seemed that everything was governed by the sheerest luck:

> There are no gods: to say Jove reigns is wrong:
> 'Tis a blind chance that moves the years along.[3]

Many felt that Chance or Fortune was some order of affairs beyond the comprehension of men. But there was nothing theoretical about her; they could see her, as Horace saw her, raising men up and striking them down:

> Fortune, that with malicious joy
> Does Man, her slave, oppress,
> Proud of her office to destroy,
> Is seldom pleased to bless;
> Still various and unconstant still,
> But with an inclination to be ill,
> Promotes, degrades, delights in strife,
> And makes a lottery of life.[4]

In other, less pessimistic moods, it seemed that her favour and disfavour were equally balanced—*today to thee, tomorrow to me*; so there was some hope in her. But meanwhile, 'gather ye rosebuds while ye may'—and in its simplest form this sort of superficial Epicureanism, the natural result of peace and prosperity, was the most widespread of all creeds. A silver goblet from Boscoreale near Pompeii, now in the Louvre (Plate 22*b*), shows human skeletons with the inscription 'Enjoy life while you are alive, for tomorrow is uncertain'. One skeleton holds a large purse full of money (inscribed 'envy') and a butterfly (representing the human soul), which he presents to his companions. Beside them smaller skeletons play the lyre, and clap their hands. The best thing, in fact, is a full purse and the amusements that it can buy—spend your money while you have a chance.

One of the most famous and influential statues of the ancient world (296–290 BC) was Eutychides' Fortune (Tyche) of the splendid, recently founded city of Antioch, which before long was to become, after Rome and Alexandria, the third greatest city of the Roman empire. The sculptor shows Fortune seated with the river-god Orontes at her feet (Plate 21). There were innumerable copies of this statue, and every community had a Fortune of its own. Every man, too, had his Fortune, and the term came almost to personify his own individuality and where it would lead him, being variously regarded as a gift at the disposal of a wise Providence, and a wholly capricious force. The Roman emperors annexed Fortune: their coins display the 'Fortune of the Augustus'—an edifying picture of the special exaltation, dedication, and labour of the ruler's momentous life. Small, private statuettes of Fortune were kept in house and palace (Fig. xi); Antoninus Pius kept a gold one in his bedroom, and his coinage calls her 'Obsequens'—indulgent to his wishes. The coins of Commodus show her as 'Manens', 'ever-remaining'—as firmly held as the horse which the design shows her as bridling. The belief in Fortune extended far and wide beyond the borders of the Greco-Roman world, and long survived imperial Rome. Dante called upon her, and people of the Renaissance in many countries showed the same fascinated devotion to Fortune, representing or symbolizing her in many paintings.

Fig. xi. Statuette of Fortune. 2nd century AD. British Museum

During the first century BC people began to talk less about Fortune and more about Fate (the statuette of one of the Fates, Clotho, appears on the Boscoreale goblet). Their relations were vague and shifting, as they are when people talk about them today: there need not always be much difference between 'chance would have it so' and 'it was fated to be so'—or the 'it was not to be' which appears so regularly in obituary notices. Both conceptions imply a denial or at least a restriction of the value of human behaviour. However, it was possible to distinguish between them if one chose. Horace apostrophizes Fortune as though Fate walks ahead of her:

> And in thy progress harsh Necessity
>   Walks still before thee, in her brazen hand
> Bearing the Tools of thy strong masonry,
>   Wedges and nails, the clamp, the lead, the band.[5]

A philosopher of the third century AD pointed out how illogical it was to believe in both Fortune and Fate at the same time.[6] Nevertheless, some people worked the two personifications, or deities, into different regions of the Universe, believing that Necessity was above the moon, and Chance and evil daemons below it. Others welcomed Fate as an escape from blind Fortune. On the whole, Fate was more respectable; at least she was a cause, 'like a fine thread', according to Zeno the founder of Stoicism, 'running through the whole of existence'.[7]

But his opponent Epicurus called it better to be enslaved to the old gods of the vulgar, useless though they were, than to the Destiny of the philosophers (p. 190); and many like him felt oppressed by its impossible, inescapable tyranny. 'Fate rules the earth and all things stand firm by a fixed law . . . the moment of our birth also witnesses our death, and our end depends upon our beginning', writes the poet Manilius early in the first century AD;[8] and 'At birth to all the day of death is set' says Ovid's teacher Arellius Fuscus.[9] Both Manilius and Fuscus are expressing belief in the inevitable, ineluctable Fate which made Stoicism, despite its apparently contradictory belief in God and in ethics, a grimly mechanistic doctrine (p. 203). But Cicero had refused to credit a blind force: 'I call Fate the order, and series of causes, in which a cause joined with another cause produces a result' and 'Fortune is brought in to cover up our ignorance of events and causes'.[10] His own view was sturdily humanistic. Conceding the very real, and indeed enormous, part which blind chance plays, nevertheless his view of great events—victories and defeats, for example—is that although they contain an element of chance, still they cannot be brought about, whether for good or for ill, without the influence and the co-operation of our fellow-men.

Virgil's deeply religious mind wove a complex web of traditional and personal beliefs round the figure of Fate. In the *Aeneid* the word has many meanings and nuances. It can refer to the lots of individuals, and these lots may well conflict. Virgilian Fate can also be the destiny guiding the whole world; and in this sense it takes on the hues of the Stoic divine guidance of the world by destiny and becomes an expression of the immanent world deity. Fate and Jupiter had been addressed separately but conjointly in the *Hymn to Destiny* of the Stoic Cleanthes,[11] and both of them appear in Virgil's poem; nor is it always clear whether the poet means Jupiter's will to be subordinate to Fate, or indistinguishable from it. But at heart Virgil was a monotheist believing, like the Stoics, in an omnipotent deity who is synonymous with Fate and whose service is not, indeed, perfect freedom, but is the task belonging to the greatest of virtues, *pietas*. This is the most important quality of *pius Aeneas*, who cried: 'where the god, where harsh Fortune calls, let us follow!'[12] *Fortuna* in the *Aeneid* can mean anything from Fate to its opposite—a protest

in favour of the individual's free-will—but in its essence Virgil's
Fate or Fortune is not a mere mechanical force arising from the laws
of nature, like the Greek *Ananke*, or an unmeaning caprice as we find
it sometimes in the Greek poets, but a deliberate purpose of the divine
being who is above the world and in the world. Happenings that
seem fatalistically destined, and other apparently contradictory
events which look like exceptions to the fatalistic pattern, are both
equally due to the agency of Providence; which is further related to
the Universe in solemn passages of the *Georgics* and the *Aeneid*
combining with strong belief the most elaborate, deeply thought and
difficult delineations of the universe (p. 220). Unphilosophical
though the Romans as a race were, it is not surprising to learn that
Virgil, if he had lived longer, was about to devote his life to
philosophy.

The response of Tacitus to the dilemma between an all-controlling
Fate and the freedom of the human will is no less thoughtful, but
more tortured, perplexed and, ultimately, indecisive. He is a fatalist,
but only makes fate the agent when other causes are not available—
the procedure of 'God in the gap'. His belief in supernatural
phenomena is hesitant and spasmodic. On the whole, perhaps, he
favours a current Stoic compromise, permitting the belief that,
although man's external circumstances are determined, his inward
life depends upon his own choice (p. 199). Tacitus's comment on
stories of the prophetic powers attributed to Tiberius's court
astrologer Thrasyllus (p. 145) is characteristic and revealing:

'When I hear this and similar stories I feel uncertain whether human
affairs are directed by Fate's unalterable necessity—or by chance. On this
question the wisest thinkers and their disciples differ. Many insist that
heaven is unconcerned with our births and deaths—is unconcerned, in
fact, with human beings—so that the good often suffer, and the wicked
prosper. Others disagree, maintaining that although things happen
according to fate, this depends not upon astral movements but upon the
principles and logic of natural causality. This school leaves us free to
choose our lives. But once the choice is made, they warn that the future
sequence of events is immutable. Yet in regard to those events they claim
that the popular ideas of good and evil are mistaken: many who seem
afflicted are happy, if they endure their hardships courageously; others
(however wealthy) are wretched, if they employ their prosperity unwisely.
Most men, however, find it natural to believe that lives are predestined
from birth, that the science of prophecy is verified by remarkable testi-

monials, ancient and modern; and that unfulfilled predictions are due merely to ignorant impostors who discredit it.'[13]

And the vicissitudes of imperial favour—that favour which had something seemingly divine about its all-powerful quality (p. 158)— lead him to a similar reflection: 'this forces me to wonder whether the favour of the emperors towards some and their dislike of others is, like all else, a matter of fate and the chances of birth, or whether something rests with our own designs.'[14]

Later in the second century AD in which Tacitus wrote, these and similar problems came under the cool, mocking scrutiny of one of the most popular and entertaining of all sceptics, the Greek or Greco-Syrian writer Lucian from Samosata on the Euphrates. The aim of his inventive, paradoxical wit was nihilistic; to have neither hopes nor fears, and to laugh at the follies and pretensions of others. Vividly employing the dialogue form for essays, short stories, mimes and parodies, in one of his *Dialogues of the Dead* he pictures the supreme Judge, Minos, cornered by the logical objections about Fate raised by a recently deceased pirate, Sostratus:

Sos.: The deeds of my life—were they in my own choice, or were they decreed by Fate?

Mi.: Decreed, of course.

Sos.: Then all of us, whether we passed for honest men or rogues, were the instruments of Fate in all that we did?

Mi.: Certainly; Clotho prescribes the conduct of every man at his birth.

Sos.: Now suppose a man commits a murder under compulsion of a power which he cannot resist, an executioner for instance at the bidding of a judge, or a bodyguard at that of a tyrant. Who is the murderer, according to you?

Mi.: The judge, of course, or the tyrant. As well ask whether the sword is guilty, which is but the tool of the anger of the man who is prime mover in the affair.

Sos.: I am indebted to you for a further illustration of my argument. Again: a slave, sent by his master, brings me gold or silver: to whom am I to be grateful? Who goes down on my tablets as a benefactor?

Mi.: The sender; the bringer is but his minister.

Sos.: Observe then your injustice! You punish us who are but the slaves of Clotho's bidding, and reward these who do but minister to another's beneficence. For it will never be said that it was in our power to gainsay the irresistible ordinances of Fate——

Mi.: Ah, Sostratus; look closely enough, and you will find plenty of inconsistencies besides these. However, I see you are no common pirate, but a philosopher in your way; so much you have gained by your questions. Let him go, Hermes; he shall not be punished after that. But mind, Sostratus, you must not put it into other people's heads to ask questions of this kind.'[15]

These convictions of an immovable or scarcely movable Fate, or of a blind Chance, created a widespread feeling of pointlessness and tedium—which Seneca describes as characteristic of his time.[16] But people reacted from the hopeless prospect by turning to a picturesque variety of more or less sensational superstitions. 'If,' said T. S. Eliot, 'there is no truth that has not been discovered by our ancestors, then there is also no possible error by which they have not been deceived.' Yet these beliefs are also significant because they are the stuff of which the thoughts and feelings of Rome's peoples and subjects were made; and because they in their turn supplied the background against which, and in reaction from which, must be seen the rise of the early Christian church (p. 182).

In the first place, an enormous majority of the population of the Roman empire, including very many of the most highly educated, believed in the stars—and their acceptance of Fate or Fortune received a great impetus from this belief. That is to say, they believed that the movements of the sun, moon and stars influence the lives and deaths, fates and fortunes, of mankind. Throughout the Roman empire this belief was so predominant and indeed universal that it must be thought of as the religion *par excellence*, at this time, of the Mediterranean world.

The basis for this belief in the stars was the general conviction that there was some sort of harmony between the earth and the other heavenly bodies—some cosmic 'sympathy' by which they all shared the same laws and behaviour. People felt—and the philosophers taught—that there was unity in this cosmos, and interdependence among all its parts. There was an impatient curiosity and desire to find a place in this system for mankind—and it seemed self-evident that mankind could not be thought of as excluded, since the Hellenistic world had rejected as blasphemy the theory of Aristarchus of Samos that the earth was not the centre of the universe (p. 74). Behind the vast and spectacular movements of the heavenly bodies, like the marchings of Homer's armies before Troy,[17] there must be some order; and surely this was an order which must prevail on earth as well. There must be a *correspondence*; heaven and earth are counterparts, and what happens above must be reproduced below, in accordance with the incessant exchange of inter-reacting molecules and effluvia between the two. For it was believed that the heavenly bodies were nourished by emanations from earth, and it seemed equally reasonable to suppose that emanations also proceeded in the opposite direction and profoundly influenced earth—and the human beings who dwelt thereon—with consequent limitations upon their power to take and enforce decisions for themselves, ruled as they were by the immutable, unfeeling, non-moral heavenly spheres.

Thus arose the governing creed of the Roman world: one of the most terrible doctrines which has ever oppressed humanity. Its pedigree was ancient and complicated. Astronomy, eventually killed by astrology, had been the only natural science for which Plato had any enthusiasm, and after him it had provided the greatest scientific achievements of the scholars of Alexandria. But both he and they uneasily disregarded irregularities and insisted that the heavenly bodies should be uniform and incapable of surprises. Following the tragic poets who described sun, moon and stars as deities,[18] Plato had insisted upon belief in their divinity, incorporating in the fabric of his ideal state a complex astral theology. Already in his time Greeks and other peoples of the Mediterranean were learning with keen interest about the ancient Babylonian worship of the stars; and soon after Alexander the Great, who left the Mediterranean world adrift from the little city-state loyalties which had absorbed so many of its earlier hankerings, professional astrologers made it their business to transmit this Babylonian lore to Greece. The first of these was said to be Berossus, translator of the *Eye of Bel* and director of an astrological school at Cos.[19] Then, in the third or second century BC, Bolus of Mendes in Egypt wrote a treatise explaining and justifying the correspondence between stars and human beings. This book, *On Sympathies and Antipathies*, was a best-seller almost unequalled in its influence on the peoples of the Mediterranean world.

Such beliefs harmonized easily with the doctrines of one of the great philosophical schools which followed Plato, the Stoics. Maintaining that man's soul contains a divine spark of the same power which rules and illumines the heavens, the Stoics accepted the divinity of the heavenly bodies,[20] and saw astrology as the proof of this solidarity of the universe and as a universalist substitute for the old city cults. So, in an age when science was beginning to fade, astrology instead took charge. It was given impressive sanction by the support of one of the outstandingly learned, prolific and influential thinkers of the ancient world, Posidonius of Syrian Apamea (*c.* 135–50 BC; Plate 20*b*), who accepted the basic principles of astrology as key to the harmony of the universe. In spite of the great range of his intellect and his boundless desire for knowledge—which indirectly helped to create a widespread new enthusiasm for physical phenomena—he accepted this as a true science, and bequeathed it as such to the centuries and millennia that followed.

Why did these beliefs enjoy such lasting and widespread support? In the first place, the worship of the sun seemed a natural and obvious procedure; the Persians had been sun-worshippers for centuries, and Plato idealizes the practice and calls the solar orb 'offspring of the first god'. Moreover, the effects of the sun on the earth present an evident example of cosmic sympathy: the sun makes the vegetation appear and perish and causes animals to sleep and rut. In spite of all our different languages, says Plutarch, every one of us sees the same sun and moon.[21] For the moon, too, which in Babylon had taken precedence even over the sun and which caused terror when it went into eclipse (p. 149), appeared to control the tide—the analogy of a magnet was often quoted—and the stars seem to control the storms and floods, which come and go according to the rise and fall of constellations; just as there was little doubt that climatic conditions, regulated by the heavenly bodies, determined men's moral and physical qualities. So it looked true enough that what happened to any part affected all the rest. It is easy to see what is arbitrary in this strange mixture of logic and fantasy; and indeed this was later pointed out in detail (p. 147)—the mixture of sun-worship with science, the fallacious associations of ideas and generalizations, and in particular the unjustified deductions from physics to human psychology: the inference which linked all human doings, as well as the physical properties of the earth, to the heavenly bodies. Yet the whole thing seemed to hang together scientifically. In fact, astrology appeared to the reason-loving Stoics an impressive manifestation of rationalism—and many alleged facts were quoted in its support. Besides, there was a satisfying neatness, completeness and indisputability about the doctrine: in the first century BC Diodorus the Sicilian compared them unfavourably to the Babylonian practitioners of astrology, who: 'by holding always to the same views, keep a firm hold on every detail, while the Greeks, aiming at the profit to be made out of the business, keep founding new schools'.[22] And by Greeks Diodorus meant philosophers, whom he as a historian disliked.

Schiller was perplexed by all this astrology, but a letter to him from Goethe in 1798 is full of profound understanding of this perennial phenomenon which reached its peak in the world of Rome:

'The superstition of astrology has its origin in our dim sense of some vast cosmic unity. Experience tells us that the heavenly bodies which are nearest us have a decisive influence on weather, on plant life and so forth. We need only move higher, stage by stage, and who can say where this influence ceases? The astronomer constantly observes that the heavenly bodies are subject to mutual disturbances; the philosopher is inclined, nay rather forced, to assume that action can take place even at the greatest distances; thus man, in his presentiment, needs only to go a stage further, and he will extend such influence to the moral life, to happiness and misfortune. Such fanciful ideas, and others of the same kind, I cannot even call superstition; they come naturally to us and are as tolerable and as questionable as any other faith.'

It might perhaps have been expected that astrology would logically abolish beliefs in heavenly immortality. But that is not what happened. On the contrary, the religious basis of astrology asserted itself. Men remembered how the Stoics, and many before them, had proclaimed that the sun, moon and stars were all divine: two Roman emperors, Elagabalus the Syrian (AD 218–22) and Aurelian the Illyrian (AD 270–5), established at Rome quasi-monotheistic state religions of the sun, and the moon had long been identified with a number of goddesses including Isis (p. 173). A poet believed to be the great astronomer and geographer of the second century AD, Ptolemy of Alexandria who wrote four books asserting his devotion to astrology, testifies to the divine spirit behind the whole heavenly order:

> Mortal though I be, yea ephemeral, if but a moment
> I gaze up to the night's starry domain of heaven,
> Then no longer on earth I stand; I touch the Creator,
> And my lively spirit drinketh immortality.[23]

Since it is Time (Aion) which brings on each propitious or unpropitious movement of the heavens, many saw Time as the personification of the Creator himself. A priestly sect among the Persians

Julius Caesar

1

Probably dating from his life-time, this head hints at the complexities of the dictator's character and foreshadows the great portrait-gallery to come.

2

(a) Augustus as awe-inspiring world-ruler; this bronze bust comes from Meroe in the Sudan. (b) Skilful use of light and shade contributes to a grand conception of Vespasian (AD 69–79).

a   b

3

Here, on the other hand, Vespasian is deliberately and vividly presented as an unpretentious middle-class Italian. These marble heads were often tinted. Nose and bust are restored.

Climax of Empire

a

b

4 a and **b**

Trajan (AD 98–117) as world-conqueror and father of his people, bearer of the unceasing burdens of government.

5

The nervous restlessness of Hadrian (AD 117–38), patron of the arts and most versatile and cosmopolitan of rulers.

New God and Philosopher-King

6

(a) Antinous, whose death in Egypt (AD 130) generated religious emotions which gave classical sculpture its last ideal. (b) His younger contemporary Marcus Aurelius, in thoughtful boyhood.

7

(a) Aurelius on horseback: in Rome's Piazza del Campidoglio. (b) The earliest of many Renaissance works that this statue inspired: Donatello's 'Gattamelata' at Padus (1453).

Tension and Crisis

a

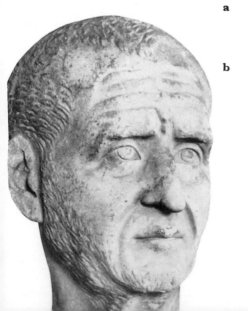

b

8

(a) Commodus (AD 180–92) extravagantly seen as Hercules, with astrological symbolism and disconcerting glance. (b) Anxious defender of a crumbling heritage: Decius, persecutor of Christians (AD 249–51).

9

Caracalla (AD 211–17) affects Alexander's sidelong pose, but the flamboyant sculptor unflinchingly portrays his tiresome, dangerous personality.

10

(a) Flamininus, 'liberator' of Greece (*c.* 194 BC): the earliest portrait of a leading Roman. (b) Mithradates VI of Pontus (120–63 BC), Rome's most dangerous foe since Hannibal. (c) and (d) P. Laeca and P. Nerva (*c.* 106–4 BC) record a citizen's rights: PRO-VOCO, 'I appeal', and the vote.

(a) Tiberius (AD 14–37) rebuilds the earthquake-shattered cities of Asia Minor: CIVITATIBVS ASIAE RESTITVTIS. (b) Ostia Harbour: Nero (AD 54–68) ensures Rome's food-supply. (c) Shekel of the rebellious Jews (AD 66–7), showing chalice and ritual plants.

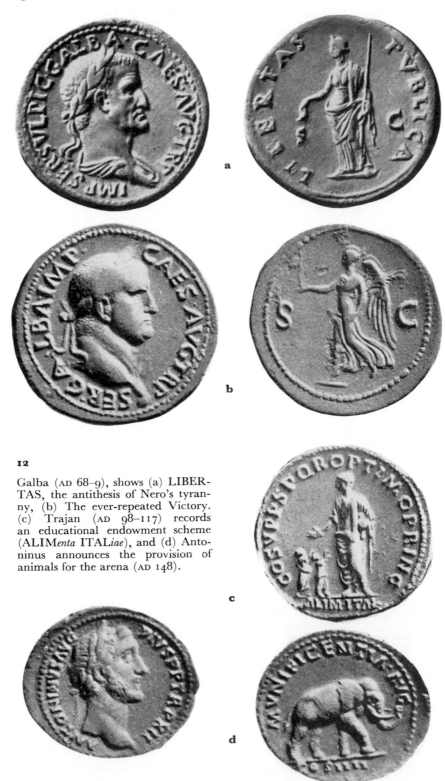

12
Galba (AD 68–9), shows (a) LIBER-TAS, the antithesis of Nero's tyran-ny, (b) The ever-repeated Victory. (c) Trajan (AD 98–117) records an educational endowment scheme (ALIM*enta* ITAL*iae*), and (d) Anto-ninus announces the provision of animals for the arena (AD 148).

a

b

13

(a) Antoninus endows girl-orphans in memory of his wife Faustina. (b) Severus celebrates his homeland AFRICA (AD 194–5). (c) His Syrian wife Julia Domna: the three figures, with a dedication to the government's fairness (AEQVITAS PVBLICA), represent the trimetallic currency.

c

Sculpture of the Late Republic

14

The dry realism of many Roman portraits is anticipated on this alabaster lid of a terracotta ash-chest at Etruscan Volaterrae (1st cent. BC).

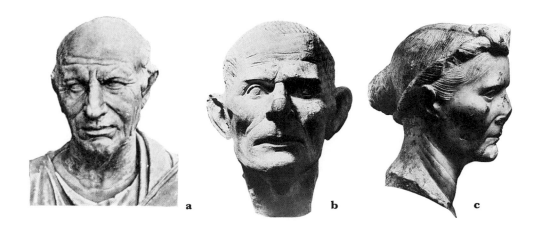

a   b   c

15

In the last years of the Republic there was a keen, documentary
interest in the features of elderly people. (b) is copied from one
of the death-masks which assisted this tendency. (d) An old
fisherman: marble copy (2nd cent. AD) of statue of late
Republican date.

d

16

This sort of figure, from the Syrian caravan-city Palmyra
(2nd cent. AD), shows a meeting of two arts and civilizations,
the Greco-Roman and Parthian.

17

The largest gallery of ancient painted portraits has been preserved by the special qualities of the Egyptian soil: heads executed in wax for insertion into the traditional mummycases. Most are of the 2nd or 3rd cents. AD.

a

b

18

(a) Egyptian society had already seen centuries of race-mixture. (b) A sentimental, whimsical study of a slave-boy, probably oriental, waiting to see his master home from a party.

19

(a) Funeral-painting from Egypt of Eutychos, a freedman of the 2nd cent. AD. (b) A sophisticated Greco-Roman theme: the young negro slave.

a

b

20

The outstanding philosophical writers
of the last century BC: (a) Cicero
(probably an early imperial copy).
(b) Posidonius of Syrian Apamea,
depicted in his lifetime, c. 85–75 BC.

21

Fortune (Tyche), venerated throughout the Mediterranean
world: a later copy of Eutychides' famed Fortune of Antioch,
shown with the god of its river the Orontes (*c.* 296–290 BC).

Death, where is thy sting?

a

22

(a) Death the Ravisher: seizure of a daughter of Leucippus by Castor or Pollux. Stucco relief in shrine seen at Plate 54a. (b) 'Gather ye rosebuds while ye may' is the theme of these skeletons on a silver cup.

b

23

(a) Aion or Time, god of the astrologers: lion, serpent, wings symbolize fire, earth, air (the serpent can also stand for the sun's sinuous course). (b) The infant son of Domitian and Domitia communes, in death, with the Seven Planets (AD 81–4). The Four Seasons emerge from the zodiac; fashionable astrology under Commodus (AD 184–5).

24

The Olympians were reinterpreted in terms of astrology: in the centre of the zodiac Jupiter himself is seated.

25

Magic abounded everywhere: (a) Bronze hands reflecting pantheistic ideas and endowed with special powers. (b) A mosaic design to deter the Evil Eye.

b

EX DONO DVCIS SPORTIAE SPORTIAE

26

A relief from Lanuvium, near Rome, showing a raptly gazing
high-priest of the Asiatic Great Mother, with ritual symbols and
vestments.

27

(a) and (b) The orgiastic worship of Bacchus-Dionysus by his Maenads passed into European art; during a visit to Florence Sir Joshua Reynolds sketched this figure, inspired by the Maenads of Greco-Roman religion.

a

b

The Mysteries

28

Wall-paintings at Pompeii (later 1st cent. BC), showing intense
feeling, hint at the secrets of the cult-drama of Bacchus,
dominant religion of the age.

29

There were terrors for the initate before he won immortality, and there were pains for the unbeliever: while a Maenad whirls, Poine (Punishment) strikes at a cowering victim.

a

b

Guarantors of Afterlife

30

The mystery-cult which most nearly became a world-religion was that of the Egyptian Isis. (a) Her rites, and (b) an entranced worshipper.

a

b

31

When cremation was replaced by burial (2nd cent. AD) as more
respectful to the husk of the immortal soul, an old near-eastern
art-form, the sarcophagus, was revived. (a) Bacchus with
Ariadne: in triumph as his followers too shall be. (b) A
15th cent. adaptation.

The ·'lives' of the Life-giver

32a

Bacchus discovers Ariadne and gives her eternal life. (This sarcophagus was found beneath St. Peter's, Rome.)

32b and 33

At Ahuramazda's behest, Mithras slays the bull from whose blood and seed the world was made (*opposite page*). In 33 the sculptor Criton of Athens (2nd cent. AD) shows the sad, dedicated serenity of Mithras as he makes this creative sacrifice.

Where Mithras was Worshipped

a

b

34

(a) A typical underground shrine at Rome: successive churches (S. Clemente) were built over it. (b) At Carrawburgh by Hadrian's Wall: the pit where initiates underwent rigorous ordeals of heat and cold.

Stucco Reliefs in House and Tomb

35

(a) Architectural decoration in religious scenes from the Augustan Villa Farnesina, Rome. (b) The Tomb of the Valerii (2nd cent. AD): elegant ceiling designs reflect doctrines of immortality.

a

b

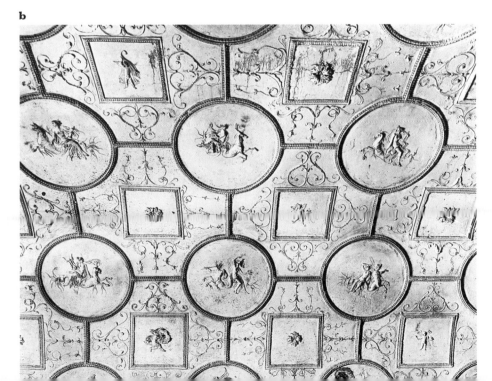

Contrasts in Historical Relief

a

b

(a) The marble sculpture of Rome's Altar of Peace: the family of Augustus in statuesque procession. (b) Mantegna modelled this scene upon the reliefs on the opposite page (37a).

a

b

37

(a) The Arch of Titus (AD 79–81) employs new techniques of lighting and movement to record his Triumph over the Jews, whose spoils are seen carried aloft. (b) The column dedicated at Mainz to Nero's welfare displays symbolic scenes in successive drums.

a

38

The spiral of Trajan's Column (once coloured) is the climax of
a dramatic documentary form. (a) His auxiliaries fight the
Dacians. (b) He receives barbarian envoys—and two worlds
meet.

b

39

(a) and (b) The style of the Column of Aurelius (*c.* AD 175) reflects the tenseness of growing crisis. (c) At Lepcis (near Tripoli) the Arch of Severus (*c.* AD 203) displays a new, hieratic frontality anticipating Byzantium.

c

40

From Boscoreale near Pompeii: architectural vistas made a
room more spacious. Compare Plate 35a for the *motif*, 63a for
some of the buildings.

41

Naturalism triumphant in an age of fashionable landscape
gardening: the House of Livia at Prima Porta, *c.* 40–25 BC.

42

Part of a series of rare, romantic landscapes from a house on
the Esquiline Hill—perhaps of Augustan date—showing the
adventures of Odysseus.

43

Architecture has become a fantasy of flashing curves in this Augustan Grove of Diana on the Palatine, with its hieratic torch-bearers and wierd, magnified ritual club.

44

(a) The waterfront of an early imperial mansion: painting at the house of M. Lucretius Fronto, Pompeii. (b) The graceful ceiling of Nero's Golden House: an inspiration to 15th century artists.

a

b

45

(a) Herculaneum, in its last years, favoured wall-paintings with the baroque, spectacular appearance of stage-designs. (b) One of the relatively few survivals of 2nd cent. AD painting: an idyllic landscape with shrines, from the Villa of the Quintilii outside Rome.

From Tyne to Sahara

46

(a) The directness of a Roman road: King Street, between Ailsworth and Ancaster. (b) A road driven through a mountain and spanned by a viaduct: the Via Domitiana linking Puteoli and Cumae.

a

b

a

47

Far south and far north: (a) Lambaesis (Lambèse in Algeria),
a fortress which became a great city in the 2nd cent. AD. (b)
Hadrian's Wall from Solway to Tyne: a view near Borcovicium
(Housesteads, Northumberland).

b

Masterpieces of Construction

a

48

(a) This granite bridge at Alcantara, erected by 11 Spanish towns in AD 106, is 630 ft. long, its maximum height 150 ft. (b) The Tomb of Caecilia Metella, Rome, provides an early example (late 1st cent. BC) of Rome's greatest structural innovation, concrete.

b

49

(a) Segovia aqueduct, of white granite, crosses the valley in mid-city, bringing water in its curved channel from springs 10 miles away. (b) These Hadrianic arches of the Aqua Claudia exert no thrust since behind their brick facing is a concrete core.

b

The Arena

50

(a) Epoch-making in boldness of design and dizzy height, the Colosseum (Flavian Amphitheatre), built to house the city's horrible amusements, is still its most imposing building. (b) This Roman innovation of many-tiered arcades was adopted by Michelangelo: the Palazzo Farnese courtyard (1546).

b

a

51

(a) The vastness of the Colosseum seen from the air. (b) Pola (Pula, Yugoslavia): as Roman cities proliferated in the empire, each had its own stone amphitheatre.

52

The historic myth-laden temple of Castor and Pollux in the Roman Forum, richly rebuilt by Augustus or the Flavians.

53

The best preserved of Roman shrines: Agrippa's 'Masion Carrée' at Nimes (16 BC), on the high base characteristic of Italian temples.

Models for Churches

54

(a) This tiny, subterranean Roman
shrine (1st cent. AD) of an unidentified pagan cult anticipates the
main architectural features of (b), the
enormous Basilica of St. Paul (engraved by Piranesi, 1720–78) before
its destruction by fire.

a

b

a

b

55

(a) Trajan's 61-ft. high arch at Ancona, built to be seen far out at sea. (b) This same arch is imprinted on a temple-front to make the novel, Renaissance church façade of Alberti's S. Andrea at Mantua (1470–2).

a

56

(a) The immense porch, with 16 monolithic granite columns, of the Roman Pantheon, inscribed in honour of its founder Agrippa, but redesigned by Hadrian. (b) One of its many offspring: the 'Tempietto' of Palladio (1508–80) at Maser near Treviso.

b

The Dome of Heaven

57

The Pantheon—'erect, severe, austere, sublime': so Byron
called this earliest and greatest of surviving domes, daringly
constructed of concrete and lit from its central opening.

a

b

58

(a) Forerunner of the Pantheon: the 'Temple of the Sibyl' (early 1st cent. BC), in a beautiful setting at Tibur (Tivoli). (b) The Mausoleum of the Julii at St. Rémy in Provence (later 1st cent. BC).

a

59
Styles of architectural decoration: (a) Lavishly ornamented Market-Gate of Miletus in Asia Minor, later 2nd cent. AD. (b) A fantastic, 'composite' capital from the Baths of Caracalla, embodying the statue of Hercules (Farnese).

b

60

The best preserved of ancient temple-interiors: the luxuriant 'Temple of Bacchus' (? 2nd cent. AD) at Heliopolis (Baalbek in Lebanon).

61

(a) In this Loggia del Capitanio at Vicenza (1571), Palladio (like Michelangelo before him) incorporates this *motif* of lofty half-columns rising above two storeys, as they had in the 'Temple of Bacchus' at Heliopolis. (b) Another view of the 'Temple of Bacchus', looking upwards within its porch.

a

b

Eastern Baroque

a

b

62

(a) A study in concavities: the delicate 'Temple of Venus' (? 2nd–3rd cent. AD) at Baalbek. (b) Its design is copied for the lantern of Borromini's S. Ivo at Rome (1642–50).

a

63

(a) A masterpiece cut out of the pink rock: the 'Temple of Isis' or 'Khazneh' at Petra (Jordan), (? 1st–2nd cent. AD). For the circular centrepiece, compare Pl. 40b. Broken pediments in two-storeyed façades were revived in Italian baroque: Rainaldi's S. Maria in Campitelli, Rome (1663–1667).

b

Through Airman's and Diver's Eyes

a

64

(a) Aerial view of Rome's enormous Baths of Caracalla. (b) A wrecked Augustan trading-ship beneath the Mediterranean near Hyères. Some jars still contained remains of tunny-bones and molluscs in fish sauce.

b

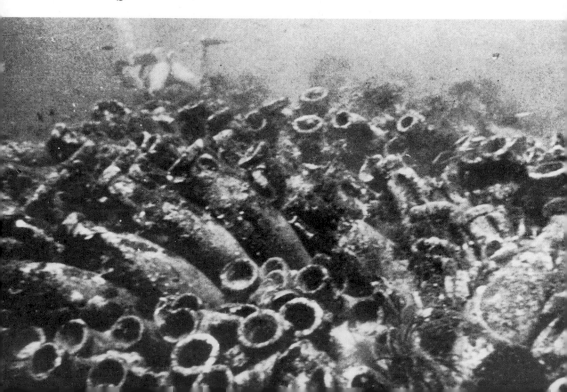

had deified Time as head of the Hierarchy and first cause, the Unlimited One of the Avesta, regulating the revolutions of the stars. The notation of time, in particular, had long been connected with ideas of a superhuman being, and most ancient calendars were religious in purpose. So Time, after at first being represented in ordinary human guise, was endowed with wings, and entwined with a serpent—because of his endless, circling, serpentine course—and his head is a lion's head, because like a ravening lion he devours all things (Plate 23*a*). Lion-headed, too, was the sinister counterpart of the Semitic Jehovah, Jaldabaoth, who was identified with Kronos or Saturn—Jupiter's father, the son of Heaven and Earth. But because of a confusion between Kronos who was Saturn and *Chronos* meaning Time (whose son Aion was supposed to be), the veneration of Time became further associated with the ancient stories and myths surrounding the primitive, pre-Hellenic Kronos. According to a more philosophical interpretation the lion stands for fire, the serpent for earth and the wings for air—the elements of which, as well as of the lives of human beings, Time is the master.

The inhabitants of the Roman world were people with an abnormally developed sense of the religious and ritual significance of Time's subdivisions, the centuries, years, seasons, hours and minutes. Under the influence of astrology and Plato, these subdivisions were conceived as bodies or deities and venerated accordingly. Zeno the founder of Stoicism deifies them, just as Egypt had for centuries worshipped the hours, the months, and propitious and adverse years. Time, therefore, is sometimes sculpturally represented—as on a late silver bowl now at Milan—within a circle of signs of the zodiac (p. 141) denoting the seasons. And the seasons too are personified. On large bronze commemorative medallions of second-century emperors from Hadrian onwards, we see them as children disposed round a globe beside Mother Earth, sometimes with the signs of the zodiac displayed above; on the medallions of Commodus—under whom such ideas especially flourished—they emerge from a circular frame held by Jupiter (Plate 23*c*). In this sort of representation Jupiter is synonymous with Time, just as Time is actually identified with a number of other gods such as the sun, and Egyptian Sarapis (p. 174).

This fantastically elaborate complex of ideas from different peoples and epochs is characteristic of the Roman age, in which the specific features of different cults and gods were ever intermingled one with another. This 'syncretism' presents a weird, unceasing series of attempts to define and explain the true nature of this godhead—who directed, or comprised within himself, the eternal and majestic movement of the heavenly bodies which controlled human lives.

So the heavenly bodies, which 'know in the midst of our laughter how that laughter will end', became powers of evil, pitilessly predestining all that will happen. But this mechanistic destiny seemed to millions of those who believed in it unendurable, and their reaction was to try to discover whether the oppressiveness of these powers could not somehow be mitigated. The first step towards such a palliative was to find out, by investigation, what heaven had in store; and then to determine and time one's own activities in such a way as to avoid subjecting oneself to its most hostile influences. But these difficult tasks could only be performed with the help of the experts—the professional astrologers, who thus became an extremely influential class in the ancient world.

Their task was to study with particular care the seven planets, as identified by the ancients—Saturn, Jupiter, Mars, the Sun, Venus, Mercury and the Moon. 'In all the religious systems of later anti-quity, if I mistake not,' observed Gilbert Murray, 'the Seven Planets play some lordly or terrifying part.' Theirs, it was believed, was the greatest influence upon all that they saw, and particularly upon the supposed centre of the system, the earth, and upon human beings. Under their chief Saturn (thought of as Time itself, p. 139), the overruling powers resided in the planets, in which moreover their decrees could be read. The identification of these planets with the gods after whom they were named gave rise to the most fantastic of all mythologies, as each star was personalized with a will, sex and character of its own, and was spoken of as 'getting up and going to bed', and so on; and each had its own colours, minerals, plants, animals and even vowels[24]—a point upon which many prayers and magical formulae play.

The influence of the planets seemed all the more cruelly decisive and inexorable because each planet was thought of as Lord of a Sphere encasing the earth itself. Each of these spheres was imagined as a translucent wall of crystal cutting off the earth from what was beyond. So seven concentric rings separated earth from heaven— and for the ever-increasing numbers of people who cherished beliefs in the afterlife (p. 159), all these rings cut off the soul from its upward flight. The system was based on the order of the planets from the earth—a concept apparently unknown to ancient Babylon, and not traceable in the Mediterranean world until the Hellenistic age. But another institution derived from the seven planets was of Babylonian origin : this was the seven-day week, which played an essential part in the astrologer's calculations since it mattered a great deal which planet was preponderant, was potent in relation to the earth, on any given day. And the same number Seven is reproduced not only in the week, but in the seven wonders of the world, seven ages of man, and much else. Men are still spoken of today, after their planetary characteristics, as jovial (Jupiter), mercurial or saturnine, and we talk of fortunate conjunctions of events, of thanking our stars, of unlucky numbers.

Alongside the planets, the second great element in this weird mixture of science and fantasy was the zodiac. 'In the starry belt that the Greeks call the Zodiac,' says Cicero, 'there is a certain force of such a nature that every part of that belt affects and changes the heavens in a different way, according to the stars that are in this or an adjoining locality at a given time.'[25] These Signs of the Zodiac, 'Houses of the Sun', were the twelve Constellations to which the most potent influence over destiny was ascribed. They are linked by artists not only with Time, Mother Earth and the Seasons (p. 139), but also with the traditional Olympian gods, by their appearance as a circular ring with Jupiter, Lord of All, in their midst (Plate 24).

These heavenly bodies, then, and particularly the seven planets and twelve signs of the zodiac, were believed by most inhabitants of the Roman empire to be the controllers of the human race. It was also felt, with profound conviction, not only that they decreed what was to happen, but that, if one possessed the necessary knowledge, their decrees could be read and discovered beforehand. Already at about 300 BC, or soon afterwards, Aristotle's pupil Theophrastus is quoted as saying that the most extraordinary thing of his age was the lore of these Chaldaeans (as astrologers were called after their Mesopo- tamian origin), who foretold not only events of public interest but even the lives and deaths of individuals; and it was at that time that such prophecies first found their way to Greek lands (p. 136). From then onwards, as the Sicilian historian Diodorus observed, they:

'predicted all changes fraught with weal or woe not only to nations and regions of the world, but to kings and ordinary men and women'.[26]

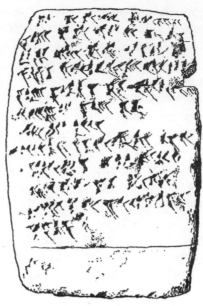

Fig. xii. Cuneiform Horoscope for morning of June 3rd, 235 BC (computed by A. J. Sachs). From Babylon. British Museum

He described the astrological signs covering the tomb of Ozymandias, the relic of grandeur that caught the imagination of Shelley, and the tomb of Augustus's client-king Antiochus I of Commagene, on the Euphrates, is of the same character. From that

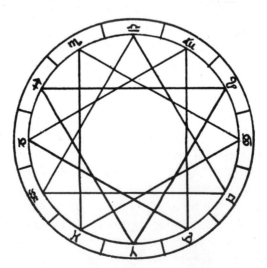

Fig. xiii. Triangles of the Zodiac

time onwards astrologers, usually oriental in origin, abounded throughout the Mediterranean world, and provided countless of its inhabitants with their main interest, consolation and excitement.

One of the principal activities of the professional astrologers was to cast horoscopes (Figs. xii, xiii, xiv). This was done by employing more or less elaborate patterns to note the disposition of the heavenly bodies and signs of the zodiac at the time of an individual's concep-

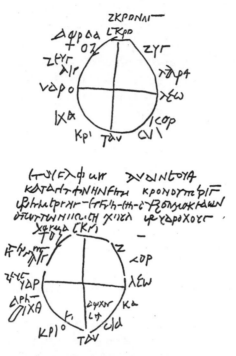

Fig. xiv. Graffiti showing horoscopes, second century AD. From Dura Europus (Salahiya, E. Syria)

tion and particularly his birth, and so to determine his future fate or fortune. Our first extant horoscope is of 410 BC,[27] but certain aspects of the technique date from the pre-Greek Babylonians. They had already foretold the fates of children from the positions of the sun, moon and planets in relation either to the earth or to the signs of the zodiac at the time of birth or conception. However, the combination of this procedure with mathematical calculations depending on the correct order of the planets (on the geocentric hypothesis) seems to have been due to the Greeks (p. 140). The great efflorescence of such horoscopes belongs to the centuries immediately before and after the beginning of our era. The home of these studies was Alexandria, but in Italy, too, in spite of complaints that astrologers were confusing shallow minds for their own financial profit (139 BC), their methods superseded the old native customs of reading the future by bird-movements and the entrails of sacrificial victims. As the histories of imperial Rome repeatedly show, the astrologers were not backward in pointing out instances when their forecasts seemed to have been justified by the event (p. 148).

But the enormous vogue of the astrologers was not only due to their alleged gifts of prophecy—to 'fatalistic' or 'scientific' astrology. That was certainly important, since it was valuable to know which constellation inexorably determined one's future. But that mere knowledge—ungarnished by hope—required uncompromising surrender to a mechanistic universe, and did not satisfy human cravings for guidance. In addition, therefore, to such investigations, there developed the subsidiary art of 'catarchic' astrology. The theory of this was that the planets or other heavenly bodies possess a strong power indeed, but not an inescapable one—so that the astrologers, by finding out the days, hours and minutes of preponderant influences, could advise their clients how to outwit the heavens by planning or avoiding undertakings at appropriate times and seasons. This art or pseudo-science, and obedience to its decrees, were carried to extraordinary lengths. The fourth century AD poet Ausonius writes of people choosing to have their nails cut under Mercury, their beards trimmed under Jupiter, their hair cut under Venus.[28]

Astrology, like other important matters of the day, was a subject for debate in the schools of Rome, where debating and speech-making were the principal activities (p. 69). We have inherited some Latin rhetorical exercises—probably lecture-notes—of a date not far from AD 100 in which the hypothetical speaker reveals the spirit of his age by refuting the contention of his father that astrology is nonsense:

'My father tries to persuade you not to believe in the art of the astrologer. He therefore contends that there is no Fate and that everything happens by accident and haphazardly. Or that even if everything were ruled by Providence, it nevertheless could not be found out by human science. . . . I, however, assume that the astrologer has spoken the truth, because certain stars, so to speak fixed and linked, shine jointly for all eternity once they were tied to each other, while others in unchanging orbits pursue their measured courses dispersed all over the sky. Do you really

believe that all of these have been casually and accidentally distributed?
. . . God, the creator of the cosmos, has placed them in their respective
positions. . . . Hence whatever is born is assigned its role, and thus accepts
the future as it does life itself. . . . I know nothing that could be more
certain than the genius of this veracious art which says what will be and
then effects what it has said. Nature, reason, and experience prove the
existence of the art of astrology. . . . Accept the basic proof of this certain
science.'[29]

Nor were such assertions restricted to school exercises: at Rome
as elsewhere, some of the cleverest men of the day maintained that the
use of appropriate techniques could discover the future and that
astrology alone was the scientific method of achieving this. Few men,
for example, were more highly educated or more intelligent than
some of the early Roman emperors. And yet every single one of them
during the first century AD (with the partial exception of Vespasian)
was a profound believer in astrology. This is overwhelmingly demonstrated by the literary record—not to speak of Augustus's dedication
of the Pantheon to the sun and stars (p. 157)—and is by no means
contradicted by the steps that some of these rulers took to expel
astrologers from Rome, since such measures were political, due to the
perils for the régime from horoscopes encouraging noblemen to aim
at the throne. Such expulsions took place under Augustus, and twice
under Tiberius: first in AD 16, after the foolish Libo Drusus, a
descendant of Pompey and relative of the emperors by marriage, had
been compelled to commit suicide after taking too keen an interest in
astrologers' predictions, magicians' rites, and readers of dreams; and
again in AD 30 when the disreputable Aemilia Lepida, descended
from Sulla as well as Pompey, had been outlawed on charges of
faking the paternity of her child, committing adultery, administer-
ing poison—and also consulting astrologers concerning the imperial
house.

It was by no means probable that Tiberius would take such things
lightly, not only because of their profound effects on public opinion
at all levels, but because he himself, though a man of high intellectual
calibre, was a profound believer in astrology. Indeed, one of his
closest friends, and one of the very few who were with him in his long
retreat at Capreae, was the outstanding astrologer of his time,
Thrasyllus of Alexandria. This man, whose personality was surrounded by a quasi-legendary atmosphere, was a grammarian by
profession, a devoted Platonist, and the author of a treatise on

numerology as well as influential astrological writings. He had worked at the philosophical centre of Rhodes, where Tiberius during a lonely period of exile under Augustus had met him and turned to astrology. Grateful to the few who had befriended him there, Tiberius raised Thrasyllus to Roman citizenship and great power, enabling him to marry a princess of Commagene, a kingdom on the Euphrates of which the monarchs had long been interested in astrology (p. 142); while Thrasyllus's grand-daughter married the Prefect of the Guard, Macro, all-powerful in Tiberius's last years. The astrologer's son Balbillus was a leading courtier and astrological adviser of Nero, and Balbillus's grandson Philopappus received a consulship under Trajan. The sister of Philopappus was the inseparable companion of Sabina, wife of Hadrian, under whom, as befitted an emperor whose grandfather was a well-known amateur practitioner of this activity, astrologers were again powerful at court.

Their advice often determined the course of events. After she had murdered Claudius with a poisoned mushroom, Agrippina's delay in proclaiming her son Nero as emperor was partly determined by considerations of this sort: she 'issued frequent encouraging announcements about the deceased emperor's health, to maintain the army's morale and await the propitious moment forecast by the Chaldaeans.'[30] But even on the official coinage there are abundant signs of their beliefs and activities. One of the favourite coin-types of Augustus was the capricorn, zodiacal sign of his conception.[31] When Domitian's infant son died, the baby is shown seated like a young Jupiter on the globe of the earth, stretching out his hands for the stars (Plate 23b). Under Commodus, upon the seventh centenary (significant planetary number) of

Fig. xv. Small gilt-bronze bust of Commodus, AD 180–92. Victoria and Albert Museum, London

the dedication of Jupiter's Capitoline Temple (AD 191), the god is shown brandishing his thunderbolt among the seven planets.[32] A bust of the same emperor rests upon a sphere inscribed with reliefs of the three signs of the zodiac governing the most important days of his life (Plate 8a). A small gilt-bronze, silver-inlaid bust, again of Commodus, displays him wearing the cosmic cap spangled with the seven stars (Fig. xv), just as the goddess Isis was seen to wear a design of moon and stars upon her robe (p. 173); and a frieze from Ephesus, now at Vienna, shows his father Marcus Aurelius led upwards to heaven in a chariot by the sun and escorted by the moon and stars.[33]

This surrender to astrology did not go completely unchallenged. Already during the second century BC there had been resistance to its fatalism in aristocratic Rome, and its triumph in the following century failed to enrol Lucretius, Cicero or Caesar as supporters. The Augustan poets were not above gentlemanly astrological consultations, modified by a degree of scepticism. But in the years that followed, the Jew Philo, the farmer Columella, the polymath Pliny the elder, and the satirist Juvenal, were no believers. Tacitus seems to suspend judgment (p. 133), perhaps accepting fatalistic astrology as true, and regarding its catarchic branch as fallible owing to the failure of individual practitioners. In his day, though the profits of astrologers were probably limited by the rise of the mystic religions (pp. 159 ff.), very few serious thinkers questioned the influence of the stars on human affairs. Yet a vigorous enemy of the doctrine actually belonged to the circle of the astrologically-minded emperor Hadrian himself. This was Favorinus of Arelate (Arles), an encyclopaedic scholar who, though he remarked that it was sheer folly not to give in to the master of thirty legions, is quoted as marshalling against astrology fourteen arguments effectively undermining the sweeping generalizations and deductions upon which horoscopes are based.[34]

Under Hadrian's successors, the less impressionable Antoninus Pius and Marcus Aurelius, astrology may have lost a little of its vogue. But it remained enormously powerful, and even St Augustine, while refusing to believe that the human soul was subject to the stars, was not prepared to deny that their emanations played a part in making one human body like another. The Byzantine scholar Stephanus still called astrology 'the most valuable of all arts and queen of the sciences'.[35] The Italian Renaissance, too, believed this overwhelmingly, and so did Tudor and Jacobean England. Sir Philip Sidney confesses his faith in the stars, the atheist Robert Greene wrote an *Apology of the Sacred Science of Astrology*. Shakespeare, who, sharing the scientific views of his time, refers frequently to astrology, believed in the influence of sun, moon and stars on matter and all life on earth. But he was perhaps one of the small minority who did not believe in the influence of these heavenly bodies upon individual destinies; it is Kent, not he, who—echoing astrological sages of antiquity—asserts in *King Lear*:

> It is the stars,
> The stars above us, govern our conditions;
> Else one self mate and make could not beget
> Such different issues.

Among great seventeenth-century scientists, too, astrology had its staunch advocates. At every epoch such convictions still rise to the surface in times of stress, spiritual tension, or boredom—for example, during the Second World War when practising astrologers were numbered by thousands; and what proportion of the general public wholly disbelieves in the astral predictions found in the daily newspapers today?

While astrology dominated the world, the ancient Italians, and most of the other peoples with whom they were in contact, continued to rely heavily on their ancient native custom of deriving prophecies from prodigies—from startling events contrary to the supposed or known workings of nature. The government made great politico-religious play with a comet that flashed across the sky after Caesar's murder,[36] and the public response to such phenomena was hysterical. This inexhaustible popular taste for prodigies was met by the freedman Phlegon, from Tralles in Asia Minor, who published an anthology of them in the reign of his master Hadrian. Phlegon reported, for example, that under Claudius a lady's maid had given birth to a monkey, that in Nero's time a child had been born with four heads, and that a woman of Alexandria had brought into the world four sets of quintuplets.[37] Readers were free to ponder the portentous significance of these alleged happenings, for such significance they were assuredly believed to possess. Then again in the fourth century AD, in defence of paganism, Julius Obsequens compiled a startlingly varied list, year by year, of prodigies recorded during the Republic.

The poetic Augustan historian Livy defends his recordings of such 'events' on the evasive grounds that current scepticism was nihilistic and that the glorious ancients had thought them worth including.[38] The disbelief of Tacitus was likewise qualified by traditionalism, as well as by his generally agnostic approach (p. 133). Besides, he realized that portents, true or false, exercised a profound influence upon the history of the period that he was describing. For example, he attributes the suppression of a formidable mutiny on the German frontier (AD 14) to the awe inspired by a timely eclipse—but here he points clearly to the subjective nature of the 'sign'.

'The night looked like ending in a disastrous criminal outbreak. But this was averted by a stroke of luck. Suddenly, in a clear sky, the light of the moon was seen to decline. The soldiers did not know why this was, and detected an omen of their own situation. The waning moon seemed to provide an analogy to their own efforts: success would only crown the measures they were adopting if the moon-goddess shone brightly again. To produce this result they made a clattering of brass instruments and blew blasts on every sort of trumpet. The light seemed stronger, and they were happy. Then it looked dimmer, and they were mournful. Finally clouds hid it from view altogether. Men's minds, once unbalanced, are ready to believe anything; and now they howled that heaven was sickened by their crimes, and endless hardships were in store for them. The emperor's son Drusus felt that advantage must be taken of this turn of events; a lucky chance could be exploited in the interests of good sense . . .'

Tacitus also describes how the sultry, thunderous atmosphere of Rome shortly before the murder of Claudius produced among the 'alarmed, excited population its crop of portents:

A series of prodigies in the following year indicated changes for the worse. Standards and soldiers' tents were set on fire from the sky. A swarm of bees settled on the pediment of the Capitoline temple. Half-bestial children were born, and a pig with a hawk's claws. A portent, too, was discerned in the losses suffered by every official post: a quaestor, aedile, tribune, praetor, and consul had all died within a few months. Agrippina was particularly frightened—because Claudius had remarked in his cups that it was his destiny first to endure his wives' misdeeds, and then to punish them. She decided to act quickly.'[39]

So there were portents—or apparent portents—but the empress

was also worried for other reasons: neither category of explanation for her rapid decision to take the murderous step is underestimated by Tacitus. A later historian, Dio Cassius of Nicaea (in north-western Asia Minor), who wrote a Roman History in Greek in the early third century AD, claims that during a critical moment of the civil wars after the assassination of Commodus he himself, while deeply apprehensive at signs of popular outcry (p. 30), almost participated in a phenomenon which seemed to be a sign from heaven (AD 196):

'Another thing that increased our anxiety was the sudden appearance of such a great fire in the northern sky at night that some supposed the whole city was burning, and others that the very sky was afire. But what I marvelled at most was this: a fine rain resembling silver descended from a clear sky upon the Forum of Augustus. I did not, it is true, see it as it was falling, but noticed it after it had fallen, and by means of it I plated some bronze coins with silver; they retained the same appearance for three days, but by the fourth day all the substance rubbed on them had disappeared.'[40]

So Dio feared that more trouble was to come and that the civil war was not over, and like all who tell such stories he is able to show that the event proved him perfectly right.

These were centuries, too, in which prophets abounded and proliferated, and each had his or her fanatical following. 'Beloved,' warns the First Epistle General of John, 'believe not every spirit, but prove the spirits, whether they are of God: because many false prophets are gone out into the world.'[41] That was written from Asia Minor, where, at a not far distant date, Christian 'prophets' Quadratus and Ammia appeared, and where after that, at Ardabau in Mysian Phrygia, there arose a new prophetic movement which turned into the austere, extremist Christian heresy of the Montanists. But there were countless pagan prophets, too, especially in that same peninsula. One of the most colourful and influential was Alexander of Abonuteichus, who, much to the disgust of Lucian (p. 134), uttered oracles accompanied by mystic pantomimes; these greatly attracted women and also gained a following among the members of leading philosophical schools, as well as eminent Roman sup-porters.[42] Alexander warned away from his rites 'any atheist or Christian or Epicurean'—the Epicureans being sceptical about such contrivances (p. 156). His own divinity was a snake which he named Glycon and proclaimed as a new manifestation of Aesculapius, the god of healing (p. 165); the city of Abonuteichus even represents the snake on its coins.

Such men accompanied their foretelling of events with panaceas that would enable their disciples to control events and avoid the hideous weight of destiny or fortune which seemed to press upon mankind. But there were also millions of inhabitants of the Roman empire, of all cultural levels from the highest to the lowest—including, inconsistently enough, a great many profound believers in astrology—who sought to exert their influence on Fate or Fortune by the more primitive means of magic. This, found everywhere at all times, is the art of influencing the course of nature by occult procedures involving constraint; thus a formula to the moon says, 'you have to do it, whether you like it or not.'[43] Such an element of constraint is not found in religion, which seeks to win the divine favour by persuasive means such as prayer and sacrifices. But the state religion of ancient Rome continued to include countless survivals of early magical practices. Such practices, in the ancient world as elsewhere, may be roughly divided into two categories—first, 'sympathetic' or 'homoeopathic', for instance when harm is devised for someone by making an image of him and piercing it with nails;[44] and secondly, 'contagious', for example when he is made to suffer by the casting into a fire of something that has been his—a lock of hair, perhaps, or a piece of his clothing.[45] There might seem to be a difficulty here for believers in astrology, because the stars were clearly not entreatable by such means, and if the gods were above (or identical with) the stars they, too, remained equally unaffected. Nevertheless, magic might still be held to give control over the somewhat less than divine, but still powerful, 'daemons' who existed below the austerely astral level. Although such practices do not have even the false rationality of astrology to recommend them, their underlying principle won the applause of Sir James Frazer. To him magic was 'the bastard sister of science', and even the mother of freedom; for its experiments at least show a sense of cause and effect, of universal sympathy—a will to freedom manifested in this short cut to getting what one wants.

Yet the influence of magic upon the peoples of the Roman Empire presents a sad picture of a deluded and fear-ridden world in which magicians of every conceivable kind found clients innumerable. The miraculous powers of Pythagoras (sixth century BC) were remembered and recounted; and as early as 200 BC the works in the library of Alexandria attributed to the most celebrated of Persian *magi*, Zoroaster, totalled as many as two million verses. As magic merged with Alexandrian philosophical speculation, subsequent centuries produced countless charms designed for utterance by the soul to each of the seven planets in turn (p. 140) as it pursued its perilous path past all of them to its ultimate home. A bronze hand (Plate 25a) represents an omnipotent God—and the symbols engraved upon its surface magically guarantee to the faithful the benefits of its protection. Strange traditions of necromancy are preserved in the sixth Book of Virgil's *Aeneid* describing Aeneas's visit to the Underworld: by way of Lake Avernus, near the cavern (now discovered) where his guide the Sibyl prophesied in shamanic trance, at Cumae from which Greek influences had first come to Rome. On a more mundane level, appropriately designed objects kept off the power, which Medea had supposedly possessed, of the Evil Eye (Plate 25b). There also arose whole schools of the 'divine and sacred art' of alchemy which, founded upon the conviction that material happenings have a spiritual basis, claimed to change base matter into silver or gold; the alleged authors of the holy books of this art have Greek, Egyptian, Hebrew and Persian names.

Greek magic papyri of the second and third centuries AD (and there were even more of them in the two centuries that followed) were mainly collections of recipes for the attainment of practical objects such as success in love, the curing of illness, and (most of all) the harming of enemies. Magic powers were ascribed to the slave leader Eunus, to Apollonius of Tyana, to Simon 'Magus' of Samaria (pp. 114, 107, 160) and to countless others. For reasons of public confidence and security the Roman authorities always set their face against the abuse of such methods, and against new growths of magical influence.[46] But when Tiberius's nephew and adopted son Germanicus succumbed to his illness (which he believed to be poisoning) in Syria in AD 19, Tacitus records that: 'examination of the floor and walls of his bedroom revealed the remains of human bodies, spells, curses, lead tablets inscribed with the patient's name, charred and bloody ashes, and other malignant objects which are supposed to consign souls to the powers of the tomb.'[47]

The curse is well known as a Hellenistic and Roman literary form; Ovid provides a lurid example.[48] But it was much more than a literary form. A surviving enchantment tablet of the mid-first century BC has been prepared on a thin lead plate (wrapped round a nail) by a professional sorcerer; it is a comprehensive curse directed against a certain Plotius, and addressed to Proserpina the Saviour (Salvia) goddess of the underworld (p. 162):

'O wife of Pluto, good and beautiful Proserpina (unless I ought to call you Salvia), pray tear away from Plotius health, body, complexion, strength, faculties. Consign him to Pluto your husband. May he be unable to avoid this by devices of his. Consign that man to the fourth day, the third day, the every day fever [malaria]. May they wrestle and wrestle it out with him, overcome and overwhelm him unceasingly until they tear away his life. . . . I give thee the head of Plotius, slave of Avonia. O Proserpina Salvia, I give thee the head of Plotius, slave of Avonia. O Proserpina Salvia, I give thee Plotius's forehead, Proserpina Salvia, I give thee Plotius's eyebrows, Proserpina Salvia, I give thee Plotius's eyelids. Proserpina Salvia, I give thee Plotius's eye pupils. Proserpina Salvia, I give thee Plotius's nostrils, lips, ears, nose, and his tongue and teeth so that Plotius may not be able to utter what it is that gives him pain; his neck, shoulders, arms, fingers, so that he may not be able to help himself at all; his chest, liver, heart, lungs, so that he may not be able to sleep; his shoulder-blades, so that he may not be able to sleep well; his sacred part, so that he may not be able to make water; his buttocks, vent, thighs, knees, legs, shins, feet, ankles, soles, toes, nails, that he may not be able to stand by his own aid.'[49]

Magic had its opponents—it was called 'unnatural', and Lucian made a great deal of fun of it. More usual, perhaps, was the attitude that its practitioners might be fakes but that the theory was not unsound. Fluctuating, like astrology, between reason and faith in support of its particular brand of universal sympathy, it found most writers credulous, or at least ambiguous. One of the greatest of them, the novelist Apuleius in the second century AD, was brought into a law court of his native north Africa on the charge of being a magician. He defends himself in a scintillating speech, the *Apologia*, but later St Augustine was by no means sure that the charge was untrue.[50]

CHAPTER 6

RELIGION

THE Roman government always realized, in the words of Field-Marshal Lord Montgomery, that 'when you command great numbers of men . . . you find that the emotional forces bottled up in them are very strong.' Drawing the appropriate deduction, they seldom failed to guide the emotions of their subjects into patriotic channels. In Rome and Italy the loyalist *mystique*, fostered by every means that government and society possessed, was immensely strong; it pervades all Latin literature.

In particular, patriotism and the state religion are indistinguishable. Although Italians like other people of the empire went, for the satisfaction of their most personal religious emotions, to exotic cults which were less formal and sterile than the antique Italian worships, it would be a mistake to underestimate the power—throughout Republic and Principate alike—of the Roman state religion as a vehicle of the patriotic emotion that was one of an Italian's strongest feelings. The glamorous potency of Jupiter the sky-god with Juno and Minerva in their Capitoline temple, and of the Household Gods (Penates), Vesta the Hearth-Goddess, Janus the Gate, and all the rest, and the care taken by the government to cherish their rites and buildings, vividly impressed a discerning Greek visitor to Rome during the second century BC, the historian Polybius:

'The quality in which the Roman commonwealth is most distinctly superior is in my opinion the nature of their religious convictions. I believe that what maintains the cohesion of the Roman state is the very thing which among other peoples is an object of reproach: I mean superstition. These matters are clothed in such pomp and introduced to such an extent into the public and private life of the Romans that nothing could exceed it, a fact which will surprise many. My own opinion at least is that they have adopted this course for the sake of the common people. It is a course which perhaps would not have been necessary had it been possible to form a state composed of wise men, but since every multitude is fickle, full of lawless desires, unreasoned passion, and violent anger, the multitude must be held in by invisible terrors and suchlike pageantry. For this reason I think, not that the ancients acted rashly and at haphazard in introducing among the people notions concerning the gods and beliefs in the terrors of hell, but that the moderns are most rash and foolish in banishing such beliefs.'[1]

There was nothing new about this hard-headed political attitude. As Plato had remarked about his ideal state: 'If anyone at all is to have the privilege of lying, the rulers of the state should be the persons, and they, in their dealings either with enemies or with their own citizens, may be allowed to lie for the public good.'[2] In his *Laws* he had gone on to prescribe in detail the religious opinions which a government should devise and impose upon the community for the national advantage. In the same spirit one of Plato's relatives, Critias, who like him hated democracy, wrote in a play that 'some shrewd and wise-thinking man' of the past had invented the deity as: 'an object of awe for mortals, that there might be some object of dread to the wicked even if they do or say or think anything in secret.'[3] Not long afterwards, again, Isocrates interpreted the Egyptian religious legislator Busiris as ordering the worship of animal deities because 'he thought it proper to accustom the mob to obeying any commands that were given to them by their superiors'.[4]

As heir to this tradition Polybius is sometimes at variance, within himself, between the seeker after truth and the supporter of a fictitious state-religion. Thus when he comments on an alleged miracle (p. 167), his scepticism is qualified in terms not unlike those later used by Tacitus (p. 133):

'Throughout the whole of my history I find myself somehow in continuous opposition to statements of this sort on the part of historians, and continuously distressed by them. . . . I admit that there are cases in which historians must be pardoned for reporting marvels of this kind in so far as their intention is to maintain the piety of the mob towards the gods; anything that goes beyond this is inexcusable. Perhaps it is not easy in every case to fix the limit; it is not, however, impossible. We must excuse a little ignorance or even a little falsification; but what goes beyond this ought, in my opinion, to be rejected.'[5]

In the next generation the jurisprudent priest Quintus Mucius Scaevola, thinking along similar lines, recommended the Stoic thesis that there were three kinds of religious teaching: the kind sung by the poets, the kind thought out by the philosophers, and the kind devised by the leading men in the state. The learned polymath of the late Republic, Varro, who quotes this view with approval, holds that the religion of the philosophers is the only one with any claim to truth, but, as regards the versions devised by statesmen, agrees with Scaevola that 'it is expedient for nations to be deceived in the matter of religion'.[6] Cicero's attitude is very similar. For example, though he does not believe in divination,[7] he recommends its maintenance because of the political function of the priestly college of augurs who were its expert practitioners, and his work with the Platonic title of *Laws* frankly sets out a Platonic scheme, modified under Stoic influence, for the employment of religion to control the people: they are to be subject to the authority of priests chosen from among the leading families, because 'the people's constant need for the advice and authority of the aristocracy holds the state together'.[8]

These late Republican thinkers Polybius, Scaevola, Varro and Cicero are stressing the impact of this patriotic religious fiction upon the common people. But there is another aspect also to be borne in mind. For Roman nobles, too, and the Italian middle-class of the Republic as well, were bound by a romantic antiquarian devotion to the old gods—and this is, roughly, what Scaevola means by the poet's religion. 'The young heir bowed shuddering before anything which his hoary ancestors had designated as worshipful.' That was the complaint of the Christian poet Prudentius,[9] but in earlier days only very rarely do we hear a dissentient note. Yet a protest had come, in the first century BC, from the passionately materialist poet Lucretius, who believed that the whole concept of religion, causing untold evils and miseries, resulted from a confusion of ideas among people deficient in a true philosophy of nature. Lucretius praises his master, Epicurus, who, a quarter of a millennium earlier: 'when human life lay grovelling in all men's sight, crushed to the earth under the dead weight of superstition whose grim features loured menacingly upon mortals from the four quarters of the sky . . . was first to raise mortal eyes in defiance, first to stand erect and brave the challenge.'[10]

But Epicurean protests did not prevail, and in the generation that followed Lucretius they were scarcely heard. On the contrary, Augustan writers of genius lovingly cherished the intermingling of patriotism with the old religion, and presented this fusion in un-equalled, unforgettable literary terms. Livy's romantic, nationalistic history of Rome incorporates illuminating myths and legends linking his story with a thousand antique religious customs and ceremonies—and he explicitly justifies what he is doing:

'Traditions relating to the period before the foundation of the city was carried out or contemplated I propose neither to establish nor refute: they belong to poetic fiction rather than to the authentic records of historical fact. Prehistory is allowed the indulgence of blending the doings of men and gods in order to make the origins of cities more impressive; and if any country is entitled to sanctify its beginnings by attributing them to divine action, that is true of the Romans. So tremendous is their military glory that, when they claim their Father, their Founder's Father, to be none other than Mars, the nations of the earth must needs endure it patiently—as they endure Roman rule.'[11]

Such, too, is the whole religious basis and background of Virgil's glorification of Italy—land of Saturn—in the *Georgics*, and of his patriotic, romantic epic of Rome's foundation, the *Aeneid* (pp. 218 ff.). Both he and Livy had, in their youth, seen a wave of fear sweep over the Roman people because the continuation of terrible civil war seemed to show that there was something wrong with the state's relations with the supernatural.[12] It was widely believed that the prosperity of Rome depended on proper ritual performances and on the upkeep of the national holy places; and Augustus devoted great pains and huge sums of money to displaying to the public that what had been wrong was being set right.[13]

> Caesar has entered the walls of Rome in triumphal procession,
> Three times a victor; he dedicates now a thanks-offering immortal
> To Italy's gods—three hundred great shrines all over the city.[14]

No one made greater use than Augustus of the traditional Roman religion in order to secure the acceptance of his régime. This endeared him to many in governmental circles at Rome, as well as providing deep satisfaction to the uneducated masses whose religious feelings and superstitions had increasingly erupted into panic-stricken demonstrations roused by portents and prophecies. In addition to restoring ancient shrines Augustus constructed magnificent new buildings such as the Palatine temple of his radiant 'patron' Apollo. Then his religious activity culminated in a resplendent celebration, accompanied by a hymn from Horace, of the often-postponed Secular Games (17 BC)—which symbolized the purification of Rome from the pollutions of the past, and the return of the long-awaited, Messianic Golden Age. Gradually, too, an innovation was introduced as the ruler, besides assuming the Chief Priesthood on the death of its long-since disgraced incumbent Lepidus (12 BC), was himself increasingly accepted as a god. For there were now many signs of ruler-worship based on gratitude and homage to the all-powerful god made manifest—an institution of later Greek religion, the only one of the world's religions in which man could aspire to become a god. In Italy corporations, including ex-slaves (p. 96), were appointed to minister to the emperor's cult, but in the capital Augustus did not become a god of the Roman state (*divus*) until after his death.

His successors utilized the state religion in similar ways, and hundreds of its traditions were kept alive by the enormously varied, persistent, abundant imperial coinages (Plates 10–13; p. 49). Thoughtful men, it is true, maintained the earlier distinction between true beliefs and this fictitious religion imposed for necessary political purposes. 'These observances,' says Seneca the younger, 'a philosopher will maintain because they are imposed by law, not because they please the gods . . . the whole base throng of gods assembled by a superstition coeval with time we must worship, without forgetting that we do so to set an example, not because they exist.'[15] Yet, far from withering away under competition from eastern cults, this official religion retained its power of national appeal. Especially devoted to its practice was Antoninus Pius, whose patriotic antiquarianism resembled, in a somewhat more contemplative and perhaps romantic fashion, that of Augustus. Even a century later, under Decius (Plate 8*b*) and Valerian, the traditional worships provided a rallying-cry, in times of crisis, against separatists and scapegoats such as the Christians; and long after Christianity became Rome's official faith there were still nostalgic, aristocratic groups in the capital who cherished the traditional paganism as the core and origin of Roman power.

But the state religion of Rome, although continuously effective in canalizing patriotic emotions, did little or nothing to soothe the care and tedium accompanying an almost universal belief in oppressive Fate or Chance (p. 129)—it could not fill the vacuum in the soul. So men and women, while retaining the forms and attending the ceremonies of the official cults, turned elsewhere. Some, as has been shown, sought to escape or avoid the decrees of Fate by listening to the advice of astrologers or by practising magic. But many relied, in this powerful, instinctive reaction of the human mind against determinism, upon a passionate belief in certain Saviours who would give them strength and holiness to endure their life upon earth, but who would also, when that life was done, endow their chosen devotees with a happy afterlife beyond and above the decrees of Destiny. For there was a new, rather desperate humility abroad, a heart-sinking from spiritual starvation, a feeling of hopeless isolation and defeat: since no faith could be placed in this world, faith must be pinned on the next instead. As the Roman principate proceeded, a very large and increasing number of men and women in its territories wanted personal, individual 'salvation'; that is, victory over evil and death in a blessed hereafter. Jesus was born at a time when there was widespread expectation of a coming Saviour, but Christianity did not become a world religion for more than two centuries to come; these were the centuries when many more people believed in the pagan Saviour Deities with the thrilling, startling, sometimes orgiastic ceremonial that comprised their Mysteries. Such mystery worships spread enormously throughout the Mediterranean world during the first three centuries AD, in the west as much as in the east from where they came.

Their guarantees for the hereafter were all-important. An epoch had begun—it lasted until the nineteenth century—when people's chief anxieties concerned the afterlife. These anxieties were assuaged by progressive initiations into the privileges of the God. Magic might alter your fate, but initiation lifted you beyond its sphere altogether: the soul of the initiate was raised beyond the reach of the hateful stars or united with them as a fellow-wanderer.[16] And so it was 'saved'. This salvation took place through personal union with a Saviour God who was believed, in many cases, himself to have died and risen again. The initiations leading to this end provided an intense emotional experience conveying a new conception of holiness and sometimes a new sense of sin. For the solemn, long-drawn process of initiation, with all its attendant purifications, magic rituals and sacramental banquets, purged human unworthiness by Ecstasis (the soul becoming clear of the body), Enthousiasmos (the God entering and dwelling within his worshippers) and suffering. Through the medium of these experiences each Mystery religion gave its initiates comforting promises of immortality.

Each claimed also to absorb and include all other cults; and here they had the help of the Stoic philosophers, who had brought all myths together in their pantheon. So the mystery cults were not exclusive, and a worshipper could belong to more than one of them at the same time. 'In Greece,' writes the novelist Apuleius, 'I took part in very many initiations. I keep carefully certain symbols and memorials of them handed to me by the priests. . . . I learnt worship upon worship, rites beyond number, a great variety of ceremonies, in my zeal for truth and my dutifulness to the gods.'[17] The second century AD, when these words were written, witnessed the climax of a three-century-old process by which the peoples of the Mediterranean world were becoming increasingly religious. The loyalist state religion of Rome was not enough, and indeed the Olympian gods, whom it worshipped in Italian guise, seemed old and tired; they were not *Ready to Aid* like the mystic saviours; they had fallen with the old city-state, and been killed by the philosophers. But the philosophers' path of the intellect only satisfied a small minority (p. 189)—for these were times when reason had become completely swallowed up in belief. The Knowledge (*gnosis*) that was sought now —some of those who sought it were known as 'Gnostics'—must come not by philosophy but by revelation. For that alone could provide the secret which would defeat the stars.

The acceptance of this revelation seemed to be something more than the faith of the mere believer. That it could be called Knowledge was an assertion that the supreme verities of religion and salvation could be known by 'reason' and demonstrated accordingly. And yet this 'reason' was the suicide of classical rationalism, for it fulfilled itself by a process of illumination, mystically revealed and conferring complete union with the god. The revealer of this light was a divine mediator, or a redeemer, or an anointed one who had himself 'known' the god—and was sometimes described as his son; or he might be a humanmediator such as Simon Magus in Samaria, whom Peter rebuked.[18] The purveyors of such 'knowledge' had their countless holy books reflecting every nuance between native beliefs and Greek philosophy, asceticism and libertinism, exaltation and abasement. Sometimes they echo versions of idealistic Greek mono-theism, but particularly typical also of Gnostic thought is the ancient oriental dualism between Good and Evil: since the problem of Evil allowed by a Good Creator seemed insoluble, and since the soul sought escape from the Evil of the world, the way was paved for great religions such as Manichaeism based on the co-existence of good and evil Powers. One especially famous and varied collection of holy books goes by the name of 'Hermes the Thrice-Great' (Trismegistos),[19] which is a rough translation of the name of the Egyptian god 'Thoth the very great'. These writings, composed in Egypt by men of Greek speech (not, apparently, formed into a religious community), were attributed to Thoth because of a prevalent belief that the wisdom of Egypt, with the prestige of its remote antiquity, could best provide the 'knowledge' which was the key to the afterlife.

There was a hankering for the absolute dependence which this knowledge could bring. This was an age in which materialism, money-making, vulgarity and often total disregard for the accepted canons of morality were combined with genuine religious belief and practice, and constant speculation about the unseen world beyond the grave; sometimes, too, there was a feeling that a well-spent, or religiously spent, life here and now could favourably affect the condition of the soul hereafter. In an epoch when the vastness of the political unit made it necessary for a man to look out for himself, he wanted something new, something exotic with poignant myths and exciting pageantry, which answered his intense curiosity about the superhuman agencies. He wanted beliefs which could comfort him and give him a new, dignified, promising relationship with the powers that ruled the world; and which, above all, could satisfy his ever-deepening conviction that the terror and power of Death the Ravisher (Plate 22a) could be overcome, and accordingly that life, after all, had some meaning. For now a widespread optimism about the aftermath of dying had superseded the Stoic doctrine that death was a welcome reabsorption in an insentient life force, or the negative, colourless ideas of the early Romans, or the pessimistic Greek view which inspires Virgil's picture of the feebly flitting, chilly souls of the dead who have not gained immortality:

> Multitudinous as the leaves that fall in a forest
> At the first frost of autumn, or the birds that out of the deep sea
> Fly to land in migrant flocks, when the cold of the year
> Has sent them overseas in search of a warmer climate.[20]

The day of such beliefs had passed, for people felt that something so independent, so complex and so subtle as the human personality could not be merely transient; and so the second century AD witnessed a widespread abandonment of cremating the dead in favour of inhumation, which seemed more reverent to the soul's earthly container (pp. 164, 251).

For centuries of ever-growing exaltation—the centuries when the Roman empire was at its zenith—the passionate Mystery religions supplied these wants, and also provided the cohesion, the community spirit, which was not available in so encouraging a form from any other source.

These emotional worships reacted, under oriental influences, towards pre-Greek cults. Yet they were also no new thing in the Greek world itself. Frenzied, tranced prophets and prophetesses, like Virgil's Sibyl (p. 219) and the Shamans in Siberia today, had lived among the archaic Greeks. For the satisfaction of their religious feelings, these people had needed not only the balanced, serene tranquillity enshrined in Attic friezes, but also the irrational ecstasy of Mysteries. The Orphic doctrines had from a remote epoch concerned themselves with the underworld and afterlife; and from very early times at Eleusis (an Athenian possession since the seventh century BC) there had been annual celebrations of the elaborate, private ritual of the earth Goddess Demeter, whom the Romans later identified with their Ceres. The secret of these rites has been well kept; but there was probably a kind of miracle-play, a cult-drama, enacting the sacred marriage of the Corn-Maiden Persephone (the Roman Proserpina), with Pluto, the god of the underworld and of the earth's increase. Originally a ceremony linked with the annually recurrent cycle of nature—its aim the fertilization and growth of the corn— this mystic ritual, accompanied by a 'sacrament' of barley-water mixed with mint, came to possess a new significance: participation ensures the favour of the deities who rule below the earth—that is to say, a happy afterlife.

The higher of the two grades of initiates were called the Beholders; what they beheld was a collection of sacred objects carried in procession from Athens to Eleusis. During this procession the participants called upon a god Iacchus, identified with Dionysus. Itinerant devotees had brought his savage, frenzied worship from Thrace. He was the Liberator of mankind (*Lysios*); in the sixth century BC his orgies may sometimes have almost threatened to undermine the structure of society itself. The Greeks of the classical epoch regularized them by incorporation in state cults, but their profoundly disturbing quality lives with us still in the *Bacchants* of Euripides. Soon the cult of Dionysus itself became the setting for Mysteries. In the huge kingdoms of Alexander's heirs these gained widespread popularity—Dionysus is the distinctive deity of that epoch of Macedonian and Greek expansion into the near east. In 186 BC the importation into Rome of the unrestrained worship of this god, identified with the Italian Bacchus or Liber, alarmed the Senate into fearing a threat to public order and taking measures of repression. But then these practices flooded into the Roman world; by the time of Caesar they had become transformed into a respectable Mystery religion. Its immense popularity in the first two centuries AD is attested by innumerable artistic representations. 'This whole little Olympus outside the greater', with its liberating influence on the art of the Renaissance and of later times (Plate 27*a*)—to which Sir Kenneth Clark has drawn attention—shows Dionysus-Bacchus and his attendant Maenads in delirious, ecstatic frenzy (Plate 27*b*), as they wildly roam and leap on their savage, wooded mountain-summits through cavernous, ivy-clad forests of oak and pine. This theme symbolizes the irrational, animal elements in human nature, the ferocious singlemindedness of the possessed, and the escape from worldly reality for which the adherents of these religions longed.

In the ceremonies it was declared that the initiate himself 'becomes a Bacchus'. The Dionysiac Mysteries have kept their secret, but from the first century BC there is a tantalizing, sinister glimpse of their rites, mixed with myth, on the wall-paintings of the Villa Item at Pompeii (p. 252). On the left is a daemonic female figure in high boots, and with powerful dark wings (Plate 28). The interpretation of this whole vivid scene is much disputed, but she seems to represent Punishment (Poine)—the penalties in the afterlife that await the uninitiated. One of these, a girl, cowers at another woman's lap (Plate 29), terrified and perhaps menaced by the wand which the winged figure raises. Such grim scenes at the Mysteries added a chill of horror to the initiation ceremonies. They also gave added bliss, by contrast, to salvation, which is represented on this scene by the figure on the right, a dancer with her back to us, on tiptoe, twisting round her head—a variant of a traditional form of Maenad dating back to the sculpture of Scopas in the fourth century BC. The Maenad is the priestess of the god, and she is perhaps purifying the terror-stricken girl by her orgiastic dance.

Bacchus punishes unbelievers but rewards devotees. The latter theme reached full artistic efflorescence when, from the second century AD, the bodies of the dead, no longer burnt, were buried in elaborately engraved sarcophagi (p. 251). On these sarcophagi we come in due course to Christianity, but before that to the old pagan myths charged with new allegorical meanings: we see the soul's fate in the underworld or among the starry spheres, and its trials and sufferings as it undergoes the purifications leading to its ultimate release. The associations of Dionysiac worshippers were particularly attentive to burials; and enormously widespread, among the themes thus treated on sarcophagi, are those relating to the story of their god.

For example, he and his train of Maenads and Satyrs—like the ecstatic crowds of worshippers whom travellers in Asia Minor actually encountered—are shown discovering, on the isle of Naxos where Theseus had abandoned her, the sleeping Ariadne; she will awaken and wed Dionysus, just as the soul of the initiate will wake from the slumber of death to a life of union with the god. Other sarcophagi show Ariadne riding in a chariot beside her divine husband, as he returns to Europe after victorious campaigns in Ethiopia and India (Plates 32a, 31a). The return is the annual return of fertility, and his partnership with Ariadne tells how the soul of the initiate, redeemed from Hades, will celebrate with her deliverer for evermore the eternal triumph and symposium of the blessed. To the human being for whom the sarcophagus was made, this mythological, mystical marriage provides promise, not only of a generally agreeable eternity, but also perhaps of the happy reunion of husband and wife in the world to come. The prominence of Ariadne is further significant because women, as successors of the Maenad train, had a special place in the worship of Dionysus. Here was a religion which, unlike the Olympian or Roman faiths, appealed to women—appealed to their emotions. One of its principal symbols, displayed in a winnowing fan filled with fruits, was the phallus. Yet, despite this feature, another peculiar characteristic of the cult was the leading part taken in its practices by children. There are many artistic representations of the birth and childhood of Dionysus himself, often shown as a newborn infant under the care of the nymphs—the mythical founders of Bacchic revelry, standing for the beneficent forces of nature. In certain circumstances a boy or girl could even be initiated into the Mysteries; while satisfying the sentimental Hellenistic love of children, this was an insurance of comfort to the parents should their child, as happened very often in antiquity, die young.

The cult of Dionysus became something of an upper-class preserve; for if these sarcophagi are the product of a new respect for human relics they also bear witness to the instinct for ostentation among the rich. The ecstatic element tended to succumb to the sensual—the afterlife was often pictured as a mere debauch, with emphasis on wine-drinking and, sometimes, upon scenes of frank sexuality. This sensual picture of a pleasant life in the next world was convenient enough for easy-going people who wanted to be free from qualms. But its materialistic weaknesses also made it unable to compete, in the last resort, with the more earnest and exacting Mysteries provided by other cults.

Another emotional religion that enjoyed great vogue was that of the healer-god Asclepius. His cult, under the name of Aesculapius, was at the instance of instructions attributed to the Sibyls—whose alleged prophecies were in the charge of a priestly college—brought to Rome in 293 BC from Epidaurus in Greece; and it spread throughout the west, enjoying particular favour in army circles, for instance in Dacia (Roumania) and Spain. It is from Asia Minor, however, that we possess strange testimony to the god's alleged gift of appearing to the sick in dreams with the power of a healer. Aelius Aristides, popular philosopher of the second century AD, who lived to the age of seventy but suffered for years from hysterical paralyses and convulsions, tells how, in a dream, the god recommended open-air bathing—though it was mid-winter—and how, to the amazement of a large crowd of spectators, this effected a miraculous cure.[21] Aristides was vain and self-centred, and believed that twice, owing to the intervention of Aesculapius, children—relations of his—had 'died in his place'.[22] But there is something striking, and characteristic of an age when even Marcus Aurelius believed in divine health-guidance (p. 203), in this learned but highly impressionable man's unconditional faith in his dream, and self-abandonment to the régime the god prescribed.

In the same sacred hours of sleep, 'the small mysteries of death',[23] a papyrus tells with much liturgical lore how this healing god Aesculapius, under the name of his counterpart Imouthes of Memphis, appears in radiant splendour to the Egyptian writer and his

mother, cures the former of his fever, and inspires him to record the
vision and miracle—an ancient custom—and then to embark on a
powerful missionary effort on behalf of the god: 'I proceeded to
proclaim the benefits which he had done to me. . . . Every Greek
tongue shall tell of thy story, Master. . . . I shall speak of his marvellous epiphanies, and of the mighty blessings of his power.'²⁴

We see Aesculapius himself, with his serpent-entwined staff and his
diminutive companion Telesphorus, on the coinage of the emperor
Caracalla, who had continually, without effect, sought refuge for his
tortured nerves and physical ailments in assiduous worship of this
and other gods. Two centuries earlier a hint of scepticism had been
recorded by the architectural expert Vitruvius, who had suggested
that the god's miracles would be more effective if his shrines were
located in naturally healthy places with a good water supply. 'So
will it happen that the divinity (from the nature of the site) will gain
a greater and higher reputation and authority.'²⁵

A conspicuous feature of many of these cults was their employment
of a professional priesthood. The novelist Apuleius gives a startling
picture of the wandering, begging, flagellant eunuch ministers of the
'Syrian Goddess' of fertility Atargatis, half-woman and half-fish,
whom Eunus, leader of the slave-revolt, had claimed as his patroness
(p. 114):

'The next morning the eunuch priests prepared to go out on their rounds,
all dressed in different colours and looking absolutely hideous, their faces
daubed with rouge and their eyesockets painted to bring out the brightness
of their eyes. They wore mitre-shaped birettas, saffron-coloured chasubles,
silk surplices, girdles and yellow shoes. Some of them sported white
tunics with an irregular criss-cross of narrow purple stripes. They covered
the Goddess with a silk mantle and set her on my back, the hornplayer
struck up and they started brandishing enormous swords and maces, and
leaping about like maniacs, with their arms bared to the shoulders.
After passing through several hamlets we reached a large country-house
where, raising a yell at the gate, they rushed frantically in and danced
again. They would throw their heads forward so that their long hair fell
down over their faces, then rotate them so rapidly that it wheeled round
in a circle. Every now and then they would bite themselves savagely and
as a climax cut their arms with the sharp knives that they carried. One of
them let himself go more ecstatically than the rest. Heaving deep sighs
from the very bottom of his lungs, as if filled with the spirit of the Goddess,
he pretended to go stark-mad. (A strange notion, this, that divine
immanency, instead of doing men good, enfeebles or disorders their

senses; but if you read on you will see how Providence eventually intervened to punish these charlatans.) He began by making a bogus confession of guilt, crying out in prophetic tones that he had in some way offended against the holy laws of his religion. Then he called on his own hands to inflict the necessary punishment and snatching up one of the whips that these half-men always carry, the sort with several long lashes of woollen yarn strung with sheep's knucklebones, gave himself a terrific flogging. The ground was slippery with the blood that oozed from the knife-cuts and the wounds made by the flying bones.'[26]

Under the influence of the local ruling classes, who utilized religion to impress or frighten the populace into obedience, the priesthoods employed every dramatic ritual aid. For example, they were conversant with the production, by conjuring tricks and scientific devices, of temple-miracles inspiring bewilderment and awe. Here it was possible to utilize the experimental research on pneumatics of Strato, a pupil of Theophrastus in the early third century BC from Lampsacus on the Hellespont, and Hero, an Alexandrian perhaps of Roman imperial date. The principle of the siphon was applied to turning water into wine; and when the congregation entered a temple, cunning systems of hydraulic bellows caused fanfares of trumpets to sound, or the altar-fire to blaze up. The expansive power of hot air, induced by burnt offerings, was employed to open the door of a shrine and to propel the statue of its god forward, so that he might greet his worshippers; and a variety of improved lighting effects included the internal illumination of statues so as to lend radiance to their perforated eyes and crowns (p. 178). Somehow or other, too, statues of Ares (Mars) and Aphrodite (Venus) were brought together in marriage; though whether this was done by magnetism or invisible cords is disputed. The historian Polybius not only approves of stage-managing religion but refuses to be wholly sceptical when he hears that a certain statue of Artemis (Diana), though standing in the open air, is never touched by snow or rain (pp. 155, 133).[27]

Some of these religions also enforced a strict moral code. This tendency increased as time went on—partly because of the need to compete with the Christians—but already in the first century BC an inscription indicating such a requirement among worshippers has been found in a private shrine of the Mother Goddess Agdistis at Philadelphia in Lydia (Asia Minor):

'Let men and women, slave and free, when coming into this shrine swear by all the gods that they will not deliberately plan any evil guile or baneful poison against any man or woman; that they will neither know nor use harmful spells; that they will neither turn to nor recommend to others nor have a hand in love-charms, abortives, contraceptives, or doing robbery or murder; that they will steal nothing but will be well-disposed to this house, and if any man does or purposes any of these things they will not keep silence but will reveal it and avenge. A man is not to have relations with the wife of another, whether a free woman or a married slave, or with a boy, or with a virgin, or to counsel this to another. . . . Let not woman or man who do the aforementioned acts come into this shrine; for in it are enthroned mighty deities, and they observe such offences, and will not tolerate those who transgress their commands.'[28]

Agdistis, whose devotees were ordered to obey these exacting ethical precepts, was a local variant of the great Mother-Goddess Cybele whose ritual, far from moralistic, carried current emotional, orgiastic tendencies to extraordinary lengths. Cybele was the timeless, immeasurably ancient Earth-Mother of Asia Minor. Just as in pre-Hellenic Crete the Mother-Goddess had been accompanied by lions, so Cybele journeys in a lion-chariot. Year by year, her ceremonial narrated the death and rebirth of her youthful consort Attis, god of things that annually grow and die. The poet Lucretius celebrates this resplendent worship (though with critical comment, p. 191):

'Earth contains the stores out of which it can thrust up thriving crops and lusty orchard trees for the races of men and provide rivers and foliage and lush pasture for the wild beasts of the mountain. . . . That is why this one being has earned such titles as Great Mother of the Gods, Mother of Beasts and progenitress of the human frame. . . . A thunder of drums attends her, tight-stretched and pounded by palms, and a clash of hollow cymbals; hoarse-throated horns bray their deep warning, and the pierced flute thrills every heart with Phrygian strains. Weapons are carried before her, symbolic of rabid frenzy, to chasten the thankless and profane hearts of the rabble with dread of her divinity. So, when first she is escorted into some great city and mutely enriches mortals with wordless benediction, they strew her path all along the route with a lavish largess of copper and silver, and shadow the Mother and her retinue with a show of roses. Next an armed band, whom the Greeks call Phrygian Curetes, joust together and join in rhythmic dances, merry with blood and nodding their heads to set their terrifying crests aflutter.'[29]

As these rites pursued their resounding, sensational course in the partly underground sanctuaries of Asia Minor—Pessinus, the two

Comanas, Castabala—the violence and excitement reached an even higher pitch than in the worship of Dionysus.

Admitted to Roman cult as early as 204 BC, the powerful cult of Cybele displayed the lengthiest and most complex pageantry ever witnessed in the ancient world, rousing hopes of immortality to a fever-heat of excitement. Seven fast-days were followed by a resplendent procession in which was carried a new-cut pine, symbolizing the dead Attis. Then, after a day of lamenting, came the Day of Blood when the priests lashed and lacerated themselves, while fanatical novices performed their own castration. When further fasting and mourning had run their course, it was proclaimed: *Be of good cheer, initiates, seeing that the god is saved: for we too, after our toils, shall find salvation!*[30] And that was the signal for frenzied rejoicing. For unlike Dionysus, Attis is not a lonely god: he is united to the goddess of the earth. Though originally a deity of vegetation born and dying with the plants, he wears a star-spangled cap as Shepherd of the Stars (p. 146)—and with astral worship, in a discordant mixture of philosophy and the crudest ancient folklore, this religion became closely associated.

A relief from Lanuvium—one of the most ancient centres, paradoxically, of traditional Roman cult—shows the solemn, visionary features of a high priest of Cybele or *archigallus* (Plate 26). Socially many grades above her mendicant priests who wandered about in rags, he is shown in full ritual vestments, with heavy medallion-studded wreath, serpent-head necklace, earrings, long woollen fillets, and scapular in the form of a tiny shrine worn on his breast, containing a miniature image of Attis. In his right hand he holds the fruit and branches of the pomegranate, symbols of life and resurrection. His left hand bears the phallic pine-cone of fertility and resurrection, in the midst of a dish full of fruit; such food, charged with holiness, the devotees consumed—to the accompaniment of music—as symbols of their rebirth. The relief also shows the magic rattle, drum, flutes and cymbals, and a whip for self-flagellation.

Though Rome received in its midst all the vertiginous anaesthesia of the dances uniting the devotees with their deity, the official policy of toning down the exuberance of foreign cults may at least have secured that the high priests were no longer eunuchs. Yet, despite preventive laws, castration in praise of Cybele continued. This modified form of human sacrifice (itself perhaps not wholly extinct, p. 178) had been the subject of very ancient stories, for example in the Hittite epic of Kumarbi, of which fragments were discovered at Boğazköy in central Asia Minor. In antique Greek myth, too, Kronos was said to have castrated his father Ouranos, whose blood had fertilized the earth while his seed fertilized the sea. Evidently this painful, violent and irremediable form of self-renunciation still struck a deep chord among the feelings of near eastern and Mediterranean peoples. One of the great surprises of ancient literature—though the subject had not been unknown to Hellenistic poets—is a long lyric of Catullus passionately telling of the castration of Attis: a poem unique in its gruesome subject, its breathless mood and its wild metre mirroring the rhythmical dance of the devotees. In this rather horrible technical and psychological masterpiece, the hero sails across the sea with a chosen band to perform this ferocious rite upon himself. Catullus tells of his frenzied dash to the summit of Mount Ida (where he himself had been), followed by exhaustion, sleep, revival, remorse—and a final sudden terror.

> Attis with the scream of a madman fled to the forest wild
> And there for ever and ever all his life's course
>   He was a slave.
>   O Holy Mother Lady of might,
>   O Holy Mother Cybele,
>   O Holy Mother Dindymus's Queen,
>   Grant that this house where I dwell
>   May never know that madness thou canst send.
>   Drive other men to frenzy—drive other men insane.[31]

The goddess, to whom he feels this unearthly devotion, had dominated Attis and demanded blood-sacrifice, to keep him her pure servant for ever. In this study of the manic-depressive, gripped after depression by mania again, is Catullus also writing, in allegorical terms, of his miserable love for Clodia, who 'leaves all men's loins limp' (p. 216)—and whose ancestor Claudia had escorted to Rome its first statue of Cybele? Perhaps, as Gilbert Highet suggests, the poet too could 'hope for nothing in the future except a succession of orgies, joyless fits of insane excitement and unsatisfied desire, separated by periods of deathlike unconsciousness and hopeless remorse'. This may have been the response evoked from a despairing poet by the terrifying, engrossing religion of Cybele.

In the second century AD the cult attained great popularity.

Antoninus Pius and his wife Faustina the elder, though a calmly respectable pair, were among its keenest followers; and the religion spread throughout Africa and Gaul, where it was adopted by the municipalities as it had been at Rome. A highly prominent place in the ceremonial, especially in Gaul, was now occupied by a repulsive rite called the *taurobolium*, a bull-sacrifice and blood-bath. After the sanction of the high priest had been obtained, the devotee descended into a hole dug in the ground, roofed with a grating. Then upon the grating a bull was slaughtered (when a ram was used instead, the ceremony was called a *criobolium*). The blood of the animal poured down upon the initiate and was received on his upturned face and on his tongue. 'Through the thousand crevices in the wood,' tells the Christian poet Prudentius, 'the bloody dew runs down into the pit.'[32] Its recipient makes sure that the torrent falls upon his head, clothes and body. He leans backward to soak his cheeks, his ears, his lips and his nostrils. He pours the wet blood over his eyes, and opens his mouth eagerly to drink.

Inscriptions show that the blood was believed to be powerfully efficacious. At first the act was 'done on behalf of the empire'. But later the initiate is specifically described as 'reborn for twenty years', and later still 'reborn for ever'.[33] The idea goes back to very early Asia Minor, where wild bulls had been caught by huntsmen and immolated with their spears—then the qualities of the bull, particularly the life-principle itself, had passed to those who drained its blood. The participants in this sanguinary procedure in the Roman empire, who were usually though not always worshippers of Cybele, had to pay for the bull themselves, and were therefore well off; and the ceremony drew large crowds of people, who bowed in veneration as the blood poured down. The last *taurobolium* known to us took place in the fourth century AD, on the site of the Vatican.

Innumerable people all over the Roman empire believed passionately in Cybele. But even more believed in the Egyptian goddess Isis. From the first century BC onwards until the triumph of Christianity four hundred years later, hers is the dominating religion of the Greco-Roman world, the only pagan religion which might have become universal. Yet its coming to Rome had been exceptionally stormy because of moral and political suspicions of Egypt and its culture. Between 59 and 48 BC the shrines of the Egyptian gods at

Rome were destroyed four times, and it was not until Caligula (AD 38) that the capital had a temple of Isis which was to survive. Her Roman processions continued until AD 394.

Egypt was still the home of countless ancient rituals of its own, and religious practices which came from there possessed the prestige of immemorial antiquity. The myths concerning Isis incorporated much of this lore and prestige, but her worship as it became world-wide developed a character of its own, absorbing general, international ideas yet adding to them a distinctive note. Thus the Egyptian god of the Underworld, Osiris, accompanying Isis in her liturgical drama, brought into the cult a tradition of former earthly rule during which civilized order was introduced into human life. He also stood, like Attis, for the birth and death of the year; and the 'Finding of Osiris', in mid-November, was the climax of the most stirring ceremony, the occasion for intense emotion and exuberant jubilation. The initiate at these Mysteries, whose tranced expression was caught by sculptors (Plate 30b), passed symbolically through all the elements, visited the lower world, and met the gods face to face: whereupon he at last assumed a triumphal robe.

An intimate ceremony of Isis is shown on a painting from Herculaneum (Plate 30a). Her major festivals included ceremonials competing with Cybele's in splendour, and perhaps exceeding them in dramatic, emotional force. Indeed, throughout the year—on a scale hitherto unprecedented, especially in the west—there were elaborate rituals daily, almost hourly; the cult of Isis was made to appeal directly and vividly to the eye, and the ear too was not allowed to forget her, as her penitents intoned hymns through the streets and performed arresting acts of piety and mortification. Yet this was also a religion of silent meditation, of the devotee's contemplative adoration before the sacred face of Isis as her magnificent image was carried in procession. She wore a linen gown with a fringed cloak on her breast, and her face was sweetly thoughtful, graciously maternal. Her worship appealed directly and powerfully —far more even than that of Dionysus—to women: she was the 'Glory of Women'[34] and gave them equal power to men. With the infant Horus or Harpocrates in her arms, she is the universal mother, the wife who understands. And Isis was also an enchantress of unequalled power, the 'Goddess of Ten Thousand Names',[35] who absorbed all other gods and goddesses into herself and could change into any shape. Her worship seemed to allow unrestrained sexuality

—her rites were said to provide rendezvous for lovers—and yet for those who wanted the opposite there were increasingly eloquent calls to purity.

The glamour comes down to us in the testimony of the African writer Apuleius, who for all his other frivolities believed absolutely in her merciful love. In his novel *The Golden Ass* (*Metamorphoses*) he tells how to Lucius, who has been turned into an ass, she reveals herself in a dream, and this vision is a prelude to his recovery of human form. Yet there can be no doubt that we are in the presence of an intense personal experience of Apuleius himself, for whom to gaze on the beloved goddess was supreme happiness:

'I had scarcely closed my eyes before the apparition of a woman began to rise from the middle of the sea, with so lovely a face that the gods themselves would have fallen down in adoration of it. First the head, then the whole shining body gradually emerged and stood before me poised on the surface of the waves. Yes, I will try to describe this transcendent vision, for though human speech is poor and limited, the Goddess herself will perhaps inspire me with poetic imagery sufficient to convey some slight inkling of what I saw. Her long thick hair fell in tapering ringlets on her lovely neck, and was crowned with an intricate chaplet in which was woven every kind of flower. Just above her brow shone a round disc, like a mirror, or like the bright face of the moon, which told me who she was. Vipers rising from the left-hand and right-hand partings of her hair supported this disc, with ears of corn bristling beside them. Her many-coloured robe was of finest linen; part was glistening white, part crocus-yellow, part glowing red and along the entire hem a woven bordure of flowers and fruit clung swaying in the breeze. But what caught and held my eye more than anything else was the deep black lustre of her mantle. She wore it slung across her body from the right hip to the left shoulder, where it was caught in a knot resembling the boss of a shield; but part of it hung in innumerable folds, the tasselled fringe quivering. It was embroidered with glittering stars, on the hem and everywhere else, and in the middle beamed a full and fiery moon. In her right hand she held a bronze rattle, of the sort used to frighten away the God of the Sirocco; its narrow rim was curved like a sword-belt, and three little rods, which sang shrilly when she shook the handle, passed horizontally through it. A boat-shaped gold dish hung from her left hand, and along the upper surface of the handle writhed an asp with puffed throat and head raised ready to strike. On her divine feet were slippers of palm leaves, the emblem of victory.

'All the perfumes of Arabia floated into my nostrils as the Goddess deigned to address me: "You see me here, Lucius, in answer to your prayer. I am Nature, the universal Mother, mistress of all the elements, primordial child of time, sovereign of all things spiritual, queen of the dead, queen also of the immortals, the single manifestation of all gods and goddesses that are. My nod governs the shining heights of Heaven, the wholesome sea-breezes, the lamentable silences of the world below. Though I am worshipped in many aspects, known by countless names, and propitiated with all manner of different rites, yet the whole round earth venerates me".'[36]

But the peculiar lure of Isis was the promise given by her religion to its initiates, a more formal and exciting promise than any other religion gave, of blest immortality in the world to come. '*I conquer Fate and Fate obeys me*'.[37] Lucius, in Apuleius's novel, had been a plaything in Fate's hands until Isis came to his rescue. Her rescue of him meant the end of an impure life and the beginning of a new one: *The Golden Ass* is a story of sin and redemption, symbolizing the greater redemption in the world to come. From the first this religion stressed that its gift was immortality, and the moving, personal message of this transcendental union between divinity and man seemed to more and more people—officials high and low, Romans, freedmen and slaves—the fulfilment of their deepest emotional needs. Throughout the west as well as the east spread the religion of Isis, particularly in lands where there was contact with Egypt and where there were military and other foreign elements.

At Delos we find Isis as the leading figure of an Egyptian Trinity: Isis, dog-headed Anubis—the god who conducts souls to immortal life—and Sarapis.[38] Sarapis was a strange phenomenon, an artificial creation of the first King Ptolemy of Egypt (d. 282 BC), calculated by him to unite the Greeks and Egyptians of his composite state in common worship—the only god, perhaps, successfully created from nothing in historical times by deliberate human thought. In the Sarapeum of Alexandria, within a darkened shrine well-fitted with miraculous effects (p. 167), was his great cult-statue, with golden head and jewelled eyes. A leading sculptor, Bryaxis, created the noble artistic type of Sarapis with a bushel upon his Zeus-like head, representing the ruler of the fertile earth. But the god was giver of life hereafter as well as upon earth. By his miracles he overruled Fate; as special patron of healing he was believed to cure blindness and, if men were born under the same constellation, to have the power of transferring diseases from one man to another. The sick Caracalla, sculpturally represented as a Pharaoh, was devoted to

Sarapis, and contemporary inscriptions identify this god with Jupiter and the Sun.[39] Yet, in general, he was an adjunct of the more important Isis.

There seemed something utterly pathetic and poignant about the deaths of the young Dionysus, Attis and Osiris. And when in the second century AD a very conspicuous human youth of striking appearance met a mysterious and perhaps tragic death, it seemed to thousands that the Mystery had truly come to pass again. This was the Bithynian Antinous. Accompanying his lover Hadrian up the Nile in AD 130, Antinous, aged about twenty, was drowned. Some said he gave his life in the sacred river to avert magical or astrological predictions of the emperor's own death. The sequel was indeed strange. Among the emotionally charged communities of the east Antinous was at once, and with evidently authentic fervour, worshipped as a saviour deity incarnate. Accepted as a god at Delphi and Olympia, he was identified with Dionysus, and at Hadrian's new city in Egypt, Antinoopolis, men worshipped him as Osiris himself. Dramatic rites were invented to incorporate a Mystery play, the Passion of Antinous, at which ceremonial dances or moving images annually represented the pathos of his sorrowful, youthful death, and the glory and ecstasy of his resurrection. He became the inspiration of a new sculptural ideal (Plate 6a; p. 242).

One age finds it hard to understand another's idols; and in this case 'an unbridgeable gulf,' it has been said, 'divides us from the emotions beneath'. They could, indeed, only have achieved so lush an efflorescence in the hysterical, amoral atmosphere of the Roman empire—or perhaps now, when an equally young popular singer still has two thousand letters posted to him every week by people who are well aware that he died a year ago. Noting that the cult of Antinous, unlike the major Mystery religions, flourished in the east much more than the west, we might feel justified in supposing that the tougher elements of society, army officers and hardened legionaries, held a contemptuous view of so sensuous, if not sentimental, a worship. Yet here too caution is necessary, for less than a century later (AD 218) the great group of armies in Syria became so emotionally excited about a bejewelled, made-up fourteen-year-old local male priest, Elagabalus, that they made him emperor of Rome.

But there were also thousands who wanted much sterner stuff, and such strange phenomena as the worship of Antinous, and an enormous number of other minor Mystery deities and saviours, were wholly eclipsed by a potent cult which laid much emphasis on austerity—the religion of Mithras. Mithras was a very ancient god of the Indo-European peoples. The Mithraic traditions and doctrines were collected in the *Avesta* or 'Law', and Mithras's name was celebrated in the Hindu Vedic hymns. But he and his Mysteries probably came to the Roman empire from Iran, where the cult spread by Zoroaster (of whom Greeks learnt in the fifth century BC) had been in the hands of the priestly clan of the Median *Magi*; the Romans regarded Mithras as Persian.[40]

Mithraism differs from most other Mystery religions in that there is a long and detailed life of the god, starting from his miraculous creation from a rock by the good power Ormazd (Ahuramazda), Lord of Life. But there is no annual cult-drama: there could be no yearly death and rebirth, since Mithras had renewed life and conquered death once and for all. Mithras attended upon Ormazd, in eternal opposition to the evil god Ahriman, Lord of Death. Both Ormazd and Ahriman originated from the First Principle, Everlasting Time (p. 139). So in the unending duality between good and evil (p. 160) Mithras was a good power, close to the divine light. Indeed, he was ally and agent of the all-powerful Sun—with whom he was later identified. Moreover, this eternal battle between light and darkness is reflected in mankind: Mithras was man's good guide, the mediator between the divinity and humanity, the protector, too, of the souls of the dead from evil demons. His name originally meant 'light'. But it came to be associated with a word signifying 'contract', and so he was also accepted as the deity of obligations, an ethical god of truth. He is also the god of herdsmen— the 'Lord of Wide Pastures', the 'Slayer of Demons and Wild Beasts'. But in Greco-Roman Mithraism the most extraordinary of his many Herculean labours, and the one that has given us his characteristic sculptural and pictorial pose (Plates 32*b*; 33*b*), is his epic struggle with the first of living creatures, the bull. After he had overcome the bull, Mithras dragged it back to a cave. Then it escaped, and the hero was ordered by the Sun's envoy, the Raven, to pursue and slay it— a harsh duty, which he carried out with a sadness or reluctance apparent on his upturned features. From the bull's blood and seed flowed corn and all plenteousness of the natural world; and these further symbolized the springing up of new life for the dead in the world beyond the grave.

After the slaughter of the bull the first human couple was born. The plagues and flames sent against them by Ahriman were overcome by Mithras; and so his mission on earth came to an end. But the Life of Mithras was closer to myth than to alleged history—and on the termination of his earthly mission he partook of a mystical love-feast and communion with the Sun. When these ceremonies were reproduced by his human worshippers, they consumed bread and wine (in the east the juice of the sacred plant *Haoma*). After the love-feast, Mithras ascended in the chariot of the Sun into heaven, whence he continued to watch over the faithful, until, according to one version, he should bring the world to an end in universal conflagration.

As his 'Phrygian cap' shows, Rome inherited him, not from Persia direct, but from a more westerly Asiatic land—namely, from Asia Minor. In the north of that peninsula, Trapezus (Trebizond) in Pontus was the great centre of Mithras-worship, and he appears as a horseman on its coins of the third century AD.[41] This divine rider is also familiar to us from St George of the Cappadocian tableland to the south-west. That was a country, not only of many horses, but of *magi*; and there were still magicians in Cappadocia in the time of the early Christian Fathers. It was also in Asia Minor, as Plutarch tells us, that Romans had first encountered the cult—among the pirates of Cilicia in the first century BC.[42] At that time Iranian and Greek elements were combining to transform the cult of Mithras, and the transformation is symbolized by his vastly reduplicated effigy. For Mithras the Bull-Slayer is not an Iranian artistic theme, but is a Hellenistic adaptation, possibly originating at Pergamum, of a well-known Greek Victory in similar pose. However, it is exceptional for Mithras to appear in Greek costume (Plate 33*b*); his dress is usually Persian (Plate 32*b*).

Mithraism, as it developed in the Roman empire, contained numerous strata of Greek as well as of Iranian religion. Chronos (Time) was believed to have formed, at the beginning of things, an egg from which the first of the gods, Aion (p. 139), was born; and Mithras, too, is sometimes represented as born not from a rock but from an egg (Fig. xvi). Like Chronos and Aion again, Mithras, as renewer of life, was associated with the seasons, signs of the zodiac, and heavenly bodies. Thus the seven grades of Mithraic initiate[43]

Fig. xvi. Birth of Mithras from egg. From Borcovicium (Housesteads)

corresponded in number with the seven planets. The name of every grade is masculine: a Mithraist's womenfolk were presumably expected to seek salvation through some other mystery-cult. And there is no mention of a priest, for the Father who presided over the ceremonies was not, in this religion, a professional but was elected for the occasion.

In the underground shrines of Mithras (Plate 34a) some of the worshippers flapped their wings like birds, imitating the cries of crows; others growled like lions;[44] and reliefs show Mithraic worshippers wearing masks depicting animals and birds. Amid these weird trappings—further dramatized by the use of gadgets, such as perforated rays, for producing dramatic lighting effects and silhouettes (p. 167)—there were rigorous and sometimes deliberately horrifying tests, ordeals and expiations, aimed at developing by harsh means that imperviousness to circumstances which was the Hellenistic ideal (p. 190). The would-be initiate had his hands bound with the innards of a chicken, which were not removed until he had been hurled across a pit filled with water. Worse ordeals were by extremes of heat and cold; a pit for the infliction of such tests has been excavated in a Mithraic shrine at Carrawburgh (Procolitia) (Plate 34b). There were also reports of tortures, brandings, and a sword dripping with the blood of a man whose violent end had been not symbolic but real. Did ceremonies of Mithras on occasion, as for example at the behest of Commodus (p. 180), include real human sacrifice? A human skeleton in chains has been found in his sanctuary at Pons Saravi (Saarburg);[45] it might have been put there by Christians to discredit the cult (p. 183), but human sacrifice— though possibly not ordered by the Roman state since 112 BC—was not extinct several centuries later in the provinces, for instance in north Africa.[46]

The importers of Mithraism to Italy were probably soldiers and traders from various parts of the east. In AD 66 Nero invited on a state visit Tiridates, King and High Priest of Armenia, who is said by Pliny the elder to have brought *magi* with him and to have initiated the emperor into 'magic banquets'.[47] The popular philosopher Lucian parodied the proceedings of Mithraism, and Celsus in his *True Discourses*, a Platonist's attack on Christianity, compared the two religions (*c.* AD 178–80).[48] During these first two centuries AD the cult of Mithras was spreading very widely indeed throughout the west. Rome, as a great cosmopolitan city, was a natural place for its development; we know of forty-five Mithraea in the city and its suburbs. The religion also flourished in other cosmopolitan ports and trading centres, such as Alexandria, the Piraeus, Carthage, Puteoli, London and Ostia—where eighteen of its shrines have come to light. The worshippers included many merchants, who favoured Mithras as patron of contracts, and imperial civil servants. Among them were freedmen and educated slaves. Yet Mithraism was not primarily a religion of the lower classes: inscriptions and works of art show that its organizers were members of a cultured and well-to-do middle-class urban society.

But it was the army that chiefly spread Mithraism—and particularly the officers, with the participation of many commanders of units. In the garrison areas on the Rhine, the Danube and the British frontier there are numerous shrines and dedications, ultimately traceable to troop movements from the east. To the military man Mithras offered irresistible appeal. For he was *invictus*—the unconquerable Herculean protector. He himself had displayed unsparing, heroic alertness and effort; and his example, in contrast to the defeatist contemplative spirit of intellectuals, stimulated these virtues in others. This sort of toughness was, indeed, all too necessary in face of the dangers and difficulties which beset the mere human warrior, as the *Pax Romana* in central and northern Europe tottered towards its dissolution. And not only must the worshippers of Mithras be tough like him, but they must also resemble him in moral purity and chastity. This aspect of the god satisfied the growing taste for asceticism—that revulsion from the body and the senses which had invaded the Mediterranean peoples, at intervals, since the archaic period in Greece and which was shortly to reach its climax among the Christian hermits. But Mithraism had no sympathy with the meditative retirement of the hermit. The asceticism for which it stood was active and militant. Indeed, one of the Mithraic grades, attainable by ordeal, was that of Soldier. At initiation ceremonies, Tertullian tells us, the aspirant to this grade was ordered to push a garland from his head so that it fell on his shoulder. As he did this he declared, *Mithras is my crown.* To those who sought to crown him he must say—*It belongs to my god.*[49]

Mithraists were always allowed to register the guilds or corporations of their religion without hindrance. Statements of their expenses for food and wine have been found at Dura-Europus in Mesopotamia. Officially, perhaps, the guilds were recognized as burial associations. At all events, the Roman authorities saw no reason to discourage them—least of all the rulers of the declining empire, who tried to harness to their support the forces of personal as well as patriotic religion. To them the hardy, un-sensual vigour of Mithraism seemed capable of stimulating the dubious morale of army and civilians alike. Nevertheless, the worship of Mithras was long regarded as too personal a faith to join the public cults; and it was not a court religion. After Nero, only a few emperors are reported as having direct contacts with its practice. Commodus, who was devoted to exotic religions from the east, extended his sanguinary favour to Mithraism—allegedly insisting that the ceremonies, when carried out in his presence, should include not merely the habitual terror and mock-killing, but authentic slaughter. Nevertheless, the worship of Mithras no doubt benefited from his support, and reached its first climax of popularity in his and the following reigns. People were now thinking of Mithras as a solar god, such as those whom in the third century AD Elagabalus and Aurelian placed at the head of the state religion. Even two centuries earlier, in Asia Minor and Italy alike, Mithras had been identified with the Sun; and from that time onwards many strands of feeling converged towards a monotheistic sun-worship.

Other pagan cults found alliance with Mithraism possible. It never refused a welcome to other gods and goddesses of kindred character, and their statues, reliefs and emblems are found in its shrines—for example in the recently excavated temple in London. Such co-operation won for its devotees the support of Cybele's powerful, long-recognized priesthood. Yet the cult of Mithras, in its development in Roman times, is unique among Mystery religions. Peculiar to itself are its lack of a professional priesthood, its exclusion of women, its rigorous moral demands, the definitive nature of

Mithras's exploits, and the consequent absence of an annual cult-drama. The religion had ideas, power and intensity. But it lacked the socially indiscriminate popular appeal, and also the tenderness and sympathy, which were needed in a religion that was to know no bounds.

The crucifixion of Jesus, as Tacitus knew, took place in the reign of Tiberius[50]—probably in AD 29 or 30 or 33. The earliest of the Christian writings, certain of St Paul's Epistles, go back to a date not very far distant from that time. His first Letter to the Corinthians, which must have been written in *c.* AD 55, refers to his visit to Corinth some five years earlier, in which he had told 'how that Christ died for our sins according to the scriptures', how he was buried and raised from the dead, and how he was then seen by many brethren and lastly by Paul of Tarsus himself[51]—whose own conversion may perhaps be dated to *c.* AD 35 or a little later. A lost collection of sayings of Jesus, at first recorded in Aramaic—a Semitic dialect—was apparently in existence before AD 60. Then followed the Greek Gospels bearing the names of St Mark (*c.* AD 65), St Matthew and St Luke (AD 80–85)—perhaps writer also of the *Acts of the Apostles* (? *c.* AD 60–2). The last Gospel is that ascribed to St John (? *c.* AD 100), of which the writer, together with Paul and the author of the *Epistle to the Hebrews* (some think it was written by Paul's Cypriot companion Barnabas), is one of the great early theologians of the Church. Not long afterwards these books, products of an exciting time of intense comradeship, experiment and spiritual adventure, had come to be regarded as canonical, and late in the second or early in the third century their texts were revised at Alexandria. Our earliest surviving fragments of any considerable portion of the Gospels probably date from soon after.

But from the various eastern countries to which Christianity had now spread came numerous other accounts of its founder, of many degrees of 'apocryphal' heterodoxy. Among them is the *Gospel of Thomas*. One of forty-nine documents in the Sahidic dialect of the Coptic language found near Nag Hamadi in Upper Egypt in 1945 or 1946, this consists of sayings attributed to Jesus, numbering 114 according to recent editors, and including, among much that is cryptic and Gnostic (p. 160), 40 hitherto unknown but not all improbable. Though the papyrus codex on which it appears is of fourth century date, this work contains elements of early second century written traditions and even earlier oral traditions; it may originate from Syria or northern Mesopotamia, where Thomas was especially venerated. Paul himself travelled most of all in his native Asia Minor, and by the second century AD the most active centres of Christian life were in that peninsula; in the following century the Church also flourished in Syria and north Africa. By then a time of consolidation, of restoration of coherence, had begun, and, foreshadowing official recognition by Constantine, Christianity was beginning to be a world religion. But during the period with which this book is concerned, the power and wealth of its adherents were still limited.

It is easy to point to resemblances between the Greco-Roman Mystery faiths and Christianity, which emanated from the same world as theirs and sought to answer the same needs. For instance, the Christian and pagan worships answered similar demands for mutual support and posthumous guarantees, and sought to satisfy many of the same cravings—for a protector who was above Fate, for a privileged status such as the world could not give, for revelation and for an effective ritual. The influence upon St Paul of the Mystery religions was perhaps only slight—though their terminology, used by contemporary Judaism, he could scarcely escape—but his followers felt their effect strongly; as did St Ignatius, bishop of Antioch (executed under Trajan), who wrote of the Breaking of Bread as 'medicine of immortality',[52] and many others who laid constant emphasis on the miraculous, emotional and mystic aspects of religious experience. Applying the fashionable practice of merging different faiths, cults on the fringes of Christianity sought to combine it with elements from the Mystery cults; for instance, in second-century Asia Minor the Naassenes and Montanists (whose Mysian founder may once have been a priest of Cybele) united Christian doctrines with a reverence for Attis or borrowings from his religion. We hear also of Alexandrians who worshipped both Jesus and Sarapis,[53] and the new conception of motherhood in representations of the Virgin Mary sometimes recalls effigies of Isis. Nor was Christian monotheism always thoroughly distinguished from sun-worship.[54]

Yet there was a very powerful opposition between Christianity and the Mystery religions, just as there was between Christianity and the religion of the state.[55] The priests of Cybele celebrated the vernal equinox in competition with Easter (which they claimed was an imitation of their rite),[56] and attributed to their bull-sacrifice (p. 171) the redemptive power of the Blood of the Lamb. The Christians, for their part, were profoundly contemptuous of the religion of Cybele because of its sordid elements and origins. The ethics and rites of Mithraism, too, with its ritual washings, sacrificial victims, solemn communal meals, and foreshadowings of martyrdom, seemed to the Church a sinister mimicry of its own moral teaching and sacraments—so that Mithraic shrines encountered actual physical attacks (p. 178). Justin Martyr of Shechem (Neapolis) in Samaria (*c.* AD 150) attacks as diabolical such parodies of the rites which stood at the centre of Christian observance, its Baptism based on the Baptism of Jesus, and its sacred meal the Eucharist or Love-Feast[57]—represented in catacomb paintings devoutly but dimly foreshadowing those depictions of the same subjects into which medieval sculptors, such as the Master of Naumburg and Andrea Pisano, put their hearts.

The original belief among Christians that the Saviour would immediately come again caused them to think of their earthly lives as transient: 'we have been enjoined as strangers and sojourners to sojourn here but not to dwell here.'[58] This conviction persisted even when the belief in an early Second Coming was replaced by a more mystic expectation of the Spirit, the Comforter.[59] At this remove Jesus might have seemed, to those of lukewarm devotion or inclined to mix their beliefs, comparable to Mithras or Attis or Osiris since they, too, were held to have tragically died in the distant past. But this very comparison would also show how great the differences were, for no faith could parallel the simple, complete assertion that, in fulfilment of the Hebrew scriptures which were now widely available in Greek translations, Jesus died *to save mankind.*[60] This transcendent doctrine of redemptive suffering—of life given to man originally, lost by man, and restored to him by the Redemption—was a concept unknown to the pagan Mysteries. And their 'eternal life' lacked the vivid urgency of the higher, more divine and more glorious destiny, the very life of God himself, which was promised to the Christian believer. The Saviour, too, was no subordinate deity, no created being endowed with human shape as intermediary between God and man, but God himself incarnate in man.

Geographically, also, Christianity and the Mystery religions went different ways, since the chief dissemination of the Christian faith was taking place in Asia Minor and Syria, where despite their eastern origins the Mystery faiths did not win most or many of their supporters. Besides, Christianity had inherited a large number of its strongest features from Judaism. For instance, there were indeed other religions of *hope*, but there was something especially thoroughgoing about the *faith*, the uncompromising monotheism, which Christianity derived from the Old Testament—and which gave its devotees a unique confidence and satisaction. Jewish in origin, too, was the regular instruction given to believers, and the inter-church organization which eventually outdid by its unified strength the local, congregational systems of paganism. Of Jewish, Old Testament inspiration again were other pillars of Christianity: the principle of authority, the belief that its followers formed a Chosen Race,[61] and above all the truly binding code of conduct. It is true that the Christians, unlike the Jews, did not have schools of their own, both for fear of persecution and because expectations of the Second Coming seemed to make the matter unimportant. Yet the occasional pagan demands—often prompted by rivalry to the Christians—for purity, austerity and goodness were no match for the continually stressed intensity of the Christian moral purpose, taught by Him whom Matthew and Luke, editing Mark with additions from other sources, see above all as the Teacher of Righteousness or Righteous Teacher.

New light has recently been thrown on the traditions behind this interpretation by certain of the numerous Hebrew and Aramaic Scrolls of leather, papyrus and copper found at intervals since 1947 in and near the Wadi Qumrân, a gorge leading to the Dead Sea seven miles south of the modern Jericho. The Qumrân settlement is believed to have belonged to the puritanical, covenanting Jewish sect of the Essenes. Their buildings at Qumrân were destroyed by Vespasian in AD 68 during the First Jewish Revolt (p. 46), although we do not know the extent to which this monastic community, prepared despite its pacifism for a world-ending Holy War, engaged in the struggle against Rome. The Righteous Teacher to which Qumrân documents refer seems to have been a heretical pre-Christian Hebrew, possibly though not certainly of the second century BC. As a Suffering Just One he may be thought of as a precursor of John the Baptist and forerunner of the Jesus of the Gospels. Yet even if, as is not unlikely, this Teacher—enemy of a Wicked Priest—died violently, his death had not been endowed with the saving, Messianic efficacy of Christ's. But in one dramatic poem the Teacher sees himself as a pregnant woman, who, in the painful 'waves of death', gives birth at the last to 'a man-child . . . a wonderful counsellor with his power'. There is no specific reference to the Essenes in the New Testament; yet the Scrolls reveal parallels to its writings, and particularly to St John's Gospel, and there has been much speculation concerning the possibility that the earlier John—the Baptist—and Jesus Himself may have had contacts with this sect and community.

But the real strength of Christianity, the truly unique and exciting feature which in the end caused it to outstrip all other religions, was its Founder's message of love—profoundly original in its emphasis despite all that it had selected from earlier Rabbinical teachings. This was a doctrine of total, revolutionary, unrestricted love, charity and sympathy—not excluding woman, since Jesus was born of a human woman; extended to children; embracing even the totally hopeless and destitute, those whom society had rejected, as it rejected and humiliated the weakness upon earth of Jesus himself;[62] and uncompromisingly proclaimed by a Son of God who, unlike Mithras, had truly and recently lived among mankind, and whose promise of immortality was firmly based upon love.

> Happy, you that are poor; for yours is the Kingdom of God.
> Happy, you that hunger now; for you shall be satisfied.
> Happy, you that weep now; for you shall laugh.
> Count yourselves happy when, on the Son of Man's account, people detest you, cast you out, revile you, and brand the name you bear. Rejoice when that time comes, and leap for joy, since your reward is great in Heaven. Did not their fathers treat the prophets so?
> But alas for you that are rich; for you have had your consolation.
> Alas for you that are filled now; for you shall hunger.
> Alas for you that laugh now; for you shall mourn and weep.
> Alas for you when all mankind applaud you. Did not their fathers do the same for false prophets?[63]

The teachings attributed to Jesus, for all their detailed affinities with Hebrew thought, made a vivid new appeal. The Greco-Roman philosophies and religions had stimulated the imaginative faculty in religious thought, had supplied the longings, had quickened men's faith and sometimes also their sense of purity. But they had not presented so gloriously definite a promise of immortality. For the Christians, this promise was concrete indeed, actually comprising a bodily resurrection; and no one was too wretched to be excluded from it. There was a great gulf between the small, prosperous, all-male Mithraic shrines, and the Christian love for all humanity, female, destitute and criminal alike. By their universal extension of the Mystery, the Christians soared beyond their pagan contemporaries. The excitement of uniting under such a love, and attempting to repay it, made them ready to disregard the unpopularity into which their apartness plunged them; to hold Roman Law and obedience as of no account beside their own allegiance; to refuse sacrifice before the statue of the emperor, since he was not their god; and so, by violating the majesty of the empire and its tutelary gods, to bring death willingly upon themselves for the sake of their faith.

After the Great Fire of Rome under Nero (AD 64), the emperor, himself suspected (no doubt wrongly) of having caused the fire, rounded upon the local Christian community and instigated the savage persecution in which, according to tradition, St Peter and St Paul lost their lives.

'So much for human precautions. Next came attempts to appease heaven. After consultation of the Sibylline books, prayers were addressed to Vulcan, Ceres and Proserpina. Juno, too, was propitiated. But neither human resources, nor imperial munificence, nor appeasement of the gods, eliminated sinister suspicions that the fire had been instigated. To suppress this rumour, Nero fabricated scapegoats—and punished with every refinement the notoriously depraved Christians, as they were popularly called. (Their originator, Christ, had been executed in Tiberius's reign by the governor of Judaea, Pontius Pilatus. But in spite of this temporary setback the deadly superstition had broken out afresh, not only in Judaea, where the mischief had started, but even in Rome, where all degraded and shameful practices collect and flourish.) First, Nero had self-acknowledged Christians arrested. Then, on their information, large numbers of others were condemned—not so much for incendiarism as for their anti-social tendencies. Their deaths were made farcical. Dressed in wild animals' skins, they were torn to pieces by dogs, or crucified, or made into torches to be ignited after dark as substitutes for daylight. Nero provided his Gardens for the spectacle, and exhibited displays in the Circus, at which he mingled with the crowd—or stood in a chariot dressed as a charioteer. Despite their guilt as Christians, and the ruthless punishment it deserved, the victims were pitied. For it was felt that they were being sacrificed to one man's brutality rather than to the national interest.'[64]

As often, Tacitus seems to hesitate between two versions. Were the Christians persecuted as incendiaries or as Christians? Our other sources know nothing of the former charge. Probably they were persecuted as an illegal association guilty of violence or subversiveness; that is, treason. Their beliefs are unlikely to have been attacked as such by Nero, whose government may not have clearly distinguished them from Jewish doctrines.

The identity of the Christians had become more clear-cut when Domitian persecuted them for refusal to accept his divinity. Early in the second century AD Pliny the younger, sent to Bithynia and Pontus with special powers by Trajan (p. 56), regards the substantial Christian community there as a serious problem, requiring meticulous study followed by reference to the emperor. Trajan's reply was as follows:

'You have followed the correct procedure in investigating the cases of those who were accused in your court of being Christians. It is not possible to lay down a rule that can be universally applicable, in a set form of words. They are not to be hunted out; any who are accused and convicted should be punished, with the proviso that if a man says that he is not a Christian and makes it obvious by his actual conduct—namely by worshipping our gods—then, however suspect he may have been with regard to the past, he should gain pardon from his repentance. No anonymous lists that are submitted should carry weight in any charges. That would be the worst of precedents and out of keeping with the spirit of our age.'[65]

This judicious ruling has been received by Christian posterity with every reaction from fierce disapproval to unqualified admiration. Later in the second century AD Marcus Aurelius wrote more critically of one aspect of Christian life, namely the readiness for martyrdom which he regarded as exhibitionism (p. 206). In his reign Christians were persecuted in Asia Minor and Gaul, where under pressure from ferocious crowds savage punishments were inflicted on recalcitrant believers at Lugdunum (Lyon) and Vienna (Vienne).[66] Again they were scapegoats; the reign had declined into plague, inflation and invasion, and men's anxiety and unhappiness were reflected in these assaults upon a separate, mysterious community, which seemed not to share the common cares and duties of humanity—and were even called 'atheists' because of their disregard for the patriotic Roman gods.[67]

Trajan's instructions to Pliny, later echoed in Imperial edicts collected by the great jurist Ulpian,[68] had in mind for the most part the uneducated Christian. However, not only were converts of higher social rank gradually attracted, but the Church began to have an intellectual background linked with Greek philosophical models. Between AD 80 and 160 almost all Christians knew Greek—it was not until AD 200 that Latin apologists arose—and just as in the lifetime of Jesus the Alexandrian Jew Philo had attempted a synthesis of Judaism and Hellenism, so in the second century AD an intellectual lay school of Christians in close touch with pagan thinkers developed under Clement and others at the same city. Already certain books of the New Testament, notably St John's Gospel had framed ideas, in Greek philosophical terms. Although there always remained a strong anti-intellectual movement, which was to bring criticism and self-torture upon Jerome for his classical learning,[69] pagan philosophy as well as pagan rhetoric (p. 71) came to be regarded as a proper preliminary training for spiritual Christian knowledge—as a natural knowledge preparing the way for supernatural knowledge. The stress of Epicurus on friendship could be regarded as a preparation for Christian love, and the humanity of Virgil, 'Prophet of the Gentiles', as a foreshadowing of Christian charity (pp. 192, 220); and St Paul himself quoted to his Athenian audience a Greek Stoic poet's assertion that we are all God's children.[70] Yet the sufferings of the poor and wretched, which Epicureans evaded, Virgil somewhat hopelessly lamented and the Stoics grimly accepted, were given a new courage and glory if one could believe the Christian doctrine that Jesus Himself had suffered supremely to save the world.

CHAPTER 7

PHILOSOPHY

EMOTIONAL religion, in one form or another, reached most of the population of the empire, but a few preferred and practised the more austere consolations of philosophy. To the peoples who inhabited the later Greek and Roman worlds, this meant practical philosophy—guidance. For since the fourth century BC all philosophers, of whatever creed, believed it the philosopher's task to provide *guidance for life*: and the thoughtful turned as anxiously to this guidance as the emotional turned to the pagan religions. These philosophically inclined people could never be very numerous because their taste demanded a degree of self-cultivation and self-control beyond most men's reach or desire. Philosophy also relied entirely on the didactic means of precept and example; its gatherings did not possess the comforting common life of the religions; its beliefs were not enshrined in sensational myths and glamorous cults; and it offered no promises for the afterlife—indeed, no rewards at all except consciousness of right. As Pascal said, the philosophers knew man's duty but not his weakness. Their story belongs to the world of Rome since they had much to offer to that world, and they buoyed up generations of educated Greeks and Romans. In regard, however, to original philosophical thought, the Roman age added very little or nothing to what had already been devised in *c.* 300 BC, or not long afterwards, by the Schools which developed as the aftermath to Plato and Aristotle. The Romans were a far from philosophical people. Yet certain of them expressed Greek philosophy more vividly than had any Greek—and they related it in compelling terms to the conditions in which they lived.

Thus Lucretius, in the mid-first century BC, gave passionately intense utterance to the doctrines of Epicurus of Athens (*c.* 342-270 BC). These doctrines were directly opposed to the pagan religious beliefs outlined in the last chapter, since Epicurus regarded sense-perception as the one and only basis of knowledge. Like Leucippus of Miletus and his atomist pupil Democritus of Abdera (*c.* 460–370 BC), Epicurus asserted that sensation contacts objects by 'effluences' thrown off by those objects through the movements of *atoms*, of which he believed everything (except the void) to consist. Yet he departed from the implied mechanistic fatalism by allowing atoms the power to *swerve* from their straight movement.[1] By this famous and much criticized device he conceded to human beings, whom like everything else he held to be composed of atoms, the power of free will; for when such a swerve occurred in the atoms of the human mind it meant that there was a conscious act of will, and the otherwise ineluctable march of Fate was diverted. For Epicurus felt an urgent need to escape the total fatalism which had spread throughout the world (p. 129): 'It would be better to follow the myths about the gods than to become a slave to the "destiny" of the natural philosophers: for the former suggests a hope of placating the gods by worship, whereas the latter involves a necessity which knows no placation.'[2]

But fear of the gods, too, if somewhat less harmful than fear of destiny, seemed to him absurd. He allowed their existence 'between the worlds'—on the grounds of universal consent, because 'Nature had impressed the idea of them on the minds of all men'.[3] But he added the provisos that they cannot be identified with the heavenly bodies,[4] and that they have no concern with the world or with men. This was Epicurus's way of working towards the peace of mind which, in a new age in which man was alone, defenceless and afraid, was the common philosophical ideal; for his aim was missionary—'Vain,' he said, 'is the word of a philosopher which does not heal any suffering of men.'[5] And one of the strangest phenomena of literary history is the appearance of that keenest of all missionaries the philosopher-poet Lucretius—of whom nothing is known except his proclamation of the faith of Epicurus in a long Latin poem of mighty, fanatical imagery and tortured dogmatic agony. Lucretius passionately praises his master's denial of religion:

'When human life lay grovelling in all men's sight, crushed to the earth under the dead weight of superstition whose grim features loured menacingly upon mortals from the four quarters of the sky, a man of Greece was first to raise mortal eyes in defiance, first to stand erect and brave the challenge. Fables of the gods did not crush him, nor the lightning flash and growling menace of the sky. . . . I will set your mind at rest with more sanctity and far surer reason than those the Delphic prophetess pronounces, drugged by the laurel fumes from Apollo's tripod.'[6]

The great saviour-religions of the Greco-Roman world attract specific criticism when Lucretius describes the worship of Cybele (p. 168). 'It may be claimed that all this is aptly and admirably devised. It is nevertheless far removed from the truth. For it is essential to the very nature of deity that it should enjoy immortal existence in utter tranquillity, aloof and detached from our affairs . . . exempt from any need of us, indifferent to our merits and immune from anger.'[7] Such religions had won their support because of widespread preoccupation with the afterlife, and Lucretius, like his master in this as in everything, sees the fear of death as the worst of the plagues which religion has brought upon men:

'Death is nothing to us and no concern of ours, since our tenure of the mind is mortal. . . . I shall drive out neck and crop that fear of Hell which blasts the life of man from its very foundations, sullying everything with the blackness of death and leaving no pleasure pure and unalloyed. . . . Life is darkened by this fear of retribution for our misdeeds . . .'[8]

> If men could perceive
> That there was a fixed limit to their sorrows,
> By some means they would find strength to withstand
> The hallowed lies and threatenings of these seers:
> But as it is, men have no means, no power
> To make a stand, since everlasting seem
> The penalties that they must fear in death. . . .
> For just as children
> In the blind darkness tremble and are afraid
> Of all things, so we sometimes in the light
> Fear things that are no whit more to be dreaded
> Than those which children shudder at in the dark.[9]

Avoid such worries, said Epicurus and Lucretius, and happiness will already be yours—without more ado. For, trusting in sensation, they argued that the highest good and supreme human aim is happiness: by which they meant pleasure, but primarily pleasure of a negative, simple kind, far removed from later associations of the word 'Epicurean'. To them happiness was *ataraxia* or freedom from disturbance: renunciation, independence, imperturbability—that escape from trouble and pain which was sought and taught by all philosophers after Plato and Aristotle.

'Do you not see that nature is clamouring for two things only, a body free from pain, a mind released from worry and fear, for the enjoyment of pleasurable sensations? So we find that the requirements of our bodily nature are few indeed, no more than is necessary to banish pain. . . . Nature does not miss luxuries when men recline in company on the soft grass by a running stream under the branches of a tall tree and refresh their bodies pleasurably at small expense.'[10]

Recline 'in company', for in spite of the aim of imperturbability and dependence, Epicurus and Lucretius speak of human association, friendship and co-operation, as a very early and essential feature of human life:

> Neighbours began to join in bonds
> Of friendship, wishing neither to inflict
> Nor suffer violence: and for womankind
> And children they would claim kind treatment, pleading
> With cries and gestures inarticulately
> That all men ought to have pity on the weak.
> And though harmony could not everywhere
> Be established, yet the most part faithfully
> Observed their covenants, or man's whole race
> Thus early would have perished, nor till now
> Could propagation have preserved their kind.[11]

However, Epicureanism could not take root at Rome (except in its most banal forms), owing to its total rejection of the moral imperative which both appealed to the minds of the Romans and harmonized with the vigilant attitude of their rulers. Its followers had been expelled from the capital in 173 BC(?) for 'introducing pleasures',[12] and even Lucretius did not succeed in making his beliefs influential.

Yet a not altogether dissimilar conclusion about human co-operation was reached, through a totally different route, by the rival school of the Stoics, which attained far greater influence at Rome. Their version of the struggle to achieve imperturbability was initiated at Athens by Zeno (335–263 BC). Another product of the new individualistic world created by the eclipse of the once all-embracing, independent city-states, Stoicism, like other Hellenistic philosophies, was more concerned with practical conduct than with abstract truth, and was at pains to make man's inmost self defensible against all threats: to make him captain of his soul. But, unlike the teaching of the Epicureans, the Stoic injunction *live consistently with nature* was meant ethically. Conscience and duty were the keynotes of Stoic ethics, and the prime duty of the soul was to realize its moral perfectibility.

The basis of this perfectibility was the belief, in opposition to the Epicureans, that the universe is animated by a divine spark, the *Logos* or Mind (or Zeus), of which every human being has a share. Since this makes all men Brothers, Zeno's ideal state must embrace the whole world—and must be governed, therefore, by the Laws of Nature which are universally applicable, and not by the laws of nations which are of purely local, particularist significance. Zeno came from Citium in a region of Cyprus where the population was of Semitic origin, and his Brotherhood of Man has something basically in common with the Jewish doctrine of the common Fatherhood of God, as exemplified in the books of *Ruth* and *Jonah*. The Greek world was now ripe for the cosmopolitan approach—of which it had already received foretastes from earlier philosophical thinkers, and a practical demonstration, in Zeno's lifetime, from the conquests and inclinations of Alexander the Great.

> We need to love all since we are
> Each a unique particular
> That is no giant, god or dwarf
> But one odd human isomorph;
> We can love each because we know
> All, all of us, that this is so.

But as W. H. Auden, writer of these words, sees, and as some of the early Stoics and their supporters also saw, this doctrine, even if not intended as fuel for political revolution, is capable of revolutionary interpretations:

> In this alone are all the same,
> All are so weak that none dare claim
> 'I have the right to govern' or
> 'Behold in me the Moral Law'.

And the leaders of a wave of rebellions in the second century BC (pp. 100, 113) tended to have the support of Stoic theory and theorists.

However, the Stoic philosophers who succeeded to the founders of the creed, and particularly Panaetius of Rhodes (*c.* 185–109 BC) and Posidonius of Syrian Apamea (Plate 20*b*), went far towards harnessing their doctrines not to revolution but to Roman imperialism. The World State could conveniently be equated with the apparently almost world-wide Roman empire; and Panaetius struck an answering chord in the minds of educated Romans. For one thing, he laid stress, not only on *absolute virtue* like his philosophical predecessors, but on *progress towards virtue*—a far more manageable and attractive prospect to the leading Roman who had to combine and compromise his moral views with the exigencies of an official career.

This moral imperative, as modified and adjusted to Roman needs and possibilities, deeply impressed Cicero (Plate 20*a*) who, although not a philosopher in the most rigorous sense, believed passionately in philosophy and found in it his inspiration and comfort. 'If the man lives,' he declared, 'who would belittle the study of philosophy, I quite fail to see what in the world he would see fit to praise.' For all his passion for public life, Cicero is said to have expressed the hope that his friends would describe him not as an orator but a philosopher. He had felt this devotion from boyhood, encouraged, in spite of an anti-Greek municipal background, by his father. And by philosophy—in spite of his immense contributions to European epistemology, logic and theology—Cicero primarily meant moral philosophy.[13]

For he enthusiastically accepted the belief of the Greek Stoics that the most important things in the world were high moral standards, and the determination to live up to them, and the emotional self-restraint needed to do so: this being the imperative command of the Law of Nature, identical with divine Providence—which is, as Zeno had pointed out, universally applicable to human relations, because all mankind possess a share of it. That is how and why, according to Cicero's *Tusculan Disputations*, Virtue joins man to God. From this belief two things follow: first, all human beings, however humble, must count for something, must have some inherent value in themselves—the basic assumption of the humanism which is fundamental to western thought—and secondly, this shared spark of divinity supplies an unbreakable brotherly bond of kinship between one man and another: and it is right and necessary that brothers should receive decent treatment from one another.[14] This Stoic conception was fundamental to Cicero's attitude and runs continuously through the writings in which he endeavours to explain the human condition and, simultaneously, to guide human behaviour. Among the later Greek philosophers he found material to reinforce his conviction that one of the first impulses in man is affection for his kind. This affection is Natural, nature is good, and accordingly man's first rule must be regard for his fellowmen and the avoidance of any personal gain when this can only be acquired by harming someone else; it is by helping others that man lives most fully according to the divinity within his soul.[15]

In his presentation of this view Cicero stands about half-way between the agnostic who asserts that men can be truly good without wholehearted adherence to a clearly defined religion, and the Christian who denies that this can be so. Cicero is concerned first and foremost with man, he throws moral responsibility upon man's shoulders, and he believes that man can make decisions without detailed interference by gods or Providence. And yet he denies complete self-sufficiency for human beings, since he assumes the existence of this supreme power which endows all men with their divine spark. But his religion varies between the patriotic godliness of the Forum and the more detached philosophizing of the study. On theology his judgment is contradictory or reserved; his prime concern is human co-operation, and his specific contribution the idea of humanity.

The theme of human co-operation which was Cicero's concern, and which Virgil illuminated with deeply-felt emotional humanity and tenderness in his picture of Aeneas rising to the Stoic ideal (p. 219), was worked out in a hundred different ways by another follower and adapter of Stoicism, namely Seneca of Corduba (Cordova) in Spain. This extraordinarily versatile man, whose attitude is often relevant to modern problems, combined in his lifetime the duties of Nero's tutor and chief minister, the responsibilities of a multi-millionaire, and the authorship—in scintillating, pointed 'Silver Latin' epigrams —of a great range of varied literature. His outstanding forensic oratory has not come down to us. But we have nine Tragedies from his pen—too rhetorical for theatrical performance, yet overwhelmingly influential upon sixteenth and seventeenth century dramas. We also have a long scientific work (*Naturales Quaestiones*) which John Milton recommended for schools; and thirteen brilliantly written, sensible ethical treatises—popularizations of philosophy with flashes of real moral grandeur, including the work *On Clemency* which Calvin began his career by editing. Seneca also composed, for his friend

Lucilius, 124 moralizing 'Letters', sermons of great charm, skill and warmth of heart, combined with tolerance of human weakness.

A new note is struck by his uncompromising insistence upon human rights and treatment for slaves (p. 115). This insistence was the logical conclusion of his belief in the Stoic Brotherhood of Man which broke down barriers of class and state and which, as interpreted by Seneca, foreshadowed St Augustine's City of God.

'Let us grasp the idea that there are two commonwealths—the one, a vast and truly common state, which embraces alike gods and men, in which we look neither to this corner of earth nor to that, but measure the bounds of our citizenship by the path of the sun; the other, the one to which we have been assigned by the accident of birth. . . . Some yield service to both commonwealths at the same time, to the greater and the lesser: some only to the lesser, some only to the greater.'[16]

And so:

'We are members of one great body. Nature has made us relatives. . . . She planted in us a mutual love, and fitted us for a social life. . . . You must live for your neighbour if you would live for yourself.'[17]

And you must regard him with charity.

' "It is impossible," says Theophrastus, "for a good man not to be angry with bad men". . . . How much more human to manifest towards wrong-doers a kind and fatherly spirit, not hunting them down but calling them back.'[18]

It is not surprising that there circulated, in the Middle Ages, a collection of letters purporting (though without foundation) to be an exchange of correspondence between Seneca and his contemporary, St Paul.

For Seneca also accepted the Stoic belief in a Divine, controlling Providence of which an element exists within all human beings—that is what makes them brothers. He believes in an immanent pantheistic, personal God, who 'has a father's feeling towards good men and dearly loves them'.[19] And the product of his love, that divinely imparted spark—that Reason which is the mirror and counterpart of the Divine Reason—must be cherished by man as his essential possession, which will enable him to practise the good life, the life of virtue, that Nature and Reason enjoin. For, God's Nature being good, men must imitate him; and that exercise of Reason is what will make them impervious to the hazards of life.

'Wherever we betake ourselves, two things that are most admirable will go with us—universal Nature and our own virtue. Believe me, this was the intention of the great creator of the universe, whoever he may be, whether an all-powerful God, or incorporeal Reason contriving vast works, or divine Spirit pervading all things from the smallest to the greatest with uniform energy, or Fate and an unalterable sequence of causes clinging one to another—this, I say, was his intention, that only the most worthless of our possessions should fall under the control of another. All that is best for a man lies beyond the power of other men, who can neither give it nor take it away. This firmament, than which Nature has created nothing greater and more beautiful, and its most glorious part which is the human mind that surveys and wonders at the firmament, are our own everlasting possessions, destined to remain with us so long as we ourselves shall remain. Eager, therefore, and erect, let us hasten with dauntless step wherever circumstances direct. Let us traverse any lands whatsoever: inside the world there can be found no place of exile, for nothing that is inside the world is foreign to mankind.'

By this realization, this concentration upon the discipline of the mind and upon the moral imperative which it enjoins, men can escape from the tyranny of Fortune which dominated so many hearts.

'Never have I trusted Fortune, even when she seemed to be at peace: all her generous bounties—money, office, influence—I deposited where she could ask them back without disturbing me. Myself I kept detached and remote from those bounties, and so Fortune has merely taken them away, not wrested them from me. . . . The man who is not inflated by prosperity does not collapse under adversity; the man of tested constancy keeps a spirit impregnable to either condition.'[20]

The power to endure so courageously could not be conferred or strengthened, in Seneca's view, by the prospects of rewards in the hereafter. Human beings, with their divinely implanted Reason, did not, according to him, need those hopes or fears of the afterlife which were the stock-in-trade of the great contemporary religions. Seneca, as a philosopher, writes of these religions with disbelief (p. 158), and claims to confer quite other means to make men endure.

'Why do you wonder that good men are shaken to make them strong? No tree stands firm and sturdy if it is not buffeted by constant wind; the very stresses cause it to stiffen and fix its roots firmly. Trees that have grown in a sunny vale are fragile. It is therefore to the advantage of good men, and it enables them to live without fear, to be on terms of intimacy with danger and to bear with serenity a fortune that is ill only to him who bears it ill. . . . "But," you object, "many things which are sad and dreadful and hard to bear do happen." Because I could not make you evade their assault, I have given your minds armour to withstand them; bear them with fortitude.'[21]

This armour is provided by the study of philosophy, and one of the many contradictions of Seneca's many-sided, perhaps schizophrenic personality is the insistence, by this chief minister of a highly unphilosophical emperor, on philosophy as the peculiar talent of mankind, as opposed to unreasoning animals;[22] perhaps his unsavoury tasks as statesman made him love it all the more as a refuge. As he writes to comfort his mother: 'I would lead you to the sure refuge of all who fly from Fortune—to liberal studies. They will heal your wound, they will eradicate your sadness.'[23] And among liberal studies it is philosophy which offers men the moral guidance they need above all. Philosophy is the panacea which gives life its only true object and pleasure; which makes old age agreeable and banishes fear of death; which teaches men to make the most of each day as it passes; which shows the true values of things and men, untwisted by irrelevant externals; and which alone can transmute the brotherhood of men from theory into some measure of reality, seeing that 'philosophy's first promise is a sense of participation, of belonging to mankind, being a member of society'.[24]

Yet human co-operation, such as Cicero and Seneca sought, were far less the concern of most other philosophers of the Roman age and their disciples. These, on the contrary, were concerned with virtue from an increasingly individualistic point of view. Basically, the schools of philosophy from which they learnt their doctrines had always been less concerned with co-operation than with arming the individual so that he may meet bravely all the buffets of Fortune and Fate. 'As free as a bird,' said Diogenes the Cynic (c. 400–325 BC) who helped to formulate this view, 'unconstrained by law, undisturbed by politicians'—immune from the worst blows.

The most widely adopted solution was that of the Stoics, who declared that this immunity could be obtained by the morally good life—and Horace, at times, echoes their view:

> Not the rage of the million commanding things evil,
> Not the doom frowning near in the brows of the tyrant,

    Shakes the upright and resolute man
      In his solid completeness of soul;

  No, not Auster, the Storm-King of Hadria's wild waters,
  No, not Jove's mighty hand when it launches the thunder;
    If in fragments were shattered the world,
      Him its ruins would strike undismayed.[25]

Here is the individual heroically at grips with the Universe; this was the preoccupation of reflective men in the Roman world. And in their quest for self-sufficiency they had guides of genius—fore-runners, for all the differences of their message, of the great interpreters of Christianity. One of these outstanding pagans was Epictetus, a lame Phrygian from Hierapolis who had been slave of Nero's powerful freedman Epaphroditus (p. 99). Liberated, Epictetus had turned to Stoic philosophy, gathering large audiences —perhaps the largest attracted by any philosopher prior to the popular 'sophists' later in the second century AD (p. 232). These listened to him lecturing in Greek at Nicopolis in Epirus; though he readily gave help and advice, he wrote nothing himself, and we owe the survival of what he said to a pupil, Arrian.

Epictetus repeatedly stressed that we must renounce everything except the one thing which it is within our power to control, namely the operation of our own will; and as for that, we must direct and control it with all the strength that we can muster. This theme, already dwelt on by Seneca, is the central feature of the message of Epictetus:

'Some things are under our control, while others are not under our control. Under our control are conception, choice, desire, aversion, and, in a word, everything that is our own doing; not under our control are our body, our property, reputation, office, and, in a word, everything that is not our own doing ... if you think only what is your own to be your own, you will blame no one, *nor is there any harm that can touch you.*'[26]

For our will is the one thing which cannot be compelled or thwarted by anything external.

'Take my paltry body, take my property, take my reputation, take those who are about me. "Yes, but I wish to control your judgments also." And who has given you this authority? How can you have the power to overcome another's judgment? "By bringing fear to bear upon him," he says, "I shall overcome him." You fail to realize that the judgment overcame itself, it was not overcome by something else; and nothing else can overcome moral purpose—it can only be overcome by itself.'[27]

In order to stand out against such encroachments we must perpetually *Endure and Renounce, Bear and Forbear*: the worst vices are want of endurance and want of self-control. ' "Yes, but what if I fall ill?"—you will bear illness well. "Who will nurse me?"—God and your friends. "I shall have a hard bed to lie on."—But like a man.'[28]

Like the religions of the time, though they were so different in their conclusions, this emphasis on choice and moral purpose represents a move away from Greek rationalism, a shift of emphasis from knowledge to non-intellectual qualities. Although the world was in Stoic theory well-ordered, its actual appearance presented a complexity so many-sided as to appear meaningless, and in this uncongenial confusion Epictetus—though in tougher, less easily consoling vein than the religions—helped men maintain their self-respect, Your best way, he said, to accept and indeed welcome the dispensations of Providence—as you must—is to shun anger, grief, desire and fear; and even—perhaps this was a potentially immoral deduction—do not admire your clothes and then you will not blame their thief. But to culture Epictetus was indifferent. Reading is no use, he felt, unless it produces serenity: 'Athens is beautiful, but happiness is much more beautiful—tranquillity, freedom from turmoil, having your own affairs under no man's control.' Yet his renunciation of worldly things did not go so far as the rejection of all social duties, for he saw that natural instincts, such as self-preservation and self-interest, can only be satisfied by making a contribution to the common welfare.[29]

Of freedom he has much to say—partly, no doubt, because of his own experiences as a slave. But as befitted a friend of emperors, a man whom Trajan listened to, Hadrian befriended, and Marcus Aurelius studied, Epictetus is not like the Stoic and Cynic anti-monarchists who had opposed the Flavian emperors (p. 28); his theme is essentially unpolitical. 'Do you philosophers, then, teach us to despise our kings? far from it. Who among us teaches you to dispute their claim to the things over which they have authority?'[30] Though conversely it must also be true—and Epictetus is not afraid of pointing it out—that the emperor's powers are limited.

Behold now, Caesar seems to provide us with profound peace, there are no wars any longer, no battles, no brigandage on a large scale, no piracy, but at any hour we may travel by land, or sail from the rising of the sun to its setting. Can he, then, at all provide us with peace from fever too, and from shipwreck, and from fire, or earthquake, or lightning? Come, can he give us peace from love? He cannot. From sorrow? From envy? He cannot—absolutely none of these things. But the doctrine of the philosophers promises to give us peace from these troubles too.'[31]

These words accepting the rights and limitations of emperors were more passive than Christ's *Render unto Caesar*, since no fundamental attacks on current poverty or corruption accompanied them—humanitarian, indeed merciful (and loving towards children) though Epictetus was. For it is enough for a man to have all things happen to himself according to his moral purpose, and he is then free. This is teaching which could not produce revolutionaries—though it might produce martyrs. Indeed, the philosopher himself, the teacher—a figure of new importance in this doctrine which stressed the will and the personality—must now himself be something of a martyr, or at least a forerunner of medieval ascetics. To be a philosopher:

'You must keep vigils, work hard, abandon your own people, be despised by a paltry slave, be laughed to scorn by those who meet you, in everything get the worst of it, in honour, in office, in court, in every paltry affair. Look these drawbacks over carefully, if you are willing at the price of these things to secure tranquillity, freedom and calm. Otherwise, do not approach philosophy. . . . Look at me! I am without house, or city, property or slave. I sleep on the ground. I have no wife, no children, no official home, but only earth and sky and my bit of a cloak. And what do I lack? Am I not without distress or fear? Am I not *free*?'[32]

Some have seen in him a pathetic, weary longing for a passive kind of happiness. To others he has seemed 'a soul aflame, and burning with love of the honourable'—and, for all their differences, a spirit approaching the basic teaching of Jesus more nearly than any Christian of the early Church. For Epictetus, although he dispenses with the need or desire for survival after death, looks to God as the creator of man's inviolable will: 'This control over the moral purpose is my true business, since this has been given by God to each man as something that cannot be hindered.'[33] Therefore, he worshipped God.

'I have submitted my freedom of choice unto God. He wills that I shall have fever; it is my will too. He wills that I should choose something; it is my will too. He wills that I should desire something; it is my will too. He wills that I should get something; it is my wish too. He does not will it; I do not wish it. Therefore, it is my will to die; therefore, it is my will to be tortured on the rack. Who can hinder me any longer against my own views, or put compulsion upon me? . . . Why, if we had sense, ought we to be doing anything else, publicly and privately, than hymning and praising the Deity, and rehearsing His benefits? . . . I am a rational being, therefore I must be singing hymns of praise to God. This is my task; I do it, and will not desert this post, as long as it may be given me to fill it; and I exhort you to join me in this same song.'[34]

Epictetus's younger contemporary and student Marcus Aurelius (Plates 6*b*; 7*a*), has left us his *Meditations*. These dramatically intimate disclosures of his deepest thoughts do not form a connected unity, and were not intended for publication. The variety of notes and reflections which they contain, written in Greek and in a highly personal style, represent a diary of his inner life over a period of ten or fifteen years—a work of self-consolation and self-encouragement, a unique self-scrutiny, each separate passage reflecting its own mood. Much of this extraordinary compilation was composed in camp, after a long day's soldiering. For it was the profound misfortune of the contemplative Aurelius that he had to spend a great part of his life commanding imperial armies in the field. He was one of the nearest approaches in world history to Plato's true philosopher-king—a man of the highest principles and intellect who, called upon to rule a great empire, consciously put his creed into practice with unremitting devotion.[35]

And yet as Aurelius turned his mild, meditative yet firm gaze upon his life, he found much that he disliked, and his most frequent mood was a melancholy resignation. At the age of forty, he said, 'A man of average intelligence will have experienced everything that has been and is to come.' Yet that was the age, when apparently he saw nothing more of interest to hope for, at which he became emperor of Rome. Although he was without false modesty, glory meant nothing to him; he hated the life of the court and was vigilant against its moral dangers for the ruler.[36] What filled his heart was something far removed from such things—the struggle to free his own character from the power of evil and from ephemeral illusions.

Like Epictetus, he differed from the predominant religions of his day by gaining no comfort, in this struggle, from hopes of a happy afterlife. 'He who fears death fears either total loss of consciousness or a change of consciousness. Now if you should no longer possess consciousness, you will no longer be aware of any evil;

alternatively, if you possess an altered consciousness, you will be an altered creature and will not cease from living.'[37] Elsewhere he offers as a possible consolation of death the suggestion that the soul will then no longer be contaminated by degrading company. The thoughts of Aurelius revolved round death as a riddle; but it was a riddle without an answer, and his strength had to be drawn from elsewhere.

Although so uncertain of a life beyond the grave, he believed in the existence of divine powers.

'To those who ask the question: "Where have you seen the gods, or from what source have you apprehended that they exist, that you thus worship them?" First, they are visible even to the eyes. Secondly, I have not seen my own soul and yet I honour it; and so too with the gods, from my experiences, at every instant of their power I apprehend that they exist and I do them reverence.'[38]

He believed that the deity, whether singular or plural, is immanent in the world in such a way that God and the world united make one whole, like the soul and body. Following the Stoics who were his teachers, he knew that man must be true to himself, that is to the highest part of himself—the deity residing in his soul. Though always a prey to doubts, Aurelius felt that at certain times of his life instructions of superhuman origin had helped him: for instance in ill-health, when he had to combat spittings of blood and giddiness.

Nevertheless, despite such occasional contacts, he had less sense of a personal God than Epictetus. Like Zen Buddhism, he should appeal to the twentieth-century intellectual who likes religions without a god. For, in common with many before and after him, he could not reconcile the beneficence of Providence with the evils of the world—a world in which he could find no joy. Every day he woke to face those evils. 'What bathing is, if you think—oil, sweat, dirt, greasy water, everything disgusting—such is every part of our life and every object.' He would have liked to pray to his God about these flaws in the world; yet he felt that even if prayer might help himself, subjectively, to attain a right state of mind, it could not alter the passage of events. For Aurelius, like earlier Stoics, was not only, in his own way, religious, but grimly fatalistic. 'Up and down, to and fro, round and round: this is the monotonous and meaningless rhythm of the universe. Whatever befalls you was prepared for you beforehand from eternity, and the thread of causes was spinning from everlasting both your existence and this which befalls you.'[39] But how to reconcile this with an all-Provident God?

'Either the Necessity of destiny and an order none may transgress, or Providence that hears intercession, or an ungoverned welter without a purpose. If then a Necessity which none may transgress, why do you resist? If a Providence admitting intercession, make yourself worthy of assistance from the Godhead. If an undirected welter, be glad that in so great a flood of waves you have yourself within you a directing mind; and, if the flood carry you away, let it carry away flesh, vital spirit, the rest of you; for your mind it shall not carry away. Does the light of the lamp shine and not lose its radiance until it be put out, and shall truth and justice and temperance be put out in you before the end?'[40]

That answer is not very comforting. Man must just strive onwards, and continue his own unremittingly laborious efforts. The direction which such endeavours should take is illustrated by Aurelius's splendid eulogy of his predecessor and adoptive father Antoninus Pius (Plate 12d).[41] What emerges from that picture is the long-suffering patience of Antoninus, and above all his endurance. And the central, practical point of Aurelius's demands upon himself is the same: turn inwards, strengthen yourself, find the courage to fulfil your task—in his own case a task of almost unendurably burdensome responsibility. The *Meditations* show classic evidence of the human power to subdue circumstances, not by forced heroism—such as many see in Seneca—but by an anxious, enduring struggle for truth. The endeavours of the Hellenistic philosopher to escape by self-reliance from the vicissitudes of Fortune receive in Aurelius their most private and deeply-felt expression. 'Be like the headland on which the waves continually break, but which stands firm and about which the boiling waters sink to sleep. "Unlucky am I, because this has befallen me." No: lucky am I, because, though this befell me, I continue free from sorrow, neither crushed by the present nor fearing what is to come.'[42] So pray not for blessings, but for the power to do without them. 'Don't be disgusted, don't give up, don't be impatient if you do not carry out entirely conduct based in every detail upon right principles; but after a fall return again, and rejoice if most of your actions are worthier of human character.'[43]

This endurance in the right cause, this avoidance of any deviation into what is insincere or superficial, is only to be achieved by the cultivation of calm. There were no oriental mysticisms and sensualities for Aurelius. Nowhere can one find a more relentlessly destructive analysis of the pleasures of eye, ear, food and sex. Cultivate, Aurelius says, a sense of proportion about your own significance, and you will acquire the right degree of detachment. 'Ponder the life led by others long ago, the life that will be led after you, the life being led in uncivilized races; how many do not even know your name, how many will very soon forget it, and how many, who praise you perhaps now, will very soon blame you; and that neither memorial nor fame nor anything else at all is worth a thought.'

The ideal then is detachment, but only 'in respect of what comes to pass from a cause outside you. In so far, on the other hand, as you control the course of events yourself—by your control of your own will—justice must be the aim: that is to say, impulse and action terminating simply in neighbourly conduct, because for you this is according to Nature.'[44] This central belief in the primacy of the social instinct, an inherited but intensely-felt version of the Stoic and Ciceronian Brotherhood of Man, confers humanity upon the convictions of Aurelius—and is related by him to the problems of empire. 'I conceived an idea of a democratic state, administered according to equality and free speech, and of a monarchy that above all honoured the freedom of the governed.'[45]Citizen of the world as well as Rome, he sees himself, like other human beings, belonging to the supreme city in which the other cities are merely houses.

Yet these ideals must be seen against an imperial system, and even an administrative framework which Aurelius did not, apparently, seek to modify. Moreover, his self-reminders warred, in his heart, with a distaste—which he ruthlessly suppressed—for the many inadequate people he encountered every day.

'Just as those who oppose you, as you progress in agreement with right principle, will not be able to divert you from sound conduct, so do not let them force you to abandon your kindness towards them: but be on your guard in steady judgment and behaviour as well as in gentleness towards those who try to hinder you or are difficult in other ways. For to be hard upon them is a weakness just as much as to abandon your course and give in from fright; for both are equally deserters from their post, the man who is in a panic as well as the man who is alienated from his natural kinsman and friend.'[46]

This is a doctrine not so much of love as of tolerance, sometimes rather remote. 'Withdraw into yourself. . . . Another's wrong act you must leave where it is'[47] lacks the startling, revolutionary humanity of 'turn the other cheek'.[48] The overwhelming responsibilities and melancholic disposition of Aurelius were alike against him. Yet he needed friendship, and he longed to treat his fellow-men well and affectionately and to forgive them their injuries. 'Have I done a neighbourly act? I am therefore benefited. Let this always be ready to your mind, and never stop. . . . Men have come into the world for the sake of one another. Either instruct them, then, or bear with them. . . . Whoever does wrong, wrongs himself; whoever does injustice, does it to himself, making himself evil.'[49] It would be hard indeed to find any monarch—almost any man—in the history of the world who, despite only a limited, impersonal degree of support from his religion, so genuinely desired to do good to his fellow-men, even if his ability to do so were limited by a social and political system that he did not reform.

The personality of Marcus Aurelius has inevitably aroused the most contradictory reactions among his readers. Some have been profoundly influenced by the knowledge that during his reign there were severe persecutions of the Christian communities in Asia Minor and Gaul (p. 187). There is no evidence that Aurelius had studied the doctrines of the Christians. His one reference to them contains a criticism of their unhesitating readiness to be martyrs, whereas death, if deliberately chosen, should be chosen 'after reflection and with dignity'.[50] But this parenthetic observation should not be related to the persecutions, which were, for Aurelius's governors, not a doctrinal so much as a civic matter, relating to the alleged danger of these communities as disobedient states within a state (p. 186).

Anyone who has revealed himself so privately and so ruthlessly makes himself vulnerable to criticism. Aurelius has been blamed for unoriginality, ineffectual mildness, weariness, doubt, insecurity, failure to reconcile religion and philosophy, too frequent remoteness on chilly Stoic heights, too little will to live, an absence of the burning passion by which the greatest prophets have won mass-support. But in the nineteenth century his morality was seen to be singularly appropriate for those ages (unlike his own) 'which walk by sight and not by faith'. To Renan, his high moral sense face to face with the universe was a gospel which never grows old. John Stuart Mill placed him at the summit of all previous attainments of humanity. For Matthew Arnold, he is 'perhaps the most beautiful figure in history'. His is that rarest combination of lofty royalty and humble humanity, of extreme purity of feeling and exceptional consistency in action. Apart from his one disastrous error of allowing his son Commodus to succeed him (p. 29), Marcus Aurelius is one of the noblest of those men who have achieved their goodness without the insistent prompting of a religious inspiration or encouragement.

Part IV

LITERATURE AND THE ARTS

CHAPTER 8

THE GREAT LATIN WRITERS

THE philosophers who have just been described culminated in a great Roman, Marcus Aurelius, who reflected the bilingual culture of his age by writing his *Meditations* in Greek. But two of his predecessors in this field, Cicero and Seneca, distilled their largely Greek learning in Latin. Their achievements in this medium recall how sharply Latin literature differs from the other, visual arts of the Roman world, since those, as Virgil knew (p. 50), did not receive their supreme expression from the hands of Romans. Virgil told the Romans to govern instead—that, he said, was their task. But they also excelled at that art of literature of which he himself was already recognized in his lifetime as the supreme master. Like the English, the Romans were a people whose often second-rate level of attainment in other arts may be sharply contrasted with the excellence of what they wrote, including above all their poetry.

This excellence was partly due to the exceptional qualities of the Latin tongue. The literature of the Romans achieved magnificent originality because their language proved able to create both resonant, vigorously compact prose and poetry of a stirringly profound, harmonious musicality. The architects, painters and sculptors of the Roman world used Greek media for their art, which thus inevitably, however bold and new its expression, formed a direct development from Hellenistic models. Latin writers, on the other hand, even when they were seeking—as they proudly desired— to model themselves closely upon Greek forerunners, were limited in the exactness of their imitation not only by convention, which demanded a variation from the model, but by the character of their own great language, which differed totally from the language of the Greeks. So literature gave the Romans their special opportunity for artistic achievement. The extent to which they took that opportunity is apparent in the contrast between the artistic merits of the Latin and Greek literatures during this period of Roman rule. Although the idiom of other arts and also the language of millions of highly educated people throughout Rome's eastern territories continued to be Greek, yet Greek literature had shot its bolt. Extensive and informative as its productions still were, they no longer compared in quality with the masterpieces of the Latin writers. Some decorative epigrams by men such as Meleager of Gadara (c. 140–70 BC), the amusing scepticalities of another easterner, Lucian of Samosata (p. 134), are now about the best, in aesthetic content, that can be set against the astonishing Latin output of the four centuries spanning the beginning of the Christian era; and with the mighty influence of Latin works upon subsequent literature and thought, Marcus Aurelius, the biographer Plutarch of Chaeronea, the third-century philosopher Plotinus, and a fresh and penetrating literary critic wrongly known as 'Longinus' are the only contemporary writers in Greek—except the authors of the New Testament—who can compete.

The opportunity given to the Romans by their language was made the more compelling and inviting by the nature of Roman education (p. 69). For all its faults, the pronouncedly linguistic and literary bent of the system seemed specially calculated to produce orators and writers; and two aspects of this educational pattern, one limiting and the other broadening in its effects, exercised powerful influences upon what was achieved. The limiting factor was the narrow social spread of Roman education: since adequate educational facilities were usually available only for the richer classes of the community, Latin literature is largely a product of those classes, and its subject-matter is restricted accordingly. So, incidentally, is its informative value for the student of history; in spite of all that it tells us, a glance at the references at the end of this book will show how often it is necessary to supplement the great Latin writers by drawing upon sources, Greek as well as Latin, which can only by the most charitable interpretation, if at all, be dignified by the name of literature. On the other hand, this same social limitation has its advantages, for it gives Latin literature a peculiar quality of intimate self-revelation and self-analysis which is absent from most Greek writings and is, indeed, something new. As Sir Maurice Bowra has pointed out, we too often think of the Greeks as arch-individualists and of the Romans as men with public minds and public faces, but the literature tells a very different story. It is, instead, the Greeks who have written for a whole people, and the Romans who write largely for small groups, for their friends and colleagues and equals—sometimes they seem almost to be writing for themselves alone. The resultant privacy, the absence of a public platform, makes it possible for them to dwell in new ways upon the human condition, and to hand down to the world new explorations of the relation of one human being to another, of man to man, and of man to woman. That is one of the greatest of their contributions.

But if the influence of Roman educational practices upon Latin literature has a narrowing effect in the social sense, its results in a geographical sense are broadening. For, seeing that Latin became the second and then often the first language of all the western regions of the Roman empire, the upper-class educational system based upon this tongue was extended throughout the same territories. Those educated in Latin, therefore, included not only Romans and other Italians, but men of mixed race from Cisalpine Gaul (north Italy), Gauls from beyond the Alps, Spaniards, and north Africans. Here are seen the finest fruits of Romanization; just as the élites of the western territories provided the greatest emperors of the second and third centuries AD, so also, long before that, they had contributed even more than Rome itself to the literature which had become their common concern.

At the outset of Roman literary history one of the leading writers is believed to have been a north African. This was the comic dramatist Terence (c. 195–159 BC), a protégé of the conqueror of Carthage, Scipio Aemilianus. To the vigorous, rowdy technique of the Umbrian genius Plautus, brilliantly adapting to Latin the unfamiliar quantitative metres of Menander (c. 341–290 BC) and other dramatists of the Athenian New Comedy, Terence added impeccable Latinity as well as Hellenic refinement. Less than a century after his death Roman literature reached full maturity—before the Roman visual arts—when Latin prose-writing was raised to its climax by Cicero. An Italian from Arpinum, he did not, in origin, belong to the charmed circle of the Roman ruling-class. But he gained admission to that class, and attained its highest honour, the consulship. For to a society dominated by debates in the Senate, Assembly and law courts, talent in oratory—to which the whole educational system was geared—provided a means of entry scarcely less effective than prowess in war. Cicero's successes prove that he was one of the most convincing orators who have ever lived. His speeches, from which quotations will be found elsewhere in this book, have contributed in countless ways to the behaviour of western societies. For instance, like Cicero's private letters, of which many have survived, these speeches reveal the many vicissitudes experienced by the Romans during the last disastrous years of the time when their government was, to a large extent, still conducted by the cut and thrust of debate. Such lessons seemed invaluable to Petrarch and to the Italian city-states of the Renaissance from which so much of modern political and social thought has developed. Moreover in his speeches against Verres, Catiline and Antony, Cicero displayed how, when gross misrule threatened, even a timid man like himself was able to rise to the occasion and fight against the menace.

But Cicero's greatest gift to humanity through his speeches is his incomparable use of the Latin language, which was to supply the people of many centuries to come with an unrivalled vehicle for effective expression and thought. The force of his oratory was strengthened by innumerable devices—endlessly studied by posterity —of word-order, emphasis, contrast, repetition, question and exclamation. It was Cicero who played the decisive part in moulding the Latin sentence into the 'period', the multiple unit in which clauses are built up into an integrated, rounded, organic whole, orchestrated by a subtle, sonorous rhythm. The Romans were intensely susceptible to such sound effects, which no one before or after him has ever been able to exploit better than Cicero. A millennium and a half later, the diction that he forged, in spite of incipient reactions towards the Spaniard Seneca's more pointed style, was still the language of governments, churches, universities and scientists. Of the theory and infinitely careful technique under-lying his oratorical triumphs Cicero himself writes in a series of treatises, particularly the *De Oratore*, *Orator*, and *Brutus*. In these, among a wealth of other material, he elaborates his conviction that the study of oratory requires as its framework, and itself should be the basis for, a truly liberal education (p. 69). But the most significant of his treatises, in their contribution to man's understanding of himself as a social animal, are the superbly written, easily flowing popularizations of Greek philosophy in which, like the versatile Seneca a century later, he sought to describe how an educated Roman can employ as his own guide that most enlightened of pagan beliefs, the Stoic doctrine of the Brotherhood of Man (p. 194).

Roman secondary education concentrated to an extraordinary extent
on the study and interpretation of both Greek and Latin poetry,
because it was felt that this was the key both to effective public
speaking and to the truly cultured life (p. 68). During the lifetime
of Cicero, after nearly a century of development based on the later
Greek models of scholarly, individualistic Alexandria, Latin poetry
reached two very different peaks under Lucretius and Catullus.
Lucretius, a mysterious figure of unknown origin, gave burning
expression, in hexameters of a force which Tennyson is not the only
man to have found irresistible, to the philosophical way of life
proclaimed by Epicurus (p. 190). Catullus, a citizen of Verona
(which only came within the borders of Italy after he was dead)
revealed a new world of personal, violent intimacy. Though an
unfailingly careful craftsman, his sense of form serves his need to
express emotion : and it is as a poet of love that he has won his fame.
The orgiastic religion of the hymn to Attis is revealing but exceptional; and this too may have had something to do with love
(p. 170). What Catullus explored with an unprecedented intensity,
reflecting his own deeply emotional character, was the relation
between the sexes. He wrote with poignant lyricism of his love for
'Lesbia'—a literary name for Clodia, the most notorious of the
women leading the smart metropolitan society to which Catullus
also belonged.

There were brief times of superlative happiness.

> Surely that man equals the gods in heaven—
> if it be not blasphemy, he excels them—
> he who sits and, constantly, in your presence,
>   watches and hears you
> laugh with sweetness such that my shaken senses
> leave me helpless. Lesbia, at the moment
> when I first caught sight of you, then my voice was
>   struck into silence,
> tongue benumbed, light delicate flame pervaded
> every limb, loud inward alarms were ringing
> through my ears, while suddenly both my eyes were
>   covered with darkness.[1]

But this love for Lesbia, the driving force behind all the poetry
of Catullus, rocked towards an ultimate, irretrievable disaster. Only
some deep-seated resource of his personality—perhaps the same
power which made him, in other poems, a ferocious satirist—saved

him from a disintegration equal to the collapse, amid the contemporary horrors of civil strife, of Rome itself. His last message to Lesbia is painful.

> You, my two old friends, who remain my comrades,
> whether I may journey to furthest India,
> where the sea-beach booms to the pounding monsoon's
>   thunderous combers,
> or among Hyrcanians, supple Arabs,
> fierce Sacae, or dangerous Parthian bowmen,
> or to where seven mouths of the Nile, debouching,
>   darken the azure,
> or perhaps may travel the Alpine passes
> towards the new-won triumphs of mighty Caesar,
> Rhine, the Gauls' frontier, and the terrifying
>   outermost British,
> you whom I know willing wherever heaven
> sends me forth, to share my adventures with me,
> take for me these words to my girl, a message
>   short and unpleasant.
> Give her my good-bye, her and all her lovers,
> whom she hugs so close to her in their hundreds,
> loving not one, yet with her constant lusting
>   leaving their loins limp.
> Gone is all my love, which she once respected—
> murdered through her guilt, as a flower blooming
> out upon the edge of the meadow falls when
>   touched by the ploughshare.[2]

Few, says Gilbert Highet who translated these passages, have said what they felt so trenchantly, have suffered such bold arrogant emotions as this poet with his 'rude violence and heartwarming affection'; few have written so little—less than 2,300 lines survive—and yet covered such a vast range of feeling, have been so outrageously direct and so maddeningly inconsistent. The fresh, lucid individualism of Catullus helped to inspire the humanist poets of the Italian Renaissance—though Rimbaud now seems closer to him in spirit. And yet these personal, subjective, intensely sincere poems were created, many of them, within the framework of the rather cold, objective, amatory epigrams of the Alexandrian Greeks: a striking example of the Roman capacity to utilize a Greek genre and its Greek exponents, and yet, through the medium of their own wholly distinct language and talent, to transmute what they found into something original.

> You poor Catullus, don't be such a crass-brained fool!
> All that is obviously lost, you must write off.
> The sun shone brightly on you once, in days gone by,
> when you would follow everywhere the girl led on—
> the girl I loved as no girl ever will be loved.
> Yes, then we had a thousand thousand pleasant games,
> and you enjoyed them, and the girl did not hold back.
> It's true: you lived in sunshine then, in times long gone.
> Now she refuses. You then must refuse, you too;
> don't follow when she runs, don't live a poor fool's life;
> control your heart, endure it all, and be steel-hard.
> Good-bye now, girl. Catullus has become steel-hard.
> He will not chase you, beg for you against your will;
> but you will surely suffer when you're asked no more.
> You devil, you. What kind of life will you lead now?
> Who will come courting you, and who will call you sweet?
> Whom will you love, and whose girl will they say you are?
> Whose lips will you be kissing now, with love-sharp bites?
> No, no, Catullus, be determined: be steel-hard![3]

Some fourteen years younger than Catullus was Virgil. He too came from north Italy: from a farm near Mantua, where there was so mixed a population of Etruscans, Celtic Gauls and Romans that the poet's racial origin is long beyond recall. Catullus had shown in sharper relief than ever before the suffering of a single human being destroyed by unhappy love; Virgil gave unequalled expression to the labours, sufferings and hopes of the whole human race. In his earlier works, the *Eclogues* and *Georgics*, there are foreshadowings of this universality. The first and ninth *Eclogues*, going beyond their pastoral subject, tell of the miseries and losses of civil war, and the fourth of these poems (40 BC) reflects, in terms that were to make Christians believe Virgil their prophet, the conviction (widespread in Mediterranean and middle-eastern lands) that a Saviour was about to come and rid the world of the miseries into which it had fallen. The *Georgics*, suggested to Virgil by his patron Maecenas, are a paean to traditional and Augustan Italy, praising—in poetry that seemed to Dryden incomparable—the beauties, labours and rewards of the rustic life. But the fourth book of the *Georgics* rises far above the countryman's world. The lives of bees, which ostensibly form its theme, are told with that incomparable Virgilian pathos which, amid a people who were far from tender-hearted, strikes so poignant and distinct a note. Living their organized lives filled with dramas and battles, the bees provide a pathetic, mock-heroic commentary on the troubles of human beings. The book culminates with the tragic legend of Eurydice and her lover Orpheus, the greatest of all singers and patrons of poetry—whom the hero of the *Aeneid* was to meet before all others in the world of the dead. The potency of song had reached its zenith in Orpheus. Yet when, leading Eurydice from the Underworld, he flouted the divine ordinance and looked behind him, no power of his was enough to save her. For Virgil, as for the Alexandrian Greeks under whose influence he and Catullus developed their original genius, this was the greatest and saddest of all tales of love; and many modern writers, especially in France, have been unable to escape from its fascination.

This sad, nostalgic note recurs in the peace-loving rural elegies of a younger contemporary, Tibullus, who belonged to the côterie of the Augustan nobleman Messalla; to Tibullus, even more than Virgil, both country life and love are, beneath their smiling surface, as precarious and insecure as men's lives were in his day, and through his pellucid verses runs an undercurrent of loss, and of the transience and deprival of happiness.

Virgil's *Georgics* fuse old traditions, semi-historical memories, literary reminiscences, folk-tale, and romance. The same threads and many more are interwoven, again so as to become something wholly new, in the twelve books of his epic poem the *Aeneid*. Escaping from the ruins of Troy, in flames and overrun by the Greeks, the devoted and deeply religious Aeneas and his followers, after an Odyssey of strange and portentous experiences, reach the shores of Italy. Resistance by the Latins and other tribes is finally quelled, and peace is made; Aeneas marries a Latin bride. The stage is set for the foundation of Rome—and the fulfilment of its destiny by Augustus who, in the poet's own time, had likewise brought peace to the war-torn Roman world. For this is a national epic, following a tradition created for Rome in the time of the Punic Wars—with the crudeness of their age—by Naevius and Ennius.

During his wanderings upon the seas, Aeneas lands in north Africa, where the Queen of Carthage, Dido, falls in love with him;

and her love is returned. But destiny calls Aeneas on to Italy, doomed in history to be Carthage's enemy. So he must abandon Dido. Their story is the climax of romantic epic. There are echoes of many forerunners, and especially of the interpretation of the tormented Medea by Euripides, and again by Apollonius the Rhodian in Hellenistic Alexandria. Yet Virgil's own unique sensibility transfuses and dominates all his sources.

> Even thus was the hero belaboured for long with every kind of
> Pleading, and his great heart thrilled through and through
>   with the pain of it;
> Resolute, though, was his mind; unavailingly rolled her tears.
> But hapless Dido, frightened out of her wits by her destiny,
> Prayed for death: she would gaze no more on the dome of
>   daylight.[4]

Dido symbolizes a harrowing conflict. As the dilemma of Aeneas has engaged the fascinated attention of readers throughout the centuries—it distracted the youthful St Augustine from thoughts of his faith—some have felt that Virgil's sympathy for losing sides is so great that the main issue is obscured: Dido is indeed human, but Aeneas, as servant of Fate, seems insipid in comparison. Yet according to the very different standpoint of Virgil, widespread among thoughtful people in his day, Aeneas represented that fusion of the Roman and Stoic ideals, the man who presses on, in unremitting endeavour, regardless of the buffets and obstacles of life (p. 198). There is also a dramatic evolution of his character. The first epic hero to be an adult human being rather than a superman or superhuman adolescent, he does not at once become the complete Stoic; he has his weaknesses, and only gradually overcomes them. Though destiny prevails, freedom of will is not excluded: the interweaving of the two is what gives poignancy to the story of Aeneas and Dido.

The turning point of the *Aeneid* comes in its sixth book when Aeneas, landing in Italy, is granted spiritual initiation into his new realm. Guided to the Golden Bough by the Sibyl, he is empowered to go down with her through Lake Avernus to the Underworld. This is a conscious echo of Odysseus's communion with the Shades in Homer's *Odyssey*. Yet the extrovert world of the oral, ballad-like Homeric epic is far away, and overladen by an amazing variety of other strata of tradition, thought, philosophy, legend and feeling. These are miraculously blended and transfigured into Virgil's profoundest expression of his own beliefs and intuitions of the universe. Like the Stoics of his day (p. 194), he recognizes the guidance of a superhuman power:

> For God (they hold) pervades
> All lands, the widespread seas, the abysms of unplumbed
>   sky:
> From whom flocks, herds, men, every wild creature in its
>   kind
> Derive at birth the slight, precarious breath of life. [5]

For Virgil this divinity thus shared among all mankind is extended, together with his own fellow-feeling, to the rest of animal creation. Yet it is man who, by reason of his greater endowments and destiny, experiences and suffers the most. When Aeneas has come to Italy, there is almost intolerable sadness in his magnificently misguided, doomed foe Turnus, and in the more youthful, frailer figures crushed in the remorseless progress of events as many had been crushed in the civil wars of his own day.

> Yes, Aeneas drove his strong sword
> Right through the young man's body, and buried it
>   there to the hilt.
> It penetrated his light shield, frail armour for so
>   aggressive
> A lad, and the tunic his mother had woven of pliant
>   gold,
> And soaked it with blood from his breast. Then the soul
>   left the body,
> Passing sadly away through the air to the land of shadows
> But when Aeneas beheld the dying boy's look, his face—
> A face that by now was strangely grey—he felt pity for
>   him,
> And a deep sigh escaped him . . . [6]

Aeneas is a truly tragic figure, in the spirit of the Attic tragedy of which there are many echoes in this poem. For his suffering comes from what is noblest in him, his humanity—from sympathy with the pain and sorrow which his divine, murderous, patriotic destiny must inflict upon others. Virgil knows the weariness and frustration of war. He knows also its inevitability, and is at one with Augustus who had fought to bring peace. Yet the poet's ultimate conviction seems to have been that military conquest mattered less than man's conquest of himself. He died at the age of fifty-one without quite finishing the *Aeneid*; if he had lived he had intended to turn to philosophy. Like those who, in their different ways, shared his deep desire for philosophical and religious guidance, he depicts the individual as uncertain of his goal and his place in the Universe, calling for some personal salvation and satisfaction in life beyond the performance of duties imposed by destiny and the state (p. 159).

By the word-pictures in which he generated these beliefs Virgil led human self-knowledge along new paths. To literature's traditional unity of action he added unity of feeling, a new dimension comparable to the use of atmosphere and light by a painter, or of harmony and counterpoint by a composer. Employing this novel complexity of design, his poetry achieves infinite profundities: hitherto unimaginably subtle interconnections, balances and undulations, and symbols interweaving sensuous, spiritual and intellectual images far exceeding any simple literal significance of the words in which they are framed. It was Virgil who created the stately rhythmical and periodic structure, the symphonic grandeur, which Milton echoed in English. Virgil's poetry attained the ultimate subtlety and sonority of which the elaborate inflections, malleable word-order and imposing musical potentialities of the Latin language are capable.

As the centuries went by, the achievement seemed of more than human greatness: the Middle Ages held Virgil to be a magician. To multitudes of others, for generation after generation, he has been a leader, halting sometimes but never failing, and a sad but faithful friend who has helped them to a better understanding of the grandeur and uncertainty, the heroism and tragic pathos, of the human condition.

One other Augustan poet rose to a universal comprehension of human problems, or at least of the problems which confronted his own segment of mankind. This was Horace, who came from Venusia in south-east Italy, and, being the son or grandson of a slave— perhaps a prisoner of war—was of as indeterminate race as his predecessor as poet laureate, Virgil. After the bitter *Epodes* of his early years spent amid the privations of civil war, Horace's *Satires* modernized a Hellenistic and Roman tradition—of which the leading native exponent had been Lucilius, friend of Scipio

Aemilianus—in graceful, familiar verse with a humane, moralizing tone. This vein achieved maturity in the *Epistles*, which have made a strong impact on many a generation as the witty and charming products of a tasteful, gently philosophical and highly civilized mind; among them is the *Ars Poetica*, notes on poetry in which Horace gave an adroit, ironic twist to what he took over from the Alexandrian Greeks. In his lyric *Odes* the poetic inspiration is richer, though modified by the conviction that Augustus the peace-bringer was admirable: a belief which Horace shared with the otherwise profoundly different Virgil. But whereas neither poet is servile, Horace, with his keen sense of humour and surprise, is markedly detached and politely—or if necessary less politely—independent; cherishing, amid all his stress on fate or fortune, the capacity to withstand their onslaughts and temptations—cherishing, that is to say, the human dignity of his own free will.

> Thy portion is a wealthy stock,
> A fertile glebe, a fruitful flock,
> Horses and chariots for thine ease,
> Rich robes to deck and make thee please.
> For me, a little cell I choose,
> Fit for my mind, fit for my Muse,
> Which soft content does best adorn,
> Shunning the knaves and fools I scorn.[7]

The seventeenth century, in which Thomas Otway and others translated such sentiments, was an age in which, after the more moral *Epistles* had long eclipsed them, there was a great vogue in England for Horace's *Odes*. In Italy they had come into their own with Petrarch, who bought a manuscript in 1347 and quoted Horace more than any other poet except Virgil.

The *Odes* adapt, with the genius of a great originator, the Greek metres of his professed models the earlier Greek poets Sappho, Anacreon and Alcaeus whom he claimed it was his patriotic mission to Romanize. The astutely grouped, expressively concise Latin of this unique craftsman in words ranges freely, in various manners that are all his own, from wine to the gods, Horace's friends, the beauty of nature, the transience of human life, the folly of exaggeration, and—sometimes in riddling terms—affairs of state. He also writes often about love. But Horace, in spite of his amorous themes and models, can scarcely be called a love-poet, for he does not usually treat the theme seriously; like Augustus, he has a double standard of feminine values, one for the true-born Roman woman—whose virtue the emperor was at pains to protect—and one for every other woman. In the hands of Horace, this distinction becomes a vehicle for tender or brutal ridicule of many a frail, Greek-named girl or hag, and of the lovers who chased them or their own desire to be chased.

> How long, old Madam, will you carry on
> This monstrous racket, which your patient lord
> so obviously can't afford?
> Your lease of life is nearly done,
> Yet, midst the golden girls you play and ply,
> A blot on their bright galaxy,
> Forgetting that what Pholoe may do
> Is less acceptable in you.
> Your daughter, now, is at the age
> To storm a bachelor's chambers, and rampage
> Like a daft Maenad with a tambourine;
> Poor darling, she's in love, and so
> Must be allowed to play the wanton roe!
> For you, 'tis time to quit the scene,
> The red rose in the wig, the violins,
> The red wine drained; for at your age, you know,
> A body stays at home and spins.[8]

Yet at other times a deeper chord is touched:

> *Horace:* When that I was acceptable to thee,
> And round thy white neck never arm would cling
> Of any young man luckier than me,
> Then was I prouder than a Persian king.
> *Lydia:* When that thou burnedst with no other flame,
> Nor Chloe was preferred to Lydia,
> Then did I live with a more splendid name
> And more renowned than Roman Ilia.
> *Horace:* Well, Thracian Chloe is my mistress now,
> Skilled in soft notes, and on the harp to play,
> For whom, if the three Sisters would allow,
> I would give up life to prolong her day.
> *Lydia:* I burn for Calais as he for me,
> The son of Ornytus in Thurii,
> And if those Sisters would allow that he
> Should so survive, twice for him would I die.

Horace :   What if the old love should come back again
        To bind us once more with its yoke of brass?
    Blonde Chloe cast off, what if should remain
        Open those lost doors where I used to pass?

Lydia :   Were he more lovely than the evening star,
        Thou lighter than a cork and more awry
    Than billows of the Adriatic are,
        With thee I'd love to live and gladly die.[9]

In this happy reconciliation Horace seems almost to desert the calmness with which he usually looks at love.

His contemporary Propertius of Assisi, the most appealing of the Roman elegists to modern ears, is rarely calm. The love of Propertius for Cynthia is passionate and disastrous:

Cynthia first enslaved me with her fatal eyes.
    I had been uninfected by desire,
but then love made me lower my proud unwavering gaze
    and placed his tyrannous foot upon my head,
remorseless, training me to hate all virtuous girls
    and lead a purposeless and wanton life.
Now for a year this madness has afflicted me
    and still I live like a damned soul in hell.[10]

Catullus, too, had known this experience of catastrophic love as a maddening magic spell and a slavery condemning man to a detestable life. Yet Propertius, on both sides—like Baudelaire—of the shifting obscure border between classic and romantic, explores whole new regions of the human spirit by his brooding abandonment to sensibility, his morbid unselfcontrolled absorption in self-pity, and the lush but sombre imagery into which the daemonic torrent of his feeling is poured. Yet ever and again, this pathological surrender to his own emotions is redeemed by a kind of mock-modest irony, evident, for example, as he tells of this unsuccessful attempt to console himself for the unfaithfulness of absent Cynthia:

After so many insults offered to my bed,
    I moved to the offensive, led the charge.
There is a girl called Phyllis on the Aventine—
    when sober, unattractive : charming drunk.
Then there is Teia—lives near the Tarpeian Park—
    a lovely thing, but hard to satisfy.

These I invited to relieve my night alone,
    and, with strange lovers, start a new intrigue.
A single couch was set for the three in a private garden,
    and I had one fair charmer at each side.
My Lygdamus served drinks in lightweight summer glasses,
    the pure juices from Methymna, rich and strong.
A Nile boy played the pipes, Phyllis the castanets;
    we scattered simple roses for our scent.
The Mighty Mite, with all his dwarfish limbs contracted,
    tossed his short arms in time to the flageolets.

Yet, though the lamps were often filled, the light kept sinking;
    the table tottered and fell upside down;
and while I diced and played always for double sixes,
    I threw the miserable double ace.
The girls sang: I was deaf: showed their breasts: I was blind:
    I felt alone and wretched, far away . . .
when suddenly the house gate opened, grating slowly,
    confused murmurs were heard out in the hall,
and in a moment Cynthia burst open both doors,
    her hair was not elegant, but neat—and furious.
My fingers lost their grip. The wine-cup clattered down.
    My lips, though loose and hot with wine, grew pale.
Her eyes were thunderbolts; she raged like a woman;
    she looked as frightful as a captured city.
She hooked her furious nails into Phyllis's eyes,
    while Teia cried 'Help! Fire!' to all the neighbours.
The lights went on all round, the sleeping Romans woke,
    the whole street raved—a midnight delirium.
The girls, with hair torn and with all their dresses disordered,
    dashed through the darkness to a neighbouring bar—
while Cynthia raved triumphantly over the loot they left,
    then turned to me, slashed a fist in my face,
left a scar on my neck, sank bloody teeth in my shoulder,
    and in particular bruised my guilty eyes.
After her muscles had grown tired with thrashing me,
    next Lygdamus, cowering beside the couch,
was dragged out prostrate, begging mercy in my name.
    (Lygdamus, I was a helpless captive too).
At last I offered unconditional surrender
    and grovelled. She *just* let me touch her foot,
and said, 'If you wish absolution for your sin,
    here are the firm conditions of my pact.

You shall not dress smartly to stroll the avenues,
   or linger round the entrance at the fights;
never look up and backwards towards the gallery;
   or stop to chat beside a lady's chair.
And, item one, let Lygdamus, my chief complaint,
   be sold in fetters on the auction block.'

Those were her conditions. 'I accept,' said I.
   She laughed, arrogant with victory.
Then, each and every spot touched by the visiting girls
   she disinfected; washed the threshold clean;
directed me to change my clothes, not once, but twice;
   and touched my head three times with burning sulphur.
So, after she had changed each separate sheet and blanket,
   I kissed her. We made peace, all over the bed.[11]

Very different was that other elegist, likewise from central Italy, who was Propertius's junior by ten years, Ovid of Sulmo (Sulmona). Too young to be seared by the civil wars, he lacked Virgil's high purpose and Horace's acceptance of Augustan morality. Innumerable Renaissance writings and paintings were inspired by his brilliantly narrated love stories—especially those of the rapid, dexterous *Metamorphoses*, prime source of classical myths; and before that, in medieval times, his works played a great part in creating the ideal of Romantic Love. Yet Ovid himself was no romantic, and had reacted decisively against the unrestrained personal feelings expressed by Catullus and Propertius. Ovid, representative of a frivolous sophisticated metropolitan society, observed love's passion coolly. That indeed is his contribution to our understanding of the human condition: of which, to him, the most important aspect was the relationship between men and women. True, Horace also had observed this relationship dispassionately, but Ovid brought to the task an Alexandrian absorption in psychology, and particularly in the psychology of women. He is the first male poet to understand, and often to understand tenderly—if not always with respect—the point of view of the females whose emancipation he likes to sponsor. In the *Heroides*, a collection of 'epistles' mostly purporting to be addressed by legendary women to their absent husbands, there is an almost sinister acuteness in the determined, and then not so determined, resistance offered by Helen to Paris, her importunate guest from Troy:

How dares a stranger, with designs so vain,
Marriage and hospitable rights profane?
Was it for this, your fate did shelter find
From swelling seas and every faithless wind? . . .
Does this deserve to be rewarded so?
Did you come here a stranger, or a foe?

For both our hopes, alas, you came too late;
Another now is master of my fate.
More to my wish I could have lived with you,
And yet my present lot can undergo,
Cease to solicit a weak woman's will,
And urge not her you love, to so much ill. . . .

My hand is yet untaught to write to men;
This is the essay of my unpractised pen.
Happy those nymphs whom use has perfect made!
I think all crime, and tremble at a shade.
Even while I write, my fearful conscious eyes
Look often back, misdoubting a surprise.
For now the rumour spreads among the crowd,
At Court in whispers, but in town aloud.
Dissemble you, whate'er you hear them say:
To leave off loving were your better way—
Yet if you will dissemble it, you may.
Love secretly: the absence of my lord
More freedom gives, but does not all afford.
Long is his journey, long will be his stay,
Called by affairs of consequence away.
To go or not when unresolved he stood,
I bid him make what swift return he could:
Then, kissing me, he said: 'I recommend
'All to thy care, but most my Trojan friend.'
I smiled at what he innocently said,
And only answered: 'You shall be obeyed.'
Propitious winds have borne him far from hence,
But let not this secure your confidence.
Absent he is, yet absent he commands;
You know the proverb, *princes have long hands.*

You court with words, when you should force employ;
A rape is requisite to shamefaced joy.
Indulgent to the wrongs which we receive,

Our sex can suffer what we dare not give.
What have I said! For both of us 'twere best
Our kindling fires if each of us suppressed.
The faith of strangers is too prone to change,
And, like themselves, their wandering passions range. . . .

Yet fears like these should not my mind perplex
Were I as wife as many of my sex,
But time and you may bolder thoughts inspire; .
and I perhaps may yield to your desire.
You last demand a private conference:
These are your words, but I can guess your sense.
Your unripe hopes their harvest must attend:
Be ruled by me, and time may be your friend.
This is enough to let you understand,
For now my pen has tired my tender hand.
My woman knows the secret of my heart,
And may hereafter better news impart.[12]

Helen's thoughts and fears, wavering into desires, are brought
before us with the skill of a professional advocate and all the devices
of school-taught rhetoric, of which Ovid was the most skilful poetic
exponent. His sexual realism was recaptured 'by the poets of the
English Restoration, but without his gaiety and amoral unconsciousness of wrongdoing. He sees love as a self-confessed indulgence, an
inevitable pathological phenomenon—often a misfortune—with
strange results upon which to ponder. 'And now,' wrote a historian
of Latin literature in 1898, 'the insidious attractions of vice were
flaunted in the most glowing colours in the face of day.' It is, indeed,
true that the principal subject of Ovid's poems is sexual gratification
with women. Such gratification, he assumes, is wanted by all—not
least, by women insisting to the contrary—and his *Art of Love*, with
clinical efficiency rather than lubricity, advises a man how to set
about it.

The birds will leave their song in spring, the crickets
    be dumb in summer, dogs will flee from hares,
sooner than women flee from tactful wooers.
    Although she seems unwilling, yet she will. . . .

Come then, take heart, you'll conquer every woman:
    hardly one in ten thousand will refuse.
Refuse or not, they'll love you more for asking. . . .[13]

Ovid's advice is to get to know them when they gather at public shows.

> Like ants who come and go in lengthy columns,
>> bearing their small provisions in their mouths,
>> like bees flying over their perfumed pastures
> and skimming flowers and herbs and scented thyme—
> the finest women crowd to the arena:
>> their numbers often set my choice at fault.
> It is a place fatal to honest beauty,
>> where women go to see, and to be seen.[14]

The women, on the other hand, are informed how to make the best of themselves:

> Care brings you beauty, and neglect will kill it,
>> though it were lovelier than Venus's self.
> If our foremothers could neglect their beauty,
>> it was because our forefathers were rude. . . .
> These were the simple days. Now Rome is golden,
>> rich with the treasures of the conquered world. . .
> Men are bewitched by elegance—your coiffure
>> should gain its beauty from incessant care.
> And styles are manifold. Consult your mirror
>> to choose the mode which decorates you best.
> A narrow face demands divided tresses. . . .
> Round faces need a knot above the forehead
>> to bind the hair and yet reveal the ears. . .
>
> If you are small, sit down, or you'll appear to
>> even while you stand. Lie often at full length,
> and then conceal your stature while reclining
>> and cast a covering above your feet.
> A slender girl should dress in solid textures
>> and wear them loosely hanging from her neck.
> A pallid girl should clothe herself in purple. . . .
> Your lover must not find the dressing-table
>> covered with lotions. Art conceals its art.[15]

But Ovid ended his days, to his continually expressed misery, with nine years of exile at Tomi (Constanta) on the Black Sea, where Augustus had sent him, as the poet cryptically asserts, for *a poem and a mistake:*

> 'Ill fares the bard in this unlettered land—
> None to consult, and none to understand.'[16]

The poem that brought down this thunderbolt may well have been one of those in which he so cynically flaunts his failure to appreciate Augustus's bourgeois standards of morality; and his sequel and antidote to the *Art*, the *Remedy of Love*, in which he tells how to avoid the encumbrance, was scarcely serious enough to win back the emperor's favour.

Ovid was the last of the great poets in Rome's literary Golden Age who broke new ground as explorers of the relation between one human being and another. He had humanized mythology and its *affaires*; he had also reduced wide areas of human relations to the level of sexual seduction. Within the framework of the antique tradition, thus strained to the uttermost, there seemed little more to be said; though many more poets tried to say it. But by the greatest of them, Juvenal, a century later (p. 41), Ovid's cool survey of the sexual predicament was transmuted into a no less detailed and much more sordid observation, biased by a biting contempt anticipating the ascetic distaste of the early Fathers.

The years in which Juvenal attacked Roman society also witnessed the culmination of Latin historical writing in the hands of Tacitus. The Roman historians have taught the world a great deal about itself; in particular they were a revelation to fourteenth and fifteenth century Italy, where their narratives were seen as a vindication of secular life and of man's power to influence heroically, indeed under God to control, his own destiny. Julius Caesar himself had provided the raw materials for history—though the form of his persuasive *Commentaries*, with their outstanding picture of Roman efficiency and discipline, is anything but raw, since their simple plainness is the product both of elaborate training and of oratorical skill second only to Cicero's. In the years following Caesar's death his supporter, Sallust, in the *Histories* (now almost entirely lost) and in his scintillating, calculatedly rugged monographs on the Jugurthine War and on Catiline (pp. 7, 9), was felt to have endowed Latin literature, for the first time, with history written in the distinguished style that this branch of the arts deserved. As a branch of the arts, indeed, it was held to need fine style no less than absolute veracity; and in his splendid glorification of the story of Rome—a prose counterpart to the epic of Virgil—the Augustan historian Livy, while providing in romantic form a greater measure of accuracy than Sallust, wrote a Latin of rich, mellifluous attractiveness. One of Livy's principal gifts towards humanity's comprehension of its potential achievements is his profound interest in great men. These men, and their deeds on great occasions, served as models for the *virtù* which was the ideal of Renaissance educationalists and has descended from them to many a modern school and college.

But Roman history attained its greatest achievements when the fluid Augustan style was out of fashion, and when even the pointed Silver Latin of Seneca had run its course. Tacitus writes in a style that is startlingly contorted and enigmatic. His individuality first appears in his monographs, the *Agricola* (about Britain) and *Germania* (pp. 59, 47), then increasingly in the *Histories* (of which the account of the years AD 68–70 survives), and most of all in his *Annals* of the early emperors. His immediate predecessors are lost; that is perhaps why we can find nothing approaching a parallel to his use of the Latin language. Examples have been quoted in earlier pages of his incisive, unique commentaries on the imperial régime. These form our earliest and most reliable account, and indeed in Latin our only substantial account, of a decisive period in the history of the western world. In spite, however, of a solemnly elevated historical conception, combined with penetrating insight into character, Tacitus betrays a bias against the unforgettably depicted Tiberius; he is seen as the forerunner of Domitian's tyranny, which—to his permanent embitterment—the historian himself had experienced. The absorbing, incisive narrative of Tacitus, with its ethical trend, pinpoints the oppressive rather than the constructive aspects of the imperial autocracy: these are studies, supremely valuable to posterity, of the evils that come from the rule of one man, even if he is at first well-meaning. However, the writer notes that things are better under Trajan, and even in dealing with grim earlier conditions he persists in the assurance that human nature, though liable to degeneration, is capable of great virtue, pertinacity and heroism. When, from the later fifteenth century onwards, the fame of Tacitus began to achieve sensational dimensions, his belief in these potentialities of the human spirit in adversity made a major contribution to humanism.

Much of Roman history, like history written elsewhere, is a tendentiously interpreted mixture of fact and rumour. Biography for instance, of which the leading Latin and Greek exponents Suetonius and Plutarch were Tacitus's younger contemporaries, had started its existence closely allied with fiction. But fiction also, in its own right, had pursued a varied career in the hands of Greeks and Romans, and the first Latin novel which has come down to us intact was written by a man born within a few years of Tacitus's death, the north African Apuleius. From an earlier date, apparently in the reign of Nero, we have extensive portions of another novel, the *Satyricon* of Petronius—in dialogue including for the first time since Plautus some Latin as it was spoken by uneducated people, it realistically describes the debauched wanderings of a group of seedy, uninhibited young men in south Italy. But the novel of Apuleius is very different. Entitled the *Metamorphoses* (or *The Golden Ass*), it tells a fantastic story about a certain Lucius who is turned into a donkey and has many weird adventures. Apuleius was the product of an age of 'sophists': versatile, well-paid, popular philosophers and lecturers, among whom his Greek counterparts were men such as Aelius Aristides (p. 52), Antonius Polemo (p. 235) and the wealthy Herodes Atticus. But Apuleius writes in Latin, employing a brilliant, luxuriant style which sometimes seems almost half-way from Cicero to the modern Latin-based tongues of Europe. Just as Petronius's novel is best-known for its 'inset' *Dinner of Trimalchio* (p. 64), so Apuleius introduces the even more famous folk-story of *Cupid and Psyche*, which, with its gay spirit, its quick response to beauty, and its frank freedom, gave Raphael a fruitful subject and appealed in England to Elizabethan and Jacobean exuberance. But most characteristic of Apuleius, and of his time, was his ecstatic belief in the Egyptian goddess Isis, to whom he bears witness in a vivid passage which brings home to us the spirit of this second century (p. 173). To convict the flamboyance of Apuleius from the viewpoint of orthodox classicism is irrelevant, because that already belonged to the past. This was not just a bad version of an old age; it was a new age.

It is right to call the Ciceronian and Augustan epochs the Golden Age of Latin literature, because of the aesthetic merit of its writers and their gifts to the human race. Yet the second century AD, in which the boldest architectural triumphs were attained, was also the time of a fresh efflorescence of Latin literature, in the hands first of Tacitus and Juvenal and then, in a rapidly changing world, of Apuleius. The next great achievements of the Latin language were again to come from his north African homeland, which was henceforward more productive of originality than any other Roman literary centre. Outstanding among its Latin writers were those ebulliently gifted converts to Christianity, Tertullian (*c.* AD 160–225) and Augustine (354–430). Among other great Christian writers of the latter's day, the poet Prudentius came from Spain, and Ausonius, Ambrose and Paulinus were of Gaul, which thus took its turn to become a world-centre of Latin culture and literary creation. St Jerome, however, came from the provinces east of the Adriatic, the home of the emperors who in the century preceding his birth had, at a terrible price, staved off the destruction which seemed to be descending upon the empire and its whole cultural heritage.

CHAPTER 9

SCULPTURE AND PAINTING

EGYPT and the Sumerian city-states on the Persian Gulf had evolved masterly techniques of portrait sculpture as early as the third millennium BC. During the centuries immediately preceding our era, a number of factors converged to stimulate the revival and development of this art in the Greco-Roman world. The Greeks of the time of Alexander and his successors liked human documents of a biographical or autobiographical nature. This biographical trend was encouraged by the growth of philosophical reflection and self-analysis, by a quickening of hero-worship, and by the new interest in personalities which such tendencies had stimulated. For this was a period of increasing interest in the individual. Whereas Greek sculptors of the classical period had sought to present man as a generalized, balanced harmony of mind and body, their Hellenistic successors wished to place emphasis on the unique pattern of the individual whom they were representing. Like contemporary biographers, they vigilantly noted contrasting elements and ambiguities, and the co-existence of apparently contradictory features. This humanist stress on the unique pattern was accentuated by the deepening conviction of personal survival after death (p. 161). For the soul, of which such beliefs enhanced the significance—the spirit of the being who was winning or losing a happy afterlife—was mirrored and reflected in the face: an additional reason for concentration, by the artist, upon the features and expressions that reflected his model's personality.

His concentration was further encouraged by a fashionable pseudo-science of this Hellenistic epoch—physiognomy. Originating as a branch of Greek medicine, attributed to Hippocrates, this study had received attention as early as the fourth century BC. One of its branches was zoological, noting human resemblances to animals, and another was racial, attempting to assess the peculiarities of peoples by examination of their physical differences. Devotees of this study

234

also noted the relations of facial expressions to character: a critic of their claims asserted that, if you applied this method to Socrates, he turned out to be stupid and fond of women. The most influential expert on physiognomy was the popular philosopher or sophist, Antonius Polemo of Laodicea in Phrygia (c. AD 88–144), whose treatises were later to influence Islamic writers.

All these factors—in addition, perhaps, to the survival of certain Egyptian portraits—contributed to a new brilliance of portrait sculpture in the later Greek world. In comparison with the large number of busts or portrait-statues of subsequent epochs that have survived, we have relatively few of the last centuries BC. But some of their artists, for instance the portrayer of the Greco-Indian military prince Euthydemus, or the originator of extant later versions of an old and brutalized fisherman (Plate 15d), or the more idealistic coin-engraver of Rome's enemy Mithradates VI of Pontus (Plate 10b), are so good that it was difficult for their successors to find fresh worlds to conquer.

The last century before our era, however, witnessed a belated artistic impact of Greece upon the aristocratic and family traditions of Rome, and this influence caused remarkable developments in portraiture. They occurred because leading Romans provided incentives on a large scale; they were among the world's great art-patrons. Surviving passages in Latin literature often refer to the decoration of their palaces and villas with Greek reliefs, decorated urns, sarcophagi, statues and portrait-busts, and to the demand for Greek gems as sealstones (p. 238). Wealthy Romans commissioned copies of Greek works of all epochs ranging from the sixth to the second century BC—thus preserving for posterity, more or less accurately, the forms of many masterpieces. But they also required originals. They had, it is true, no great awareness of an artist's methods and problems. Nor does surviving art-criticism show much insight. Perhaps its best exponent, though there are many gaps in his knowledge and taste, is Pliny the elder. The greatest of sculptors, in his judgment, is Lysippus, the lively, virtuoso portrayer of Alexander the Great,[1] but the finest work of all time he believes to be the unbridled, tormentedly baroque Laocoon group, one of the last original Hellenistic masterpieces, executed by Rhodian sculptors in the second or first century BC.[2]

Most Roman patrons knew infinitely less about art than Pliny, yet they 'knew what they liked' and set a great and inspiring task for the sculptors of the last century BC onwards. Portraits were what they wanted above all. The mentality of upper-class Romans contained an ingrained sense of history and of factualism and was deeply attracted by portraits which would record and analyse the features and expressions of the individual in his own social and historical setting and without sparing his physical oddities. These Roman patrons, even more than their Greek forerunners, wanted a sculptural biography chronicling and summing up a man's peculiarities, achievements and experiences. They endowed the art not only with an incentive and with funds but with a Roman definiteness, purpose and dignity and with an inspiring, challenging new range of subjects—namely their own resolute, tough, square faces, vigorously displaying every blend between northern endurance and southern exuberance (Plates 1–9; 20*a*).

The Roman interest in portraiture had specific social causes. From an early date the patricians had been granted the exclusive right of keeping in their houses, and parading at family funerals, the death-masks of their ancestors. Polybius[3] and Pliny the elder[4] describe such funeral displays of the mid-second century BC. Polybius suggests that these masks, which had no doubt originally been of a generalized and unindividualized character, had by his time already become realistic likenesses. Terracotta, stone and marble portraits of the next few generations have facial structures suggesting that they are copies or reminiscences of death-masks (Plate 15*b*), since they stress prominent bones and cartilages rather than the surface irregularities which were smoothed out by death; and the frequency with which old men and women are represented may be prompted not only by the desire to sum up a biography but by the existence of such masks. Vivid portraits of the dead had already appeared on Etruscan funeral urns since the third or second century BC, and their masterpiece, an alabaster study in marital relations from Volaterrae (Volterra) (Plate 14), is probably of the last century before our era. But the country where funerary portraiture reached its greatest distinction was Egypt—the medium, however, being not sculpture but painting (p. 241). At Rome there was an increasing demand for realistic portraits of the living as well as the dead. Italian portrait-painting has completely disappeared (except for a few murals from Pompeii), but we know that, during the final century of the Republic, the Greek custom of erecting statues in honour of famous men was extended to Rome[5] where senior officials ('curule magistrates') became entitled to set up portrait-statues of themselves in public places. This custom fused with the aristocratic funerary tradition to create a special demand; and that is what the portraits of the first century BC, with their drastic probing after expression and strong gift for characterization, supply.

The sculptors of the Roman portrait gallery that now began—one of the chief glories of Roman civilization—were only very infrequently Romans or Italians; they were nearly all Greeks, or orientals of Greek culture and training. Rome provided the market, the money and the faces, and the artists came, as hitherto, from the coastlands of the eastern Mediterranean and Aegean. Nor did these sculptors, even the greatest of them, achieve high social status or position (p. 76).[6] In common with other artists, they had gained in esteem under the monarchies which followed Alexander, when a sculptor gained a fraction of the fame he was able to bestow; but they remained below architects, and much closer to tradesmen than to senators or senior civil servants. That is to say, the profession did not attract educated Romans. In this most Roman of all achievements it was Greek-speaking non-Romans and easterners who were the experts. In particular, the employment of marble, used for sculpture and wall-decoration in Roman homes from the first century BC onwards, involved techniques with which only those brought up in near-eastern traditions were familiar.

They found massive employment at Rome, and their style at its best does not seem to have undergone marked geographical variations, becoming truly international. It is true that on the borders of the empire, for example in Egypt (Plates 17, 18a, 19a) and at Palmyra in the Syrian desert where Greek and Mesopotamian traditions met (Plate 16), distinctive schools retained an easily recognizable element of the regional tradition (p. 241). But the output of noteworthy schools within the central Greco-Roman region, for example on the island of Paros with its marble quarries, or at Ephesus, Miletus and Aphrodisias in Asia Minor, is only distinguishable with difficulty from the rest of the cosmopolitan and imperial sculpture of the day, of which it formed an integral part. However, what is lacking in purely regional deviation is made up for by a marked variety of portrait styles, often co-existing, or radically changing from one fashion to another within the shortest space of time. Indeed, every school of sculpture throughout the Roman empire seems capable of veering, at a moment's notice, from archaic to classical, from turgid emotion to delicate rococo or brutal realism; and often, under the impact of Roman life upon these Hellenistic themes, an individual stamp is set upon the adaptation.

The most characteristic style that emerged in Rome during the first century BC displayed a quality which has been described as *verism*, and defined as a somewhat dry realism: the subject is portrayed as he really is, without idealizing his physical peculiarities, and with the expression not of a philosopher, poet or visionary but of a man of affairs. The later Greeks had originated an energetic, intense, realistic manner which was the forerunner or first stage of this veristic style. Under additional influence from Etruscan traditions of bronze casting (with strong reflections of light on the bronze), and possibly even under Egyptian influences, the opportunities existing at Rome caused the fashion to reach its full development there. During the centuries since Alexander, the Greeks had evolved other portrait styles, too, notably one laying stress on pathetic emotion and others adopting the purely idealistic trends of earlier times. But though signs of these styles sometimes emerged in Republican Rome they achieved less favour. Verism rather than pathos or idealism was what, in this brutal age of individualism turned to violence, the leading Romans demanded; and the Greek and Asian artists, as they satisfied the demand, simultaneously achieved the education and emancipation of Roman taste.

Early signs of these new developments at Rome appear on the coinage. An isolated and remarkable coin-portrait of Rome's 'liberator' of Greece, Flamininus, had occurred on a Greek commemorative piece of the 190's BC (Plate 10a). Then, nearly a century and a half later, the Roman coinage itself shows posthumous heads of Sulla and other notables,[7] and finally portraits of the living Caesar and his slayer Brutus. This last, together with at least one bust, may have contributed to the complex inspiration behind Michelangelo's bust of Brutus, as a strong and resolute tyrant-slayer rather than Dante's arch-criminal. Another source was probably a gem: like Pompey and other men of the time, Brutus was portrayed in this medium, which now became fashionable as Romans employed the best artists—the name of a certain Dioscurides has come down to us— to engrave intaglios (where the design is sunk) and cameos (where it is in relief) for their sealstones and signet-rings. Likewise during the mid-first century BC we find portrait-busts of outstanding quality, for example of old and elderly men (Plate 15a and b), and of a woman (Plate 15c). Busts of the Stoics Posidonius (Plate 20b) and Cato the Younger are originals, or go back to originals, dating from before their deaths. The finest surviving portraits of Cicero (Plate 20a) are probably early imperial copies of heads executed in his lifetime, but at least one outstanding representation of Julius Caesar (Plate 1), showing grandiose will and vigour—and perhaps beneath its calmness a discreet irony—may well belong to the years of his dictatorship.

This head of Caesar inaugurates a new, imperial tradition, raising its subject above the mere, photographic accuracy of aged fisherman and the like. For the advent of mighty rulers provided the occasion to infuse an element of the idealism and grandeur which had been apparent in earlier Hellenistic sculpture but had not yet received their opportunity at Rome. For purposes of publicity, the Roman emperors took the portrayal and distribution of their own features very seriously indeed. No modern dictator distributes photographs of himself so thoroughly as the rulers of the Roman empire circulated theirs; their portraits reached millions (who could see their ruler in no other medium, except the coinage) and were accorded respect and veneration to an extent perhaps paralleled only in Japan.

So an emperor ensured that there should be a variety of sculptured figures and heads of himself in great numbers in every town and village of the empire. Local authorities were not encouraged to offer their own approximations; the innumerable surviving busts stem from relatively few central models. The Greek and oriental sculptors employed to design these were encouraged to interpret their master in various ways. Sometimes they showed him with complete realism and no nonsense about it, in the tradition of late Republican Rome. Or they returned, with improvements, to the idealistic splendours of the Hellenistic kingdoms. But the most frequent formula of all was a mixture between these two main themes; and the history of imperial portrait sculpture is a story of the different forms and nuances of such mixtures, in the hands of the most talented artists of their day—on the results of whose efforts very much was believed, by the imperial government, to depend.

Under Augustus, with his classicizing tastes and his claim to civilize Rome by contact with the highest classical traditions, the tendency was to idealize his features. But this was done in an enormous variety of different ways, and with varying amounts of realism infused. He was represented as Roman man of religion, as democratic statesman, as Greek thinker or hero-god, as world-conqueror. The Roman sorts of bust were intended chiefly for the west, and the Greek sorts for the east. For the east, too, was a bronze bust, found in Meroë in the Sudan, which shows him with the imperial features, heavy frown, and glaring eyes of the Greco-oriental autocrat (Plate 2a).

Augustus's immediate successors proceeded somewhat less ambitiously on similar lines, until a new, impressive synthesis was found for the heavy, invitingly baroque features of Nero. These are cleverly rendered on his coinage, which exceeds those of his predecessors in artistic skill (Plate 11b). An essential element in the propaganda for which the coinage was abundantly employed (p. 49) was the effective portrayal of the emperor, the empress and their family. The coinage itself was attributed to the patronage of the gods, and was, in due course, even described as 'sacred';[8] so that the portraits on these coins had their share of the veneration accorded to imperial statues. Although there had been fine portraits of Greek monarchs and their consorts, the Roman series of coin-portraits is pre-eminent. Throughout the principate, the sculptural interpretations of each emperor are paralleled by a rich series of numismatic portrayals—all inspired, to a varied but never insignificant extent, not only by the emperor's actual facial characteristics, but by his character, tastes and general policy. This point is illustrated by the emperors who followed Nero. For instance, his immediate successor, Galba, was a grim, economical, elderly soldier who deliberately reacted from the extravagances of Nero's reign. So the fine portraits on Galba's coins reflect the same theme. One of them shows him as the heir of the old Republican tradition of austerity (Plate 12a). But this stern representation might well have seemed to make him look a little senile, and another designer attempts a more regal, grandiose portrayal (Plate 12b). On this coin he looks years younger; but the two interpretations, the veristic and the idealistic, are contemporary, since his reign only lasted a few months. The coin-portraiture of this period—to which was added, in the second century AD, a superb series of commemorative medallions (Plate 23c)—exercised great influence on the Renaissance medallists, after directly inspiring in 1390 the earliest known departure from current frontal portraiture, a medallion of Francesco II of Carrara, ruler of antiquity-loving Padua.

Portrait-busts as well as coins[9] illustrate, in very much the same way as the coins of Galba, the rival, ambivalent interpretations of Vespasian's appearance. One such bust is an outstanding achievement of the dry realistic style (Plate 3)—unflinchingly irreverent to imperial shams. This kind of relentless Republican version had not hitherto been employed for imperial portraiture, but it had continued to be employed for numerous non-imperial personages, and its return to the most expensive patronage under Vespasian is fully in keeping with his frequent jokes about human weaknesses, including his own.[10] Each emperor, like everyone else, wanted to be recognizably unique and his sculptor wanted to make him unique—and employed the methods and traditions of verism to do so. But another means of stressing the emperor's singularity was provided by a more elevated manner, which was likewise employed for Vespasian (Plate 2b). Such masterpieces as this were made possible by novelties and improvements of technique, and particularly by a new, fluent, more atmospheric texture brightened, in illusionist fashion, by colourful designs of strong light and shade. Portrait sculpture has now taken to itself some elements from the comedy of manners, exemplified by the fashionable novelist Petronius. The sitter is presented as a personality with a social context, with emphasis upon tricks of gesture and amusing details, or—in the case of imperial women—upon their frequently changing fashionable hair-styles.

The second century AD, which produced outstanding masterpieces of architecture, did not, in portraiture, to the same extent improve upon the achievement of the preceding age; though it produced notable innovations and changes of emphasis. Special mention should be made of a national Egyptian or Greco-Egyptian tradition of portrait-painting. This school, painting panels for mummy-covers, had been gradually developing during the past century and more, and reached its climax now in a series of exciting and sympathetic pictures of men and especially women, plastically treated with bright highlights (Plates 17; 18a; 19a). In sculpture, too, there is an occasional vivid, hieratic, Egyptian work; but the principal sculptural school of markedly regional character was to be found at Palmyra in the Syrian desert, where artists observed a piquant balance, anticipatory of the Byzantine age, between the styles and fashions of the Greco-Roman and Parthian worlds (Plate 16).

These eastern schools display local residents, and in the metropolitan workshops also—and those throughout the empire which are stylistically indistinguishable from them—private citizens continue to be finely portrayed. But the best efforts of sculptors are lavished upon the features of emperors and their relatives. In depicting the impressive countenance of Trajan, imperial dignity and virile heroic virtue have, as in the age of Augustus—but with the aid of recently improved techniques—reasserted their ascendance over individuality (Plate 4a); though a bronze bust, in a dedicatory shield, now discovered at Ankara seems to represent him less as the second Alexander than as a thoughtful, careworn sage dutifully bearing the burdens of empire (Plate 4b). Bronze busts such as this had long acquired added vitality from the drilling of the eyes, sometimes varied by the insetting of separate, coloured eyeballs (Plate 2a). As early as the time of Tiberius, drilled eyeballs occur in marble statues from Aphrodisias, and in the second century of our epoch the custom was gradually extended to imperial portrayals in this medium. One such portrait is among the few which succeed in reproducing the energetic nervousness of Hadrian (Plate 5).

Of the same reign are statues of the emperor's favourite boy Antinous (Plate 6a), whose dramatic death led in the east to a wave of religious feeling and his deification (p. 175). For the portrayal of the new god, the classical Hellenic tradition, to which Hadrian was so devoted, summoned up all its force once more to give form to a new ideal in the voluptuous contours, low unintellectual brow, heavy lips and dreamy gaze of Antinous; expressing not an overfed, spoilt boy, but eternal sorrow for youth which passes, beauty which fades, and perfection which dies. This ideal, represented with every device of romantic sensuousness, and reduplicated on many amulets —and even on coins and medallions issued by the governor of Egypt and Asian cities—was to play an important part in the process by which Renaissance artists rediscovered the nude as a leading field of their activity. For example, a statue of Antinous figured prominently among the subtly selective influences which contributed to Donatello's 'David'.

Strangely contrasted in style, as in the personality of its subject, is a portrait of another second-century youth, Marcus Aurelius at about the age of fifteen (Plate 6b). This masterpiece of psychological interpretation displays a pensive abstracted melancholy characteristic of Aurelius (p. 202), and characteristic also of a time when portraits were somewhat withdrawn and remote, although (at their best) with significant undercurrents of feeling. The outstanding representation of Aurelius in his maturity, his bronze equestrian statue on the

Capitoline Hill (Plate 7a), shows him not as the philosopher he wanted to be, but as emperor and conqueror; under the raised fore-foot of his horse once lay a barbarian, with hands bound behind his back. This is our earliest complete example of an imperial equestrian statue, and the forerunner of medieval achievements in this genre, such as the thirteenth-century royal rider at Bamberg Cathedral symbolizing Hohenstaufen chivalry. More than two hundred years later, this Marcus Aurelius is the model for Donatello's Erasmo da Narni (Gattamelata) at Padua (Plate 7b)—the first great bronze cast in the Renaissance—and for the Bartolomeo Colleoni of Verrochio and Leopardi at Venice.

As the age of the Antonines continued, marble surfaces were increasingly polished, or deliberately left rough, so as to secure dramatic effects of light and shade. The drill, no longer merely an adjunct to lighten the work and reach recesses, came to be used for its own sake to achieve decorative contrasts. Flesh was shown with a brilliant, porcelain-like surface, and this smoothness, especially of the face, is contrasted with ever curlier, more intricately undercut hair and beard. These tendencies, already apparent in Asia Minor more than a century earlier, reach their climax in imperial art under Aurelius's son Commodus (Plate 8a). Commodus reacted profoundly against Aurelius, in the directions of luxury, cruelty and emotional religion. His religious boldness is suggested here by a direct identification with Hercules, whose lion's skin and club he bears. But in his handsome features there is only the subtlest suggestion of a changed atmosphere. The portraiture is still contemplative, severe and self-contained. Yet the subdued Antonine soliloquy of man and his soul about the burden of the world is replaced by a more attentive glance under heavy-lidded, deeply drilled eyes; and there is a faint raising of the eyebrow, curl of the lip, and inclination of the head—a slight, enlivening touch of unpleasantness. The position of the heavy half-bust on its fragile, elaborate support has been criticized, but should be judged by baroque rather than classical standards. The torso rests on an Amazon's shield, recalling the emperor's name, 'Amazonius'. This shield is flanked by two cornucopiae standing upon a sphere displaying reliefs of the three signs of the zodiac governing the three most important days of Commodus's degrading life. The same keen interest in astrology also appears in a bronze, silver-gilt bust at the Victoria and Albert Museum, London, which shows Commodus wearing a cosmic cap dotted with stars (p. 146).

The cap, like the sphere which carries his marble bust, symbolizes world-domination. With this, and with open divinization, the concept of the emperor as some sort of a human being, however extraordinary, is beginning to give way to more extravagant conceptions. Yet first other tendencies were still to have their way, and some of the most brilliant of Roman portraits were still to come. At the outset there is a real break with the past under Caracalla (AD 211–217). Though noting his model's boasted resemblance to Alexander the Great (whose head-pose is copied), the Michelangelesque sculptor give full rein to the emperor's violent, neurotic character (Plate 9). Caracalla, who regarded himself as a soldier (p. 19), eliminates the previous light-and-shade style of sculpture by wearing his hair shorter than his predecessors. In about AD 220 there was a further complete change of fashion, in which the hair becomes a mere cap, and, amid ever-increasing grimness and turbulence, expressions remain distrustful, careworn, pessimistic and tormented; such is the face of the persecutor of Christianity, Decius (Plate 8*b*).

Then Byzantine immobility took control; the sense of human strain gives place to a kind of ecstasy, and the inner man who has been disturbingly apparent in third-century portraits becomes spiritualized, with enormous eyes staring from enormous hollows their message of the impotence and insignificance of human effort.

In the sculptural reliefs which decorate their monuments, the Romans, and their Greek or eastern artists, achieved real originality. But the conception of such a relief was not new. Scenic reliefs had many centuries earlier been a conspicuous feature of Assyrian, Babylonian and Egyptian art, and in the fifth and fourth centuries BC the Greeks had gone beyond the technique of Phidias's Parthenon frieze by experimenting with figures placed at different levels in battle-scenes and other elaborate low-relief compositions reminiscent of paintings. Then, in the official sculpture (as well as painting) of the monarchs who succeeded to Alexander's heritage, attention was increasingly devoted to narrating past and present events of national significance. At first the approach to current affairs was somewhat indirect. For example, when King Attalus I of Pergamum celebrated his successes against the Gauls (*c.* 200 BC) by reliefs on the wall of the Athenian acropolis, he did this by depicting the ancient triumphs of Greeks over Persians, and mythical victories of Greeks against Amazons, and of gods against giants. But then in 168 BC another Greek artist adorned a monument at Delphi with a partially documentary relief depicting a contemporary event—the victory of the Romans over the Macedonian king Perseus at Pydna.[11] This sort of subject was already not unfamiliar to the Romans from paintings which they commissioned to grace their triumphal processions; half a dozen such paintings of the third and early second centuries BC, undertaken by Greek immigrants—or perhaps in some cases by their Italian pupils—are mentioned by literary authorities, the earliest celebrating victories of the First Punic War (264 BC).[12] Such paintings were in Virgil's mind when he tells of the pictures of the Trojan War seen by Aeneas in Dido's palace.

> —the sons of Atreus
> Were there, and Priam, Achilles too, hostile to both.
> Aeneas, stood; wept—
> Oh, Achates, is there anywhere,
> Any place left on earth unhaunted by our sorrows?
> Look!—Priam. Here too we find virtue somehow rewarded,
> Tears in the nature of things, hearts touched by human
>   transience.[13]

Many of the ingredients in this past history of the sculptural relief were utilized, in original fashion, by the Greek sculptors of the Altar of Peace (Ara Pacis) erected by Augustus at Rome, where its reconstruction is to be seen today (Plate 36a). Consecrated in 13 BC to commemorate the emperor's safe return from Gaul and Spain, this structure was completed and dedicated four years later. The altar itself, adorned with reliefs reproducing sacrificial scenes, stands in a walled precinct (thirty-eight by thirty-five feet, height twelve feet six inches) sculptured with reliefs in two tiers; the general design may well owe inspiration to an Altar of Pity erected in the Athenian market-place during the Peloponnesian War (420–410 BC). In addition to rich and luscious floral decoration, the designs engraved upon the Augustan Altar include set-pieces of legendary patriotic scenes, and another personifying Mother Earth or Italy. The principal reliefs, however, show the procession which took place when the altar was consecrated. The emperor himself appears—marked off from the rest by subtle distinctions, yet participating in the ceremony in modest guise, as befitted the human, non-autocratic picture of the principate which, in Italy especially, he was at pains to make known. There are, however, strong dynastic implications, since the company attending him includes not only the priests, Vestal Virgins, and great officers of state but many members of what, although no dynasty officially existed (p. 28), was coming to be thought of as the imperial family. The portion of the frieze illustrated here includes two of Augustus's nieces, both called Antonia, with their husbands and children—a girl and two smaller boys, Germanicus and the slightly older Gnaeus Domitius Ahenobarbus, father of Nero.

Linear perspective has registered no advance on Greek relief-work (p. 248); and the style of the Altar of Peace is grave and tranquil to the point of stiffness. This gravity is deliberately reminiscent of the old Republican traditions, which Augustus was seeking to recapture. It is also intended to echo the classicism of the Parthenon, since the Greek culture to which the emperor devoted so much encouragement was classical rather than Hellenistic—it is the classic poets of Greece rather than their Alexandrian successors whom the Augustan poets claim as their models (p. 222). Besides, the scene was a religious one which lent itself to such treatment rather than to borrowings from vigorous Hellenistic battle-scenes. The prevailing classical calm of these reliefs does not permit expressive portraiture; the heads of the adults are ideal, with scarcely more individuality than heads by Phidias, or than the imperial personages grouped upon great gems of the early principate, the Gemma Augustea at Vienna and the Paris Cameo. But on the Ara Pacis an exception must be made in respect of the children, whose personalities emerge with greater distinctness. They look more like real, different, children than the fat cupids of Hellenistic art or the children whom earlier Greeks had depicted as miniature men and women. The older of the two boys (if one may judge despite the fact that his head is modern) seems to be suffering a little from stage-fright at this official parade, as he grasps the cloak of his uncle Drusus the elder, while his elder sister looks down at him reassuringly. Another curious note of intimacy is provided by the evident admonition that the younger Antonia and her husband are receiving, because they talk on so solemn an occasion, from an elderly lady who is probably Augustus's sister Octavia. Such few homely or sentimental touches remind us that this was a human gathering, and that the Romans were a vivacious people. They are elements of informality which combine curiously with the general air of serene, if unpretentious, stateliness.

The Altar of Peace incorporated many of the traditions of relief-sculpture and transformed them into a new creation in Italian soil. All its reliefs can be directly linked with a single, definite occasion. Here, instead of the somewhat loosely-anchored myths of earlier artistic monuments, we have, translated into sculptural terms, a concrete moment of recent time. Admirers of the Altar see it not only as a classicizing monument but as an Augustan classic in its own right, a sculptural *Aeneid*. However, its historical position soon became very different from that of the *Aeneid*. For the quality of the latter was never again even approached, whereas relief-sculpture rapidly advanced beyond the achievements of the Altar. A strikingly different technique, for example, is displayed by the sculptor of the Arch of Titus. This single-spanned monument was erected across the Sacred Way, near the entrance of the Roman Forum, to celebrate the capture of Jerusalem by Titus in AD 70. The elaborate decoration includes, on one side of the deeply-recessed and coffered opening of the Arch, a carved relief of the prince in his triumphal chariot, and on the other a procession of soldiers carrying the spoils taken from the Temple at Jerusalem (Plate 37a). Among these spoils are the table for the shewbread, the seven-branched candlestick, and the trumpets for summoning the Jewish people.[14] These objects had been brought by Titus to Rome and remained there until the Vandals seized them in AD 455; later they were removed partly to Constantinople and partly to Jerusalem, from both of which they disappeared. The sculptor on the Arch sought his inspiration from paintings depicting triumphal scenes of this kind. In fifteenth-century Padua it was again a painter, the 'archaeologist of genius' Andrea Mantegna, who— utilizing antique models in a more direct fashion than other Renaissance artists—drew upon this scene for his murals of The Triumph of Caesar now at Hampton Court (Plate 36b).

Both the Arch of Titus and the Altar of Peace show processional scenes, but the difference is very great. The decorator of the Arch, like contemporary portrait-sculptors (p. 241), employs deep shadows and the vigorous interplay of light and shade—though the soldiers are in such low relief that they themselves cast no shadows. The effect aimed at, as in certain mural paintings (pp. 254 ff.), is complete illusion: the illusion of a procession seen through an open frame, with merely air and no wall behind it, and with all its members silhouetted against the sky. Although not wholly unknown to the Etruscans, the third dimension could not be seriously attempted until sculptors had acquired, in the employment of these unpliable

materials; the technical dexterity which they now possessed. In this
bold experiment, the product of a century of effort, the problem of
perspective is cleverly attacked. However, it is not yet conquered.
It remained for Ghiberti and other fifteenth-century Florentine
workers in relief, after studying their Roman forerunners, to understand fully the sculptural rendering of spatial depth. But the sculptor
of the Arch of Titus plays a significant part in the story.

Soon relief-sculpture embarked on wider ambitions. One of its
most astonishing monuments is the Column of Trajan (AD 114),
which stands in the Forum of Trajan adjacent to his Basilica; perhaps
like them it was designed, if not partly executed, by the great
Apollodorus of Damascus (p. 266). Its pedestal, ornamented with
sculptured trophies (a favourite though ugly motif of imperial art),
contains the entrance to the tomb-chamber of Trajan and his wife
Plotina. The shaft of the Doric column, twelve feet two inches in
diameter, is covered by a spiral band three feet six inches wide and
over eight hundred feet in length, its twenty-four windings engraved
with reliefs depicting Trajan's War against the Dacians (Plates 38*a*,
b). This spiral, a development from the successive horizontal drums
such as appear on a Column of Nero at Moguntiacum (Mainz)
(Plate 37*b*), is new. The climax towards which, as on a parchment
scroll, the design unwinds, is a hemispherical plinth that formerly
supported a statue of Trajan (now replaced by St Peter).

> The sculptures wind aloft
> And lead, through various toils, up the rough steep
> The hero to the skies.

The scenes, as they unfold, contain no fewer than 2,500 human
figures. Much of the labour that went into these close-packed designs
seems to have been doomed to wastage since they could never be
properly seen and appreciated. But the column was originally
surrounded by an open colonnaded court carrying galleries at
different levels, from which the reliefs could at least be viewed more
easily than they can now. Furthermore, their scenes, numbering as
many as 118—or according to another interpretation 155—did not
look as flat or overcrowded as they do today, when they fuse at a
short distance into an unreadable arabesque. For like much of
ancient sculpture these reliefs were originally picked-out with gilding,
painting and metalwork, of which numerous traces exist or have
been recorded. Whatever the aesthetic disadvantages of this form of

composition, its artists skilfully adapted their considerable talents to the medium. Rejecting the illusionistic attempts that had culminated in the Arch of Titus, they ignore experiments in perspective, arbitrarily altering sizes of figures and buildings in accordance with a 'map technique' reminiscent of the bird's-eye views on archaic and early classical Athenian vases. This technique, with its anticipations of early Christian and Byzantine art, has been employed with a purpose, since, by enabling the designers to accumulate deep blocks of figures it achieves feats of composition which vividly express the characteristic Roman sense of history: the past is unfolded as a basis and guide for the present and future.

This problem of depicting continuous events initiated a new era in representational relief and called for new qualities. Above all, the designers have infused into their work a strong dramatic content expressing itself, beneath the even majestic flow of the whole design, in antitheses and gradations between high and low emotional intensity. The themes of Roman triumphal paintings and Greek reliefs are recalled by battle-scenes of concentrated power (Plate 38a) providing special opportunities for the masterly groupings upon which the symmetries, contrasts and rhythms of the designs on the Column are based. Yet only a relatively small proportion of the total space—less than one-quarter—deals with actual fighting: greater interest is shown in the results, and meanings, and backgrounds of each battle. Many varied incidents, therefore, are selected for illustration—imperial addresses, sacrifices, works of fortification, marches and journeys, envoys and prisoners. In this richly detailed and skilfully unified epic, man is still the measure of all things, and the scene is dominated by his doings and emotional reactions; repeatedly we see the feats of the Romans, the solicitude and clemency of the emperor, the hardships of the troops who bore the heavy burden of empire. One relief (Plate 38b), in which violent movement is not needed to heighten the impact, shows Trajan and his staff, in civilian dress, standing in front of a fortified city with an amphitheatre, and receiving a delegation which consists of at least eight groups of enemy chieftains of different races from beyond the frontiers. In this 'triumph of psychological intuition', as Michael Rostovtzeff (a Russian) called it:

'two worlds face each other—the proud world of the Romans . . . and the barbarians who were ready to take up the heritage of the Roman empire and start a new life on the ruins of the ancient cities. They have come to greet the great Roman not as slaves or subjects but as equals, no less proud and self-confident than he. The duel between the two worlds has begun, and its deep significance was well understood by the artist of genius who created this scene.'

Another column, likewise with spiral reliefs, was erected by Marcus Aurelius (AD 174) to commemorate his victories on the Danube (Plate 39*b*). Still standing in the Piazza Colonna at Rome, it is a little broader (thirteen feet two inches in diameter) than the Column of Trajan, but not so high (ninety-seven feet three inches), and with larger substructure, base and capital. Its summit, on which once stood a statue of Aurelius and now stands St Paul, is reached by a stairway of 197 steps. Its twenty tiers of relief are simpler, stronger and less crowded in design than those of Trajan's column, with less gradations and variations, so that the scenes are most distinct, more plastic and shadowed, and more easily readable at a distance. The end of the Antonine Age had been heralded by ominous barbarian threats, and the anxious and serious character of these times, soon to be reflected in portrait-busts (p. 244), finds strong expression here in tortuous, wind-blown hair and draperies, strained bodies, and troubled, pathetic expressions (Plate 39*a*).

The triple Arch of Septimius Severus in the Forum (AD 204) is unfortunately in a poor state of preservation. Dedicated to the emperor and his two sons Caracalla and Geta to commemorate their Parthian victories, it resembles the columns in containing narrative description on several superimposed registers, but in an epoch of rising crisis, centralization and autocracy (p. 19) the human element is eclipsed. On the Column of Aurelius the soldiers listening to the emperor's address had indeed been listening collectively, but they were still psychologically differentiated individuals. On the Arch of Severus the whole reaction of the listeners is collective and impersonal: they are a single undulating mass in a narrow layer between the foreground plane and the neutral background, concentrated without any real individual differentiation. The process goes further on the reliefs of Severus's four-faced Arch at his birthplace Lepcis Magna in Tripolitania. Here again there is a whole series of crowded scenes—battles, groups of cavalry, sacrifices, proclamations and a triumphal procession (Plate 39*c*). But the whole spirit has changed. This is no longer narrative but representational sculpture, heralding the late-classical reliefs on the Arch of Constantine. The figures at Lepcis are forcibly twisted out of the planes of action into rigid frontality. They show the map technique in its extreme form, utilized so as to give the spectator a maximum view of the scene. The design has been attributed to the school of Aphrodisias in Asia Minor (p. 237), but its peculiar and evidently oriental features seem to come from Parthian territory beyond the eastern frontiers of the empire. The more immediate model may have been a panoramic landscape-painting with a high viewpoint, painted for the triumphal occasion; when the Thracian emperor Maximinus (AD 235–8) had pictures of his exploits set up before the Senate House,[15] they may well have been of the same kind. On the Arch of Severus at Lepcis, the emperor is a very different sort of being from the 'first citizen' on Augustus's Altar of Peace. Severus stands elevated above his puppet-like entourage in rigid, hieratic glory. As the shadows closed round the Antonine Golden Age, the epoch of undisguised autocracy is heralded by the sculptors.

These arches of Severus, on which the narrative technique is so greatly modified, display the last continuous narrative reliefs known to us. But incentives for reliefs of another kind had now appeared. In an age when, among other signs of interest in the afterlife, inhumation had replaced cremation (p. 164), many artists, good and bad, had begun to devote their talents to decorating the private sarcophagi of prosperous people. At first the designs were religious (Plates 31a; 32–3a). Already before AD 200, however, the martial tradition of relief-sculpture is perpetuated by the growing custom, amid rapid stylistic evolution, of ornamenting sarcophagi with elaborate scenes of battle. In these as well as the earlier, religious designs there are survivals of the artistic traditions of Asia Minor and lands farther east from which the sculptors mostly came; among their forerunners are the artists of sarcophagi of the fifth century BC, found at Sidon in Phoenicia, and now, more than six hundred years later, a special, architectural version of the religious sarcophagus had its home at Sidamara in Asia Minor. Bernard Berenson sees in Greco-Roman sarcophagi only a 'certain wistful, crepuscular charm'; yet certain reliefs show real skill in their grouping of figures and interplay of light and shade. From the thirteenth century onwards they exercised great influence upon the Italian artists who utilized and adapted their designs so as to achieve either original relief compositions, such as Pisano's 'Last Judgment' or Donatello's 'Cantoria', or sometimes quite close adaptations (Plate 31b).

Of the panel-paintings of triumphal scenes which inspired Roman sculptural reliefs nothing is now extant. Portrait-painting has chiefly survived in mummy-portraits of the Egyptian school (p. 241; Plates 17; 18a; 19a). Otherwise the bulk of the Greco-Roman painting that has come down to us is on the walls of those upper-class houses at Pompeii and Herculaneum which are partly preserved owing to their burial in lava during the reign of Titus (p. 260). Their rediscovery in the eighteenth century, inspiring the wall- and ceiling-decoration of the architect-designer brothers Adam, helped the interior decorator's profession, developed if not invented earlier in the century by William Kent, towards the prosperous *chic* which has been its ideal ever since. Furniture, and pictures hung on the walls, were among these decorators' stock-in-trade. Yet the furniture of Pompeians and Romans had been simple and portable, and it would have seemed wrong to spoil the organic structure and *décor* of their houses by fixing pictures to their walls. Instead, they commissioned men to construct vivid mosaics for the floors—a picturesque art which led the way to medieval church decoration—and to paint light, graceful frescoes upon the surface of these walls. Since the painters (like the architects and sculptors) whom they commissioned were mostly Greeks or easterners, they painted—with modifications due to the houses and tastes of their patrons—in styles which were familiar in the Greek world. They also incorporated in their murals more or less free reproductions of earlier pictures ranging in date all the way from pre-classical to late Hellenistic times.

Some of the most dramatic of their achievements were found at the Villa Item not far from Pompeii (Plates 28; 29), where a whole series of wall-decorations represent religious scenes concerned with the worship of Dionysus (p. 163). Although precedents for certain of these themes cannot yet be traced, they are probably of traditional character; but the artist, who shows a masterly avoidance of superfluity, interpreted a number of the scenes in his own way. These paintings cover whole walls; others form mural panels. By the first century BC such panels are often incorporated within a painted architectural framework—a natural development seeing that the primary function of these mural paintings was architectural and decorative rather than pictorial, their design being adjusted and subordinated to the availability of wall-space. Thus murals from Boscoreale, near Pompeii, display not only what appear to be copies of earlier paintings but also imaginative architectural designs, avoiding monotony by the use of complex vistas and an abundance of detail; the enclosure of perspective within perspective creates a sense of limitless space and a mysterious beyond (Plate 40). These painted architectural frameworks harmonized the panels with the structure of the room, and by seeming to extend the range of vision beyond the wall gave it an added spaciousness, appropriate for crowded towns where the high cost of land limited the size of rooms and thus encouraged decorative schemes conveying illusions of space.

The colours employed, on these ill-lit walls, are generally brilliant; the technique rapid, since this process of painting 'frescoes' on wet lime plaster precluded refinements. Thus, though figures are foreshortened, there are no great explorations of perspective (p. 246). The names of the artists are nearly all lost. Pliny the elder does record a painter of Augustan date, but the text is corrupt and we cannot tell if he was called Ludius or Studius (neither of them, incidentally, Roman names). In addition to undertaking portraits and historical subjects, this artist introduced 'a very pleasing style' by including in his pictures 'villas, porticos, landscape gardens, sacred groves, woods, hills, fish-ponds, straits, rivers, and shores'.[16] Ludius or Studius has been described as the inventor of landscape-painting, but what he probably did was to adapt Greek prototypes, now lost, by transforming them into views of actual Italian villas and maritime scenes. Surviving paintings, though we have no reason to attribute any of them to this man or to any other whose name is known, include a number of graceful landscapes and townscapes (Plate 44a). For example, the Farnesina House just outside Rome has provided nine rooms of very well-preserved paintings (Fig. xvii)— probably a connected religious sequence—with a fidelity of landscape technique almost anticipating the Dutch school. The same mansion was decorated with extremely graceful low reliefs in stucco (Plate 35a), the white lime plaster—used since Mycenaean times—which artists of this and the following century employed for decorative purposes with excellent results (p. 259). A house on the Esquiline Hill was decorated with pictures, perhaps of Augustan date, telling the story of Odysseus. With their skilful suggestions of natural effect, these are the most remarkable intact examples of continuous ancient landscape-painting (Plate 42). Their artist, blending naturalism, mythology, genre and still-life, effectively exploits his colours and sharply contrasts light and shade.

The same period shows a desire for the faithful portrayal of flowers

Fig. xvii. Wall-paintings of Sanctuary of Dionysus, later 1st century BC.
From Villa Farnesina; Museo Nazionale, Rome

and fruits. Thus a house on the Palatine, known as the 'House of
Livia', wife of Augustus, but perhaps originally the home of Cicero's
legal opponent Hortensius, contains paintings with rich floral
designs; paralleled in other media (Fig. xviii), these blooms are
reminiscent of an Altar erected at Pergamum early in the second
century BC. Prima Porta on the outskirts of the capital—a villa
which probably belonged by inheritance to Livia—displays this
naturalistic style at its full efflorescence in a masterpiece of illusionism, the garden enclosure painted upon its walls (Plate 41). This
rich bird-filled shrubbery of trees, fruit-trees and flowering plants is
conceived by the artist as railed off from a strip of flower-beds by
a balustrade; and a low trellis is inserted to separate the scene from
the actual room. In such pictures Eugenie Strong acclaimed the

Fig. xviii. Silver mixing-bowl, Augustan period.
From Hildesheim Treasure; Berlin

conquest of the 'space beyond' as an accomplished fact. 'The sense of
the confining wall is annulled; it is as if the closed door, beyond
which in certain Pompeian paintings we see trees waving and birds
flitting, had suddenly burst open.' Augustan notables such as
Maecenas had developed a taste for landscape gardening, and Virgil
devoted to the Italian garden of his retired pirate from Corycus in
south-eastern Asia Minor one of the most famous passages of his
Georgics:

> Indeed, were it not that already my work has made its landfall,
> And I shorten sail and eagerly steer for the harbour mouth,
> I'd sing perhaps of rich gardens, their planning and cultivation,
> The rose beds of Paestum that blossom twice a year . . .
>
> . . . I'd not forget
> Late-flowering narcissus or gum arabic's ringlet shoots,
> Pale ivy, shore-loving myrtle.[17]

Even in urban surroundings, such as those in which Virgil lived,
Romans retained a keen affection for the countryside; and prosperous Italian domesticity of this period gave the Greek or oriental
artist his chance to respond to this taste and to endow his rich
patrons' houses with a romantic spaciousness with which, sometimes, is infused the contemporary sense of man's littleness within
the world of nature.

So numerous and varied, then, were the styles of painting which

Fig. xix. Wall-painting, late Augustus or Tiberius. Pompeii (House
of Spurius Maesor)

flourished in the Augustan age. During the same period the fashionable architectural design was sometimes modified into a more ornate
and unrealistic decorative system, in which the architectural divisions remained as frames for panels but no longer served a functional
purpose (Fig. xix; Plate 43). Such exercises of the imagination,

applied to stucco-work in which similar tendencies appeared, earned adverse comment from the conservative Roman architect and military engineer Vitruvius:

'Imitations based upon reality are now disdained by the improper taste of the present day. On the stucco are monsters rather than definite representations taken from definite things. Instead of columns there rise up stalks; instead of gables striped panels with curled leaves and volutes. Candelabra uphold pictured shrines and above the summits of these, clusters of thin stalks rise from their roots in tendrils with little figures seated upon them at random. Again, slender stalks with heads of men and of animals attached to half the body. Such things neither are, nor can be, nor have been. On these lines the new fashions compel bad judges to condemn good craftsmanship for dullness.'[18]

Under Nero and the Flavians, if not earlier, there came a new brilliance and richness of colour. Figure-painting achieved fresh successes, and a partial return was also made to the original architectural manner. That is to say, the structures framing the panels at least recover their canonical members and their sense of gravity (Fig. xx). But now a new baroque spirit is abroad, a scenic illusionism experimenting with effects of spatial recession inspired by stage designs (Plate 45a). These fantastic structures, often anticipatory of Piranesi, infuse into earlier architectural styles the emotional temperamentalism of Neronian taste. Beams curve, designs seem to flash into nervous movement, there are menacing storms in the air. Nero's great Roman Golden House (p. 278) in the capital was decorated with unprecedentedly intricate patterns and arabesques. Its elegant ceiling-paintings (Plate 44b), when they were rediscovered, greatly attracted the artists of the Renaissance such as Raphael, who, since Pompeii and Herculaneum were not yet uncovered, knew little other ancient painting. Nero's master-painter Famulus—whatever his racial origins—seems to have intended to 'Romanise' his art, since, even on the scaffolding, he always wore the toga.

In the second century AD, though no fundamental changes occurred, the various styles and tendencies of Greco-Roman painting achieved new masterpieces of grace and sophistication. Since Pompeii and Herculaneum had already ceased to exist before that date, we have no substantial body of second-century painting with which to illustrate the developments that continued to occur. It seems, however, that special merit was achieved in a manner already

Fig. xx. Wall-painting, second or third quarter of 1st century AD.
Pompeii (Casa della Caccia)

evolved in the late Republican and Augustan periods, notably the
combination of pastoral, landscape motifs with little shrines, tombs
and sacred enclosures. Of this 'sacred idyllic' theme, so much in
keeping with the antiquarian religious interests of leading Romans
during the second century (p. 158), a fine example has survived from

258

the Hadrianic Villa of the Quintilii (the Villa Albani) on the Appian Way, five miles outside Rome (Plate 45*b*). At the same period decorative stucco work reached new heights (Plate 35*b*). Then, soon afterwards, the painters of the catacombs begin to utilize and modify the available traditions; and the long history of the Christian mural has begun (p. 183).

CHAPTER 10

ARCHITECTURE

THE paintings that have been described were intended for the decoration of rich men's houses. The eruption of Vesuvius in AD 79, which overwhelmed and thus partly preserved commercial Pompeii and residential Herculaneum, and the country-houses of Stabiae, has not only given us most of the paintings that have survived but has made it possible to reconstruct the main features of the houses which they

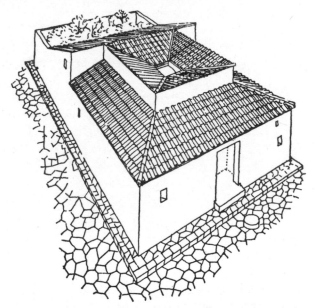

Fig. xxi. Reconstruction of house at Pompeii (exterior)

graced (Figs. xxi, xxii). Their houses were perhaps not unlike those of well-to-do Greeks of preceding epochs. But there is one apparently un-Greek feature, the long and lofty *atrium*. Half court and half front room, containing the family altar and the ancestral statues, this, together with parts of the rooms beyond, could be glimpsed as one entered the front door. At the other end of the atrium was the peristyle, the centre of the private part of the building, surrounded by bedrooms, reception rooms, kitchens and dining-rooms—usually made to accommodate nine people, and including rooms with different aspects for summer and winter. The peristyle sometimes contained a small garden, but on larger properties the garden lay beyond.

Fig. xxii. Reconstruction of another house at Pompeii (interior)

These dwellings at Pompeii and Herculaneum presented plain façades to the street; and when the towns had begun to go down in the world, if not before, the frontage on either side of the entrance was let off as shops. The absence of windows towards the street—as in Arab houses of old Cairo—was probably for the sake of privacy; glazed windows, though known, were little used. The rooms were lit by openings on internal courts, but except in the peristyle these were not large, since the sun was often strong—the house was heated by braziers when it was cold. In some houses at Pompeii, and more at Herculaneum, there seem to have been upper floors, to which the domestic water supply, when it existed, was carried by leaden pipes. These upper floors were made of timber which, painted and gilded, was also used for the ground floor ceilings.

These were the residences of prosperous people, in a single locality, during a fairly brief period of time. In most large Roman cities conditions were very different. In addition to fine houses and monuments, there was a great deal of squalor. Houses were ramshackle, streets narrow, noisy and filthy, and nights sleepless and smelly. Seneca—who himself possessed gigantic palaces well insulated by great estates—suggests how it felt to live over a bath house (p. 280):

'I can't for the life of me see that absolute quiet is as necessary to the studious recluse as it seems. Here am I in the middle of roaring babel. My lodgings are right over a bath. Now imagine every sort of outcry that can revolt the ear. When the more athletic bathers take their dumb-bell exercises, I hear grunts as they strain or affect to strain, hissings and raucous gasps as they expel their breath after holding it: when I run against some sedentary soul, who is content with the mere humble massage, I catch the smack of the hand as it meets his shoulders, with a different note according as it alights flat or hollowed. But if a tennis professional comes along and starts scoring the strokes, all's up. Next add the quarrelsome rowdy and the thief caught in the act and the man who loves his own voice in a bath; after that, the people who jump into the plunge-bath with a mighty splash. Besides those whose voices are the real unvarnished thing, if nothing else, you must imagine the remover of superfluous hair emitting from time to time a thin falsetto howl to advertise his presence, and never silent except when he's removing the superfluous hair and making someone else do the howling in his stead. Then there is the cordial-seller with a whole gamut of yells, and the sausage-vendor, and the puff-pastry man, and all the eating-house hawkers crying their wares each with a distinctive melody of his own.'[1]

Nero seized the opportunity provided by the Great Fire of AD 64—in which ten out of the fourteen Augustan Regions of the city were destroyed—not only to build his own fantastic palace, the Golden House (p. 278), but to impose upon the capital some of the orderly ideas of town-planning which the Romans had, it seems, inherited from the Etruscan cities across the Tiber, and had already utilized for their own colonies.

'In such parts of Rome as were unoccupied by Nero's palace, construction was not—as after the burning by the Gauls (c. 390 BC)—without plan or demarcation. Street-fronts were of regulated dimensions and alignment, streets were broad, and houses spacious. Their height was restricted, and their frontages protected by colonnades. Nero undertook to erect these at his own expense, and also to clear debris from building-sites before transferring them to their owners. He announced bonuses, in proportion to rank and resources, for the completion of houses and blocks before a given date. Rubbish was to be dumped in the Ostian marshes by corn-ships returning down the Tiber. A fixed proportion of every building had to be massive, untimbered stone from Gabii or Alba (these stones being fireproof). Furthermore, guards were to ensure a more abundant and extensive public water supply, hitherto diminished by irregular private enterprise. Householders were obliged to keep fire-fighting apparatus in an accessible place; and semi-detached houses were forbidden—they must have their own walls. These measures were welcomed for their practicability, and they beautified the new city. Some, however, believed that the old town's configuration had been healthier, since its narrow streets and high houses had provided protection against the burning sun, whereas now the shadowless open spaces radiated a fiercer heat.'[2]

If, however, we can believe Juvenal—whom Samuel Johnson adapted to write of London—Rome was not immediately transformed.

Most sick men here die from insomnia (of course
their illness starts with food undigested, clogging
the burning stomach)—for in any rented room
rest is impossible. It costs money to sleep in Rome.
There is the root of the sickness. The movement of heavy wagons
through narrow street, the oaths of stalled cattle-drovers
would break the sleep of a deaf man or a lazy walrus.
On a morning call the crowd gives way before the passage
of a millionaire carried above their heads in a litter,
reading the while he goes, or writing, or sleeping unseen:
for a man becomes sleepy with closed windows and comfort.
Yet he'll arrive before us. We have to fight our way
through a wave in front, and behind we are pressed by a huge mob
shoving our hips; an elbow hits us here and a pile
there, now we are smashed by a beam, now biffed by a barrel.
Our legs are thick with mud, our feet are crushed by large
ubiquitous shoes, a soldier's hobnail rests on our toe. . . .
Newly mended shirts are torn again. A fir-tree
flickers from the advancing dray, a following wagon
carries a long pine: they swing and threaten the public.
Suppose the axle should collapse, that axle carrying
Ligurian stone, and pour a mountain out over the people—
what would be left of the bodies? the arms and legs, the bones,
where are they? The ordinary man's simple corpse
perishes like his soul.[3]

The basic structure in this vast, noisy agglomeration was the tenement house, already long familiar at Rome and apparently a local Italian creation. With its shops, workshops and flats united in a single unit, this type of building carried trade and production to any part of a town, by way of contrast to the segregated residential and bazaar quarters of cities in the near east. In Republican Rome there had been repeated attempts to build second storeys, with planks, mud-brick, wattle and (later) more durable materials. Vitruvius, whose treatise *On Architecture*, backward-looking though it was, contained information on materials, methods and proportions which exercised great influence when it became known at the end of the fifteenth century, shows that in Augustan times his contemporaries were already building impressive tenement-houses of a number of storeys; Augustus limited their height to sixty feet, but Vitruvius did not think that they would be safe for more than eighty years.[4] The construction work undertaken and encouraged by Nero was more permanent in character, and henceforward tenement-blocks achieved ever-increasing size and solidity. Of these there is little trace now at Rome, but the surprisingly modern appearance of its large, residential buildings erected in the first and particularly the second century AD can be reconstructed from the extensive remains at Rome's port of Ostia (Fig. xxiii). In such great cities, including no

Fig. xxiii. Reconstruction by I. Gismondi of house at Ostia,
2nd century AD

doubt Rome itself, streets had continuous rows of open shops under several floors of tenements. Within each block main staircases generally led to the upper floors independently of the shops. On these higher floors the windows facing the street often had built-out balconies with bases of brick-faced concrete. A few large houses possessed arcaded courtyards like Italian Renaissance palaces; for these blocks housed both rich and poor. This was the first great social architecture, showing how houses as well as public monuments could be constructed with dignity for the needs of almost all ranks of a great organized society. Yet houses fulfilled less varied purposes than they do today, since sanitation and the more complicated forms

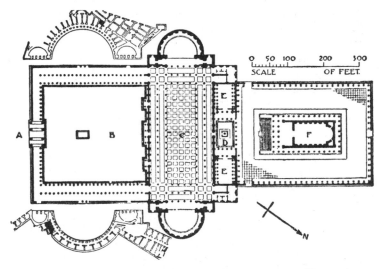

Fig. xxiv. Plan of Forum of Trajan, AD 111–14. Rome

of heating were generally left to communal buildings, in which much social life took place—much also being reserved, as in southern Italy today, for the open air.

To provide for these needs, combined with the requirements of trade and patriotic religion, the emperors lavished their most grandiose attention upon the construction of elaborate monumental town-centres (*Fora*). At Rome itself, where several of these were successively built side by side as extensions of the Roman Forum itself (Plate 52), the Forum of Trajan (Fig. xxiv) was the most spectacular (see Plan of area). This was planned, and in large part designed or supervised—as were other great buildings of the time—by the Greco-Syrian town-planner, engineer and architect, Apollodorus of Damascus. The Forum of Trajan contains his Basilica (Figs. xxv, xxvi). The Roman Basilica, a magnified adaptation from Hellenistic models—perhaps originally from the Greek temple —was a rectangular roofed hall serving as a social and commercial meeting-place and a law court. The remains of two earlier structures of this kind, the Basilica Julia and Basilica Aemilia, can be seen in the adjacent Roman Forum. Pliny the elder described the Basilica Aemilia, reconstructed by Augustus, as one of the three most beautiful buildings in the world.[5] But it was far outdone in splendour

Fig. xxv. Reconstruction of Basilica of Trajan

by the Basilica of Trajan. The central hall of this edifice was 80 feet in breadth and 280 feet long. It was divided into double aisles (on all four sides) colonnaded with monolithic granite columns and surmounted by clerestories of light construction, under a wooden roof which was probably of local larch. At each of the shorter ends there was a raised dais, enclosed within an apse and containing a tribunal. The apses show a subsidiary use of the characteristic Roman arch or vault in a type of building which is, otherwise, of typically Greek, rectilinear construction (p. 271). The Roman Basilica had a remarkable future as a Christian church. Indeed, almost all the characteristic features of the Christian place of worship—portico (narthex), nave, aisles, terminal apse, central seat of chief officiant—

are already found in a tiny, subterranean Basilica of the first century AD, near Rome's Porta Maggiore. This small building, devoted to some not certainly identified non-Christian cult (Plates 54*a*, 22*a*), provides a remarkable contrast in size to some of the immense Christian Basilicas of later centuries (Plate 54*b*).

The Basilica of Trajan, as splendid as these great churches, was only one element in the mighty complex of buildings comprising his Forum. For that also incorporated, with every visual magnificence and comfort, not only shops and a great market hewn out of the rock (Fig. xxvii), but the Column of Trajan (p. 248), law courts, libraries

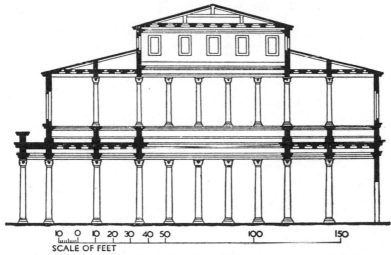

SCALE OF FEET

Fig. xxvi. Cross-section of Basilica of Trajan (alternative plan)

and places of worship, all served by wide thoroughfares and colonnaded promenades. The creators of such grandiose designs were usually Greeks or easterners, yet they interpreted the tastes and aims of their imperial patrons in producing these bold axial plans, gigantic structures and symmetrical vistas utilizing great sweeps of surrounding town or country landscape (Plate 44*a*). The Romans who prompted their architects to such forceful, spacious achievements had a gift and passion for organization which inclined them, not to the perfection of single buildings like the Greeks, but to strong combined movements and splendidly conceived unities. The decoration which they or their architects included was not always refined or delicate, yet the compositions taken as a whole displayed a strong feeling for architectural harmony and effect. During the Augustan

Fig. xxvii. Market of Trajan

age, contemporary trends towards classicism had somewhat repressed this dynamic temper, which reasserted itself to reach its climax in constructions of the second century AD such as the Forum of Trajan.

The most characteristic and original achievements of Roman architecture were due to the availability and utilization of a clean, sandy earth known to us as *pozzolana* and to the ancients as 'pit sand'. This chocolate-red earth, a finely pulverized volcanic product found in thick strata at Puteoli (Pozzuoli) as well as to the north and east of Rome, was mixed in a kiln with lime—limestone ($CaCO_3$) reduced to quicklime (CaO), the best binding material available until the nineteenth-century discovery of Portland cement. Early Italian mortar, perhaps introduced through the Greek colonies of south Italy, had been lime mixed with ordinary sand, but then the superiority of *pozzolana* to sand was discovered: it contains a vitreous element which, after mixing with lime, has the property of forming exceedingly consistent and cohesive hydraulic concrete, setting with almost imperishable hardness even under water. This mixture of *pozzolana* and lime was then added to an aggregate (*caementa*), often made of chips and waste from polished facing blocks—broken stone, brick or even marble, and (where light weight was an important consideration) pumice-stone. When the mixed *pozzolana* and lime had been poured over it, this aggregate was bound together in a compact, monolithic mass, solid and exerting no thrust when set—a wonderful material for architects.

From the late second century BC, foundations and cores made of various blends of concrete already formed masses capable of bearing as much weight as the rock itself (Plate 48*b*)—though the Romans did not at first fully realize its tenacious properties. By the time of Augustus the red *pozzolana* was already in use, but still timidly, and it was during the next centuries that this was employed for the most daring constructions—thanks to the genius of Greek or oriental architects who, in order to fulfil the requirements of Roman patrons, mastered the humble materials to hand and exercised due care in their choice, preparation and mixture. The consequent employment of the excellent, inexpensive *pozzolana* revolutionized the construction of Roman walls. These were formed by the pouring between boards of liquid concrete in watertight layers alternating with sections of aggregate. This was the technique which enabled the walls of tenement houses at Rome to achieve a new many-storeyed height and massiveness from the Augustan age onwards (p. 264); and in the second century AD there was a greatly increased facility and confidence in handling this medium.

Concrete walls, with their coarse surfaces, demanded a disguise, and except below ground were normally covered with layers of facing materials—thus constituting an essentially different phenomenon from the homogeneous stone walls of the Greeks. At Rome they possessed a more or less elaborate covering of brick, produced by brickyards which often made fortunes. Before the end of the Republic crude brick had already been replaced by the more durable kiln-baked brick, at first taking irregular forms, then square or diamond-shaped (reticulate) and then rectangular. Its heat-resisting quality was proved in the Great Fire of Nero's reign. At first this brick, with concrete behind it, was faced—when above ground—by stucco or plaster at the very least; on the more splendid buildings a delicate purity of line and variety of decoration was introduced by the utilization of marble, granite, porphyry, alabaster or bronze. The removal of these expensive materials during the plunderings of the Middle Ages accounts for the misleading appearance of so many Roman buildings today—all that can be seen is their massive core of brick-faced concrete, none of which was meant to be visible. It was not until the early second century AD (except in purely functional structures) that Ostia and other towns show brick employed as the outermost facing, and even used—in final rejection of the Greek heritage of stone façades—to make mouldings and decorative features.

The exploitation of the arch was a Roman achievement. The Greeks had made no use of arches in design; but the Etruscans had, and the arched Great Drain (*Cloaca Maxima*) of Rome is still visible as a record of their domination of the city during the sixth century BC. From *c.* 150 BC semi-circular stone arches are often found in Italy. This Italian speciality, with its endless opportunities and varieties of plan, caused great changes in architecture. Owing to its construction with wedge-shaped blocks (*voussoirs*), an arch exerts at its spring not only a downward weight, but a tendency to spread or 'thrust'. For the arch to remain stable this thrust must normally be resisted by abutments or buttresses or by a reinforcement of the wall in which the arch is placed. These difficulties were eliminated by the employment of thrustless concrete (p. 269). To make an arch, the liquid concrete was spread over temporary timber centrings or permanent brick centrings, which might later be faced with stone or tile. These brick centrings had a very practical part to play during the pouring and setting of the concrete core, but thereafter it was the core that did the work.

But from early days, before concrete was known, Rome knew free-standing arches, forming no part of any wall and originally used for ceremonial purposes. A notable example in the Roman Forum was the now vanished Arch or Temple of Janus, god of gates and beginnings, through which armies marched to war. In the Imperial age a favourite form of monument was the Triumphal Arch erected to an emperor and bearing his dedicatory inscription. Built with one or three openings, these arches were adorned with statuary and bas-reliefs relating to his victorious campaigns. Thus the Arch of Titus near the entrance to the Forum shows reliefs commemorating the capture of Jerusalem by that prince in AD 70 (Plate 37*a*; p. 247). This sort of monument provides classic examples of the characteristic Roman achievement of combining the Italian arch with the traditional post-and-lintel, rectilinear Greek Orders comprising columns or pilasters which support Doric, Ionic, Corinthian or 'composite' capitals (p. 287) surmounted by horizontal architraves: the arch is the fundamental structural unit, whereas the employment of the Orders is wholly decorative. The columns are wholly, or half, or threequarters detached; on the Arch of Tiberius at Arausio (Orange) the two last-named formulas appear together. Trajan's Arch at Ancona (AD 115; Plate 55*a*), where he constructed new harbour works, stresses the plasticity of its grouped columns; they strive upwards from markedly offset plinths, while the powerful angle-blocks of the base prolong the upward sweep. On the causeway which it bestrides with a ten-foot span, this arch, sixty-one feet high, tops a lofty flight of steps and was visible to ships far off. The fifteenth-century architect Alberti used the Arch at Ancona as his model in experimenting with the affixation of arch and column to wall in the façade of his Church of S. Andrea at Mantua (Plate 55*b*). The Arches of Septimius Severus at Rome and particularly at Lepcis Magna display new decorative motifs (p. 250), but the favourite quarry of Renaissance architects, sculptors and painters alike was the Arch of Constantine at Rome (AD 312) which displayed reliefs dating back over the two previous centuries.

However, the Romans used their new mastery of the arch for far more practical structures than these. Their bridges, for instance—simply and solidly constructed, indispensable adjuncts to the great network of roads (p. 32)—were designed to offer a well-calculated resistance to the rush of water. The bridges of the empire, like other arches, do not always employ concrete. An early example is Rome's Milvian Bridge (Fig. xxviii). Uncemented volcanic stone tufa is used for the core, travertine (the deposit of calcium carbonate—Rome's principal building stone) for the *voussoirs* (p. 270), *peperino* from Gabii (a tufa containing fragments of basalt and limestone) for the rest of the facing. The span of the arches, unprecedented at their

Fig. xxviii. Reconstruction of Milvian Bridge, 109 BC. Rome

early date (109 BC), is sixty feet—with which may be compared the forty-six feet of the vault in Ely Cathedral's Lady Chapel. Likewise the six-arched bridge which, under Trajan, the Spanish communities of the district combined to erect across the Tagus gorge near Alcantara (Plate 48a) is wholly of granite. Its six vast semi-circular arches, the largest of which is just over ninety feet wide, extend for a total length of 630 feet, and stand over 150 feet high at their loftiest point. Although in the deep ravine only the centre pillars were in water, all spring from about the same level, with impressive artistic effect. Trajan's 3,000-foot Danube bridge of AD 104 below the Iron Gates, now vanished except for portions of the foundations, has stone piers that are no less than 170 feet apart; but their superstructures, like those of other large bridges, were segmental arches of timber.

Just as the arches of bridges spanned water, the arches of aqueducts carried water over land. Here again a magnificent surviving example from Spain makes no use of concrete. This is the aqueduct at Segovia (Plate 49a), believed to have been erected under Augustus or one of his first successors—and still conveying water today. Its two-storeyed row of 128 arches, reaching a maximum height of over ninety feet and crossing the valley for half a mile in the middle of the town, is constructed of white granite, uncemented. The masonry of the finely proportioned Pont du Gard near Nemausus (Nîmes), with arches possessing a span of seventy-five feet, is again laid dry without cement. But it was equally safe, and much more economical, to use concrete, as exemplified by Hadrianic portions of the Aqua Claudia (Plate 49b), one of the eleven principal aqueducts which supplied Rome with more than one million cubic metres of water every day. Here the concrete was faced with brick, elsewhere with tufa or limestone, or sometimes, in such functional constructions, the facing was omitted. For the sake of economy again, the Romans employed masonry channels rather than pressure-resisting metal pipes, since cast iron was unknown and lead or bronze was costly. They could have created a pressure-supply by constructing siphon-conduits in this material, for the resisting powers of their hydraulic cement exceed the figure now accepted as safe. But they did not do this, cautiously refraining from imposing on their concrete the full strain that it would bear. The Romans aimed at using a gravitational flow, aided by small falls in the conduits; Vitruvius records a fall of 6 in 100 feet. Aware of the law that water rises to its own level, but greater as builders than as hydraulic experts, they in no sense anticipated high-pressure methods—although the use of these for

Fig. xxix. Public lavatory. Thugga (Dougga, Tunisia)

pumps, water organs and the like was known and they sometimes supplied the upper rooms of houses with water by 'rising mains' (p. 261).

In spite of some costly failures by local authorities (p. 56), an expert on the construction of aqueducts, Frontinus, describes these proudly as 'a signal testimony to the greatness of the Roman empire. . . . With so many indispensable structures for all these waters you are welcome to compare, if you will, the idle pyramids or all the useless, though famous, works of the Greeks.'[6] And indeed the Romans had a respect amounting almost to adoration for running water. Their admirable water supply, with its provision for Public Baths (p. 280) and continuously flushing lavatories (Fig. xxix) (still

273

not improved upon in many of the regions where they are found), was intended primarily, not for the private consumer—although there was a good deal of unlawful private tapping of conduits—but for the general public.

The employment of arches, and of concrete, led to a peculiarly Roman achievement: the amphitheatre. These gigantic oval buildings represent a doubling of the semi-circular Greco-Roman theatre of which the first permanent Roman version, constructed of stone and *pozzolana*, was completed by Pompey in 53 BC. An amphitheatre is the equivalent of two theatres with their flat ends (Plate 51*a*, p. 286), as it were, laid together, so that, as in its direct

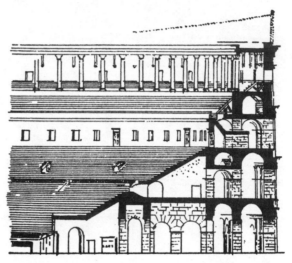

Fig. xxx. Diagram of Colosseum, AD 72–80. Rome

offspring the bull-ring of Spanish cities, the auditorium wholly surrounds an elliptical 'arena'—the Latin word for sand or beach, used because of the sand which was strewn to absorb the blood of the combatant human beings and animals. The architecture of the Romans includes great religious monuments, too, but their vast amphitheatres provide a reminder that, unlike the same art among the Greeks, it was also, to at least as great an extent, secular; though its description, for that reason, as an architecture of humanism requires some qualifications when the appalling purposes of these magnificent structures are recalled (p. 121).

It was unsafe for such buildings to be made of wood; Tacitus records the collapse of a wooden amphitheatre at Fidenae in AD 27.[7]

Before that, in the reign of Augustus, the first permanent amphitheatre partly of stone had been constructed in the capital. Nero
laid the foundations for one made wholly of stone; and the largest
and most famous of all amphitheatres, the Colosseum, was initiated
soon afterwards by the Flavian emperors, and opened for use in
AD 80 (Plates 50*a*; 51*a*; Fig. xxx). The span of the Colosseum is 620
by 500 feet, the space for its arena measuring about 290 by 180.

Fig. xxxi. Arches without classical entablature, beginning
of 4th century AD. Salonae (Split, Yugoslavia)

The travertine-faced exterior, with its combination of solidity,
grandeur and grace, is in its final form four storeys high. The three
lower storeys are pierced with arches, and display attached three-
quarter columns of the Doric, Ionic and Corinthian Orders respectively. The top tier—between corbels to support the masts of the huge
awning drawn across the auditorium—is not arcaded, and its
engaged columns, with Corinthian capitals, are rectangular (pilasters). Yet the essential constructional units, organically linking
exterior and interior (in contrast to modern ornamental stone-work

veiling the steel skeletons within), are not the Greek Orders—which are there to give scale and ornamentation—but the massive arch-bearing piers. Already in the House of Fortune at Pompeii, as later in the Severan forum at Lepcis and in Diocletian's early fourth-century palace at Salonae (Split) in Dalmatia (Fig. xxxi), Romanesque, Islamic and Renaissance architecture is foreshadowed by a novel springing of the arches directly from the capitals. But in the Colosseum, although the Roman arch is already the basis of the structure, the Greek Orders with engaged columns and pilasters nevertheless remain as its decorative frame (p. 271).

The cumulation of these arches one above another to the unprecedented height of four tiers, greatly exceeding the two-storey halls of the Greeks, was made possible by the use of concrete. The construction of these tiers shows how the Romans exploited their discovery that such concrete-cored arches could be used for im-

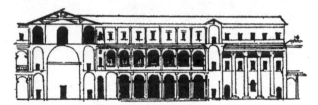

Fig. xxxii. Palladio's design for Carità Convent, Venice, 1561

pressive decorative effect. Here is a much more significant development than the single or triple Triumphal Arch (p. 271): namely the arcade, a great row of arches forming a single composition. These almost interminably repeated arcades show in its most majestic form the instinctive Italian capacity for dramatic presentation. The formula, reduplicated in many amphitheatres throughout the empire (e.g. at Nîmes, Arles, Verona, Pula: Plate 51b) exercised an immense effect on the Renaissance, inspiring for example—perhaps in conjunction with the Augustan Theatre of Marcellus—the Courtyard of Michelangelo's Farnese Palace at Rome (Plate 50b), and Palladio's design for the Carità Convent at Venice (Fig. xxxii). Similarly the architect of one of the earliest great Roman *palazzi*, the Cancelleria, imitated for its façade the non-arcaded, pilastered fourth storey of the Colosseum. And this most influential of all memorials of Roman power also provided the palaces of Italy and Europe with models for the design of their staircases.

Concrete was again employed in the corridors and cells of the

Colosseum, as well as underneath the arena. It appears again, mixed with lightweight pumice-stone, in the raking vaults which form a complex series of covered ambulatories and support the four tiers of seats reared one above another, in a mighty ellipse, up to the fantastically lofty crowning colonnade. The employment by the Romans of the vault—the arch produced sideways—is one of their most original and enduring contributions to architecture. Long known in Egypt and Mesopotamia but not much used in Greece, it was found by the Romans to be the perfect expression for their new ideas and imperial aspirations. Cautiously, however, as if their concrete were stone, they at first tended to provide cross-walls or relieving arches, as well as brick bonding-courses or brick-lined compartments in the concrete itself; although the lateral thrust which they seemed to fear, while perhaps a possibility before the concrete had set, was not thereafter a danger (p. 269). The completed structure had the rigidity of a porcelain cup—the exact antithesis of the vaults of Gothic churches. Yet hesitations gradually diminished, and the first and second centuries AD witnessed vaulting of ever more ambitiously light and thin construction, of which the boldness remained unequalled until the introduction of steel in the nineteenth century.

The Romans used both the semi-circular barrel or tunnel vault and the much more elaborate intersecting cross-vault. Simple tunnel vaults had been built in Etruscan tombs as early as the sixth century BC, and the practice had become extensive by the time of Augustus. Intersecting vaults (also called 'groined', the groin being the line of intersection) occur on a relatively small scale in Greek buildings soon after the time of Alexander. This sort of vault, over a square or polygonal compartment, gives much more scope; for example it facilitates lighting, through windows which can now be placed high up immediately under the vault. The Colosseum contains several successful large-scale experiments in this branch of design.

Earlier Greek buildings had used many small points of support; the architects of the Romans needed a few major ones, since their aim was to provide a large, unencumbered floor space. Those ready to construct huge, increasingly daring vaults for such purposes found their opportunity in the grandiose imperial palaces. Augustus and his successors gradually developed an elaborate complex of buildings of which the labyrinthine sub-structures can still be seen on the Palatine Hill. After greatly extending this Palace, Nero profited by the Great Fire of AD 64 to commission his chief architects Severus and Celer—whose origins we do not know—to undertake the construction of his unprecedented Golden House, designed to cover a sizeable proportion of the whole city. Remains of this palace on the Esquiline Hill indicate that it played a pioneer role both in the exploitation of brick-faced concrete as a building material and in the employment of new sorts of vaulted and domed halls, including rooms of elaborate polygonal shapes. In these searches for novel formulas, as John Ward Perkins has observed, 'we meet for the first time the modern attitude to architecture as the organization of

Fig. xxxiii. Reconstruction of throne-room in Domitian's Palace, AD 81–96. Palatine Hill, Rome

space rather than the composition of masonry masses'. Some slight idea of the general appearance of the Golden House may be obtained from sketches of contemporary mansions (Plate 44*a*), from the paintings which appear on its groined vaults (Plate 44*b*), and from the gossip of Suetonius:

'A huge statue of Nero himself, one hundred and twenty feet high, stood in the entrance hall; and the pillared arcade ran for a whole mile. An enormous pool, more like a sea than a pool, was surrounded by buildings made to resemble cities, and by a landscape garden consisting of ploughed fields, vineyards, pastures and woodlands, where every variety of domestic and wild animal roamed about. Parts of the house were overlaid with gold and studded with precious stones and nacre. All the dining-rooms had ceilings of fretted ivory, the panels of which could slide back and let a rain of flowers, or of perfume from hidden sprinklers, shower upon his guests. The main dining-room was circular, and its roof revolved slowly, day and night, in time with the sky. Sea water, or sulphur water, was always on tap in the baths. When the palace had been decorated throughout in this lavish style, Nero dedicated it, and condescended to remark: "Good, now I can at last begin to live like a human being".[8]

But not for long, for the Golden House was still unfinished at his death and was mostly destroyed by the Flavian emperors. However, they greatly extended the Augustan imperial palace on the Palatine. In this, as the surviving ground-plan shows, there were immense, vaulted halls (Fig. xxxiii), the sweep of their imaginative curves straining the horizontal, Greek post-and-lintel Orders almost to breaking-point. The breaking-point was still more clearly approached in Hadrian's 'Villa' at Tibur (Tivoli). This vast conglomeration of apartments, terraces, colonnades, wrestling-grounds, theatres and baths extended over seven square miles. Its architects displayed great novelty and daring in their vaults, hemicycles and niches, umbrella half-domes over apses, and an experimental octagon (Piazza d'Oro).

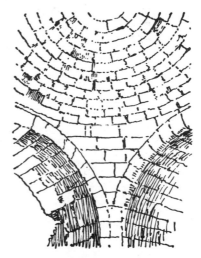

Fig. xxxiv. Pendentive in Baths, late second or early third century AD. Gerasa (Jerash, Jordan)

When vaults were placed, as they now were, over hemispheres, experiments had to be made with pendentives (Fig. xxxiv). The Romans also achieved extraordinary skill and delicacy in decorating their vaults not only with paintings, as in Nero's Golden House, but with tiles, and particularly with panelling and coffering of stucco (Plate 35; pp. 253, 259).

All these techniques were lavished not only on the imperial residences but on the superb Baths constructed for the general public, in Rome and every other town that could afford them. As characteristic of Roman materialism as the more gruesomely employed amphitheatres, these Baths were designed not only for comfortable and luxurious bathing but for club-life, sport, permanent art-exhibitions, and all and more than all the activities of the most elaborate community centre—as Seneca, complaining of the noise, describes (p. 262). Although the expenses, including the upkeep of a very numerous staff, must have been enormous, the entrance-fee amounted to a fraction of a penny, and even this was waived by emperors eager to make a good impression.

The remains of Baths at Stabiae in Campania show that already in the first century BC the practical Italian mind had invented, in place of braziers, furnaces (hypocausts) under the floors to give a controlled heat by conveying the warmed air through flues behind the walls of the various compartments. Agrippa's census of 33 BC records 170 Baths. In the capital, the Baths of Agrippa, Titus and Trajan probably contained many of the features which we can reconstruct from the still existing ground-plan of the gigantic Baths of Caracalla (Plate 64a). Its once sumptuously ornamented main building (750 by 380 feet), flanked by an elaborate enclosure with garden and open-air gymnasium, included a huge-vaulted Central Hall (185 by 79 feet) with clerestory windows (Fig. xxxv)— prototype of the great medieval churches with their vaulted naves— in addition to a circular, domed hot-room (115 feet in diameter) and a large swimming pool, surrounded by apartments containing every possible amenity.

The luxuries of such a building in the second century AD are described by an unidentified Greek writer:

'The building suits the magnitude of the site, accords well with the accepted ideas of such an establishment, and shows regard for the principles of lighting. The entrance is high, with a flight of broad steps of which the tread is greater than the pitch, to make them easy to ascend. On entering one is received into a public hall of good size, with ample accommodation for servants and attendants. On the left are the lounging rooms, also of just the right sort for a bath, attractive, brightly lighted retreats. Then, besides them, a hall, larger than need be for the purposes of a bath, but necessary for the reception of richer persons. Next, capacious locker rooms to undress in, on each side, with a very high and brilliantly lighted hall between them, in which are three swimming pools of cold water; it is finished in Laconian marble, and has two statues of white marble in the ancient style, one of Health (Hygeia or Salus), the other of Asclepius (Aesculapius). On leaving this hall, you come into another

which is slightly warmed instead of meeting you at once with fierce heat;
it is oblong, and has an apse on each side. Next to it, on the right, is a
very bright hall, nicely fitted up for massage, which has on each side an
entrance decorated with Phrygian marble, and receives those who come
in from the exercising floor. Then near this is another hall, the most
beautiful in the world, in which one can stand or sit with comfort, linger
without danger, and stroll about with profit. It also is refulgent with
Phrygian marble right up to the roof. Next comes the hot corridor, faced

FIG. xxxv Reconstruction of Great Hall in Baths of
Caracala, AD 211–17. Rome (see scale
from figures).

with Numidian marble. The hall beyond it is very fine, full of abundant
light and aglow with colour like that of purple hangings. It contains three
hot tubs. When you have bathed, you need not go back through the same
rooms, but can go directly to the cold room through a slightly warmed
chamber. Everywhere there is copious illumination and full indoor
daylight. . . . Why should I go on to tell you of the exercising floor and of
the cloak room? . . . Moreover, it is beautified with all other marks of
thoughtfulness—with two toilets, many exits, and two devices for telling
time, a water clock that makes a bellowing sound and a sundial.'[9]

Developing from experiments with half-domes over niches, the egg-shaped or hemispherical dome—an arch rotated on its axis—played a novel part in Roman architecture. We possess a marvellous example in the best preserved of all Rome's ancient structures, the Pantheon (Plate 56*a*). Originally erected by Agrippa in the time of Augustus, but in its present version dating from a reconstruction by Hadrian (AD 120–4), this extraordinary building has undergone

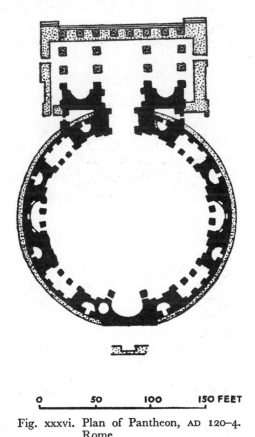

0   50   100   150 FEET

Fig. xxxvi. Plan of Pantheon, AD 120–4.
Rome

many losses and many changes, yet the walls and vaulting of the round temple, and its huge colonnaded portico, still remain.

The one-hundred-foot high, brick- and tile-faced concrete exterior of the circular structure was originally coated with stucco and marble and decorated with a marble frieze. But the architect devoted his most masterly efforts to the inside of the rotunda (Plate 57, Fig. xxxvi). This measures 142 feet both in height and in width. Its interior wall, which is of brick-faced concrete twenty feet thick, does not repeat the uninterrupted circuit of its external counterpart, but contains eight recesses—five rectangular (including one which forms the door) and three semi-circular. The existence of these recesses and of various vaulted niches shows that by now the Romans had full trust in their monolithic concrete and could therefore boldly lighten what they built. Semi-circular brick arches seen in the upper stages of the wall were probably built to serve as a frame into which the liquid concrete was poured (p. 269). The recesses are separated by eight huge piers: their great columns have little structural significance, but,

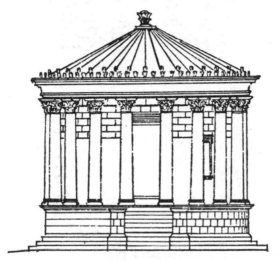

Fig. xxxvii. Reconstruction of round temple ('of Sibyl'), early 1st century BC. Tibur (Tivoli, near Rome)

even more strongly than in their use for the Colosseum, give an effect of scale.

They lead up to the lower of the two cornices. Above this cornice is a series of panels alternating with niches under a second cornice, from which rises the semi-circular dome. Its inner surface is ornamented by coffering in five ranges, in each of which the mouldings (once decorated with bronze rosettes) are adjusted or foreshortened in mock perspective with regard to their appearance from below. These coffers diminish the weight of the dome, which being of concrete exercised no thrust, and was even strong enough to survive the removal of its gilded bronze roof-tiles in AD 663; it is built up of successive horizontal layers made from concrete containing progressively lighter materials, from the large pieces of travertine (p. 271) at the base to the volcanic rubble at the top. The whole building is boldly lit by a single circular opening, twenty-seven feet wide, at the summit of the dome. Through this opening, the light is always regularly diffused; only the two cornices are strongly shadowed.

The circular form chosen for this temple was of remote Italian antiquity, going back to the primitive mud and wattle huts of which specimens still survived on the Palatine in the time of Augustus.

Fig. xxxviii. Caradosso's Foundation Medal of
St Peter's, 1506

Round temples of late Republican or early imperial date (but of far earlier origins) such as the Temple of Vesta in the Forum and other shrines in the Velabrum and at Tibur (Tivoli) (Plate 58a; Fig. xxxvii) —buildings which inspired Bramante's wonderful Tempietto (S. Montorio)—may in some cases have had their little domes, like those of certain small-sized buildings of the Greeks. But we know of no precedent for the vast, breathtaking dome of the Pantheon. This arouses powerful emotions in its viewers. In its absence of mystic shadows and patches of light some find a cheerful, restful brightness. Byron called it 'simple, erect, severe, austere, sublime'. Others see it as stern, unsmiling and cavernous; unlike an earth-bound Greek temple, the Pantheon dwarfs mankind in its immensity. Its majestic spaciousness warns worshipping mankind that they are in the presence of the gods.

For this, as its name the Pantheon suggests, was a temple: the Temple of All the Gods. We know that it originally contained statues of Mars, Venus and the deified Julius Caesar. But ancient uses of this word Pantheon often have a special relation to the sun, moon, planets and other stars. These heavenly bodies were regarded as divine by most of the inhabitants of the empire (p. 140)—among them Augustus who sponsored the foundation of the Pantheon, and

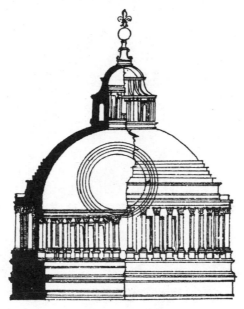

Fig. xxxix. Serlio's woodcut of Bramante's
Dome of St Peter's

the no less astrologically-minded Hadrian who replanned the building. There can be no doubt that this dome represents heaven, its central light represents the sun, and seeing that a temple's form 'should be analogous to the character of its divinity'[10] the harmony of the dome, with its star-like rosettes, was intended to reflect the majestic rhythm of the heavenly bodies.

Of this most influential among all Roman religious buildings every feature has served as a model to subsequent architects, including the greatest of them. The fundamental forms of the Pantheon guided Bramante in his design for the dome of St Peter's (Fig. xxxviii, xxxix), later superseded by Michelangelo's. Palladio, too, who believed that round churches were best owing to their simple, uniform spaciousness demonstrating the uniform unity, infinity and justice of God, gave his Tempietto at Maser near Treviso (Plate 56*b*) the cylinder and dome of the Pantheon—without even including the drum by which Bramante, at St Peter's, had intended to separate them. Bernini uses the same form for his church of S. Maria dell' Assunzione at Ariccia. But in Bernini's Christian dome of Heaven, the celestial messengers are waiting to receive the ascending Virgin; the architectural framework has become a setting for sculptural revelation.

Fig. xl. Reconstruction of stage of theatre, *c.* AD 200. Sabrata
(in Tripolitania, Libya)

The huge columns and entablature of the Pantheon's portico (Plate 56*a*) recall that the great majority of Roman temples were not round, but still obeyed, with variations and magnifications, the rectilinear principles of classical Greek architecture. The portico of the Pantheon is one of the most ambitious Roman endeavours within this canon. Its pediment—much sharper than Greek pediments—has lost its elaborate marble reliefs and statuary, including at the apex Jupiter hurling thunderbolts from his chariot. Nevertheless, the façade is still substantially intact. It is inscribed with the name of the Pantheon's founder, Agrippa, and, although what we see today dates from Hadrian, this portico at least (unlike the rotunda behind) may perhaps go back to Augustus in its essential plan. The main doorway, forty feet high and twenty feet wide, is approached by a mighty porch of sixteen unfluted monolithic granite columns— each forty-six and a half feet high. These columns are disposed in three rows, of which the first has eight columns, in contrast to the usual figure of six. Behind are two rows of four columns each disposed so as to divide the whole structure into three divisions (or a nave and two flanking aisles) reminiscent of the ancient triple-shrined temples of the Etruscans, and the temple of Jupiter, Juno and Minerva which they had built on Rome's Capitoline Hill. The capitals surmounting the columns show a somewhat immature form of the favourite Roman Order, 'Roman Corinthian', which adds various kinds of elaboration to the basic Corinthian design of *acanthus* leaves as well as to the carved mouldings of its architraves and entablatures (Plates 52 and 53). Elsewhere the Romans also utilized a Composite Order representing an ornate combination of Ionic and Corinthian (Fig. xli), and subsequently branching out into many intricate varieties (Plate 59).

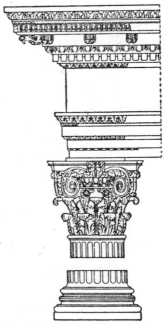

Fig. xli. 'Composite' entablature of Arch of Titus (frieze omitted), later 1st century AD. Rome

The most grandiose of all Roman rectangular temples was the Temple of Venus and Rome, for which Hadrian was again responsible. Of this, as of the Temple of Concord reconstructed from a Republican building at the other end of the Roman Forum (Fig. xlii), little but the ground-plan survives. But remarkable examples of rectangular temple construction are still extant both in the capital itself—for example, the surviving portions of the Temple of Castor and Pollux (Plate 52)—and in many other parts of the empire. Some of the best preserved and most magnificent of these temples are to be seen far away on the eastern frontier, at Heliopolis (Baalbek) in Syria. There the principal temples form part of a complex

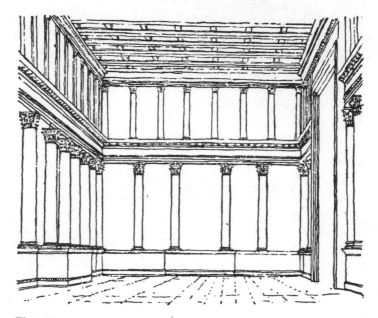

Fig. xlii. Reconstruction of Temple of Concord as restored under Augustus. Forum Romanum

Great Sanctuary (880 by 440 feet) upon an artificial, vaulted terrace within the city's acropolis (Fig. xliii). This group of buildings achieves one of the architectural triumphs of the Roman empire by its superb axial planning and its adaptation of the Forum-formula to the temples, bazaars and cults of the east. Instead of concrete, in these outlying provinces enormous stone blocks are employed; three such blocks, forming part of the terrace, are each over sixty feet long (Fig. xliv). Beside the huge central Temple of Jupiter and the Sun (Helios) is another temple, of which the interior is the best preserved of any in the Roman world (Plates 60; 61b). With its flights of stairs rising to an altar platform above a crypt, this interior seems to foreshadow a Christian church. But the temple may have been dedicated to Dionysus-Bacchus, and its platform used to stage performances of his Mysteries (p. 163). The colossal fluted pilasters, rising above not one but two tiers of niches, anticipate a favourite design of the Italian sixteenth century: Michelangelo's palaces on Rome's Capitoline Hill and Palladio's Loggia del Capitanio at Vicenza (Plate 61a) likewise employ unusually lofty columns to knit together, in a single organic design, the two storeys of their façades.

But Baalbek also shows how Greco-Roman architecture sometimes

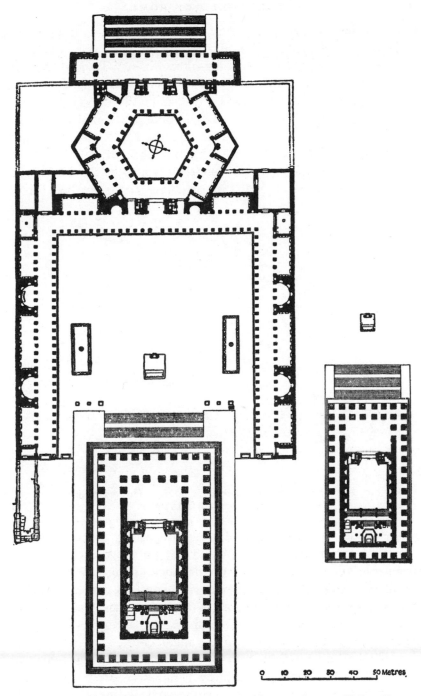

Fig. xliii. Plan of Great Sanctuary, 1st-3rd centuries AD. Heliopolis
(Baalbek, Lebanon)

foreshadows even more directly the seventeenth-century Italian architecture. For a small round temple at the same Syrian city perhaps of the third century AD—the so-called Temple of Venus (Plate 62a; Fig. xlv)—was known to Borromini and closely imitated by him (after he had also studied Hadrian's Villa at Tibur) for the Lantern with which he crowned the dome of his masterpiece, the bee-shaped Church of S. Ivo della Sapienza at Rome (Plate 62b), with its twisted spire suggested by the horn of a Sicilian goat. This Lantern and its graceful model at Baalbek, though circular, display entablatures curved inwards in five recessions between the

Fig. xliv. Huge stones in wall of sanctuary enclosure. Heliopolis (see scale from figure to left)

columns—straining, without entirely departing from, rectilinear classicism to an extent which could not fail to attract a baroque architect. The same adoption yet defiance of the Greek Orders is found at another Levantine border-city, Petra, at first capital of the semi-independent client-kingdom of the Nabataean Arabs and then, from the second century AD, chief town of the Roman province of Arabia. Its elegant, flamboyant temple-façades—hewn out of the rose-coloured rock—include, at the entrance of the gorge which was the city's only approach, a shrine (Plate 63a) that is sometimes identified as a Temple of Isis or a Treasury (Khazneh). Its façade displays the broken pediment so dear to seventeenth-century architects—a feature in ancient times much commoner in the east than in Rome, though it had occurred at Tiberius's Arch of Arausio (Orange) and was copied therefrom in Alberti's church of S. Sebastiano at Mantua (1460).

But more important is the superbly bold combination, in this Petra temple, of rectangular and circular themes. This sort of experiment with concave and convex surfaces anticipates the façades of baroque Roman churches, such as Rainaldi's S. Maria in Campitelli (1659; Plate 63b) with its two storeys of strong pediments upon harmoniously grouped columns, and its two niches in the shape of rounded shrines. This interplay of curves with classical horizontality goes back to the sophisticated designs of the Roman world. Enlarging

Fig. xlv. Reconstruction of 'Temple of Venus', mid-3rd or partly 2nd century AD. Heliopolis

the classic formula and combining grace with power, traditional stability with dynamic movement, they had displayed a spirit of decision, release and fulfilment. The Romanesque architects toned down Greco-Roman convexities, and the designers of the early Renaissance softened and straightened them, but in the seventeenth century Bernini, Borromini and Rainaldi at Rome, and Longhena at Venice, accepted this boldness, adding their own stamp. So Rome looked forward and led to the seventeenth century, just as in a host of different ways it has fathered every generation between its colossal achievements and our own time.

EPILOGUE

So the foundations of the medieval and modern west and near east were now established. Surviving the partial disintegration of this unprecedented Mediterranean empire, Roman law and citizenship, Roman agriculture and administration and toughness, became the bases of the nation-states into which, one after another, the western provinces began to change; and in Aegean coastlands and oriental borderlands these same Roman institutions merged with surviving Greek and eastern trends to give a thousand years of life to the empire of Byzantium.

No one would ever be able to outdo Marcus Aurelius in his demonstration of what a moral code, unbacked by strong religion, could achieve as a remedy for human weakness. Yet in his time the Roman peace, created by Roman arms, had created the material conditions in which spiritual emotions could thrive; and Christianity, already powerful in western Asia and gaining power in northern Africa, was about to achieve the stature of a world religion. The art which gloriously served its Churches in the Middle Ages sprang direct from the sculpture and painting and architecture of the Roman world. Ever and again, too, these provided revivifying draughts to the artists of Italy, who in their turn, between the fourteenth and seventeenth centuries, created and led the arts of modern Europe— further adorned, as the next century neared its end, by the decorative designs learnt from recently disinterred Pompeii and Herculaneum.

In the generations immediately preceding these discoveries, classical Roman patterns of writing had been found so inspiring that many of its products have been called Augustan. Yet by then Virgil had dominated the minds of poets and readers, first for one millennium (during which a vast public had believed him a magician), and then for threequarters of another. Throughout most of the same period, also, the medium of intercourse between one educated man and another had been Latin: the Renaissance of the fourteenth and fifteenth centuries was above all a Renaissance of Cicero, and even when, for purposes of communication, the national vernaculars superseded his language, they long remained, like the morality and oratory which they expressed, beneath Cicero's spell. This spell prevailed as potently upon traditionalists as upon leaders of the French and American Revolutions.

But from then onwards, for the first time in nearly two thousand years, the fascination of Rome began to be dimmed. To some the achievements of classical Greece appeared so incomparable that Rome seemed little more than a transmitter. But I have attempted in these pages to show how the transmission was also a transformation —how the atmosphere and achievement of the Roman world contained important elements that were original, indeed almost unrecognizably novel.

And yet this new synthesis was the work of Greeks living in the Roman world, almost as much as of Italians. A large part, in many fields of human activity, was also played by the great numbers of partially or wholly Hellenized or Romanized persons who came from the outlying regions of the empire—and particularly from its eastern territories, not well known today. The world of Rome, which generation after generation of these diversified peoples created and maintained, was a new world, and it was a world both wonderful and horrible, as startling and enlightened in many ways as it was grey and brutish in others. But it was a world which we can scarcely ignore, since in many ways it made us what we are.

THE FAMILY OF AUGUSTUS

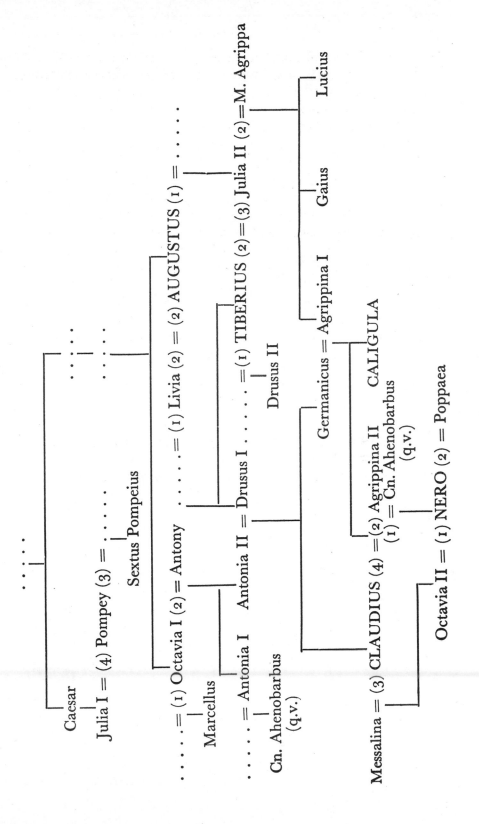

1. THE WEST
at the death of Augustus
A.D. 14

Firth of Forth
F. of Clyde
Borcovicium
Procolitia
R. Tyne
Solway F.
BRITANNIA
R. Severn
R. Trent
ICENI
Wheathampstead
Londinium
Dubrae
R. Seine
Colonia
Agrippina
TREVERI
R. Rhine
Moguntiacum
Pons Saravi
R. Neckar
Alesia
GERMANIA
R. Elbe
R. Danube
Rheinzabern
NORICUM
RAETIA
GAUL
Lugdunum
Lezoux
Vienna
HELVETII
Rhône
Graufesenque
CALLIA NARBONENSIS
Arausio
Arelate
Narbo
Aquae Sextiae
Massilia
HISPANIA
TARRACONENSIS
R. Ebro
Segovia
R. Tagus
Alcàntara
LUSITANIA
Vipasca
Córduba
BAETICA
Munda
Gades
MEDITERRANEAN SEA
MAURETANIA
Utica
Carthage
Cirta
Saltus
Lambaesis
Burunitanus
NUMIDIA
Thugga
Thapsus
Theveste
AFRICA
Sabrata
Lepcis
Magna

Scale of Miles
0   100   200   300   400   500

F. V. Botley

2. ITALY & SICILY
at the death of Augustus
A.D. 14

ALPS
CISALPINE
Comum
Mediolanum
Vercellae
River Po
Verona
Maser
Aquileia
Patavium
Mantua
Pola
GAUL
Mutina
Pistoria
Luca
R. Rubicon
Florentia
Ariminum
R. Arno
Ancona
Volaterrae
Arretium
UMBRIA
Assisium
ETRURIA
R. Tiber
SABINI
CORSICA
Sulmo
Rome
MARSI
LATIUM
Arpinum
SAMNITES
Ostia
Minturnae
Capua
CAMPANIA
Neapolis
ADRIATIC SEA
Brundisium
Velia
Thurii
SARDINIA
MEDITERRANEAN SEA
Naulochus
SICILY
Henna

CAMPANIA
Capua
L. Avernus
Cumae
Puteoli
Mt. Vesuvius
Neapolis
Pompeii
Herculaneum
Stabiae
Capreae

Scale of Miles
0   50   100   150   200

LATIUM
R. Tiber
Tibur
R. Anio
Rome
Gabii
Praeneste
Alba Longa
Ostia
Aricia
Albanum
Lanuvium

F.V. Botley

3. EASTERN EUROPE
at the death of Augustus
A.D. 14

	Imperial Frontier
	Provincial Boundaries

MARCOMANNI
BOHEMIA
QUADI

R. Danube
Carnuntum

PANNONIA

DACIA

ILLYRICUM

IRON GATES

M O E S I A

R. Danube

Salonae
DALMATIA

ADRIATIC SEA

Serdica

THRACE

MACEDONIA

Philippi

Thessalonica
Pydna

Apollonia

EPIRUS

Pharsalus

AEGEAN SEA

Nicopolis
Actium

ACHAIA

Delphi

Chaeronea

Corinth
Athens
Piraeus
Eleusis
Epidaurus

Olympia

Delos
Paros
Naxos

PELOPONNESE
Messene
Megalopolis

MEDITERRANEAN
SEA

Scale of Miles

| 0 | 50 | 100 | 150 | 200 | 250 | 300 |

CRETE

F. V. Botley

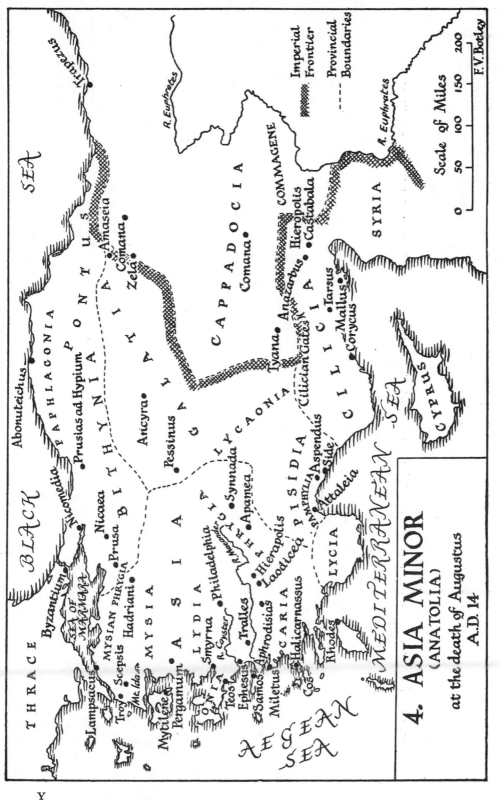

4. ASIA MINOR
(ANATOLIA)
at the death of Augustus
A.D. 14

Scale of Miles

F.V. Botley

Imperial Frontier
Provincial Boundaries

BLACK SEA

THRACE

Byzantium

SEA OF MARMARA

Lampsacus

Troy
Mt. Ida

Mytilene

Pergamum

Scepsis
Hadriani
MYSIAN PHRYGIA

MYSIA

IONIA
Smyrna
Teos
Samos
Ephesus
Miletus
Cos
Rhodes

LYDIA
Philadelphia
Sardes
R. Cayster
Tralles
Aphrodisias
Halicarnassus
CARIA

R. Maeander
Laodicea
Hierapolis
PHRYGIA
Apamea
Synnada

Prusa
Nicaea
Prusias ad Hypium
BITHYNIA

Nicomedia

PAPHLAGONIA
Abonuteichus

Amaseia
Comana
Zela

PONTUS

GALATIA
Ancyra
Pessinus

LYCAONIA

PISIDIA
Laodicea
PAMPHYLIA
Aspendus
Attaleia
Side

LYCIA

Tyana
Cilician Gates

CAPPADOCIA
Comana

Anazarbus
Mazaca
CILICIA
Tarsus
Mallus
Corycus

COMMAGENE
Hieropolis
Castabala

SYRIA

R. Euphrates

R. Euphrates

CYPRUS

MEDITERRANEAN SEA

AEGEAN SEA

Trapezus

Y

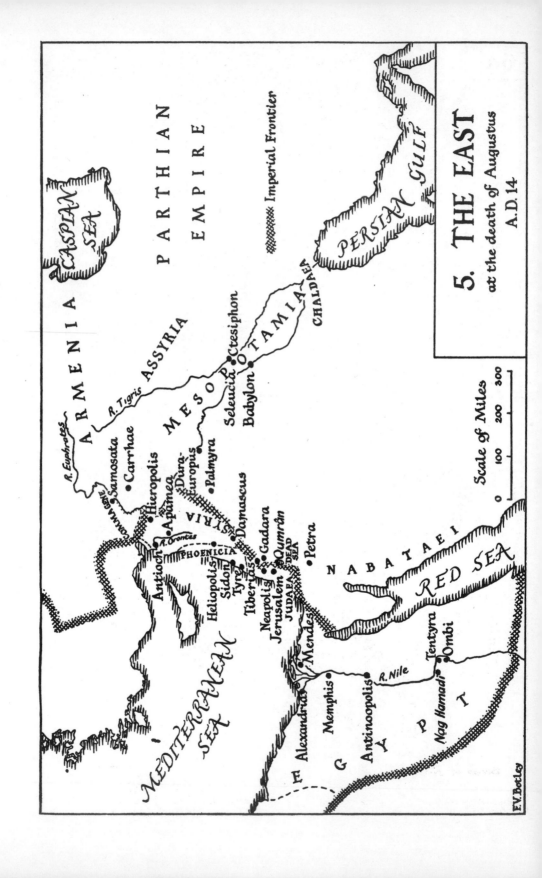

5. THE EAST
at the death of Augustus
A.D. 14

⁕ Imperial Frontier

Scale of Miles
0   100   200   300

CASPIAN SEA

ARMENIA

PARTHIAN EMPIRE

R. Euphrates

R. Tigris

ASSYRIA

MESOPOTAMIA

Seleucia Ctesiphon

Babylon

CHALDAEA

PERSIAN GULF

Samosata
Carrhae

Hieropolis
Apamea
Dura-Europus
Palmyra

COMMAGENE

SYRIA

Antioch
R. Orontes
PHOENICIA
Damascus
Gadara
Qumrân
DEAD SEA
Petra

Heliopolis
Sidon
Tyre
Tiberias
Neapolis
Jerusalem
JUDAEA
Mendes

NABATAEI

RED SEA

MEDITERRANEAN SEA

Alexandria
Memphis
Antinoopolis
R. Nile
Tentyra
Ombi
Nag Hamadi

E   G   Y   P   T

E.V. Botley

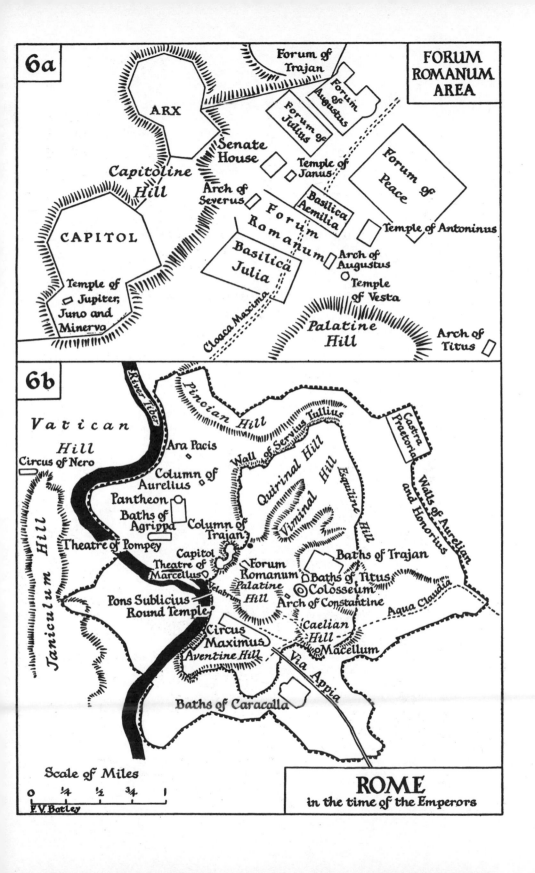

6a

FORUM
ROMANUM
AREA

Forum of Trajan

Forum of Augustus

Forum of Julius

ARX

Senate House

Temple of Janus

Forum of Peace

Capitoline Hill

Arch of Severus

Basilica Aemilia

Forum Romanum

Temple of Antoninus

CAPITOL

Basilica Julia

Arch of Augustus

Temple of Vesta

Temple of Jupiter, Juno and Minerva

Cloaca Maxima

Palatine Hill

Arch of Titus

6b

River Tiber

Pincian Hill

Wall of Servius Tullius

Castra Praetoria

Vatican Hill

Ara Pacis

Quirinal Hill

Circus of Nero

Column of Aurelius

Pantheon

Viminal Hill

Equiline Hill

Walls of Aurelian and Honorius

Baths of Agrippa

Column of Trajan

Theatre of Pompey

Janiculum Hill

Capitol

Theatre of Marcellus

Forum Romanum

Baths of Trajan

Baths of Titus

Palatine Hill

Colosseum

Pons Sublicius
Round Temple

Velabrum Hill

Arch of Constantine

Aqua Claudia

Circus Maximus

Caelian Hill

Macellum

Aventine Hill

Via Appia

Baths of Caracalla

Scale of Miles

0   ¼   ½   ¾   1

F.V.Batley

ROME
in the time of the Emperors

NOTES

CHAPTER 1: HISTORICAL SKETCH

1. Polyb., *Hist.* I, 1, 5.

CHAPTER 2: THE RULERS AND THE EMPIRE

1. Polyb., *Hist.* VI, 11–18.
2. *Comm. Pet.*
3. Pollio, *Hist.* (60 BC –), cf. Hor., *Od.* II, 1, 1f; Lucan, *Phars.* I, 84ff.; Florus II, xiii, 8 ff.; Vell. Pat. II, xliv, 1.
4. Suet., *Caes.* 77 f. (R. Graves).
5. Sydenham, *Rom. Rep. Coinage*, p. 177, no. 1063.
6. *Fast. Praen., Laud. Turiae*, cf. Vell. Pat. II, lxxxix, 3 f.
7. *R. G. Divi Aug.*, 6, 34.
8. E. g. *BMC. Emp.* I, p. 59, nos. 322, 333 ff.
9. Hor., *Od.* III, vi, 45–8 (E. Marsh); cf. Sall., *Cat.* 51, Livy I, praef.
10. Cic., *Imp. Cn. Pomp.* xx, 60.
11. *BMC Emp.* I, p. 112, no. 691.
12. Tac., *Ann.* I, 2.
13. Suet., *Tib.* 27 f.
14. Tac., *Ann.* 1, 3 f.
15. Dio Cass., *Epit.* lxxxvi, 4 (E. Cary).
16. Polyb., *Hist.* VI, 56, 6–12 (W. R. Paton).
17. Cic., *Q. Caec.* xx, 66 (L. H. G. Greenwood).
18. Cic., *I Verr.*, xiv, 40.
19. Cic., *Att.* V, 21; VI, i.
20. Cic., *Att.* V, 16 (E. O. Winstedt).
21. Suet., *Tib.* 32.
22. *CIL.* xiii, 1668.
23. Cic., *II Verr.* iv, 4; 5; 134 (L. H. G. Greenwood).
24. Cic., *II Verr.* ii, 7 f.
25. Cic., *Arch.* x, 23 (N. H. Watts).
26. Cic., *Flacc.* 9 f., 11 (L. E. Lord).
27. Hor., *Epist.* I, xix, 32 f., cf. II, ii, 99; *Od.* I, xxvi, 11.
28. Juv., *Sat.* III, 72–5, 77 f., 101 ff., 104–8, 109–12 (R. C. Trevelyan).
29. Ibid. 67 f.
30. Str. XIII, xii, 1 ff., 629.
31. Cic., *Flacc.* 65.
32. Pl., *Lach.* 187B.
33. Juv., *Sat.* III, 62 ff.
34. *Anth. Lat.* I, 353 f. (Riese).
35. *App. Verg., Mor.* 31–6 (R. C. Trevelyan).
36. Cic., *Flacc.* 69.
37. P. Lond. 1912 (Hunt and Edgar, *Select Papyri*, no. 212).
38. *Act. Isidor. et Lampon.* (Musurillo, *Acts of the Pagan Martyrs*, pp. 18–26).
39. Tac., *Hist.* V, 5.
40. Str. V, ii, 7, 224.
41. Str. III, iv, 18, 165.
42. Tac., *Germ.* 33.
43. *BMC. Emp.* I, p. 351, no. 237.
44. Ibid. III, pp. clxxi ff.
45. Vell. Pat. II, 126 (F. W. Shipley).
46. Virg., *Aen.* VI, 847–53 (Rolfe Humphries).

47. Tac., *Hist.* IV, 74 (C. H. Moore).
48. Ael. Aristid., *Or. Rom.*, 94, 96 f. (J. H. Oliver).
49. Tac., *Ann.* I, 2.
50. *BMC. Emp.* I, p. 92, nos. 548 ff. (AD 176).
51. E.g. Oliver and Palmer, *Hesperia*, XXIV, 1955, pp. 328 ff.
52. *CIL.* VII, 10570 (Souk-el-Khemis).
53. Plin. jun., *Ep.* X, 37 f. (W. Melmoth–W. M. L. Hutchinson).
54. Juv., *Sat.* XV, *passim.*
55. Plut., *Praec. Reip. Ger.* 813 f.
56. Dio Prus., *Or.* XXXVIII, 36 ff.
57. Ibid. XXXXI, 8–150.
58. M. Aur., *Med.* VI, 54.
59. Cic., *II Verr.* iii, 207, *Imp. Cn. Pomp.* xxii, 65.
60. Cic., *Off.* II, viii, 27.
61. Sall., *Cat.* 10.
62. ap. Gell., *NA.* VI, iii, 16.
63. Sen., *Ep. Mor.* xci, 13; Plin. sen., *NH.* XXXIV, 43.
64. Dion. Hal., *Ant. Rom.* I, V, 1; I, xc, 1 ff.; VII, lxx, 1 ff.
65. Tac., *Ann.* III, 40: XIII, 56; XIV, 31.
66. Tac., *Agr.* 15; 19; 31.
67. *Or. Sibyll.* VIII, 1–3, 37–42, 91–5, 121–9 (M. S. Terry).
68. Ibid. III, 350 ff. (H. N. Bate).
69. Cic., *Off.* I, xlii, 151 (W. Miller).
70. Suet., *Aug.* 98.
71. Ptol. I, xi, 7.
72. Petr., *Sat.* 76 (M. Heseltine).
73. Plin. sen., *NH.* XII, 84; cf. IX, lviii, 117, 119 ff., etc.

CHAPTER 3: CITIZENS OF ROME

1. Suet., *Rhet.* 1, *Gramm.* 2.
2. Quint., *Inst. Or.* VI, praef. 3; VIII, iii, 76; II, iv, 42; II, x, 3 ff.; V, xii, 17–23; VIII, iii, 57 f.
3. Ibid. II, xvi, 12–19; XII, xi, 30, etc.
4. Sen., *Ep. Mor.* cvi.
5. Tac., *Dial.* 40 (W. Paterson).
6. Basil, *Ep.* 335–49, *Ad Iuv. passim*; Greg. Nazianz., *Or.* 43, *Carm.* 8; Greg. Nyss., *Ep.* II.
7. Cic., *Rep.* IV, 13.
8. *Ber. Rab.* 65, *Babyl. Shabbat* 119B, Jos., *C. Apion.* I, 12, Philo, *Leg. ad Gaium*, 31.
9. Plin. jun., *Ep.* IV, 13.
10. Plin. jun., *Pan.* 26–28.
11. Veget., *De Re Mil.* II, 19.
12. *ILS.* 1825–36, *BGU.* 1125, *P. Oxy.* 724, Ditt. *Syll.* 479.9.
13. *L'Ann. Ép.* 1936, no. 128.
14. Ditt. *Syll.* 523a, cf. *CIG.* 3062, 3086.
15. Cic., *Att.* XV, 11 (44 BC).
16. Sen., *Cons. ad Helv. matr.* XVII, 3.
17. Plin. sen., *NH.* XIV, 117 f.
18. Jer., *De Vir.* III, 54.
19. Ar., *Pol.* I, xiii, 13, 1260a.
20. Cic., *Off.* I, xlii, 150 f.
21. Plin. sen., *NH.* XXXVI, 26, Dio Cass. LVII, 21.
22. Suet., *Vesp.* 18.
23. Quint., *Inst. Or.* I, x, 31, cf. 22–6.
24. Tac., *Ann.* XIV, 20.
25. Plin. sen., *NH.* XXXV, 77.
26. Lucian, *Somn.* 9.
27. Tac., *Ann.* XI, 25.
28. *R. G. Divi Aug.* 8.
29. Virgil, *Georg.* II, 173–6 (C. Day Lewis).
30. Tac., *Ann.* I, 17.
31. Livy II, 15, 3.
32. *Acts*, XXV, 9–12.
33. Plin. jun., *Pan.* 65.
34. Cic., *Clu.* liii, 146 (H. G. Hodge).
35. ap. Gell., *NA.* XI, iv, 1 (from Eur., *Hec.* 293 ff.).
36. Cic., *Leg.* III, xvii, 38 f.
37. Cic., *Rep.* I, xxxii, 53 (C. W. Keyes).
38. *R. G. Divi Aug.* 15.

39. *R. G. Divi Aug.* 22 f.
40. *BMC. Emp.* II, p. 262, no. 190.
41. A. Alföldi, *Die Kontorniaten*, I, p. 152, nos. 218 ff.
42. Suet., *Gaius*, 30.
43. Hor., *Od.* III, i, 1.
44. Tac., *Ann.* XV, 44.
45. Juv., *Sat.* V, 1 f., 5, 170–4 (G. Highet).

46. Arr., *Diss. Epict.* IV, 4, 27.
47. Matt. IV, 36.
48. Tac., *Hist.* II, 37, 87 etc.
49. Dio Cass., *Epit.* LXXIV, 10.
50. *SHA. Ael. Caes.* III, 3.
51. *BMC. Emp.* I, p. 166, no. 8.
52. Plato, *Rep.* IV, 434B.
53. Tac., *Ann.* XIII, 27.

CHAPTER 4: SUBJECTS AND SLAVES

1. Cic., *Flacc.* VIII, 18 f.
2. Ael. Aristid., *Or. Rom.* 64 (but ci. 39).
3. Tac., *Ann.* XV, 20.
4. Ibid. XI, 24.
5. *SHA. Hel.* 20, 1.
6. Plut., *Praec. Reip. Ger.*, 16 ff.
7. Ael. Aristid., *Or. Rom.* 65.
8. *IGRR.* III, 69.
9. E.g. *P. Oxy.* 744 (G. Milligan, *Selections from the Greek Papyri*, p. 33), Stob., *Ecl.* 75, Longus, *Pastor* 4, p. 126.
10. Tac., *Ann.* XIII, 48.
11. Petr., *Sat.* 44 (M. Heseltine).
12. Plut., *Praec. Reip. Ger.*, 19, 32.
13. Ibid. 17.
14. Plin. jun., *Ep.* X, 34.
15. Dio Prus., *Or.* XLVI, 6 f.
16. Ditt. *Syll.* 850.
17. Buckler, *Anat. St. to Ramsay*, 30 ff.
18. Ibid. 34 ff.
19. Philostr. *Vita Apol.* I, 15 (Paul McKendrick).
20. Luke XVI, 19; Matt. XIX, 24.
21. *Rev. de Phil.*, 3rd ser., XVII, 1943, p. 111.
22. Plin. sen., *NH.* XXXIII, 135.
23. Ar., *Pol.* I, v, 2, 1254a; cf. I, viii, 12, 1256b.
24. *ILS.* 7710.
25. *Lucr.* VI, 806–15.
26. Cato, *RR.* 56 f.
27. Plut., *Cato*, 21 (B. Perrin).
28. Athen., *Deipn.* VI, 272 f.
29. Diod. Sic. XXXIV, 25 ff. (N. Lewis and M. Reinhold).

30. *Florus* II, 7 (19), 4.
31. E. S. G. Robinson, *Num. Chron.*, 4th ser., XX, 1920, p. 175.
32. Posid., *fr.* 108 (c) and (f) Jacoby.
33. Johnson and Jotham, *Excavations at Minturnae*, 1933, 2 (1).
34. Varro, *RR.* I, iv, 1 f., I, xvi, 1–xvii, 7; II praef. 3–4, 6; II, x.
35. Cic., *Att.* I, 12.
36. Cic., *Clu.*, lxiii, 176 f.
37. Sen., *Ep. Mor.* xlvii, 1, 10, 13 (E. P. Barker).
38. Plin. jun., *Ep.* VIII, 16.
39. Gaius, *Inst.* I, 9.
40. Tac., *Ann.* XIV, 45.
41. Just., *Dig.* XLVIII, xviii, i, 1.
42. Gaius, *Inst.* I, 5; Just., *Dig.* I, vi, 2; *Inst.* I, viii, 2.
43. Florentinus ap. Just., *Dig.* I, v, 4.
44. Just., *Dig.* L, xvii, 32.
45. M. Aur., *Med.* IV, 4.
46. Cic., *Tusc.* ii, 17; *Fam.* vii, 1.
47. Petr., *Sat.* 45 (M. Heseltine).
48. Tac., *Ann.* XII, 56.
49. *Fast. Ost., L'Ann. Ép.* 1933, no. 30.
50. Plin. jun., *Pan.* 33.
51. Sen., *Ep. Mor.* vii, 2; cf. xc, 45.
52. Aug., *Conf.* VI, 8.
53. Sen., *Brev. Vit.* 13.
54. Suet., *Gaius*, 27 (R. Graves).
55. Galen, *Protrept.*, 9 ff.
56. E.g. Oliver and Palmer, *Hesperia*, XXIV, 1955, p. 333.
57. Tert., *Spect.* 30.

CHAPTER 5: FATE AND THE STARS

1. Plin. sen., *NH.* II, 22 (G. Murray).
2. Polyb., *Hist.* II, 38, 5; X, 5, 8; XVIII, ii, 5; XXIX, 21.
3. Lucan, VII, 445-7 (M. L. Clarke).
4. Hor., *Od.* III, 3, 29-44 (John Dryden).
5. Ibid. I, 35, 17-21 (E. Marsh).
6. Alexander Aphrodis., *De Anima Mantissa*, p. 182, 18 Bruns.
7. Zeno 87 Arnim.
8. Manil. IV, 14.
9. Sen. sen., *Suas.*, ii, 2.
10. Cic., *Acad.* I, vii, 30.
11. Cleanthes 528 Arnim.
12. Virg., *Aen.* XII, 676.
13. Tac., *Ann.* VI, 22.
14. Ibid. IV, 20.
15. Lucian, *Dial. Mort.* 30 (F. H. Cramer).
16. Sen., *Tranq.* 2.
17. Ar. *fr.* 12 ff.
18. Aesch., *Ag.* 6; Eur., *Hipp.* 530.
19. Sen., *Nat. Quaest.* III, 29, 1.
20. Chrysippus 1076 Arnim (Philodem., *De Pietate*, 11).
21. Plut., *De Is. et Os.* 67.
22. Diod. Sic. II, 29 ff.
23. *Anth. Pal.* IX, 577 (R. Bridges).
24. 574 Suppl. Grec., Bibl. Nat. = *Dieterich, Eine Mithrasliturgie*[3], (ed. Weinreich).
25. Cic., *Div.* II, xlii, 89.
26. Diod. Sic. I, 49, 5.
27. R. Campbell Thompson, *Late Babylonian Tablets in the Bodleian Library*, pl. 2.
28. ap. Auson. VII, 26.
29. Pseudo-Quint., *Decl. Mai.* IV, 13 ff. (F. H. Cramer).
30. Tac., *Ann.* XII, 68.
31. *BMC. Emp.* I, p. 56, no. 305 etc.
32. *BMC. Emp.* IV, p. 754, no. 349; p. 833, no. 679.
33. Strong, *Art in Ancient Rome*, II, p. 119; fig. 422.
34. ap. Gell., *NA.* XIV, 1.
35. Steph. Byz., *Cat. Codd. Astr.* II, p. 235.
36. *BMC. Emp.* I, p. 59, no. 323 etc.
37. Jacoby, *FGH.* II (B), no. 257, p. 1179.
38. Livy, XLIII, 13.
39. Tac., *Ann.* I, 28; XII, 64.
40. Dio Cass., *Epit.* LXXVI, 5, 7 (E. Cary).
41. John, *Ep.* I, iv, 1.
42. Lucian, *Alex.*, passim.
43. Wessely, *Greich. Zauberpapyrus von Paris and London*, p. 31, no. 2242 (p. 32, lines 11, 16).
44. Pl., *Leg.* 933 B; Theocr. ii; Virg., *Ecl.* viii; Ov., *Her.* VI, 91.
45. Theocr. ii, 53 ff.; Virg., *Aen.* IV, 494 ff.
46. Jul. Paul. Sent. V, 23, 14 ff.; *Cod. Theod.* IV, 10; Just., *Dig.* ix, 18.
47. Tac., *Ann.* II, 69.
48. Ov., *Ibis.*
49. *CIL.* I[2], 2520 (N. Lewis and M. Reinhold).
50. Aug., *Civ. Dei*, XVIII, 18.

CHAPTER 6: RELIGION

1. Polyb., *Hist.* VI, 56 (adapted from W. R. Paton).
2. Pl., *Rep.* III, 389 C.
3. Critias, *fr.* 25 D Nauck.
4. Isocr., *Busiris* 26 f. (B. Farrington).
5. Polyb., *Hist.* XVI, 12.
6. Varro, *Ant.* ap. Aug. *Civ. Dei*, IV, 32.
7. Cic., *Div.* II, lxxii, 148.
8. Cic., *Leg.* II, xii, cf. vi, x.
9. Prud., *C. Symm.* I, 199 f.
10. Lucr. I, 62-7 (R. E. Latham).
11. Livy I, praef., 6 f.
12. Hor., *Od.* III, vi, 1-8.
13. *R. G. Divi Aug.*, 19 f.
14. Virg., *Aen.* VIII, 714 ff. (C. Day Lewis).

15. Sen. ap. Aug. *Civ. Dei*, VI, 10.
16. 574 Suppl. Grec., Bibl. Nat. = Dieterich, *Eine Mi hrasliturgie*[3] (ed. Weinreich), 4.
17. Apul., *Apol.* 55.
18. *Act. Apost.* VIII, 9, 18; Just. Mart., *Apol.* I, 26.
19. *Corpus Hermeticum*, ed. Nock-Festugière.
20. Virg., *Aen.* VI, 309–12 (C. Day Lewis).
21. Ael. Aristid. XLVIII, 19–23 Keil = XXIV, 295 Dindorf (M. and B. Parry).
22. Ibid. XLVIII, 37–44 Keil, LI 18–25 Keil.
23. Mnesim. *fr.* 11.
24. *P. Oxy.* 1381, 90 ff.
25. Vitr. I, ii, 7.
26. Apul., *Met.* VIII, 27 f. (R. Graves).
27. Polyb., *Hist.* XVI, 12.
28. Ditt. *Syll.* 985.
29. Lucr. II, 589 ff., 598 ff., 611–32 (R. E. Latham).
30. Firm. Mat., *De Err. Prof. Rel.* 22 ff.
31. Cat. LXIII, 89–93 (F. O. Copley).
32. Prud., *Peristeph.* X, 1011.
33. *CIL.* VI, 510 = *ILS.* 4152.
34. *P. Oxy.* 1380, l. 130.
35. *ILS.* 4361 (note).
36. Apul., *Met.* XI, 3 f. (R. Graves).
37. Ibid. XI, 6, 15.
38. Roussel, *Les Cultes Égyptiens à Délos*, p. 277; cf. *IG.* XII, 3, 43.
39. *CIG.* 2716, 4683, 4713; *CIL.* XIII, 7610; *ILS.* 4393.
40. Stat., *Theb.* I, 719.

41. *BMC. Pontus*, pl. VII, no. 8.
42. Plut., *Pomp.* 24.
43. Jer., *Ep.* 107, 2; cf. Porph., *De Abstin.* IV, 16.
44. Cumont, *Textes et Mon. Mithr.* II, p. 8.
45. Vermaseren, *Corp. Inscr. et Mon. Mithr.* I, p. 327, no. 983.
46. Tert., *Apol.* 9.
47. Plin. sen., *NH.* XXX, 16.
48. Origen, *C. Cels.* I, 9.
49. Tert., *Coron.* 15.
50. Tac., *Ann.* XV, 1–8.
51. Paul, I *Cor.* XV, 1–8.
52. Ignat., *Eph.* 20.
53. *SHA. Quadr. Tyr., Firmus*, etc., 8.
54. Lact., *De Mort. Pers.* 46.
55. Firm. Mat., *De Err. Prof. Rel.*, etc.
56. Pseudo-Aug. (Ambrosiaster), *Quaest. Vet. Test.* lxxxiv, p. 145, 13 Souter.
57. Just. Mart., *Apol.* I.
58. *Martyr. Polycarp.* 6, cf. Cypr., *De Mort.* 26, Aug., *De Doctr. Christ.*, ii, 4.
59. John XV, 26; cf. I. *Thess.* I, 10; II, 19.
60. I Pet. II, 21, 24; cf. Isaiah LIII.
61. *Gal.* VI, 16; I Pet. II, 9.
62. I. *Cor.* I, 23–5.
63. Luke VI, 20–6 (E. V. Rieu).
64. Tac., *Ann.* XV, 44; cf. Suet., *Nero*, 16.
65. Plin. jun., *Ep.* 97 (L. A. and R. W. L. Wilding).
66. Euseb., *Hist. Eccl.* V, 3–iii, 3.
67. *Martyr. Polycarp.* 9.
68. Lact., *Div. Inst.* V, ii, 19.
69. Jer., *Ep.* xxii, 30; cf. *Epp.* l, lxx.
70. Arat. Sol. ap. *Act. Apost.* XVII, 28.

CHAPTER 7: PHILOSOPHY

1. Diog. Laert. *fr.* 33 col. ii, 3; cf. Lucr. II, 289–293, Cic., *Fin.* I, vi, 19.
2. Epicur., *Ep. Menoec.* 134.
3. Ibid. 123; cf. Cic., *Nat. Deor.* I, xvi, 43, Diog. Laert. x, 134.
4. Epicur., *Ep. Herod.* 77.
5. Epicur., *fr.* 54 Bailey.
6. Lucr. I, 62–9; V, 110 ff. (R. E. Latham).
7. Lucr. II, 644–8, 650 f.
8. Lucr. III, 830 f., 37-40, 1011–5.

9. Lucr. I, 107–11; II, 55–8 (R. C. Trevelyan).
10. Lucr. II, 16–21, 23, 29 ff.
11. Lucr. V, 1019–27.
12. Athen. XII, 547A.
13. Cic., *Tusc.* II, 11; V, 3–5, 19.
14. Cic., *Fin.* II, 45; III, 62 ff.
15. Cic., *Lig.* 38.
16. Sen., *De Ot.* IV, 1.
17. Sen., *Ep. Mor.* xcv; xlviii.
18. Sen., *De Ira*, I, 14.
19. Sen., *Prov.* II, 6.
20. Sen., *Cons. ad Helv. matr.* VIII, 3 ff. (J. W. Basore).
21. Sen., *Prov.* IV, 12 f.
22. Sen., *Ep. Mor.* lxxvi; xc.
23. Sen., *Cons. ad Helv. matr.* XVII, 3.
24. Sen., *Ep. Mor.* v.
25. Hor., *Od.* III, 3, 1–8 (Lord Lytton).
26. Arr., *Enchir.* I, 13 (W. A. Oldfather).
27. Arr., *Diss. Epict.* I, xxix, 9.
28. Ibid. III, xxvi, 37.
29. Ibid. IV, iv, 36.
30. Ibid. I, xxix, 9 ff.
31. Ibid. III, xiii, 9.
32. Ibid.
33. Ibid. IV, v, 34.
34. Ibid. IV, i, 89 f.; I, xvi, 15–21.
35. M. Aur., *Med.* X, 16 (A. S. L. Farquharson).
36. Ibid. VI, 30.
37. Ibid. VIII, 58.
38. Ibid. XII, 28.
39. Ibid. X, 5.
40. Ibid. XII, 14 f.
41. Ibid. VI, 30.
42. Ibid. IV, 49.
43. Ibid. VI, 9.
44. Ibid, IX, 30 f.
45. Ibid. I, 14.
46. Ibid. XI, 9.
47. Ibid. VII, 28; IX, 20.
48. Matt. V, 39; Luke VI, 29.
49. M. Aur., *Med.* XII, 20; VIII, 59; IX, 4.
50. Ibid. XI, 3.

CHAPTER 8: THE GREAT LATIN WRITERS

1. Cat. 51 (G. Highet).
2. Cat. 11 (G. Highet).
3. Cat. 8 (G. Highet).
4. Virg., *Aen.* IV, 447–51 (C. Day Lewis).
5. Virg., *Georg.* IV, 220–4 (C. Day Lewis).
6. Virg., *Aen.* X, 815–23 (C. Day Lewis).
7. Hor., *Od.* II, 16 (T. Otway).
8. Hor., *Od.* III, 15 (Sir E. Marsh).
9. Hor., *Od.* III, 9 (Lord Dunsany).
10. Prop. I, i, 1–8 (G. Highet).
11. Prop. IV, viii, 27–88 (G. Highet).
12. Ov., *Hor.* xvii, 3 ff., 105 ff., 143 ff. (Lord Mulgrave and John Dryden).
13. Ov., *Ars Am.* I, 272 ff. (G. Highet).
14. Ibid. I, 93–100 (G. Highet).
15. Ibid. III, 105 ff., 113 f., 133 ff., 139 f., 209 f. (G. Highet).
16. Ov., *Trist.* V, 12 f. (W. Cowper).

CHAPTER 9: SCULPTURE AND PAINTING

1. Plin. sen., *NH.* XXXIV, 61 ff.
2. Ibid. XXXVI, 37.
3. Polyb., *Hist.* VI, 53.
4. Plin. sen., *NH.* XXXV, 5.
5. Ibid. XXXIV, 10, 32.
6. Cf. Plut., *V. Pericl.* ii, 1; Lucian, *Somn.* 9.
7. Sydenham, *Rom. Rep. Coinage*, pp. 147 f., nos. 891 f.; p. 150, nos. 907 f.; p. 153, no. 919;

p. 158, no. 943; p. 162, no. 970.

8. Grant, *Roman History from Coins*, pl. 5, nos. 3, 6.

9. *BMC. Emp.* II, pl. 30, no. 2; *Ars Classica* sale, No. XVI, 1933, no. 1612.

10. Suet., *Vesp.* 22 f.

11. *Fouilles de Delphes*, IV, pl. 78.

12. Plin. sen., *NH.* XXXV, 22.

13. Virg., *Aen.* I, 458–62 (C. Day Lewis).

14. Exodus XXV, 23, 31; Numbers, X, 2.

15. *SHA. Duo Maximini*, XII, 10 f.

16. Plin. sen., *NH.* XXXV, 116 f.

17. Virg., *Georg.* IV, 116–19, 122 ff.

18. Vitr. VII, 3 f.

CHAPTER 10: ARCHITECTURE

1. Sen., *Ep. Mor.* 56.

2. Tac., *Ann.* XV, 43.

3. Juv., *Sat.* III, 232–48, 254 ff. (G. Highet).

4. Vitr. VI, viii, 1–5.

5. Plin. sen., *NH.* XXXVI, 102.

6. Front., *De. Aq.* II, 119.

7. Tac., *Ann.* IV, 62.

8. Suet., *Nero*, 31.

9. Pseudo-Lucian, *Hippias*, 5 f. (A. M. Harman, abridged by N. Lewis and M. Reinhold).

10. Vitr. VI, viii, 9.

NOTES FOR FURTHER READING

OUT of the vast literature on ancient Rome mention will be made here of a few books—in English only—of a more or less general character, which may be found suggestive and useful for reference. Nothing will therefore be said of the equally extensive writings in other languages or of the great array of articles, reporting the conclusions of research, in periodicals.

PART I (HISTORICAL SKETCH). Our most important survey of the whole field is provided by successive volumes of the *Cambridge Ancient History* (IX-XII, 1932–39). There is also the shorter *History of the Ancient World* of Methuen (146–30 B.C., F. B. Marsh, 2nd ed., 1953; 30 B.C.–A.D. 138, E. T. Salmon, 1944; A.D. 138–337, H. M. D. Parker, 1935). One-volume histories are provided by M. Cary, *History of Rome* (2nd ed., 1957), and A. E. R. Boak, *A History of Rome to A.D. 565* (4th ed., 1955); *The Legacy of Rome*, ed. Cyril Bailey (1924), covers a wide field briefly. We have nothing to compare with A. Piganiol's *Histoire de Rome* (4th ed., 1954) in which a historical survey is supported by detailed bibliographical notes indicating the sources of the research upon which it is based. For the first part of our period see especially H. H. Scullard, *From the Gracchi to Nero* (1959), and for the later years C. G. Starr, *Civilisation and the Caesars* (1954). General works of reference include the *Oxford Classical Dictionary* (1949), P. Harvey's *Oxford Companion to Classical Literature* (3rd ed., 1946), and A. A. M. van der Heyden and H. H. Scullard, *Atlas of the Classical World* (1959). Excerpts from ancient sources are collected in translation by N. Lewis and M. Reinhold, *Roman Civilisation* (2 vols., 1951, 1955), E. Barker, *From Alexander to Constantine* (1956), and (more briefly) Paul Mac-Kendrick, *The Roman Mind at Work* (1958), M. Grant, *Roman Readings* (1958).

PART II (STATE AND SOCIETY). On politics R. Syme's *Roman Revolution* (1939; reprinted) is fundamental; see also F. E. Adcock,

Roman Political Ideas and Practice (1959), L. R. Taylor, *Party Politics in the Age of Caesar* (1949), R. E. Smith, *The Failure of the Roman Republic* (1955). The Knights are discussed by H. Hill, *The Roman Middle Class in the Republican Period* (1952), the franchise by A. N. Sherwin-White, *Roman Citizenship* (1939), and the government of the provinces by G. H. Stevenson, *Roman Provincial Administration* (1939). The army is the theme of R. E. Smith, *Service in the Post-Marian Roman Army* (1958), H. M. D. Parker, *The Roman Legions* (1928), and G. L. Cheesman, *The Auxilia of the Imperial Roman Army* (1914); and the fleet of J. H. Thiel, *Studies on the History of Roman Sea-Power in Republican Times* (1946), and C. G. Starr, *The Roman Imperial Navy, 31 B.C.—A.D. 324* (1941). For Roman law see F. Schulz, *A History of Roman Legal Science* (1946), *Classical Roman Law* (1951), W. W. Buckland, *A Textbook of Roman Law from Augustus to Justinian* (2nd ed. 1932), H. F. Jolowicz, *Historical Introduction to Roman Law* (repr. 1939), and *Roman Foundations of Modern Law* (1957); and for the education of a Roman, A. Gwynn, *The Roman Education from Cicero to Quintilian* (1926), H. I. Marrou, *A History of Education in Antiquity.* D. L. Clark, *Rhetoric in Greco-Roman Education* (1957). The scientific and technological situation is described by B. Farrington, *Greek Science* (1944), O. Neugebauer, *The Exact Sciences in Antiquity* (1951) and F. W. Walbank, *The Decline of the Roman Empire in the West* (1946).

For the relation of politics and economics there is the much-discussed *Social and Economic History of the Roman Empire* by M. Rostovtzeff (2nd ed., revised by P. M. Fraser, 2 vols., 1957). Material is collected in the *Economic Survey of Ancient Rome*, ed. T. Frank, 5 vols. (1933–40). For aspects of trade see M. P. Charlesworth, *Trade-Routes and Commerce of the Roman Empire* (2nd ed., 1926) and R. E. M. Wheeler, *Rome Beyond the Imperial Frontiers* (1954), and for the coinage H. Mattingly, *Roman Coins* (1928), C. H. V. Sutherland, *Coinage in Roman Imperial Policy* (1951), M. Grant, *Roman Imperial Money* (1954) and *Roman History from Coins* (1958).

General surveys of Roman society are provided by M. Cary and T. G. Haarhoff, *Life and Thought in the Greek and Roman World* (1946), S. Dill, *Roman Society from Nero to Marcus Aurelius* (1928), W. Warde Fowler, *Social Life in Ancient Rome* (repr. 1929), F. R. Cowell, *Cicero and the Roman Republic* (1948), H. Mattingly, *Roman Imperial Civilisation* (1957), R. W. Moore, *The Roman Commonwealth* (1942), H. Grose-Hodge, *Roman Panorama* (1944). See also H. H. Tanzer,

The Common People of Pompeii (1929), and A. M. Duff, *Freedmen in the Early Roman Empire* (1928), and the good fictional reconstructions of Rex Warner, *The Young Caesar* (1958) and Marguerite Yourcenar, *Memoirs of Hadrian* (English ed., 1955). The status of slaves is discussed by R. H. Barrow, *Slavery in the Roman Empire* (1928) and W. L. Westermann, *The Slave Systems of Greek and Roman Antiquity* (1955). Full information concerning gladiatorial and other amusements is given by L. Friedländer, *Roman Life and Manners under the Early Empire* (7th ed., translated), and conclusions are summed up by Jérôme Carcopino, *Daily Life in Ancient Rome* (English ed., 1956).

For the Greek and eastern regions of the empire see especially W. W. Tarn–G. T. Griffith, *Hellenistic Civilisation* (3rd ed., 1952), M. Rostovtzeff, *The Social and Economic History of the Hellenistic World* (3 vols., 1941), A. H. M. Jones, *Cities of the Eastern Roman Provinces* (1937) and *The Greek City* (1940), D. Magie, *Roman Rule in Asia Minor* (2 vols., 1950). There are also numerous studies of single territories of the empire.

PART III (BELIEFS). On the stars there is F. H. Cramer, *Astrology in Roman Law and Politics* (1954) ; see also Gilbert Murray, *Five Stages of Greek Religion* (1935 ed.). For the national Roman beliefs, H. J. Rose, *Ancient Roman Religion* (1949), W. Warde Fowler, *The Religious Experience of the Roman People* (ed. 1922), and the more speculative *History of Roman Religion* of F. Altheim (English ed. 1938). For the mystery faiths F. Cumont, *The Mysteries of Mithra* (from 3rd ed., 1913) and *After Life in Roman Paganism* (1922), A. D. Nock, *Conversion* (1933), A.-J. Festugière, *Personal Religion among the Greeks* (1954). Emperor-worship is discussed by L. R. Taylor, *The Divinity of the Roman Emperor* (1931). The chapters by A. D. Nock in the *Cambridge Ancient History*, Vols. X-XII, give an invaluable survey, and comparisons with other religions are provided by E. O. James, *The Ancient Gods* (1960). For Judaism see S. W. Baron, *A Social and Religious History of the Jews* (2nd ed., 1952). No special bibliography of early Christianity can be attempted here, but up-to-date information is summarised by Van der Meer and Mohrmann, *Atlas of the Early Christian World* (1958) ; a vast new literature is now accumulating round the Dead Sea Scrolls and 'Gospel of St Thomas'. The relation of Christianity to paganism is discussed by C. N. Cochrane, *Christianity and Classical Culture* (1940) and W. Barclay, *Educational Ideals in the Ancient World* (1959).

The Hellenistic philosophies have received little adequate modern treatment in English; for their atmosphere and background see W. W. Tarn—G. T. Griffith, *Hellenistic Civilisation* (op. cit.). Studies of various aspects include E. Bevan, *Stoics and Sceptics* (1913), R. D. Hicks, *Stoic and Epicurean* (1910), W. J. Oates, *The Stoic and Epicurean Philosophers* (1940), B. Farrington, *Science and Politics in the Ancient World* (1939), A.-J. Festugière, *Epicurus and his Gods* (1955). On the Roman followers of these schools see E. V. Arnold, *Roman Stoicism* (1911), M. L. Clarke, *The Roman Mind* (1956), H. A. K. Hunt, *The Humanism of Cicero* (1954). On Seneca, Epictetus and Marcus Aurelius there are no comprehensive up-to-date studies in our language, but their works can be read in translation.

PART IV (LITERATURE AND THE ARTS). General works (which alone can be cited here) on Latin literature are by J. W. Duff, *A Literary History of Rome from the Origins to the Close of the Golden Age* (2nd ed., 1953), and *The Literary History of Rome in the Silver Age* (1927), J. W. Mackail, *Latin Literature* (1895), H. J. Rose, *Handbook of Latin Literature* (1949), W. A. Laidlaw, *Latin Literature* (1941), M. Hadas, *History of Latin Literature* (1952) and M. Grant, *Roman Literature* (revised ed., 1958). For the classical literary tradition see J. E. Sandys, *History of Classical Scholarship* (1903), R. R. Bolgar, *The Classical Heritage and its Beneficiaries* (1954), G. A. Highet, *The Classical Tradition* (1949), and J. A. K. Thomson, *The Classical Background of English Literature* (1948). Translations of most of the leading classical authors are now available in the Loeb and Penguin Classics series.

Recent discussions of the art and architecture of Rome and the empire have in many cases not yet reached readily accessible book form. On the arts in general, see E. Strong, *Art in Ancient Rome* (2 vols., 1929), H. B. Walters, *The Art of the Romans* (2nd ed., 1928), P. G. Hamberg, *Studies in Roman Imperial Art* (1945), A. Hauser, *Social History of Art* (1951), E. H. Swift, *Roman Sources of Christian Art* (1951) and W. Oakeshott, *Classical Inspiration in Medieval Art* (1959). Sculpture is discussed by A. W. Lawrence, *Classical Sculpture* (1928), A. Hekler, *Greek and Roman Portraits* (1912), R. P. Hinks, *Greek and Roman Portrait Sculpture* (1935), M. Bieber, *Sculpture of the Hellenistic Age* (1955), G. M. A. Richter, *Three Critical Periods in Greek Sculpture* (1951) and *Ancient Italy* (1955), J. M. C. Toynbee, *The Hadrianic School* (1934) and K. Clark, *The Nude* (1956). For paintings and the houses which they adorned see A. Maiuri, *Roman Paintings* (1953), and *Pompeii* (1931), M. Borda, *La Pittura Romana* (1958), A. W van Buren, *A Companion to the Study of Pompeii and Herculaneum* (2nd ed., 1938). General works of reference on architecture are B. Fletcher, *History of Architecture* (16th ed., 1956), D. S. Robertson, *Greek and Roman Architecture* (2nd ed., 1945), H. Plommer, *Ancient and Classical Architecture* (1956) and G. T. Rivoira, *Roman Architecture* (1926). Building materials are discussed by M. E. Blake, *Ancient Building Construction in Italy* (1947), and Roman monuments by S. B. Platner and T. Ashby, *A Topographical Dictionary of Ancient Rome* (1929), D. M. Robathan, *The Monuments of Ancient Rome* (1950), M. R. Scherer, *Marvels of Ancient Rome* (1955), J. Lees-Milnes, *Roman Mornings* (1956). See also E. Nash, *Roman Towns* (1944), and articles in *The Legacy of Rome* and *Cambridge Ancient History*.

INDEX